Social Policy in a Changing Europe

HN 373.5 .S728 1992
Social policy in a changing
                    172701

DATE DUE

FEB - 7 1996	
NOV 1 2 1996	
APR - 8 2000	
JUL 2 3 2003	
BRODART	Cat. No. 23-221

Public Policy and Social Welfare
A Series Edited by Bernd Marin

 European Centre
for Social Welfare Policy and Research

Volume 10

Zsuzsa Ferge, Jon Eivind Kolberg (Eds.)

OKANAGAN UNIVERSITY COLLEGE
LIBRARY
BRITISH COLUMBIA

Social Policy
in a Changing Europe

Campus Verlag · Frankfurt am Main
Westview Press · Boulder, Colorado

Published in the United States by Westview Press.
5500 Central Avenue
Boulder, Colorado 80301

Library of Congress Cataloging-in-Publication Data

CIP data available upon request

ISBN 0-8133-1589-1

Die Deutsche Bibliothek – CIP-Einheitsaufnahme

Social policy in a changing Europe / [European Centre for
Social Welfare Policy and Research]. Zsuzsa Ferge; Jon Eivind
Kolberg (eds.). – Frankfurt am Main: Campus Verlag; Boulder,
Colorado: Westview Press, 1992
   (Public policy and social welfare; Vol. 10)
   ISBN 3-593-34656-7 (Campus Verlag)
   ISBN 0-8133-1589-1 (Westview Press)
NE: Ferge, Zsuzsa [Hrsg.]; Europäisches Zentrum für
Wohlfahrtspolitik und Sozialforschung <Wien>; GT

© 1992 by European Centre for Social Welfare Policy and Research, 1090 Vienna, Berggasse 17.
Composition: Michael Eigner. Printed by Druck Partner Rübelmann, Germany.

Contents

List of Tables and Figures

Tables

Figures

Chapter 1

Introduction:
Social Policy in a Changing Europe[1]

Zsuzsa Ferge
Jon Eivind Kolberg

Nowadays change is so fast that even the most recent events have to be seen in a historical light. When the idea of the meeting ultimately giving birth to this volume was first coined by the Director of the Finnish Board of Social Affairs, *Vappu Taipale*, at the Board Meeting of the European Centre for Social Welfare Policy and Research in 1989, it was accepted as the "First *East-West* Dialogue on Social Policies". When it took place in March 1990, many real and symbolic walls had already fallen down; and the meeting went under the title of the "First *All-European* Dialogue on Social Policies".

At that time, the feeling of liberation was very strong, even though the future of Europe was hazy. The unification of Germany was unsure; and *perestroika* in the Soviet Union was less in jeopardy than it is one year later (March 1991), when this introduction was written. The terms of the European integration, or at least some problems surrounding integration, were less clearly recognized than they are now. Most importantly, the tremendous difficulties which the post-totalitarian countries have to face were not fully perceived.

The objective of the East-West dialogue was originally to deal in a comparative way with the welfare systems of "market" and "planned" societies. In 1989, when the authors were first asked to make a contribution, they were requested to deal with the question of whether the two systems could mutually learn something from each other in terms of welfare politics.

Meanwhile, the situation has altered to such an extent that mutual teaching or learning is no more on the agenda.[2] The new democracies will have to learn the language of the market and of political democracy – without too much to offer. They will have to study in detail the Western experiences in welfare politics, too. Perhaps

first of all, they will have to understand their own past. Thus, history has reformu-
lated the initial objective of the All-European dialogue. The present volume puts
forth a confrontation of the social experiences and expectations, the successes and
the failures of the different political systems and welfare regimes of postwar Europe,
attempting to throw light on the reasons of the collapse of Eastern socialism and
offering to the newcomers some more or less attractive models of welfare capitalism.

Despite their "winning hand", the Western contributors dealing here with welfare issues are far from buoyant. No doubt, most of them belong to the left-liberal
tradition. They are simultaneously proud and critical of the former record of the
welfare state, and they are very much aware of the current threats endangering it.
Most importantly, none of them has essential doubts about the economic and social
rationality of (improved) welfare politics. What they attempt to do, over and above
new analyses of recent processes, is to find fresh arguments in support of this policy.
This may imply the presentation of the consequences of market failures (such as
lasting unemployment), or of the cuts of welfare funding (such as increasing poverty
and marginalization), or positive statements about the (economically) beneficial
functions of welfare spending. Their diversified approaches to contemporary reality
– offering some new insights and some more indirect than direct lessons for the
Eastern block – are presented in Part I.

In the case of the Eastern countries, the year which has elapsed since the meeting
has finalized the downfall of state socialism. It has become both possible and
necessary to look at the past in a new light. Right now, it seems that – despite
tremendous efforts and tremendous sufferings – almost nothing is worth saving
from the débâcle. The uncertainties of the future also loom darkly. Therefore Part
II, containing mostly the recent experiences of post-totalitarian systems, does not
offer particularly cheerful reading. The most encouraging piece in this section is
the Spanish record. In fact, Ana M. Guillén, from Spain, was asked (after the
conference) to share with the "newcomers" the historical experiences about welfare
issues of a Western dictatorship and its transition to democracy. The lesson of this
story is exceptionally important for the East, because Spanish society has succeeded
in overcoming dictatorship and has acceded to a genuine parliamentary democracy – without going overboard in the negation of its past history.

As for possible futures, there again is no unanimity. The chapters in Part III describe the different visions about this future. The thorough analysis of implications
for welfare policy and social stratification of European integration forms the core
of this section. Stephan Leibfried's "inside" analysis (from Germany) is completed
by an "outsider's" assessment (Kåre Hagen from Norway) of the processes under
way.

Some "guesstimates" about what Europe is likely to look like in the future,
complete the picture. Bold projects are not often on the agenda. The host country
of the meeting, Finland, is one of the few countries with innovative welfare poli-

tics: namely, the model of the "welfare society", a de-bureaucratized and flexible variant of the social democratic welfare state (cf. Wiman). The scenario of a "citizens' Europe" (cf. Balbo), is also a completion and improved version of the welfare state. Moreover, the basic income scheme is offered by several authors as the mechanism which could overcome the growing gap between a changing economic organization and the traditional instruments of social policy which prove to be increasingly inadequate (cf. Atkinson, Leibfried).

Apprehension regarding the evolution of the recent trends is, however, more widespread than optimistic visions. Several scenarios emerge in the discussions of this volume. One of the possible futures is described as "a workers' Europe", introducing fundamental segmentation within the integrated continent. Other projections are the "Latin-Americanization" of the former socialist block; or of Europe as a fortress against the underdeveloped outside world; or a savage, intolerant "Blade Runner" Europe.

1   Western Experiences

The revolution in the East, with its adoption of democratic institutions and rights – together with the intent to promote private ownership of the means of production within a market framework – could, of course, be regarded as the triumph of capitalism over socialism. And at one, albeit very aggregate level, this is true. However, the chapters in this volume – on the dynamics of the welfare state under advanced capitalism and on the prospects of a welfare state at a supranational level – are not written in a self-congratulatory style. Instead, the authors emphasize problems, tensions, challenges, and change. Several of them strongly underline the divergence of the Western experience. They point out that there are not one, but several types of markets, welfare state regimes, and different conceptions of democracy; and that markets and welfare states are linked in different ways.

The first contribution, written by *John Myles* and *Robert J. Brym*, focuses on the burning issue of the complementary and conflictual relationship of democracy and the free market, on its dynamics both East and West, and on the ambiguities of the terms in question. Democracy, the market, the welfare state – all are historically changing, politically and ideologically overloaded terms: hence, a number of possible misconceptions and contradictions both East and West.

Drawing attention to the slow and difficult emergence of Western democracies, the authors warn against two assumptions widely held in the West. On the one hand, both public opinion polls and recent events in the formerly socialist countries show that these countries are not at the end, but just at the beginning of the struggle for democracy. On the other hand, the Western countries have to understand that they themselves are not at the end of their history. While the duality of democratic versus totalitarian states lasted, Western democracy could be defined in terms of its absence elsewhere. The end of the duality presents new challenges and will force many to rethink and question the perfection of the Western model. Similar problems arise in the case of the market.

Myles and Brym emphasize that the new "love affair" of the Eastern intelligentsia with a self-regulating market and a democracy based on negative freedoms (implying also a minimal state), may not be shared by those who are forced to bear all the costs of the transition. The lesson from the West ought to bring home to them that without democratic limits on market forces, on property rights, and on distributional issues, social tensions might run so high as to invite violence and repression – which in turn may jeopardize or even defeat the current experiment.

The welfare state has emerged as the instrument to implement the democratic limits referred to above. Its form and force have continually changed; and it varies largely in contemporary capitalism, too, from the largely market-reliant (mostly English-speaking) democracies to the two types of "planned markets" (the "corporatist" type like Sweden or Germany, and the "market nationalist" type exemplified by Japan). The debates of the late 1980s and early 1990s were not about whether there should be a welfare state or not, but rather about the type and kind it should be – implying also the type and kind of democracy and market. The lesson for Eastern Europe is, in the view of these authors, that if they want to avoid the Latin American experience (with its economic and political underdevelopment), they should struggle not only for the market, but also for strong democratic institutions which complete and control it.

Jean-Pierre Jallade's contribution is the most optimistic chapter in Part I. In his paper, he presents a balanced assessment of the literature on the so-called crisis of the welfare state which was the dominant and fashionable theme of public discourse 10 years ago. Jallade specifies the crisis in terms of three dimensions: a financial crisis, a crisis of legitimacy, and an institutional crisis. His conclusions are in several ways promising. A retrospective look on what happened during the 1980s informs us that our welfare states, apparently on the verge of bankruptcy in 1980, have survived. Their financial difficulties have been eased considerably, and the so-called crisis has evaporated. Jallade claims that the systems of social security have turned out to be more flexible than expected, and the adjustment process did not disrupt the range and level of benefits fundamentally. In his study, Jean-Pierre Jallade discusses a set of other related topics. Here, we will only highlight three important additional elements. First, he claims that the welfare state will survive the increasing globalization of the economy. High labour costs in some countries reflect high standards of living and sophisticated economies where cost is only one decisive factor among others (cf. Kåre Hagen). In addition to this, welfare states employ a large number of people (cf. Kolberg and Uusitalo) and redistribute incomes, which contribute to maintaining demand on a smooth level. According to Jallade, this means that the welfare states can also be seen as an engine of growth.

In line with Kolberg and Uusitalo and on the basis of research findings, Jean-Pierre Jallade rejects the widespread argument that the redistributional impact of the welfare state is negligible and that we could do away with the whole apparatus of taxes and transfers with no significant consequences for social stratification. However, he argues that the redistributional ambition of the welfare states in the West has eroded over time, and he indicates that this bolsters the middle-class support for it. The last point is that this chapter also contains a warning which is important beyond Western Europe: namely, that unemployment rather than low rates of growth is the Achilles' heel of European welfare states. This is the basis for his recommendation for job creation in all sectors.

Frances Fox Piven and *Richard A. Cloward*'s conclusion is far less optimistic. Their story is that of an intellectual battle between business on the one hand, and the liberal establishment on the other. The basis for this battle is the mobilization of American business, prompted by the shock of the 1970s. This put an end to the politics of fractionalized business interests in the US. One of the results of this class mobilization was the hardened resistance towards union activity; another were the tax cuts on business and the better-off. A third outcome was a campaign against welfare state programmes.

The resulting change in public policy strongly affected the distribution of income and well-being in American society, to the detriment of the bottom part of it. The mobilized business community claimed that the campaign against the welfare state was a response to popular sentiment; that the programmes of the welfare state sustain poverty, lead to marital breakdowns, and thus do more harm than good. Most importantly, it was argued that the attack on the welfare state (cutting taxes and slashing programmes) was necessary to fuel profits and investment to enable US business to compete successfully on the international market.

The second part of the chapter discusses the liberal and left-wing response to this attack. The traditional supporters of the welfare state were caught off guard. They had no powerful counter-arguments and were unable to refute the assaults. One aspect of this retreat is presented as a shift in the intellectual climate. Welfare state politics was traditionally conceived of by American liberals in terms of class politics. This is no longer the predominant approach. Instead, a new intellectual "habitus" has emerged, focusing on issues such as post-modernism or the cultural determinants of poverty and the underclass. Thus, the authors conclude, the large-scale attack on the welfare state was indeed successful: it did dismantle, albeit only temporarily, the liberal left in the US.

Jon Eivind Kolberg and *Hannu Uusitalo* emphasize that some welfare states – i.e. the Scandinavian ones – have been success stories in terms of redistribution and in terms of reducing the level of poverty. Secondly, they argue that the conventional wisdom which regards the welfare state as the root cause of economic problems under capitalism, is inconclusive at best. And finally, they also maintain that the functions of the modern welfare state by far exceed its original format. In this sense, the Western welfare states are overloaded. However, according to Kolberg and Uusitalo, this is not because of the postulated revolution of rising expectations, but because the welfare state is being increasingly used to reduce labour supply – and thus to bolster firm productivity and boost competitiveness on the international market.

This chapter concludes by spelling out a series of challenges for future research, out of which we highlight here only the most relevant ones. For one thing, the development at the interface of the economy and welfare states appears to contradict the idea that the single dominant substance of modernization is functional differentiation. Instead, contemporary reality may be better described in terms of functional integration. Secondly, our conventional understanding of social policy as a response to problems created in other areas needs to be modified. In the view of the authors, the welfare state is an active agent in the structuration of contemporary capitalist societies. Thirdly, there is a warning here against unidimensional theoretical frameworks, based on the observation of the authors of highly divergent patterns of welfare state/labour market relationships in Western Europe. The last point flowing from their analysis, is the apparent need for a re-specification of the trade-off between efficiency and equality. This should include both a better specification of what is meant by efficiency, and its micro and macro context.

Adrian Sinfield's contribution contains a careful summary of the research literature on unemployment in the West. Besides his discussion of methodological issues and of the striking variation on unemployment experiences in Western capitalist countries, the author argues that the rise of unemployment has a very significant impact at three different levels: the individual level, the level of the welfare state, and the societal level. He first documents beyond any reasonable doubt that unemployment is harmful for those who experience it – in terms of poverty, health risk, and even mortality. He shows, secondly and also convincingly, that unemployment is harmful to the welfare state itself. It increases expenditure and decreases revenue, which produces financial pressure on other programmes. This effect is exacerbated in situations when tax concessions for private arrangements (for the better-off) further erode the financial base of the welfare state. Sinfield finally argues that high unemployment affects the character of society as a whole. He shows that unemployment disproportionately hits the bottom of society – and in addition, that the class-specific profile of unemployment has increased with the rising level of unemployment. One quite obvious consequence of high and persistent unemployment is the shifting balance of power between the employing and the working classes.

Since Adrian Sinfield explores the darkest side of the development of contemporary advanced capitalism, it seems no wonder that he warns the countries of Eastern/Central Europe not to overlook the importance of high unemployment.

1.1   Shared Preoccupations

While each author explored his/her subject independently and with a different theoretical framework, there are some issues of pragmatic or theoretical relevance which point to shared preoccupations:

1.1.1 The Role of the State

As already mentioned, there is by and large a consensus of the contributors of this volume not only about the necessity of the welfare state, but also about its peculiar feature of combining stability and resistance to onslaughts on the one hand, and flexibility and adaptability on the other. The thesis about the "incompressibility" of state activity may be substantiated by Table 1.1.

No doubt, there is currently a widespread view according to which welfare states bread helplessness and immorality, and they "are in the name of solidarity destroying those social networks which are the 'infrastructure' of the 'community' as meta-reciprocal collectivity" (cf. Rus; see also Segalman and Marsland, 1989). Most authors in this volume held an opposite view. They tend rather to think that welfare policies were put in place *because* traditional communities were weakened or destroyed in the last two centuries: because people were helpless in meeting new risks; because there were no traditional instruments to fulfil new and urgent needs; and, last but not least, because they were beneficial for the economy.

They also think that while the achievements of the welfare state in terms of basic securities solved some fundamental problems, there was always a tremendous need for what remained of the former "natural" networks, which have been unceasingly complementing the activity of the state.

This may be the reason why we presently simultaneously witness both the in-compressibility of welfare state spending, and a multiplication of new welfare arrangements – from privatized and marketized social services to self-help groups

Table 1.1:   Current Receipts of Government and Social Security Transfers as a Percentage of GDP in EEC Countries

	Averages for				Only
	1960-1967	1968-1973	1974-1979	1980-1988	1988
Government Receipts	27.6	32.2	37.2	42.4	42.6
Social Security	10.6	12.3	15.1	17.5	18.8

Source: OECD, 1990: 66-67.

and grass-roots helping communities. In other words, welfare needs seem to increase so that a stable, but no more rapidly-expanding welfare state has to be complemented by other societal resources. It is an open question whether a strong welfare state hinders, or rather promotes, the unfolding of other forms of social solidarity. The evidence is certainly multifaceted. The question has to be further explored.

1.1.2 The Changing Intellectual Apparatus

The papers reflect in various ways not only the ever-changing ideological climate, but also, and more importantly, the (epistemological) changes in the intellectual tools of exploring and analysing social reality.

The changing ideological climate is part of the background. It is sometimes made explicit: for instance, when one author notes that equality is no more a legitimate concern of social policy, "egalitarian policies having lost support in recent years both among policy makers and public opinion" (cf. Jallade). More often, it is implicit in the writings, in the way the authors have to follow the prevalent public discourse – even if they themselves do not adhere to new tenets.

The change in the cognitive tools or in the intellectual habitus is interesting not only in itself, but because it opens up new vistas for research. The need for the critical rethinking of the well-known, and usually unquestioned, thesis about functional differentiation (treated by Kolberg and Uusitalo), is one case in point. A more general, and more frequently appearing concern, is the approach to the structuring factors of society. In contemporary sociology, there are competing paradigms for the structural analysis of society. They cover a range from a traditional Marxist approach in terms of social classes to the so-called "post-modern" conceptions of social structuration, where various structuring and dividing forces are identified. From the post-modern perspective, the traditional approaches are thought to have lost their validity. The authors of this volume who analyse welfare politics or policies in structural terms, seem to adopt an intermediary position. None of them rejects the importance of new structuring factors – but they implicitly recognize the heuristic value of more or less traditional class concepts. This surfaces in the evaluation of the role of the middle class(es) in defining or in appropriating welfare policies (Jallade, Sinfield) or in the formulation of the conflicts either between the business élite and other factions of society (Piven and Cloward), or again, the inclusion in the analysis of new modes and ways of labour market structuration and segmentation which combine the more traditional conception of "good" and "bad" jobs, and the more recent recognition of the importance of the division between the public and the private sector, or between "insiders" and "outsiders" of the labour market (Sinfield; Kolberg/Uusitalo; see also Atkinson, Part III). A similar concern, and a similar understanding of the importance of a complex approach, is apparent in some of the chapters in Part II (Ferge; Kolarska-Bobinska).

2   Hopes and Fears in the East

One year after the "First All-European Dialogue", social researchers in the East are wiser and in some respects more, in some others less optimistic. Optimism is warranted in as much as the impossible seems to have happened: totalitarianism has been overcome without (at least as yet) major trouble. Also, as shown in Zaslavskaya's paper for the Soviet Union – or at the first free elections in Hungary, in Czechoslovakia and in Poland – the overwhelming majority of citizens (about or over 95% in each case) have rejected the Stalinist past, the totalitarian system, and all its political corollaries. In other words, *almost nobody is grieving for the past system in the former Eastern block*, and practically none of its "civilian" citizens want it back. However, as history unfolds itself, new fears and new hopes are arising.

The aim of *Ana M. Guillén's* chapter is to assess the significance of the changes in social policy during the Spanish transition from dictatorship to democracy. Hence, her contribution fills a glaring gap in the research literature on cross-national variations in welfare state regimes. It contains a rich and most valuable account of the welfare system that was built up under Francoism. The major programme of social protection in this highly-fragmented system, was directed to low-income industrial workers and their dependants. But this core was complemented by a whole series of schemes for specific occupational categories – and also by a complex of worker's mutual aid associations.

Guillén uses three indicators to examine the social policy implications of the transition from dictatorship to democracy: (a) the existence, or absence, of reforms in the macro-institutional design and the organization of the welfare state; (b) changes in coverage and expenditure; and (c) changes in the character of the decision-making process. She shows that the most salient feature of social policy during the period of democratic transition, was its high degree of continuity *vis-à-vis* the *ancien régime* in all three fields. Democratic practices were institutionalized, and standards were improved without dismantling widely-accepted structures. Also, instead of denouncing unfulfilled promises of the former regime, the new system implemented them.

Guillén explores three sets of possible explanations for the continuity, and the lack of radical reform in social policy. In case of one of them, the Francoist inheritance, it seems that changes in social policy started already before Franco's death, so that incremental improvements were sufficient. As for the second issue, the character of the political process of democratization, Guillén underscores the ghost of a potential military *coup d'état*, which made imperative the emphasis on consensual politics. The third explanation is offered by the contextual aspects of the transition, out of which the most important element was the economic crisis of the 1970s, which hit Spain especially hard, and warranted cautiousness in change.

Two articles give a flavour of the problems the Soviet Union has to face. Both emphasize the utter failure of 70 years of socialism in fulfilling the early promises, and the inhuman system which supplanted the first dreams.

Vladimir Shubkin's chapter provides a helpful addition to labour market theory, although it does not deal with the labour *market* at all. Indeed, Shubkin specifies the essential characteristics of labour relations under Stalinism, when there was no labour market. Instead, there was a specific type of industrial relations regime, which was characterized by: (1) extreme hierarchization: the complete subordination of workers to a powerful commanding and punitive apparatus; (2) the broad use of brutal force, in the form of purges, concentration camps, and imprisonments; (3) the effective ban of territorial mobility; (4) the transformation of the trade unions into the "executive arm" of the power élite; (5) the elimination of private ownership and the institution of state feudalism; and (6) curiously but understandably, steeling as a form of labour relations.

Shubkin explores some of the reasons for the creation of the above system, its consequences, and some of the challenges for the future. He finds the reason for this "production regime" in the political system and in the repercussions of the former on the moral fibre of society. Hence, he discusses such factors as the non-existence of democratic control and the persistent assault on moral restraint (Christian faith). Shubkin also underlines the role of the military setting with its real or unreal ingredients: such as the preparation for the world revolution, the pervasive idea of being surrounded by enemies, the experience of World War II, the postwar arms race, and – in particular – the effort to maintain nuclear parity. The remedies spelt out in this paper are to be found in a transition to property rights, which will form a basis for the articulation of interests through parties and, hence, the development of a multi-party system. However, in addition to economic and political components, Shubkin also stresses the importance of spiritual values for a decent future in the Soviet Union.

Tatiana Zaslavskaya broadens and substantiates this picture by new insights as well as by means of detailed and up-to-date public opinion poll data. Her starting point is also the inevitability of the change of the system, but she emphasizes the prime importance of the radical change of the political structure, among other reasons because the polls show the complete loss of confidence of the citizens in the state and the party. According to the author, this lack of confidence may hinder *perestroika*, because there is no legitimate social force to make people accept the new, often unpopular sacrifices. Zaslavskaya then points out (on the basis of data from 1990) that a second major source of political conflicts is the "inter-ethnic" situation, the strong, and often opposed views on the future of the various republics.

The polls related to economic and social issues are of extreme importance. Despite assumptions to the contrary, a strong majority supports the Shatalin plan of marketization, and more and more people are beginning to get used to the idea of private ownership and entrepreneurship. No doubt, people accept with less equanimity the consequences of the market in the field of increasing inequalities. In the absence of a deliberate policy for more "social justice", and more social protection for the vulnerable groups, social tensions may grow because of these changes.

The conclusion of the author is that without the imminent radical democratization of social, economic and political life there is not even hope to overcome the current and increasing difficulties. She thinks that the support for radical change would be there, even though the former "reforms initiated from above" have gradually become a "revolution from below", with often uncontrollable and dangerous consequences.

Jan Hartl and *Jiri Vecerník* are also struggling with the problems of social transformation. Before the war, Czechoslovakia – unlike the other Central and Eastern European countries – had a prosperous capitalist system characterized by democratic humanism and a relatively developed early welfare state. This legacy was fully rejected in the 1950s and replaced by a particularly harsh variant of state socialism, which destroyed extremely valuable traditions and institutions. Since this past cannot be readily revived, the return to "Europe" is not easy.

The renewal of the economy by means of the transition to a market economy, is a basic condition of societal improvement. But there are various obstacles to this renewal. There is the resistance of the former bureaucratic apparatus which has much to lose in the transition, and the difficulty to change mentalities: to accept a new, more entrepreneurial ethos; to overcome psychosocial barriers to social change entailing increasing inequalities; individualism, etc. One has to reckon also with the fear of losing acquired social securities which were based, however, on the absolute centralization of power.

The "functional prerequisites" of social security were a bureaucratic system of employment ending up in brutal exploitative practices; a paternalistic state mixing up economic and social policy, rendering the economy ineffective, leaving social policy in a residual status, and leading to a shabby egalitarianism; and a "liberated household" ideology, forcing women out of the home and ruining the foundations of family life.

All three fields had to be transformed. In all of them, there is need for the recognition of the autonomy of the institutions (the economy, the labour market, the family, etc.); for far less centralized redistribution; for spontaneous developments, autonomous initiatives of the citizens, and for giving up the former attitude to expect improvements only "from above".

A new social policy is clearly on the agenda. It should break with the centralized, uncontrolled practices, and unclear relationships of the past, and should be rooted in a strong "civil society". The authors believe that the new social policy should be pluralistic, completing the activity of the state with the other formal and informal sectors (the local community, the voluntary sector, the family, etc.).

Pluralism is necessary here as elsewhere. Also, the welfare system should be transparent and have a subjective meaning for people, i.e. the relationships between taxes and social services should be restored.

It seems to the authors that the historical gap created by state socialism may be overcome, and the sense of social security may be preserved only by the combination of three main strategies: decentralization, de-etatization, and marketization.

The preoccupations and the outlook of *Lena Kolarska-Bobinska* are not far removed from those of the previous authors. Because Poland had a headstart over the other countries, she can identify more clearly some of the problems; and she already has some empirical data on the impact, or the difficulties, of change. Also, because the contours of the change are slightly clearer, Kolarska-Bobinska identifies a single core problem – the emergence of civil society – and focuses on the factors promoting or hindering it. In her assessment, civil society is the key to the success of the transition; but, in her view, it is far less active than would be desirable. She identifies two causes of apathy. On the one hand, she asks whether society will be able to completely redefine its relationship to the state and become more active. On the other, she shows that the process of transformation itself has psychosocial effects and is not necessarily curing the anomic state and the apathy of society.

In the case of the state, the difficulty is that while society is alienated from the former state, the massive withdrawal of the state from the sphere of social protection is not seen favourably. The gap left by the state should be filled by self-organizing movements of civil society. However, this would mean that initiatives which should come from below are, in fact, pushed forward (by necessity) from above. Also, it may be the case that, instead of genuinely redefining the mutual roles of the state and of civil society, people will qualify the withdrawal of the state merely as a new form of "unfriendliness".

As far as the psychosocial price of the transformation is concerned, important changes are noted in the causation of anomy. While in the former system, anomy was bred by a non-legitimate government and the impossibility to reach socially accepted goals, under the new, legitimate conditions goal-attainment is prevented by new, harsher economic conditions. Also, there are many elements which breed confusion and anomy. Thus, among others, there are many losers because of the structural change; and even the winners feel insecure: bad economic conditions increase self-centredness and have a generally disruptive effect on self-organization; it is exceedingly difficult to adjust to the complete reversal of the value system, and so forth.

Civil society will take shape only if there are movements and organizations starting from below and centred not only around immediate economic interests, but also around other shared values. But it is uncertain whether these processes can start vigorously enough under the conditions described above. The author is therefore doubtful whether civil society will be able to fill the gap left by the state. In any case, the rebirth of civil society will be slow and difficult; and many social spheres and groups will be adversely affected by the change.

Veljko Rus builds up a philosophical-theoretical framework to prove the inevitable demise of existing socialism. His basic couple of concepts is positive and negative equality. The socialist utopia is built around the negative concept of equality, which refers to both its inorganic emergence (a negation of capitalism) and its negative consequences in distribution as well as in shaping human relations. Further theoretical flaws in the socialist concept of equality are also identified by the author. It is essentially limited to economic equality, which impoverishes social objectives. However, in this impoverished interpretation, it is an unlimited or maximizing concept, confusing the theoretical difference between justice and equality and thereby ruining the basis of solidarity. In fact, solidarity cannot be conceived of as the automatic outcome of an "equalized" division of labour (without private ownership), because it would also need a moral basis.

According to the author, socialist social policy had to fail because it never made clear the concept of equality on which it was based. It did not make a distinction between differentiation ("just inequality" leading to marginalized groups) and discrimination (unjust inequality leading to unprivileged groups). Because of this, social policy did not recognize that poverty could have other than structural – namely, cultural – roots and therefore could not cope with it.

Because of the dominant role of the concept of negative equality, politics started to dominate the economic and the social sphere. The abolition of private ownership and the market necessarily followed. However, it turned out that not only the market, but also planned redistribution could generate important inequalities; and the Yugoslavian third option, self-management, did not improve the situation, either. From the failures of all known distributive mechanisms, the author concludes that social policy should in fact not aim at all at social equality, but only at the redistribution of a very narrowly defined set of public goods.

Finally, one of the main problems with the socialist concept of equality is its exclusivity, i.e. the worship of equality at the expense of freedom and solidarity. In the view of the author, existing socialism – but also Social Democracy, or the modern welfare state in general – promoted more negative than positive freedom, by promoting more negative than positive equality; and they also destroyed social solidarity, by making it institutionalized and compulsory. It was by the means of institutionalized solidarity that modern welfare states have invaded and destroyed civil society and its collectivities. In the view of the author, only a freely-organizing civil society could promote positive freedom and positive equality.

The chapter of *Zsuzsa Ferge* tries to connect societal transformation to the probable changes in social policy. She first reviews the former and the prospective welfare regimes of Hungary. Using the welfare regime types of Esping-Andersen

(1990), the pre-war system is identified as one similar to the continental European conservative-corporatist-statist model. The model of the former state socialist system is described as an (unprecedented) antiliberal-statist-hierarchized-socialist mix, with conservative bits thrown in.

The social structure is currently undergoing change, passing from a "repressed" structure to an authentic one. Two groups of the new middle class – the state bureaucracy, and the entrepreneurial class – are heading towards consolidation and towards a well-established position in the upper echelons of the social hierarchy. The third faction of the middle class, the "intellectuals", are losing out. The working class is divided, and the future of the rural population is still uncertain.

Under the current conditions of societal change, two of the three main models (conservative and liberal) are strongly represented in parliamentary politics, and the social forces in their favour start to organize also outside Parliament. Out of the groups supposedly in favour of a liberal-socialist model of welfare, those inside Parliament are weak and on the defensive; and those outside Parliament are either unshaped or disorganized. Therefore, despite the processes of democratization and new opportunities for engaging in real politics, the welfare system may evolve in a way contrary to the will and interests of a majority. Because the economic and social conditions are tragically deteriorating and (re)distribution of shrinking resources works in favour of the better-off minority and forcefully against the worse-off majority, the prevailing processes may either lead to a weakened welfare state, or to social trouble.

2.1   General Assumptions

Some common themes emerge also from the chapters on the transition from dictatorship to democracy, which may help to formulate some general assumptions about the systemic change taking place in these countries.

2.1.1 Economy and Politics

It appears to be an important fact that practically all reform movements in "existing socialism" from the "NEP" – the New Economic Policy in the Soviet Union in the early 1920s – on, started as endeavours to reform the economy. It is an unanswered theoretical question whether the economic start has been due to the "nature of things", because – after all – the economy is the foundation of social life (as orthodox Marxists would have it), or because criticisms about the economy were the only outlet left to civil society by the dictatorial power (as we prefer to think). After all, a better economy would have been beneficial for the existing power structure, if it could have been attained without endangering the political system.

The advocates of economic reforms, consciously or not, have usually accepted, at least provisionally, the terms of the trade offered by the central power. They acted and talked as if the economy alone, if marketized, could redeem society, adding (almost as an afterthought) that more market inevitably means more democracy, too. In other words, the reformers instrumental in preparing the way to the collapse of "existing socialism" have believed, or have long made themselves believe, that the system was reformable: that "democratic socialism", "socialism with a human face", were genuine historical alternatives in Central and Eastern Europe.

And history has repeated itself each time. When the "top" realized that economic reform would not stop at the borders of the economy but would spread to politics and jeopardize their power directly or indirectly, they instantly tried to kill the innovative ideas, as often as not together with those conceiving them – and the story started again. (This was the case – to mention only the most momentous events – of the NEP; of the first economic reform movements in the early 1950s in Hungary, East Germany, and Poland "overflowing" to politics; that of the Prague Spring in 1968 which did the same; of the second Hungarian economic reform, also starting in 1968 and nipped in the bud in 1972 without ever reaching politics.)

Whatever the case, the recognition that society could not function without some form of the market is almost as old as the banning of the market from social life. Because of the former lessons, in later periods the political corollaries of the market had to be played down by the reformers in order to dissipate the fears of the power élite. In the last years, the idea of the market as the saviour of society has been underpinned by the victorious march of neo-liberalism in the West. It is not surprising, therefore, that many social scientists have become firm believers not only in the economic, but also in the politically liberating virtues of the market.

Signs of the (almost) unconditional adherence to a pure market economy may be found in the majority of the papers originating from the former state socialist countries. (The most convincing illustration is probably the chapter by Veljko Rus). However, most authors point out the confusion in the minds and attitudes of people, who are simultaneously expectant and afraid of the market (Hartl; Kolarska-Bobinska).

2.1.2 The Heavy Legacies of the Past

POLITICS   It is brought home (almost) everywhere with painful clarity that the legacy of the political oppression of totalitarianism is heavier than one would have assumed. The forebodings of Zaslavskaya about the right-reactionary forces and the possible failure of *perestroika* are now more than an unformed fear. Unsuspected depths of nationalism, of social conservatism, of all forms of racism including anti-Semitism, are now surfacing practically everywhere. Two fearful political corollaries may follow. On the one hand, the passions turning against the past are trying to delegitimate not only "existing socialism" as a political system (which would be a normal reaction), but also all those who have "collaborated" to make it survive. And the definition of "collaborators" may be very flexible, engulfing at the end all those who do not declare openly their allegiance to the new system.

This means a repetition of the dictatorial past in terms of the intolerance of pluralism, and it may instill fear in the majority of citizens. Democracy cannot work if the citizens are afraid of the consequences of their free choices and free actions.

The other consequence of the new passions is that the (abstract) idea of socialism (or social democracy), is equated with the reality of existing socialism; and left-wing thinking or movements are also completely delegitimated. This means that the newly-elected Parliaments may have no significant left wing, or that what is left of the left is so markedly on the defensive that it has no real impact. This imbalance of the political field of forces is not boding well in a newborn and shaky democracy.

Observing the newly emerging passions and ideologies, one has the impression that existing socialism was really a "non-system" (Ferge), or that what we observe right now is a "reinvention of the past" (Hartl/Vecerník). In this respect, it seems that 70 years of "socialism" in the Soviet Union, and 45 years in the other countries, did not leave any impact on the mentality of people – or worse, it seems as if the darkest passions had been strengthened by the aggressive oppression. It is not yet clear whether the negative passions affect the majority or only a tiny, but very vocal minority of the newly liberated societies. It is even less evident how the conflicts activated by these passions will end.

OWNERSHIP   Another element of the riddle concerning the future is the problem of ownership. It has become clear that while the "nationalization" of private ownership could be achieved in a very short time, the abolition of the state monopoly is much more difficult. On the one hand, people have become unused to entrepreneurship, to really managing property – although it seems that this difficulty may be overcome relatively smoothly. The real problem is that practically everywhere private ownership was confiscated without so much as a symbolic or partial compensation, and that many of those whose property was (to speak bluntly) stolen, are still living and are asking their property back. However, so many things have changed in the meantime, that it is impossible to restore a state of affairs prevailing half a century ago without causing new injustices and without inflicting new pains, not to mention the fact that the costs of compensation can be financed only by the taxes of former non-owner citizens. Thus, the issues of (re)privatization and of compensation for all past sufferings, are inextricably merged. By now, it seems (taking into account the disastrous economic conditions of the countries involved) that there is probably no really satisfactory solution to this dilemma.

SOCIAL ANOMY   Another legacy of the past, looming large in Central and Eastern Europe, is a very high level of social anomies and of literally sick societies. Several authors point out that, while one of the main reasons of the anomic state – the forced adjustment to a non-accepted system – disappeared, there are new factors breeding anomy and preventing social integration. Adjustment to radically new challenges and a diametrically changed value system, is stressful for many.

The current transition would require, in fact, many changes in attitudes and mentalities. Lost social skills, both in the economy and in democratic political behaviour, should be brought back to life. Perhaps more importantly, the learned attitudes acquired under state socialism (like bad work ethics) should be overcome (cf. Kolarska-Bobinska; Shubkin; Hartl/Vecerník).

In this respect – unlike in the case of the "dark passions" – the "non-system" seems to have made its imprint on society. The explicit objective, a thorough change "in the personality of socialist man", was attempted by direct indoctrination – and proved to be completely ineffectual, or, rather, counterproductive. Meanwhile, the "learned helplessness" in the public sphere, in politics as well as in the economy, seems to be there for keeps.

It may well be that the impact was greater in the latter case because it was unintended. The outcome (like bad work ethics, "cheating" the state, expecting directives from above) has formed part of the defensive strategies of people and was developed absolutely spontaneously, "under cover" of the private sphere – in which very different strategies were surreptitiously developed. It is not easy, though, to transform covered and private strategies into open and public attitudes.

2.1.3 Perception of the Limitations of the Market

One of the new developments is the realization that the market, especially in the shape of that of an early capitalist society, is not an unmitigated blessing. The unchecked increase of income differentials under conditions in which the majority are losers, is irritating – if not intolerable – for many. Of course, state socialist societies were not genuinely egalitarian. Major studies emphasized the huge privileges and inequalities saddling "existing socialism" (see, e.g. Konrad/Szelényi, 1978). But on the one hand, there was a forceful ideology; and, on the other, there were genuine – if misplaced – attempts to contain inequalities (e.g. in case of salaries and wages). In other words, equality, even if absent or abused, was an explicit and endorsed objective – while at present it is negated as a legitimate social concern. There is a confusion in people's minds because of this fundamental reversal of values.

2.1.4 The Changing Role of the State

One aspect of the transition to a market economy is the changing role of the state. The problem is different from that of the Western countries, partly because the state was very different, and partly because the institutions which are supposed to replace the state – namely the market and, more broadly, civil society – are only *in statu nascendi*. In both cases, talk is about de-etatization. But in the West, this is essentially an economic argument (emphasizing the increasing role of the market); and in the East, the approach is essentially political. The cardinal question in the East seems to be to what extent should the former, all-invading state be replaced by "civil society", without emphasizing the role of the market in this connection. There is a complete agreement among the authors about the necessity of the revival of civil society, and everybody knows that the total withdrawal of the state is impossible. Still, there is a difference in the faith put in the potentialities of civil society in replacing the state. This divergence is the other side of the differing evaluation of the relationship between market and democracy.

Some of the Eastern authors believe that the withdrawal of the state from *all* walks of life, social policy included, is a condition *sine qua non* of the systemic change. In this view, the "learned helplessness", which prevents people to cope with the new challenges and to function adequately under the new conditions, cannot be unlearned if the state continues to perform its former social role. The gap left by the state in social protection should be filled mainly by self-organization, self-help, and other non-state institutions of civil society – even if this entails the temporary increase of social problems. The states themselves – or rather, the governments –, all in great financial trouble, seem to follow this precept. As Hartl and Vecerník put it: "To dare to speak of social policy or even of social justice is seen as a traditional "leftist" deviation, tolerable perhaps in case of a scholar, but suicide in case of a politician.".

Others make a difference in the desirable role of the state in different sectors. While a marked curtailing of the state's power and activity is seen as warranted in politics and in the economy, they make an exception for social protection. Of course, the character of the state should markedly alter: from an undemocratic and paternalistic state, it should become a democratic partner. If Zaslavskaya is right in advocating a renewed social policy for winning people over for the cause of systemic change and for preventing their utter impoverishment, then the rejection of welfare policy as a means of consolidating the new democracies – and the rejection of the financial and legal responsibilities of the state in shaping this policy – may entail disastrous consequences.

2.1.5 Changing Social Structures

Practically all the Eastern authors realize that the former social structure will inevitably and radically change, even if few deal in some detail with this issue. It is widely recognized that social inequalities will increase, that a wealthy group will appear alongside increasing poverty and marginalization. Some authors (Kolarska-Bobinska; Ferge) make an attempt to generalize this common observation. They expect the formation of a "middle class" or *bourgeoisie*, and both of them think that the newly-shaped economic interests will be one of the strongest factors leading to the formation of a social group (or perhaps class). As for the global structural impact of the changes – namely, the possibility of the emergence of an upper class, the potential structuration of the middle class, the fate of the workers and peasants – only some theoretical attempts are made in this direction. And there are only hints about the structuring factors of a "post-modern" society. This is probably due to the fact that the new societies are more similar to early capitalist class societies than to the so-called post-modern structures.

2.1.6 The Nature of Dictatorships

Fascism and Bolshevism are usually both qualified to be totalitarian systems. In an abstract sense or if Fascism is embodied by Hitlerism, the equation may be true. However, if one compares the aftermath of Francoism and that of "existing socialism", the similarity ends. Admittedly, late Francoism was a mild dictatorship – but so was late Kadarism in Hungary. Nonetheless, Spain succeeded to build a new society on the ruins of the old without liberating passions for vengeance and without wanting to destroy all remnants of the past, even those which were by and large working. Of course, the history of the transformation of Eastern European socialism is not yet completed; but resentment against the former system seems much stronger than in the case of Francoism.

We cannot offer a satisfactory explanation to this apparent difference. We suspect, however, that part of the explanation lies in the simple fact that Francoism left more or less intact the basic system-integrative mechanism, the market, and did not fundamentally alter one of the basic structuring forces of capitalism, property relations. Therefore, the transition to a new, democratic society was easier. It may also be the case that Spain was for many centuries much "closer to Europe" than the Eastern periphery. And we also suggest that the psychosocial distortions induced by the Stalinist type of totalitarianism were more cruel. People were more deeply deceived: their primeval dream about a just and equal society was cruelly destroyed, but they had to act for a long time as if the dream had come true.

3 New Instruments, Institutions and Scenarios in the West

Anthony B. Atkinson focuses on a possible instrument for renewing social policy, the basic income scheme, which has been on the agenda since some time in Western Europe (cf. also Leibfried). The starting point of Atkinson is the observed close correlation between the form of economic organization and the role of social policy. To prove this point, he first compares two "pure" economic types: "centralized socialist" and "market capitalist". He shows that social policy, or at least minimum income support, is related more to the workplace in the first case, and more to "social insurance" (completed by social assistance) in the second.

Of course, "pure" types do not exist in reality. Eastern socialism is on its way to disappearing and to "returning to Europe". As for market capitalism, it seems that the operation of the traditional tools of social policy is endangered by widespread, long-term unemployment and by new forms of segmentation due to the increase of "atypical" forms of employment (part-time work, self-employment, etc.). Social insurance is not well-prepared to cope with the new trends. Social assistance cannot properly supplement it, partly because of the increasing dimensions of the problem, and partly because of its old flaws: incomplete take-up, low levels of assistance, and the erroneous assumption that assistance can be based on the family and on strong family ties.

Because of the failure of Eastern socialism, and the flaws of market capitalism, there is a good cause for searching for a "third way" – not only in terms of economic organization, but also in terms of social policy. In Atkinson's view, the "basic income" scheme could usefully replace social insurance and assistance. It would not only overcome the shortcomings of these two systems, but would also be more consistent with the new forms of economic organization. The problem is, however, that a sufficient level of the basic income would imply excessively high tax rates. In Atkinson's view, this difficulty could be overcome by a limited reform of the economic organization. Following James Meade's lead, he suggests that the state should be endowed, as owner, with a sizable fraction of the capital stock.

Atkinson also thinks that the Eastern countries are in a good position to experiment with this scheme. In any case, they should take into account, when deciding about their own future, the limitations of Western arrangements and the close connection between social policy and economic organization, and they should at least make informed choices.

Ronald Wiman's chapter, "From the Welfare State to a Welfare Society", echoes some of the contemporary worries of benevolent and visionary bureaucracies, such as the Finnish National Board of Social Affairs, and takes up an important thread about the future of European social policy. He starts from a critical assessment of the welfare state, claiming that the welfare state harbours certain basic and outdated conceptions of man, of social problems, and of the role of social policy in society at large. Wiman argues that the conventional understanding is definitely too passive on all these counts: we need to replace Social Darwinism and the therapeutic outlook with a new actor-oriented model of man which emphasizes the potential for an active role inherent in every human being. Thus, this chapter speaks of the innovative capacities of the whole population, and especially of the neglected innovative ability of clients.

On a more general level, social policy should be more than a trash bin for problems that are created in other sectors. There should be a much more active role for social policy in the future. Large-scale preventive efforts are needed, where social welfare policies should cease to be subordinate to economic policy. Instead, social policies should become aggressive tools in overall societal policy-making for generating economic and social processes, which would lead to greater well-being for all citizens.

Finally, there is advice in this chapter concerning international collaboration. The author strongly recommends the "Health-for-All" strategy to the entire field of social policy. This strategy – by means of appropriately-selected indicators and priorities – has designed strategies applicable to social development strategies across a whole spectrum of cultures. It has had stimulating effects both in intellectual terms and in relevant policies.

Stephan Leibfried – as well as all the remaining chapters of this part – switches to the global dilemmas of the future of Europe. He first provides the reader with several sensitizing distinctions which help to organize our understanding of the uncertain steps towards a *"Social Europe"*. Thus, he sets apart negative and positive integration, and argues that the move towards common constructive action is different from the former negative ambition of removing the obstacles to a free common market. He then spells out the main difference between two historical models for European integration in the social policy domain: the German *Reich*, and the United States of America. In the former case, integration was promoted through social reform (the establishment of social rights in Bismarck's Social Insurance), whereas the US model was marked rather by an "underdose" of social rights.

In contemporary Western Europe, Leibfried identifies and analyses four social policy regimes: the Scandinavian Welfare State; the "Bismarck" countries; the Anglo-Saxon countries; and the "Latin Rim" countries. He discusses how these regimes could be affected by the introduction of a basic income scheme and attempts to judge the integrative potential of reforms in this area.

There are other options, though. Thus, poverty policy may remain the main domain of national legislation; the different systems will integrate from below; or they will be harmonized from above. A likely scenario seems to be the Europeanization of poverty policy and the maintenance of social security as a national responsibility. The Europeanization of poverty policy could mean intensive targeting towards certain (deserving) groups. This would create a division of labour between the supranational level and the national level and be a step in the direction of the categorical approach to welfare (to treat different categories differently). The most likely development in the view of Leibfried is that all poverty policy will remain at the sub-European level. The three main reasons identified are: the difficulty to standardize needs-oriented policies; that present poverty regimes are incompatible in Europe; and that such policies have no strong lobby in the European context.

Kåre Hagen's approach to the same issue is slightly different. He starts from the assumption about a potential new type of welfare state regimes: a welfare regime at the supranational level. He sets out clearly the different motivations, conceptions, and the underlying logic of the so-called social dimension of the common market. He explores at a supranational level the relationship between capitalism, democracy, and the welfare state. This analysis goes to the heart of social policy by his discussion of the different, currently debated models on how the relationships between market, nation-state, and super-state, and between individuals, organized interests, and democracy should be (or not be) institutionalized within the framework of the European Community.

Hagen sets out five approaches to the social dimension of European integration that could be regarded as different outlines of possible supranational welfare-capitalist models. The first of these, economic liberalism, regards a social dimension as undesirable because it distorts the very market mechanisms the common market was designed to promote. The second approach rejects a social dimension by arguing that there is no need for it: social standards are seen as rewards for productivity, rather than as rigidities imposed on the market. In the third outlook, a supranational social polity is desirable but it is superfluous, because the market by itself will produce convergence. These three arguments against the need for a social dimension all confine the role of supranational bodies to that of creating and enforcing conditions for optimal economic efficiency. The two remaining views do not accept leaving social issues to the nation-state or market forces. One of the strategies is the "social market economy" approach, and the second the creation of a "European welfare super-state". In both views, the single integrated market is not a guarantee of the more effective realization of social goals than is possible by the institutions of the nation-state. Economic efficiency is no goal in its own right, but must be balanced by welfare and distributive objectives. Both views call for supranational institutions to implement this, but differ as to whether corporatist cooperation or democratic decision-making processes should produce these institutions. Consequently, their coverage differs. The social market economy sets out to establish a welfare regime for workers, whereas the ambition of the second approach is to include the entire population.

If the European Community is to become something more than economic cooperation between nation-states, the members will have to agree on an institutional edifice which combines to an acceptable degree core values of social welfare, democratic decision-making procedures, and politically-disciplined welfare capitalism. A European Community without these three traits is, of course, conceivable (in principle) but highly implausible. Hagen's own assessment for the medium-term future, is that the social dimension will in the coming years emerge as a framework for a Euro-corporatist variant of the social market economy with moderate ambitions.

Laura Balbo brings a refreshing feminist perspective into the picture, without being overly optimistic. In a thorough assessment of the bad and good fortunes of the postwar welfare state, she claims that (among many other trends) a "needs-oriented culture" has evolved, linking people more closely than before to their political system. Women, due to their daily experiences with unmet needs and their crucial role in fulfilling those needs, have been instrumental in building up this culture. Throughout this process, they have become "strategic actors" – a fact which may have importance for shaping the future. One of the key concepts of the needs-oriented culture is entitlement. Balbo believes that the centrepiece of the postwar European experience was an increasingly widespread acceptance of the fulfilment of people's needs as a basic right.

The conservative/neo-liberal turn of the tide, embodied in Thatcherism, has undermined this culture and has weakened or abolished social citizenship. Its impact is so strong that the strategy of social citizenship, which seemed to have been a shared European vision, cannot be considered as a common objective any more. In fact, Europe is now at a crossroad, with several scenarios in perspective.

Two of these are rather bleak. One starts from the fact that Europe is a privileged world, with her accumulated wealth, culture, and democratic traditions. Europe has much to loose and is therefore afraid of threatening worldwide processes. In defence of her advantages, she might become a "fortress", inimical to other cultures, and increasingly closing her borders. It may be feared that – paradoxically – the will to defend the values of Western democracy puts at risk the democratic tradition itself. The "Blade Runner model" is still worse. It is a gloomy vision of an anomic society, in which a small minority tries to keep control over the destitute, alienated, powerless masses.

Balbo's own choice would be the "user-friendly society", a caring society, a "welfare society", a natural continuation of the needs-oriented culture. Unfortunately, in contemporary Europe, where pervasive economic reductionism seems to rapidly gain ground, the other two models have a better chance to win. Currently, only the Nordic countries seem to retain this vision of a "good society", and it is an open question whether they may be able to maintain their fully autonomous policies under the conditions of an increasingly harsh economic competition and of European integration.

4   Generalizations about the Future

All in all, the prospects of social policy are not very bright in the near future. It seems to us that, while the alleged reason for cuts and withdrawals in the field of welfare is always economic (and therefore seemingly "objective" and irrefutable), the real reasons are social and political. This story is long and involved. We will just mention, without going into detail, some of the factors which may account for the real reasons.

There is, for one, the weakening of the former "strongholds" of the dominated class – of the trade unions, in the first place. There are countless new organizations, but they do not replace the old ones. Many of them, products of the postmodern society, are dealing with "post-modern" issues; and the traditional problems of poverty, unemployment, and insecurity are not their first concern. Also, they are extremely fragmented and do not join force easily (perhaps because of the pervasive individualism also on the agenda).

There is also the downfall of Eastern socialism. Many have observed for a long time that the Western countries profited more from the existence of socialism in the East than the Eastern countries themselves. Whatever the real records of existing socialism, it represented a challenge while it lasted. Capitalism had to prove itself even on those grounds which were supposedly the main attractions of socialism. The challenge has gradually weakened with the shortcomings and failures of socialism becoming more blatant, and it has completely disappeared with the downfall of "existing socialism".

Finally, we mention the new and shifting relationship between the respective power of capital and labour, and the consequences of this change. Apparently, the strength of capital is rapidly increasing with its "globalization", with its becoming more international and more impersonal. At the same time, labour – or the employed population in general – is weakening, for several reasons. One of them is their increasing fragmentation with new forms of employment, related to a large extent to the new technologies (economies of scale are probably of decreasing importance: small independent ventures are proliferating, etc.) The new forms of segmentation – atypical forms of employment, long-term unemployment – hinder the crystallization of common interests and also prevent unification or self-organization by divisive, competitive elements.

As a consequence of the above processes, the newly-emerging, strengthened middle or upper classes seize their opportunity to back out of the concessions to which they consented in the heyday of the postwar welfare state. It remains to be seen how far this process can go, and how the field of social forces will evolve in the future. We believe that, for many objective reasons, welfare policies and institutions have to change. But we do not believe that a society deprived of its institutions offering existential security, and of institutions offering a sense of belonging, is an acceptable alternative for the majority.

Notes

1 The editors based the introduction not only on the contents of the present book, but also on the lively discussions having taken place during the "First All-European Dialogue on Social Policies" in Helsinki, Finland, 15-19 March 1990.
2 Because of the changes, the majority of the authors rewrote their article, following the processes up to the end of 1990 or even up to early 1991.

References

OECD (1990) *Historical Statistics 1960-1988*. Paris.
Segalman, R., Marsland, D. (1989) *Cradle to Grave*. Macmillan.
Szelényi, I. (1983) *Urban Inequalities under State Socialism*. Oxford: Oxford University Press.

PART I

THE DYNAMICS OF THE WELFARE STATE IN ADVANCED CAPITALISM

CHAPTER 2

Markets and Welfare States:
What East and West Can Learn from Each Other

John Myles
Robert J. Brym

1 Democracy versus the Free Market?

The USSR and the countries of Eastern Europe have embarked on experiments of world-historical significance. Just what those experiments will produce, is as obscure to us now as the results of past revolutions were to those who were present when they occurred. We are in a period of transition, a time when "the parameters that create regularity in routine periods are themselves in flux and unsettled" (Cohen and Zysman, 1987: 88). The result is that outcomes are even more unpredictable than under conditions of relative stability. In these circumstances, as Mahon (1989: 1) concludes, the best we can do is attempt to discern the broad outlines of possible alternatives from the contradictory tendencies at work. Bearing that caveat in mind, what are some of the "contradictory tendencies" at work in the USSR and Eastern Europe? What are their implications for the West? And what, if anything, can the East learn from the Western experience?

Soviets and Eastern Europeans are in love at the moment with two ideas: democracy and the free market – so, at least, it seems when the East is viewed through the eyes of the Western media and therefore through the eyes of much of the Western public, including large segments of its intellectual stratum. Let us dwell briefly on these two ideas, on their connections and contradictons.

The word *democracy* is one of those terms like "class", "freedom", and "equality" that bears a heavy conceptual burden in Western thought. It has taken on different meanings in different historical periods and can be attached to a wide variety of political forms. As Marshall (1964) pointed out, the history of democracy in the West has been the history of the accumulation of rights – civil, political and social. These rights were accumulated slowly and were the product of enormous struggles. In most countries, universal adult suffrage is an achievement of very recent vintage; and few democratic rights – civil, political or social – were won painlessly (Therborn, 1977).

With the demise of the Stalinist state in the USSR and Eastern Europe, it has become fashionable in the West to conclude that this historical evolution of democracy has now come to an end; indeed, that we are at "the end of history". With the arrival of multiparty, or at least multicandidate, elections in the USSR and Eastern Europe, the evolution of democracy is allegedly being brought to completion.

Recent public opinion polls confirm that in the USSR, for example, about two-thirds of the adult population favour democracy. However, closer inspection of the data suggests that the Soviet population is confused about what "democracy" means – or, perhaps more precisely, that many definitions of democracy uncomfortably exist side by side in the USSR. Thus, according to a 1988 poll taken in Moscow, 28 per cent of respondents believe that the USSR is more democratic than the USA (compared to 35 per cent who hold the opposite opinion) (Project Understanding, 1988). Evidently, opinions about the nature of democracy vary widely in the USSR; and the large demonstrations and riots that regularly take place in the republic and national capitals show that different groups are prepared to vote with their feet for their versions of democracy. What these observations suggest to us, is precisely the opposite of the commonly-held Western view: the Soviet Union and Eastern Europe are not at the end of the democratic struggle, but at the beginning. We are at the threshold of a new historical experiment in democracy, the outcome of which will quite possibly bring forth new forms and new understandings of democracy.

Furthermore – and paradoxically – the West has much to learn from the East about democracy. In many respects, the era of the Cold War brought with it a temporary freeze in the development of Western democracy. Every Western school child knew that democracy existed in the West and not in the East. The United States, Canada, and France were democracies; the Soviet Union, Hungary, and Poland were not. Western democracy was defined in terms of its absence elsewhere – not as an historical project still in the process of unfolding but as an historical project successfully completed. However, with the demise of the Stalinist state and with the creation of parliamentary forms in the East, democracy once again becomes a contested concept in a double sense. New experiments in democratic politics will surely lead to novel political forms in the East. And new institutional expressions of popular sovereignty in the East will challenge traditional understandings of democracy in the West. People in Western societies may be free once again to ask fundamental questions about the democratic character of their own political institutions.

What of *markets*? Here the Eastern experience has already had an enormous impact on the West. The clear failure of the Eastern European experiment in centralized planning has disabused all but the most ardent Western socialists of the desirability of an economy where toothpaste production is planned and organized by a central state apparatus. And the Western business press is in a state of euphoria over what they read to be the clear victory of capitalism over socialism. For the time being at least, the dramatic events in Eastern Europe have distracted many in the West from the fact that Western capitalism is also in a period of transition, the outcome of which is by no means certain and which will have enormous significance for the future evolution of Western democratic political forms.

Recent public opinion polls suggest that in the USSR and Eastern Europe, the intelligentsia is as enamoured with free markets and classical liberal conceptions of democracy as the Western business press. However, the Soviet and Eastern European population as a whole is decidedly less enthusiastic about these ideas (Zaslavskaya, 1989: 19). Thus, while approximately two-thirds of the Soviet adult population favour a market economy, when asked what they understand by the term only 28 per cent indicate that they mean a market free of state intervention. In contrast, some 41 per cent of Soviet adults mean a system that promises affluence with low levels of social inequality and unemployment – apparently a sort of Swedish welfare state written large. The more concrete the question, the more anti-market the response. Thus, 75 per cent of the adult population resent the incipient capitalist class in the USSR (the owners of so-called "cooperative enterprises"), only 32 per cent of urban dwellers would like a business of their own, and barely 4 per cent of people in the countryside aspire to become independent farmers. Tatiana Zaslavskaya, the Soviet Union's foremost sociologist and public opinion pollster, concludes that the majority of Soviet citizens feel that "most of their daily problems should be decided not by themselves but, above all, by organs of the state" (quoted in Pipes, 1991: 80).

In their love affair with classical nineteenth-century conceptions of democracy and the free market, large segments of the Soviet and Eastern European intelligentsia seem to lack an appreciation of the more fully developed Western conceptions of social citizenship of the latter part of the twentieth century, conceptions that may be more in line with the sentiments of the Soviet and Eastern European population as a whole.[1] Here the Eastern intellectuals have much to learn from Western comparative welfare state studies. What seems to be missing from much of the intellectual debate in the East is an awareness of the inherent tensions and contradictions between the pursuit of more democracy, on the one hand, and capitalist forms of economic organization on the other. Reflecting on the Western experience, then, it might be useful to highlight some of those tensions and contradictions.

Nineteenth-century liberal notions of democracy were based on largely negative conceptions of freedom. They were concerned mainly with the absence of restraint or interference especially with respect to the use of one's property. The objective of classical liberal struggles was to expand the rights of property over and against the rights of the state, whether feudal or mercantilist. These struggles against the old order were often accompanied by considerable violence. It seems, however, that we are less prone to recall that the violence did not end with the overthrow of the old order. The rights of property did not only have to be wrested from the aristocracy; they also had to be imposed upon the propertyless. And, again, this frequently required the use of violence and repression. Albeit to a lesser degree, Henry Ford as well as Stalin found it necessary to use armed violence in order to compel people to work. Capitalist labour markets did not just evolve. They had to be created and, once created, they had to be maintained. Both their creation and maintenance historically required considerable use of public and private violence, judicial compulsion, and public regulation.

If the use of violence and repression is less frequent in contemporary capitalist economies, it is because the history of Western democracy has been accompanied not only by the expansion of property rights but also of personal rights that in varying degrees place boundaries upon and compete with property rights as the basis for both political participation and economic distribution. And the postwar welfare state, as Marshall (1964) pointed out, was one of the more critical ingredients in abating, if not eliminating, the class warfare that characterized previous generations.

There is an obvious economic logic to this development. The creation of social rights is one way of redistributing the costs and benefits of economic modernization. It is simply irrational for workers to participate willingly in such a process if they absorb all of the costs while all of the benefits go elsewhere in society. Under some conditions, this rational resistance will turn to violence. One should assume that Lech Walesa or other popular leaders will, in Walesa's words, "go back over the fence" if market reforms do not bring tangible improvements to their constituencies.

The history of Western capitalism suggests there is also a political logic here. To ensure that appropriate limits are placed on property rights, it is necessary that the propertyless have the capacity to exercise sufficient power to prevent the abuse of property rights. The postwar compromise between capital and labour in the West, was more than just a distributional compromise. In many countries, the basic democratic right of "freedom of association" was for the first time extended to include the rights of labour to organize. To varying degrees, labour in most countries acquired new powers both in the market and in the political system. The increased power of labour to impose constraints on the exercise of property rights by employers reduced the need for labour to turn to non-institutional forms of conflict to achieve their goals (Korpi and Shalev, 1979).

It seems to us, then, that the first lesson which the Soviet and Eastern European intelligentsia can learn from the history of Western capitalism is that negative concepts of democracy based simply on notions of limiting the role of the state in economic and social activity, provide an inadequate political environment for both economic and social renewal in the Soviet Union and Eastern Europe. If the lessons of the West are of any relevance today, they suggest that in the absence of positive democratic limits on property rights – both in the exercise of power and the distribution of wealth and income – the result will be a return to violence and repression that could quite possibly bring about an early demise of the current experiment.

The deeper and more fundamental lesson to be learned from this experience, is that while capitalism and democracy are clearly able to coexist, it is a coexistence fraught with tension and contradiction. The nineteenth-century liberal state, offspring of the bourgeois revolutions, was a state in which political participation and individual rights were based on economic capacity and ownership of property. The liberal democratic state of the twentieth century, the product of a century of conflict, also vests rights in people. But this marriage between a democratic state and a capitalist economy is a union of opposites, requiring accommodation between two opposing logics of social participation and distribution – one that attaches rights to the possession of property and another that attaches rights to people in their capacity as citizens. In adopting democratic principles of participation and distribution, the state did not abandon its liberalism. Rather, these two opposing doctrines were subsumed within a single structure. And it is this tension that has been the source of dynamism and change in the capitalist democracies during the twentieth century.

For a while, during the quarter century following World War II, it appeared that a relatively permanent accommodation had been reached. With an appropriate blend of Keynes and Beveridge, the rights of property and the rights of people could be reconciled to the advantage of both. During the 1970s, however, a contrary view began to take form. The capitalist democracies, it was argued, were suffering from a severe case of "democratic overload" (Huntington, 1975). The proliferation of citizenship entitlements, it was argued, had become a fetter on capital accumulation and democracy would have to be tamed if capitalism were to survive. As Marshall (1964: 134) had anticipated, capitalism and democracy were at war again.

We will take up the details of this conflict in the section that follows. Our purpose here is simply to highlight the fact of its existence and to note that Soviets and Eastern Europeans do not have to look far to find an explanation for this tension in democratic capitalism. It was Karl Polanyi (1944) who taught us about the impossibility of social survival when people (or nature) are treated as though they are commodities: that is, produced for sale in the market. Unlike pots, pans, or ships, the supply of people is determined not by their saleability in the market but by "nonstrategic demographic processes and the institutional rules of human reproductive activity" (Offe, 1985: 16). More simply, people are not produced or destroyed because of their expected value on the market; and some people, such as those with severe disabilities, have no labour to sell. Accordingly, to allow income distribution to be shaped by the market mechanism alone – to organize society as though people are produced exclusively for sale in the market – would, as Polanyi argued, result in the self-annihilation of society. Hence, labour markets need welfare states; without welfare states people will die, revolt, or both. It was also Polanyi's genius, however, to recognize that the problem is not markets *per se*. Throughout history there have always been markets. The problems begin only when a social inversion occurs and the social is subordinated to the market, where market logic becomes the logic of all social and political life.

2   What Kind of Welfare State? What Kind of Market?

Bismarck notwithstanding, the welfare states of Western Europe and North America are social institutions of very recent vintage. For the most part, modern systems of income security developed slowly after World War II and acquired their present form only in the late 1960s and early 1970s. It was also during that time – from the late 1960s to the mid-1970s – that the welfare state became a major focus of social scientific analysis in the West. In the first wave of comparative welfare state studies research questions were framed in terms of the growth of the welfare state, which is not surprising in view of the dramatic expansion of the welfare state in all capitalist democracies in the preceding decades. And despite wide variation in theoretical orientation, this first generation of studies generally agreed that the welfare state was the inevitable result of industrial (Wilensky, 1975) and/or capitalist (O'Connor, 1973) modernization.

   However, no sooner had the academy proclaimed the historical inevitability of the welfare state than the critics began to announce its demise. With the unhappy economic experience of the late 1970s and early 1980s, capitalism – and with it, the capitalist welfare state – were pronounced to be in a state of "crisis" (OECD, 1981). As in the welfare state growth literature, research problems were constructed in linear terms of more or less spending or of bigger or smaller welfare states (Esping-Andersen, 1990). Should we have a welfare state or not? Would the welfare state be forced to wither away as a result of demographic, economic or political pressures or would it survive more or less intact?

   Now, at the beginning of the 1990s, it seems fairly clear that a purely linear conception of the problem is at best misleading. The critical issue is not whether we shall have a welfare state but, rather, what kind of welfare state we shall have. As long as there have been states there have been welfare states, that is, political institutions for regulating the distribution of wealth and income. The nineteenth century brought the "poor house welfare state", the early twentieth century brought the "social assistance welfare state", and the postwar era brought the "social security welfare state". And each of these broad historical types contained considerable diversity of institutional forms (Leibfried, 1990).

For example, contemporary Western welfare states vary in the degree to which they rely on the market or the state for determining how wealth will be produced and distributed. At one extreme are largely market-reliant countries such as the US, the UK, and Canada. In such countries, decisions about what to produce, how to produce it, how many people to employ and just who those people will be tend to be dictated by competitive forces – more accurately, by competition between the economically powerful and the economically weak – and the vagaries of supply and demand. Central economic planning is widely regarded as a vile phrase. Thus, in the three largest English-speaking democracies, it has been especially fashionable for the past decade to blame all economic difficulties precisely on too much state involvement in the economy; and Republican and Conservative administrations have sought to improve their countries' economic standing by "liberating" free enterprise, selling off state-owned corporations, eliminating rules and regulations that do not favour large private business interests, reducing social expenditures, and changing the tax system with the aim of encouraging private saving and investment (without, we might add, passing laws which ensure that savings will be domestically and productively invested). The neo-conservatives argue that the liberation of capitalism will generate more jobs and, therefore, more wealth for all. But the record of the past decade reveals a less rosy picture: a trend towards greater economic inequality, new jobs in abundance only at the low end of the wage scale, an eroding manufacturing base, a mounting balance of payments problem, and a crushing debt burden.

The variety of Western welfare states also includes two types of what may be called "planned markets". These are widely regarded as the economic powerhouses of the next century.[2] First are the corporatist political economies of countries such as Sweden, Norway, Austria, and Germany (Katzenstein, 1985). There, the production and distribution of wealth are shaped by the ship of the market combined with a considerable degree of consultation and planning among government, business, and labour representatives. In those countries, workers have, for example, agreed to moderate their wage demands – thereby keeping strike action and inflation in check – in exchange for government guarantees of expanded welfare services and the manipulation of fiscal and monetary policy to ensure low unemployment rates. The second type of planned market, typified by Japan, may be called "market nationalist" (Courchene, 1986). There, government agencies coordinate much private research, development, investment and trade, but labour plays a consultative role only in large factories, not at the level of planning national economic strategy (Shalev, 1989). Thus, the long-range plans to dominate the world steel, consumer electronics, and automobile industries were designed and coordinated by the Japanese Ministry of International Trade and Industry (Johnson, 1982); and that ministry is now performing the same function with respect to the world aviation industry.

On closer inspection, the debates of the 1980s have been less about whether or not to have a welfare state than about what kind of welfare state we should have in the future. What kind of welfare state is politically and economically desirable? What kind of welfare state is politically and economically feasible? In a particular political-economic context, does it make sense to follow the model typified by the Englich-speaking democracies, the continental Northwestern European example, or the Japanese prototype?

These debates on the welfare state, as we can all recognize, are debates about democracy or, more specifically, about what rights and entitlements, obligations and duties we should attach to citizenship. But they are also debates about markets, especially labour markets. Western European discussions of a "basic income", for example, are inseparable from the Western European experience of low employment growth in the 1980s. Conversely, Canadian enthusiasm for some variant of a guaranteed annual income to provide wage subsidies to the working poor is inseparable from high employment growth in low-wage jobs in the 1980s and some expectation that this trend will continue in the future (Myles, 1988).

In effect, debates about what kind of welfare state we should have are simultaneously debates about what kinds of markets we should or are likely to have. And this, we think, is the second major lesson that the Soviet and Eastern European intelligentsia may learn from the Western experience: not all markets are the same. As any comparison of the major Western economies will show, there is a variety of ways of combining capital, labour, and technology. There is perhaps no better evidence for this than the frustration expressed by American economists and business analysts with the fact that the West Germans or Japanese do not share the American understanding of what a market "really" is. The reason for this diversity among Western markets, of course, is that all are subject to political and social regulation. And this diversity is not simply a matter of the degree of regulation but also of its institutional form. The Pentagon has been as important in the construction of America's postwar industrial strategy as MITI has been for the Japanese.

In short, the choices facing the USSR and Eastern Europe are not simply about whether to have markets or not, or to have welfare states or not. The more fundamental issues have to do with what kinds of markets and what kinds of welfare states they will have. These are the choices that will determine the future relationship of Eastern and Western Europe, both economic and political. Many of our more sceptical colleagues are predicting that the relationship may come to resemble that of Latin American underdevelopment and dependence on the United States. The Latin American experience would suggest that the way to avoid such an outcome is the formation of strong democratic institutions to regulate what will surely be a long historical process of market formation.[3]

Notes

1   Differences of opinion on state intervention are evident not just along class lines, but also along regional lines. For example, in the USSR, people in the heavily state-subsidized economies of Kazakhstan and Tadjikistan favour state intervention much more than people in the rich Baltic republics.
2   Following the 1981-82 recession, the gap closed somewhat between planned-market and free-market societies on several dimensions of economic activity, while in terms of annual increase in GDP, the planned-market societies appear not to have performed better than the free-market societies in the postwar period. For details see Martin (1986) and Panitch (1986), although Panitch's analysis should be treated with caution because he examines bivariate relations only.
3   The contrast between Latin America and the Asian NICs (Taiwan, Korea, Singapore, Hong Kong) is instructive. Though hardly exemplars for would-be democracies, the success of the latter countries is closely related to the capacity of their social and political institutions to direct and regulate capitalist development and relations between their home economies and foreign capital.

References

Cohen, St., Zysman, J. (1987) *Manufacturing Matters: The Myth of the Post-Industrial Economy.* New York: Basic.
Courchene, Th. (1986) 'Market Nationalism', *Policy Options* 7 (8): 7-12.
Esping-Andersen, G. (1990) *The Three Worlds of Welfare Capitalism.* Cambridge: Polity Press.
Huntington, S. (1975) 'The United States', pp. 59-118 in Crozier, M., Huntington, S., Watanuki, J. (eds.) *The Crisis of Democracy,* New York: New York University Press.
Johnson, Ch. A. (1982) *MITI and the Japanese Miracle.* Stanford: Stanford University Press.
Katzenstein, P. (1985) *Small States in World Markets: Industrial Policy in Europe.* Ithaca: Cornell University Press.
Korpi, W., Shalev, M. (1979) 'Strikes, Industrial Relations and Class Conflict in Capitalist Societies', *British Journal of Sociology* 30 (2): 164-187.
Leibfried, St. (1990) *Income Transfers and Poverty Policy in EC Perspective: On Europe's Slipping into Anglo-Saxon Welfare Models.* Paper presented to the All European Dialogue on Social Policies, Helsinki.
Mahon, R. (1989) *Post-fordism, Canada and the FTA: Is There Room for the Left to Manoeuvre?* Prepared for the conference on Export-Led Growth, Uneven Development and State Policy: Canada and Italy. University of Pisa, April.
Marshall, T.H. (1964) *Class, Citizenship and Social Development.* Chicago: University of Chicago Press.
Martin, A. (1986) 'The Politics of Employment and Welfare: National Policies and International Interdependence', pp. 157-241 in Banting, K. (ed.) *The State and Economic Interests,* Vol. 32, Studies of the Royal Commission on the Economic Union and Development Prospects for Canada. Toronto: University of Toronto Press.
Myles, J. (1988) 'The Expanding Middle: Some Canadian Evidence on the Deskilling Debate', *Canadian Review of Sociology and Anthropology* 25 (3): 335-64.
O'Connor, J. (1973) *The Fiscal Crisis of the State.* New York: St. Martin's.
Offe, C. (1985) *Disorganized Capitalism.* Cambridge, MA.: MIT Press.
Organization for Economic Cooperation and Development (1981) *The Welfare State in Crisis.* Paris.
Panitch, L. (1986) 'The Tripartite Experience', pp. 37-119 in Banting, K. (ed.) *The State and Economic Interests,* Vol. 32, Studies of the Royal Commission on the Economic Union and Development Prospects for Canada. Toronto: University of Toronto Press.
Pipes, R. (1991) 'The Soviet Union Adrift', *Foreign Affairs* 70 (1): 70-87.
Polanyi, K. (1944) *The Great Transformation.* Boston: Beacon Press.

Project Understanding: Surveys of Residents of New York and Moscow: Tabular Report (1988) Boston: Marttila and Kiley.

Shalev, M. (1989) 'Class Conflict, Corporatism and Comparison: A Japanese Enigma', pp. 60-93 in Eisenstadt, S.N., Ben-Ari, E. (eds.) *Japanese Models of Conflict Resolution*. London: Kegan Paul International.

Therborn, G. (1977) 'The Rule of Capital and the Rise of Democracy', *New Left Review 103* (May-June): 3-41.

Wilensky, H. (1975) *The Welfare State and Equality*. Berkeley: University of California Press.

Zaslavskaya, T. (1989) 'On the Strategy of Social Management', *Soviet Sociology* 28 (4): 16-23.

CHAPTER 3

Is the Crisis Behind Us? Issues Facing Social Security Systems in Western Europe*

Jean-Pierre Jallade

1   Introduction

The presence of a large, well-developed social security system – the so-called welfare state – is often considered as a distinctive feature of Western Europe when compared with other industrialized societies in Asia and America. These systems, which developed as a result of both historical and political traditions, have become part of the fabric of these societies and affect the daily life of most Europeans.

At the beginning of the 1980s, it was commonplace to speak of a "crisis" in European welfare states. The combination of slow growth, high unemployment and huge deficits in social budgets led some observers and politicians to predict the bankruptcy of social security systems, while others argued further that the growth of those systems was one of the main factors explaining poor economic perfor-mance in Western Europe. As economic recovery in this part of the world is now largely under way, it is worth looking back and examining the performance of those systems during adverse economic circumstances. The experience gained throughout the 1980s may teach us a more sober view about what social security systems can and cannot do, about what can be expected from them, and perhaps also about the conditions that have to be met for them to perform efficiently.

The purpose of this paper is thus to review some of the key issues faced by social security systems in light of recent developments and present trends. It draws mostly on the experience of Western European systems, although occasional references may be made to the US situation. It also sets out to provide some exploratory ideas about the potential and limitations of those systems in the wake of the new challenges of the next century, among which the most conspicuous are the demographic challenge arising from falling birth rates and the trend towards the "globalization" of world economies, including the single economic market in Western Europe from 1993 as a first step.

2   The Welfare State in Crisis: Is the Crisis Behind Us?

One of the most far-reaching consequences for European societies of the two oil shocks of 1973 and 1979 and of the ensuing economic disruption, has been the emergence of a permanent crisis in their social security systems. In all countries, the high level of social protection achieved over the preceding 30 years has been threatened by slow growth and the resulting constraints on social budgets. The nature and dimensions of this crisis were fully discussed at a major conference on "Social Policies in the 1980s", convened by the OECD in October 1980. The proceedings of this conference were published in 1981 in the form of a widely publicized book, *The Welfare State in Crisis* (OECD, 1981), which helped to put the notion of a "crisis" in the forefront of the international scene. Other books, such as Rosanvallon's *La crise de l'Etat-providence*, also published in 1981 (Rosanvallon, 1981), helped to elucidate the political and sociological aspects of the crisis.

Ten years later, it is worth taking a retrospective look at what happened during the 1980s. Social security systems that were apparently on the verge of bankruptcy in 1980 have survived; and although they are still wrestling with the consequences of past economic recession, their difficulties have eased considerably. The so-called crisis has evaporated or, perhaps, our perceptions of the crisis have changed now that non-inflationary economic growth is back. This is indeed a first lesson to remember: namely, that the judgements made about the welfare states at the beginning of the 1980s were to a large extent dictated by the adverse economic circumstances prevailing at that time. In retrospect, one may even say that social security systems have proved to be more flexible than expected, allowing for a necessary adjustment to be made but on the whole maintaining a diverse range of benefits to many segments of the population. To be sure, many other adjustments in both taxes and benefits are still necessary, but confidence has been restored and there is a widespread feeling that the difficulties still faced by social security systems can be solved by cautious management.

The conspicuous change of mood *vis-à-vis* these problems throughout the 1980s deserves further scrutiny. The crisis of social security had three dimensions. It was first of all a financial crisis; then doubts were expressed about its legitimacy; and lastly, there was a loss of confidence in the institutional arrangements governing social security. Each aspect of the crisis is examined below.

2.1   The Financial Crisis

The main feature of the financial crisis affecting social security systems during the 1970s was the widening gap between rising expenditure and stagnating resources. Social budgets began to grow faster than usual as a result of larger outlays for unemployment compensation and new social programmes designed to increase benefits to those worst affected by the crisis. At the same time, fiscal revenue did not continue to grow as fast as expected because of economic stagnation. Raising taxes might have solved the problem; but it was a very unpopular course of action at a time when taxpayers in California were engaged in a "tax revolt" against soaring public expenditure, while European governments were more and more concerned about the ever-increasing size of the public/social sector in their economies.

The OECD summed up the situation in the following words:

> In the past – meaning between 1960 and 1980 – growth of social expenditure has been rapid, outstripping that of national income throughout the OECD area. Social expenditure now averages about one quarter of gross domestic product. It is inevitable that such rapid growth should eventually have been called into question, although the passage of time would probably have seen some automatic moderation as the major social programmes approached maturity. In the event, economic developments forced a more urgent re-examination of social expenditure than might have been necessary if the strong economic growth of the 1960s had persisted through the 1970s and into the 1980s.
>
> Economic growth slowed down, abruptly following the two oil shocks of 1973-1974 and 1979-1980. This was accompanied by a greatly increased rate of inflation which in turn required a much restrained attitude towards inflation and recovery. In these circumstances economic and social policies were brought into apparent conflict. Social programmes appeared to have developed a momentum which was difficult to check, and this was being aggravated by additional demands for income support from a growing number of unemployed. At the same time, the exigencies of stagflation demanded the restraint of public expenditure growth and the reduction of government deficits. As far as the welfare state and its material requirements were concerned what might have been an evolutionary social process began to assume aspects of an immediate budgetary crisis (OECD, 1985).

In retrospect, two features of the financial crisis, overlooked a few years ago, are now clear. First, social deficits that perhaps seemed large in absolute terms were actually rather small when compared with the enormous size of total social budgets. This is not to say that no remedial action had to be taken, but simply that the problem was one of matching expenditures and resources and not a structural issue which would jeopardize the very existence of social security. Second, lagging economic growth was a more important factor than soaring social expenditure in explaining the apparently uncontrolled increase in ratios of public expenditure to GNP which caused so much alarm among policy-makers. In other words, it was primarily because GNPs had stopped increasing and not so much because social security systems had suddenly become overly generous that the "crisis" developed. What was presented as a crisis in the welfare state was above all the failure of economic policy to deal with a new international environment.

Of course, there was no lack of people to argue that oversized welfare states were one of the reasons why Western European economies were so sluggish and that social policies had become over-extended at the expense of economic policies favouring growth. To be sure, most policy-makers were slow to understand the nature of the economic crisis and kept reacting by granting new benefits, hoping that economic recovery was around the corner. But, on the whole, recession was caused by other factors than the welfare state – such as the two oil shocks, the emergence of new technologies and the geographical relocation of smokestack industries. Furthermore, present levels of economic recovery in Western Europe cannot be explained by cutbacks in social security benefits. Levels of social expenditure have started to look more manageable, simply because growth has returned.

So, may we say that the crisis is behind us? A cautious "yes" is in order, provided that European economies keep investing and growing at the same pace as in the last two years, and that good management, including the trimming of unnecessary benefits if necessary, becomes normal practice and not a last resort policy when deficits become threatening. But the crisis might come back if those conditions are not met. One of the lessons which has perhaps been learned from the recent past is that social security systems in Western Europe cannot function effectively with rates of economic growth much below three per cent a year!

2.2   A Crisis of Legitimacy

Great things are expected from the welfare state. Greater equality and, specifically, greater income equality than that yielded by market forces, ranks high among expectations associated with the growing and complicated array of social programmes developed in all European countries since the war. But the extent to which European welfare states achieve this equality objective by redistributing income, is still an open question. Some say that they are ill-equipped to do so; others, that they should refrain from doing so, since the struggle against inequality is not their prime objective; yet others, that they would fail to do so even if they were willing to try, because past experience has shown that this objective is both technically and politically out of reach.

Today, scepticism regarding the redistributive efficiency of social security systems is based on the fact that the slight progress towards greater equality which may sometimes result from social programmes, is in no way commensurate with the very high level of spending required to achieve it. Not only are the high and increasing costs of equality looked upon with suspicion; there is also growing public sensitivity about the possible negative effects of social programmes on other parameters of economic life – such as labour costs, innovation, and allocation of resources. A troubling question lurks behind those concerns, "How equal a society do we want and/or can we afford?" In short, egalitarian policies have lost support in recent years both among policy-makers and public opinion, creating a serious legitimacy crisis for social security.

But equality has never been the sole or even the main purpose of the welfare state. Although in some countries the eradication of poverty ranks very high, the principal concern is for security – or, in other words, protection against such risks as loss of income, old age or accidents. This duality of objectives – security and equality – clearly implies the possibility of conflict, since one may take precedence over the other in certain social programmes or at certain times. Periods of economic constraint and uncertainty – such as the one which lasted from 1975 to 1985 – are *not* conducive to the "equality objective" of the welfare state, since they exacerbate the feeling of insecurity and the need to strengthen the income maintenance side of social programmes.

In other words, social security systems have experienced a shift of objectives over the past 15 years. They have become less egalitarian and more centred on income maintenance, and public opinion is generally supportive of this trend – thus giving a new political legitimacy to social security.

2.3 An Institutional Crisis

During the 1980s social security systems have also been affected by a mounting loss of public confidence in the capacity of central government to deliver adequate welfare services. Anti-bureaucratic attitudes have been fuelled by what was perceived as the decreasing quality of these services and their failure to adapt to changing needs. Individuals feel increasingly powerless *vis-à-vis* bureaucratic regulations that are impersonal, remote, and ill-adapted to specific situations. They are put off by the bewildering complexity of rules governing social programmes. They want "customized" programmes adapted to *their* local situation, not blanket initiatives coming from the top.

To remedy this situation, it has sometimes been proposed to take the delivery of social services away from central government and to bring it closer to beneficiaries by using community networks, local authorities, voluntary associations, etc. – what the French would call *"nouveaux réseaux de solidarité"*. Such a development is considered well-suited to the growing concern to reduce government bureaucracies and increase participatory democracy.

The issue was spelled out by the 1980 OECD conference in the following terms:

> The competing strategies appear in large part to boil down to the relative weights assigned to the traditional centralist ("Welfare State") option as compared to a much more decentralized disaggregated and selective ("Welfare Society") approach. The traditional centralized approach depends on tax/transfer mechanisms, uniformity in the delivery of social services, universalities and the protection of individuals through impersonal transactions with non-discriminatory eligibility conditions. The disaggregated approach, which has emerged in the 1970s, is based on more selectivity (to target groups) in income transfers and the delivery of services; greater decentralization and localization of services; greater responsibilities by local authorities, community groups, employers and trade unions, and of "third sector" institutions; tighter eligibility conditions and income-testing; and more monitoring of effectiveness. This latter strategy presumably has political appeal because of its capacity to cater to the needs of a more diverse set of interests – but does it not run the risk of undermining the principles of equity inherent in the "Welfare State?" (OECD, 1981).

Have social security systems during the 1980s contributed to this trend away from the "welfare state" towards the "welfare society", thus helping to solve the institutional crisis? On the whole, this is an area where only minor progress has been recorded. There is, to be sure, a drive towards diversification and decentralization which takes the form of *local provision* of some social services, but major income maintenance programmes such as retirement benefits, sick pay or unemployment compensation are still managed centrally. It is also true that new local partners often drawn from voluntary bodies are now involved in the delivery of local social services, but these people cannot substitute for the groups of highly qualified professionals (doctors, nurses, social workers, etc.) built up during the high growth years of social security systems. The "local" welfare state is more of an add-on phenomenon than a substitute for centrally-designed social policies. It provides services at a reduced cost because it relies on lowly paid quasi-volunteers instead of highly paid professionals, but it does not maintain incomes.

3   Will the "Globalization" of World Economies Kill the Welfare State?

"Globalization of world economies" is taken to mean a process whereby economic forces are progressively freed from the constraints of national policies and which subverts the power of sovereign nation-states, thus posing a threat to the mainte-nance of the "social contract" prevailing in any given country. There is no need to insist here on the powerful forces at work in this area. Technology, being in-ternational by nature, is one of them. It gives industrial companies the capacity to affect entire regions far beyond the confines of individual countries – for better (employment creation, higher productivity) or worse (pollution). Capital is another: it can move faster and faster from one place to another, hence virtually beyond the control of nation-states. New, transnational networks of communications already function at the global level, treating the entire industrial world as a single entity.

Not only is this process also at work in Western Europe, but one may say that it is an explicit policy objective set up by the EEC for the 12 member states. In this respect, the achievement of the single economic market should be seen as a step towards the globalization of European economies. In addition, a similar concern is arising: will the social standards of the most advanced industrial nations be eroded as a result of this process which, it is feared, may lead to the "dismantling" of the most advanced – and costly – social security systems? German union leaders are concerned by the social consequences of the single market, which might induce big companies to create jobs in Southern Europe where salaries are lower and du-ration of working time longer than in Germany – not to mention smaller social benefits. Overall, Portuguese hourly salary costs are about one sixth of Germany's – a situation which may lead to pressure to reduce social benefits in Germany. Hence, there arises the new concern for building a "social Europe" alongside the single market to mitigate its effects on working conditions and social security systems, and for increasing solidarity among European labour unions.

But what may be negotiable among EEC countries within the framework of a unified European labour market, will be seen as a competitive factor at the world level. In other words, a weak and cheap welfare state in the US and Japan may give them an edge over Europe in international competition and induce European leaders to lower social standards to restore the competitive situation of their economies. In short, the fundamental question remains: will the globalization of world economies lead to a downward equalization of social security rights and benefits, i.e. to a dismantling of European welfare states?

Many of the arguments heard about this problem turn on the (disputed) effects of labour costs on investments and exports. On the one hand, it is true that low labour costs attract foreign investment: most Japanese investment in the EEC is concentrated in Portugal and Great Britain, which have below-average labour costs. In the same way, part of the economic boom enjoyed by Spain and Portugal in recent years, is due to investment by Northern European companies looking for cheap labour. On the other hand, low labour costs are only one factor to be considered by domestic or foreign investors. Communications facilities, environmental situation, closeness of major markets, presence of intellectual "centres of excellence" (universities, science parks), and regional policies also play a role in the decision to invest or not. Moreover, modern industry does not need much cheap, unskilled or semi-skilled labour. The crucial factor as far as labour is concerned, is the availability of specialists who are in scarce supply, and of highly-skilled production workers who can be found only in countries where labour costs are high.

In the same way, low labour costs are only one of the factors – and perhaps not the most important one – affecting trade performance. European countries with the highest labour costs – i.e. West Germany and the Netherlands – also rank highest in the exporters' league. Other factors such as quality, after-sales service, and types of product are as important as costs. It is true, however, that when all those other factors are equal – although they seldom are in our modern economies, where tastes and styles change constantly and where product innovations are often a more decisive factor than price – high labour costs may undermine competitiveness; but the relationship between the former and the latter is not as simplistic as employers' representatives like to argue.

Thus, the often-expressed fear that the global economy will kill the welfare state, rests on dubious grounds. Furthermore, one should not lose sight of the positive effects of high labour costs on the modernization of European economies. Countries with high labour costs are under constant pressure to use labour in an efficient way and to invest in new machinery, both of which lead to higher productivity and lower prices. Furthermore, social security systems do employ a large number of people and redistribute income – which contributes to demand. Thus, from a dynamic perspective, the welfare state can also be viewed as an engine of growth.

In crisis periods, when public opinion becomes very sensitive to the "burden" of social contributions on labour costs, it is always possible to resort to a new balance between direct salaries and social contributions in order to keep total labour costs down. This is indeed what happened in some European countries during the first half of the 1980s. In an attempt to keep labour costs down, direct salaries levelled off and, in some cases, even decreased – while social contributions kept increasing to finance additional social outlays. In other words, European workers were more willing to accept a (small) sacrifice in their present income than put in jeopardy their health insurance systems or their pension schemes. In doing so, they expressed a preference for deferred income and welfare over present maximization of living standards, demonstrating once again that Europeans are deeply attached to their long-term economic and social welfare.

To sum up, the globalization of world economies is unlikely to lead to the disappearance of European welfare states. High labour costs in some countries reflect high standards of living and sophisticated economies where cost is only one decisive factor among others, and the recent crisis has shown that Europeans are quite conscious of the possible trade-off between present living standards and future incomes.

4   Employment and the Supply of Labour

During the ten-year period of economic uncertainty and stagnation from 1975 until 1985, unemployment in Western Europe hovered around 10 per cent of the labour force, with peaks at 15 or even 20 per cent in some countries. Unemployment was the prime cause of social deficits, both because of increased outlays to the unemployed and because of foregone taxes and social contributions. In countries like France, calculations using simulation techniques were made in 1985 showing that, had employment levels been maintained, the growth of social expenditure would have been perfectly manageable. The so-called "crisis" in the welfare state was actually the direct result of the employment crisis affecting European economies.

European governments reacted to this situation in two ways. First, unemployment compensation systems were adjusted to reduce the gap between resources and expenditures: benefits were reduced and eligibility conditions tightened, while unemployment contributions from workers and employers increased. Unemployment schemes aimed at young workers who had never contributed, were often the target of budget cuts – and when all this was not sufficient, state funds were pumped into the system. Second, governments sought to reduce the number of unemployed by launching programmes designed to take people out of the labour market: young people, by inducing them to stay in education or training; and old people, by encouraging early retirement.

However, these policies were very costly; and whether they can be sustained in the long term, is questionable. As a result of economic recovery, unemployment has fallen considerably in the United Kingdom and Germany; but it is still high in France, Italy, Spain, and the Netherlands. Unemployment compensation systems are under less pressure than in the recent past, but the progress achieved so far is fragile, as most European economies are still far from the full-employment growth path which would enable them to sustain costly social policies.

It was argued earlier that a minimum growth rate of three per cent was perhaps required to provide a solid economic base for social security systems. In addition, this growth rate should lead to job creation so as to reduce unemployment rates to "manageable" levels. Opinions differ across countries and over time as to what "manageable" means. During the 1960s, a three per cent rate of "frictional" unemployment was considered as a minimum norm in Europe, while five to six per cent was considered appropriate in the US. There is no hope of achieving such low rates again in Europe but, all in all, it appears that a seven per cent unemployment rate might be set as a suitable and feasible target. This target will seem out of reach at present in some European countries; others may find it too timid and plan for lower unemployment.

Obviously such a target is somewhat arbitrary, all the more so in that unemployment rates cannot be discussed without discussing activity rates which determine the size of the labour force. What matters most is a suitable overall employment level – which can be achieved either via a low unemployment rate applied to a small labour force or a high unemployment rate applied to a large labour force – and, above all, an adequate ratio between the number of employed persons and the number of social security beneficiaries. This ratio has been decreasing in most European countries, less as a result of demographic decline (as is often believed) than of economic policies favouring labour productivity at the expense of job creation. In this connection, the European experience between 1975 and 1985 is in sharp contrast with the US situation, where millions of jobs were created – especially in the service sector of the economy – while the overall employment level in Europe stagnated or even declined. Not only was American growth more vigorous than in Europe, but it created many more jobs.

Should the ratio of employed persons to social security beneficiaries deteriorate further, social security benefits will have to be revised downwards, especially in the health and retirement area. Postponement of the retirement age, indexation of pensions linked to prices rather than to salaries, and increased users' charges are some of the means contemplated to offset the declining ratio of employed persons to beneficiaries. Further erosion of social security benefits will come unless European economies put "growth-*cum*-employment" creation at the centre of economic policy.

European welfare states are sometimes criticized for providing disincentives to work, thus having adverse effects on the supply of labour. Social transfers, it is argued, amount to income without work, encouraging "free-riding" attitudes and destroying the work ethic of European societies. In a country like France, which is by no means an exceptional case in Europe, social benefits amounted to about 35 per cent of disposable household income in 1985 – a high percentage indeed, which is often said by critics to demonstrate that the welfare state is dangerously eroding the traditional connection between work and income. This line of argument is voiced most insistently in the area of unemployment compensation and sick pay, where concrete cases of free-riding if not outright fraud, are often mentioned. According to critics, many people receiving these benefits are paid to do nothing – hence, the need to tighten the screws on the system.

In all European welfare states, however, most social transfers benefit people who are not of working age: pension benefits, which typically amount to 45-50 per cent of all social transfers, but also the major part (from 60 to 80%) of health outlays benefit older people who are not expected to work. For the working age population only, the proportion of transfer income in total income hovers around five per cent in France – hardly a disincentive to work.

The often-made case that unemployment compensation and sickness benefits may have been overly generous and encouraged people to stay away from work, rests on more solid grounds. In many European countries, these benefits have been lowered at least once and sometimes several times during the crisis period 1980-1985.

Eligibility conditions have also been tightened gradually to make sure that those who receive those benefits actually need them. As a result of the crisis, European welfare states have surely become less lavish than in the past.

The impact of the welfare state on the supply of labour deserves to be analysed in a comprehensive way. On the one hand, social policies enhance the labour supply: gainfully employed females are more numerous than ever, partly as a result of improved day care facilities. Despite the unemployment crisis, increasing labour force participation of women has been observed throughout the 1980s, leading to fast-rising numbers of two-income households. On the other hand, some social policies are explicitly aimed at reducing the labour supply: early retirement schemes adopted in France and Germany around 1983, made it possible for many workers to retire before the normal retirement age. More people take part in educational activities as a result of longer initial education and lifetime education, causing activity rates for both young people and older workers – especially males – to fall in recent years.

Overall, European welfare states have not reduced the labour supply – rather the contrary, as is shown by the growth of labour forces. But more important, they are increasingly used as a policy tool to manage the labour supply, i.e. reducing it where the demand for labour is low and increasing it when it is high. In other words, the welfare state may be used as a "buffer" to smooth the "ups and downs" of economic growth.

In this process of labour supply management, European welfare states also help to redistribute work among groups: both from men to women and from young and older workers to adult workers. This redistributive process could conceivably go in the opposite direction if need be. For example, the need to keep an appropriate ratio of contributors to beneficiaries in the future, may mean increasing the number of gainfully employed by postponing the retirement age. Alternatively, more older people would be at work while the number of adult workers temporarily absent from the labour force for retraining purposes, would rise as a result of a plan to grant educational leave to employed adults.

To sum up, the welfare state has no mechanical, negative effect on the supply of labour. It is a combination of sophisticated social policies which can be used by governments in an effective way to manage the supply of labour and redistribute work among people.

5 The Welfare State Does Redistribute Income and Contributes to Equality

Equality is not a policy objective that can be clearly spelled out so as to enlist enthusiastic political support; and, unlike "the reduction of inequalities", it is seldom referred to as such. This is because, while reducing inequalities is a readily understandable policy course, its final aims are never very clearly described: reduction of inequalities, yes, but up to what point and at what cost? Surely, the goal is not absolute equality? Yet acknowledging this hardly makes the "egalitarian" case any easier to defend. While the strength of the latter lies in a general, vaguely formulated demand for less inequality in European societies, it is weakened by the impossibility of determining precisely the *degree* of equality pursued. In short, the course of action may be clear but the final goal is not.

The debate is often confused because the notion of equality is often ill-defined in the literature on the welfare state; and this leads to misunderstandings about its redistributive potential. There are basically two conceptions of equality which can be used to assess the redistributive efficiency of the welfare state. The first can be labelled equality of opportunity or of *access to welfare benefits* and services, and it takes the form of identical social rights or treatment for everybody in a given situation regardless of the use that will be made of those rights. It is generally measured by means of social indicators – benefits received or services rendered – which can be considered as inputs into the process of equalization. The second conception, far more ambitious, focuses on the degree of equalization achieved by the welfare state or, in other words, on the *outcome of the process*. Success or failure is assessed in terms of the changes that have occurred, as a result of social programmes, in the positions of people or of a group on a scale of income or well-being.

Obviously, equality of access to benefits does not guarantee that inequalities in income or well-being will be reduced. Besides, the fact that some sort of positive discrimination – that is, inequality of access to benefits favouring those at the bottom of the scale – is needed to overcome *initial* inequalities in incomes or well-being, many factors other than social benefits have a bearing on inequalities of this kind. As long as these factors are not considered, equalizing access to benefits may not be enough to bring about equalization of outcomes.

In the case of health insurance, for instance, ensuring that everybody receives free health care (equality of opportunity) does not imply that everybody will be in the same individual state of health (equality of outcome). The fact that people's state of health or life expectancy varies widely in spite of the provision of 40 years of state-funded health services, is considered by welfare state critics as a proof of failure; but it simply demonstrates that equality of access to these services is not the only factor accounting for "equality" as regards health matters. Clearly, it is absurd to criticize the welfare state for persistent wide variation in individual health (life expectancy etc.) because many other factors (drinking, smoking, etc.) and working conditions (office, mine or factory environment, etc.), not to mention heredity, are responsible for determining a person's health. Unless the welfare state is requested to intervene in *these* areas, it can hardly be blamed for their adverse effects on health inequalities.

The standard method of assessing the redistributive efficiency of the welfare state is to compare the distributions of income *before* and *after* transfers and taxes. Redistribution takes place if the latter (also called the distribution of "final" income) is more egalitarian than the former (also known as distribution of "economic" or "market" income). Simple as it is, the tax and transfer method is fraught with many theoretical and empirical difficulties which are beyond the scope of this paper. Some general conclusions on redistributive efficiency are summed up by Ringen (1987):

1) The entire system of transfers and taxes is redistributive in favour of the poor in the sense that there is less inequality in the distributions of disposable and final income than in the distributions of market and gross income.

2) This redistribution is caused primarily by the effects of direct transfers. The most important form of their redistribution is between households in the economically active population and households in the economically passive population, the largest net receiving group being old-age pensioners.

3) Taxes have, all together, little or no impact on the distribution of income. Direct income taxes are generally moderately progressive, payroll taxes (employees' social security contributions) flat or moderately regressive, and indirect taxes moderately regressive.

In assessing redistributive efficiency, due consideration must be paid to the economic background behind the social security system. In his sophisticated study of the redistributive efficiency of the welfare state in the United Kingdom,

O'Higgins shows that over the 1976-1982 period, inequalities in market income have increased significantly during the recession and that social incomes (i.e. social security transfers and benefits) have played a significant role in combating these inequalities. In his own words, *"social welfare had an important redistributive impact: it has not brought about greater overall equality over the period studied, but it has combated and significantly modified the impact of pressures towards increased inequality. However, while transfer incomes are markedly more egalitarian than income distributed through the market, the market – and employment in particular – is still the major determinant of inequality. During the recession, (market) inequalities have grown. Income transfers have significantly stunted this growth"* (O'Higgins, 1988).

In France, social security does contribute to income redistribution but benefits and taxes had opposite effects up to 1978: the former reduced income inequalities, while the latter increased them. Because the pro-poor bias of benefits is stronger than the anti-redistributive effect of taxes and social contributions, the overall effect is redistributive. Since then, attempts have been made to set rates of social contributions uniformly across all income levels, thereby enhancing the impact of social security on income distribution (Jallade, 1988). The French situation provides interesting insights as to which branch of social security contributes most to income redistribution. Thus, the health insurance system contributes to a significant narrowing of income differentials in two ways: first, by distributing the same level of benefits regardless of income levels and, second, by raising contributions proportional to wages. The pension system, although largely based on past earnings, also allows for a significant degree of income redistribution thanks to indexing policies and to the stronger weight given to basic pensions *vis-à-vis* supplementary pensions. By contrast, family policy – which is usually expected to be strongly redistributive – is almost neutral from the viewpoint of income distribution, both because some benefits are provided in the form of tax allowances that increase as income rises and because family benefits are financed not out of general taxation but out of a nine per cent employers' contribution levied on low wages.

In the Netherlands, the overall impact of social security contributions and benefits also helps to redistribute income. There was the problem to reduce some benefits – essentially the unemployment and disablement benefit – considered as too high and thus endangering the whole social security system, without negative effect on the distribution of income. According to the study done by the *Sociaal en Cultureel Planbureau* in 1986, such a reform is technically feasible, although politically difficult to implement (de Kram et al.,1988). Another interesting case is that of Sweden. Söderström reaches the conclusion that "Swedish social policy has a progressive effect on income distribution, but also that a relative decline in the redistribution efficiency of the Swedish welfare state is taking place". In his own words *"the growth of social policy expenditure in recent years has tended to favour the maintenance of an individual's customary standard of living. The elements of Swedish social policy that provide a basic minimum income guarantee have been well established for many years and by and large are not subject to a great deal of change. Hence the growth of the welfare state has tended to gradually weaken the progressive nature of social policy"* (Söderström, 1988).

Thus, the evidence collected from various European countries suggests that the welfare state does redistribute income and does contribute to equality although its redistributive impact has tended to decline during the past 30 years as a result of the following trends:

a) From flat-rate to earnings-related benefits:

Flat-rate benefit was the first fundamental principle of the Beveridge Plan for social insurance in Britain at the end of the War. In Scandinavia, too, one of the principles of Nordic social policy after the war was that benefits should respond to present needs and be divorced from contributions. Significant moves away from flat-rate towards earnings-related benefits have taken place in those countries since the war. In the early 1960s, Sweden adopted a compulsory earnings-related pension scheme to complement the existing basic pension system. The United Kingdom followed suit in 1975 with the Social Security Pensions Act, under which pension benefits are very much the products of pre-retirement household earnings. What happened to pension systems – which amount to by far the most important single area in modern welfare states – was bound to exert an influence on other areas of social policy. In the words of Korpi and Esping-Andersen: *"The ATP pension reforms stand as a watershed in postwar Scandinavian social policy since they symbolize a novel principle in the welfare state. The honoured ideal of equal benefits to all gives away to the ideas that citizens should be guaranteed against income loss, and that benefits should be closely related to accustomed earnings or income, ideas which already to some extent had been realized in connection with reforms of sickness insurance. During the 1960's, all four Scandinavian countries moved from the flat-rate to the earnings-graduated principle in sickness, accident and unemployment compensation, as well as in the pension systems"* (Esping-Andersen and Korpi, 1984). It thus appears that Beveridge's postwar dreams of a flat rate of insurance benefit to all, have in many ways been shattered by current practice. The basic contradiction concerning the level of social security benefits in European welfare states – best expressed as "How can a benefit represent at one and the same time a fair return on past contributions and a sum related to the present need of the household?" – is now increasingly resolved by giving preference to the first option in the alternative.

b) From taxes to social contributions:

The rising share of social security contributions in the financing of the welfare state over the past 20 years, is a well-known phenomenon. This general trend

– the United Kingdom standing as the only important exception – illustrates the inability of traditional tax systems to support fully-developed welfare states. In this connection, the rapid growth of social contributions and, above all, of the employers' contribution can be interpreted as one way of transferring the financing of the welfare state away from visible forms of tax, such as personal income tax, to less visible forms, such as payroll tax, in an attempt to defuse opposition to taxation.

What this trend means from the point of view of redistributive efficiency, is less clear. It was mentioned above that social contributions levied on wages are usually less progressive than income tax, in which case the redistributive potential of European welfare states may be declining. But the true redistributive effects of social contributions cannot be assessed without making assumptions about "shifting". As far as employees' contributions are concerned, no shifting is possible and the burden of these contributions rests on the employees themselves. Employers' contributions, which account for an ever-increasing share of total social security financing, may be shifted "forward" to consumers or "backward" to employees in the form of lower salaries. In the former case, they can be considered as a tax borne by consumers; in the latter, they are a direct tax on earnings. Studies have shown that the redistributive effects of social security are very sensitive to these assumptions: if contributions are assumed to be borne by consumers, social security helps to reduce income inequality; if they are borne by wage earners, little redistribution takes place among the latter, who also appear to subsidize high-income independent workers.

In practice, employers' contributions are assumed to be shifted backward to wage earners because they are considered as part of total labour costs. They are indirect or "deferred" wages which top up – and may even compete with – the direct wage.

c) Towards the emergence of collective, non-state schemes:

The rise of modern welfare states following the demise of Mutual/Friendly Societies and private (mostly church and family) involvement in welfare activities, is usually viewed as part of an historical trend aimed at transforming and improving the ways of coping with insecurity and poverty. In this connection, nation-wide, state-controlled arrangements are considered by most as "the best" (and even final) way of organizing collective protection. It is unlikely, though, that social history will stop there. Rather, there are increasing signs that the monopoly of nation-states in the welfare area is losing ground to a variety of collective, non-state arrangements. It was mentioned earlier that this trend is clearest in the area of pensions and health insurance – by far the two biggest programmes in European welfare states. Sometimes encouraged through tax relief, sometimes only tolerated, the development of occupational, company-based pensions or private life insurance contracts represents a significant chal-

lenge to the state monopoly over welfare. Although public authorities are seldom willing to acknowledge it, these arrangements are usually welcome – at
least as long as their development does not call state schemes into question –
because they are a cheap way of catering for the desire of high-income groups
for high replacement incomes.

Needless to say, these non-state programmes rest on the insurance principle
among participants and have limited, if any, redistributive ambitions.

The three changes described above have significantly contributed to eroding the
redistributive edge of European welfare states which have become progressively
more middle-class oriented. As they gained in coverage reaching all parts of society
and diversified their programmes to provide a comprehensive spectrum of benefits,
they tended to lose their sharpest "anti-poverty" thrust.

6   Poverty: Still There

The elimination, or at least the reduction, of poverty has always been an important
goal of European welfare states. This goal can be achieved by targeting benefits
on those population groups who need them most, the idea being to provide a "safety
net" to everybody by means of "pro-poor" social programmes. Selective, means-
tested benefits granted according to needs have a higher redistributive potential
than universal benefits given to everybody. In some countries – the United States,
for instance – income-testing is used in almost all social programmes. In the United
Kingdom, means-tested benefits are also widespread.

Selective social policies are difficult to implement on a large scale. First, the
concept of poverty is a matter of dispute (i.e. are we talking in terms of absolute
poverty or relative poverty?) and the correct identification of the poor is not easy.
For practical reasons, most countries use the concept of *poverty line*, defined as
a given income level – although this concept does not provide an adequate measure
of the necessary resources, capabilities and motivations to achieve what is defined
as a minimum living standard. Second, administrative efficiency to deal effectively
with poorly educated and motivated populations, is a must. Central government
civil servants, however well-intentioned, are often ill-trained to take care of difficult cases. Their action has to be backed up by that of social workers and voluntary bodies who know those populations best. Fraud is always possible and
difficult to eradicate.

A third difficulty lies in the fact that the beneficiaries who are a minority, may
be stigmatized by the majority and are often offered low-quality services. This may
account for the low take-up rate recorded for some social benefits.

The overall effectiveness of the welfare state in eradicating poverty, is a matter
of dispute. In some countries, like Belgium and the Netherlands, minimum income
provision has proved to be an effective policy tool; in the United Kingdom,

supplementary benefits are distributed to millions of low-income families to help them reach the poverty line. In France, the 1988 decision to provide low-income families and individuals with a "minimum income" benefit, is a move in the same direction. Still, there is no lack of official reports, both at national and EEC level, showing that poverty still exists in rich countries – although it is generally agreed that it is less severe among low-income groups, thanks to these social assistance programmes.

There are two explanations for this apparent paradox. The first, already mentioned, is that poverty is not only a matter of low income but also has to do with poor housing, bad health, cultural maladjustment, insufficient education and training, etc. Only a set of policies aimed at curing all those handicaps has a chance of success. The second, stressed by modern research, is that poverty is the result of a *process* of accumulated deprivation whereby economic, social, and cultural exclusion is built up over the years. This process can only be reversed by another cumulative process whereby poor individuals or families are put in a position to regain each of the attributes or capacities required for adequate self-management in modern industrial societies. Needless to say, this concept of poverty is much more demanding than the low-income criterion. European welfare states may yet have to come to grips with it in an appropriate way. The point can be illustrated by the recent French discussion about the minimum income benefit which is to be granted as a right to all low-income individuals who agree to enter into a contract whereby they will take some sort of action (training, small job, etc.) to start their re-entry – *insertion* as it is called in French – into society. The French initiative is still too recent to provide any insight into this process of re-entry. What is clear however, is that the welfare administration finds it much simpler to give money to people than to disentangle effectively the intricate nexus of handicaps that has led them to poverty.

In the long run, the political acceptance of selective, means-tested programmes targeted towards the poor, may be difficult to sustain: what a given political majority has done, can be undone by the next one. These programmes are also very vulnerable to extended periods of economic and budgetary austerity, as witnessed by the evolution of the American and British social security systems during the first half of the 1980s. There might be a trade-off between *redistributive efficiency* by means of means-tested social programmes, and *political acceptance* in the long run. Enacting strong pro-poor social programmes at the expense of the dominant middle classes, may be a self-defeating business if it triggers an anti-poor political backlash a few years later. During those crisis years, most continental welfare states have actually chosen to go slow on redistribution in order to retain political acceptance among the dominant middle classes.

7   The Socio-Political Legitimacy of the Welfare State

The difficulties faced by European welfare states over the redistributive issue have led some observers to question their legitimacy. Despite those difficulties, European welfare states still enjoy widespread support because redistribution from rich to poor is only one objective among the many they pursue. Actually, the prime objective of the biggest social programmes – unemployment compensation, basic pension schemes, sick pay, etc. – is now *income maintenance over the life cycle* rather than income equality. These programmes are expected to help individuals and families maintain a proper balance between their high- and low-earning years over a lifetime. In other words, lifecycle income redistribution is becoming the hallmark of the modern welfare state, which is expected to provide an adequate range of institutional arrangements to perform this function effectively and safely.

In essence, the mechanisms to achieve this are rather simple. In all areas where social benefits take the place of lost earnings, both benefits and contributions should be related to earnings. This is what happened in many unemployment compensation schemes where benefits became progressively more closely tied to past contributions. The implications of this trend for redistributive efficiency are twofold. First, pro-poor income redistribution will probably be less strong than in the past because there is less room for enforcing redistributive policies when there is an explicit link between contributions and benefits. In other words, the insurance principle will be strengthened at the expense of the assistance principle in devising the regulations governing social programmes. But second, what is lost in terms of pro-poor redistribution is gained in terms of political support. Acceptance of social security systems providing adequate devices ensuring the redistribution over the lifecycle, is high – because everyone, and not only the poor, expects to derive some benefit from it.

In all Western European countries, there is a growing demand from the dominant middle classes for effective and safe devices to redistribute income over time, as the ongoing debate over the future of old-age pensions shows. This demand provides a solid basis for the social and political legitimacy of the modern welfare state. Ensuring a clear, *visible* connection between contributions and benefits is also important to strengthen acceptability. During all the crisis years, increases in social contributions explicitly devised to maintain future benefits have been far more easily accepted than increases in general taxes to finance public budgets. While this change in the focus of redistribution may signal a retreat from earlier, more ambitious, redistributive objectives, it can also be taken as a guarantee of survival, as the demand for lifelong income redistribution is very strong in all European societies.

Furthermore, to say that contributions and benefits have to be related to earnings does not mean that they have to be proportional to earnings. Progressive rates for social contributions can be devised, and indexing policies can be differentiated according to income to ensure some degree of income equality. Indeed, the political legitimacy of the welfare state in the future will rest on its ability to manage social programmes, combining income maintenance over the lifetime and social benefits to the poor. Some may argue that redistributing income over time is more effectively done on an individual rather than a collective basis and that therefore, only a small welfare state catering for the needs of the poorest is necessary. But the quest for safety in income maintenance is a priority concern among European middle classes and, in most countries, this means that the state has to be involved to guarantee and regulate the system. It is therefore highly probable that European welfare states will remain large, both because they are expected to cater to the varied needs of many groups and also because this ensures their political legitimacy.

8 Conclusions

The recent history of European welfare states provides some lessons which highlight their future prospects.

First, they have adjusted remarkably well to the adverse economic and social conditions which have prevailed during the past 15 years. The crisis has put heavy demands on them and, far from being a factor of rigidity, they have responded to these demands in a flexible way. They are no longer expected to provide ever-increasing benefits. Flexibility means responding to new urgent needs but also scaling down unnecessary benefits in line with circumstances.

Second, unemployment rather than low rates of growth or declining birth rates is the Achilles' heel of European welfare states. Hence the need for economic policies supporting job creation in all sectors.

Third, the welfare state will survive the global economy and increasing international competition. This does not mean that no adjustment has to be made, but that it is all a matter of choice between present and deferred income. So far, European populations have proved mature enough to adjust their choice to changing conditions.

Fourth, European welfare states are an instrument for human resources management. They play an essential part in managing the supply of labour and in redistributing work, especially between men and women and among people of different age groups.

Fifth, the welfare states do redistribute income and contribute to equality, thanks to taxes and transfers; but their redistributive ambitions have eroded over the years. They play a significant role in the struggle against poverty, although their ability to understand and tackle modern deprivation leaves much to be desired.

Sixth, income maintenance for all has become the hallmark of the modern welfare state, thus ensuring that not only the poor but also the middle classes benefit from social policies and programmes. The legitimacy of the modern welfare state rests on its ability to respond to the needs of the majority of the population.

No doubt our perception of the welfare state has changed as a result of nearly 20 years of economic difficulties. Both its potential and its limitations are now clearer than before, leading to relativism in the sphere of social policies. But the welfare state is here to stay because it fulfils some essential functions in modern European countries.

It is unlikely that the achievement of the single economic market in 1992 within the European Community, will require sacrificing existing differences in social security and welfare arrangements. Harmonization and deregulation policies will not lead to a centralized wage bargaining system in Brussels in the foreseeable future. Present EC efforts to establish a European social charter refer only to the setting up of *minimum* norms in the area of industrial relations (working time, workers' representation, and so on), but they also leave more advanced EC countries entirely free to enact whatever regulations they wish to adopt in the social field. National idiosyncrasies about social security are strongly institutionalized and will not be given up easily. The more so because, as this chapter has shown, the adaptability of social security systems, grossly underestimated in the past, is sufficient to prevent a frustration of the ongoing – but very slow – harmonization process.

Note

* The present chapter was originally published in the collection of papers submitted to the *Conference on Globalization of Industrial Economy – Challenge to the Social Contract* (Z. Suda, ed.), FAST programme, Brussels, 1991. The article is reprinted here with the kind permission of the publisher.

References

de Kram et al. (1988) 'Economic Crisis and its Aftermath: The Reform of Social Security in the Netherlands, 1984-1986', in Jallade, J.-P. (ed.) *The Crisis of Redistribution in European Welfare States.* Trentham Books.

Esping-Andersen, G., Korpi, W. (1984) 'From Poor Relief Towards Institutional Welfare States: The Development of Scandinavian Social Policy', Swedish Institute for Social Research.

Jallade, J.-P. (1988) 'Redistribution in the Welfare State: an Assessment of the French Performance', in Jallade, J.-P. (ed.) *The Crisis of Redistribution in European Welfare States.* op. cit.

OECD (1981) *The Welfare State in Crisis.* Paris.

OECD (1985) *Social Expenditure 1960-1990.* Paris.

O'Higgins, M. (1988) 'Inequality, Social Policy and Income Distribution in the United Kingdom', in Jallade, J.-P. (ed.) *The Crisis of Redistribution in European Welfare States.* op. cit.

Ringen, S. (1987) *The Possibility of Politics. A Study in the Political Economy of the Welfare State.* Oxford: Clarendon Press.

Rosanvallon, P. (1981) *La crise de l'Etat Providence.* Paris: Seuil.

Söderström, L. 'The Redistributive Effects of Social Protection: Sweden', in Jallade, J.-P. (ed.) *The Crisis of Redistribution in European Welfare States.* op. cit.

CHAPTER 4

Welfare State Politics in the United States

Frances Fox Piven
Richard A. Cloward

The recent upheavals in Eastern Europe have been based, ideologically, on the fusing of symbols of market and democracy, as if each were the essential concomitant of the other. This is curious, and from an American perspective, ironic. Despite Jeffersonian notions that democracy rested on the economic independence of small landholders, market or *laissez-faire* ideas were invoked historically to justify limitations on the state – and necessarily, therefore, on democratic politics. State interference presumably risks distortions of market processes or market "laws". And in the contemporary period, especially in the United States, a strong revival of *laissez-faire* ideology cast in the terms of international markets has become a powerful weapon in an assault on public programmes that had been won in part through democratic political influence.

1   American Welfare State Programmes

The United States is often characterized as a welfare state laggard. The main programmes to ensure economic security for the old, the unemployed, the disabled or the poor were not inaugurated until the 1930s, some decades after such programmes were begun in the leading welfare states of Western Europe. And once initiated, the US programmes trailed behind Western Europe in benefit levels and scope of coverage. Moreover, the concatenation of mass movements and electoral instability which made these limited initiatives possible during the Great Depression, naturally did not last. After World War II, many of the limited programmes that had been established were allowed to languish, and new programmes proved impossible to win in the Congress, largely owing to the combined resistance of southern Democrats and business-oriented Republicans. In response to this resistance, organized labour gradually turned away from politics and government as the arena for solving problems of economic insecurity. Instead, a still-militant and still-strong labour movement bargained with employers for health and old-age protections, and later for unemployment protections as well. The result was that core working class groups came to rely less on state programmes, and more on privately provided employment-based benefits, than in most other welfare states.

Nevertheless, the public programmes eventually did expand, and new programmes were added, particularly during the 1960s when welfare state programmes in other Western countries also rapidly enlarged. This convergence suggests similar political dynamics at work – perhaps the combined influence of growing beneficiary groups and the protest movements of the 1960s. Popular images of these movements depict them as mainly the creation of the children of opulence. However, student protests were sparked by the protests of other groups, and in turn helped spark them: discontented workers broke out of the strait-jacket of their union compacts, and marginalized groups generally erupted in protest, including racial minorities and the very poor. Notwithstanding the iconography of the 1960s as a "youth movement", it was these linked and spreading protests which gave the movements their great force.[1] Of course, the specific dynamics were different in different countries. In the United States, the seedbed of the spreading movement was in the black protests which began early – in the 1950s in the South – and focused not on economic grievances but on political rights.

These extraordinary protests by an impoverished people living in the shadow of the lynch mob, helped inspire the early phase of the American student movement – and also spurred protests among blacks in the ghetto communities of the north. The administrations of John F. Kennedy and Lyndon B. Johnson depended on the electoral support of the South, where the trouble was initially concentrated, and of the big cities, to which the protests rapidly spread. From the very start of the 1960s, Kennedy and then Johnson tried to quiet the forces that were being unleashed by initiating new social programmes directed specifically at impoverished minorities, and by liberalizing the social welfare programmes inherited from the 1930s (thus also sealing the allegiance of the enlarging numbers of recipients of the then-miserly old-age pensions). As a result, new programmes targeted specifically to the poor were initiated in the areas of health, education and housing; and existing income maintenance programmes were expanded. By the early 1970s, while the United States still lagged well behind such spending leaders as Sweden or Germany, it nevertheless could be said that it had joined the family of welfare states, some distinctive features of its programmes notwithstanding.[2]

It is worth mentioning the intersection of this development with large-scale changes that were occurring in the circumstances of American women, an intersection that has parallels in a number of other countries. The American welfare state was forged in the 1930s in response to mass protests by the unemployed which unfolded in an unstable electoral context and thus made the national government vulnerable. It was expanded in the 1960s in response to a similar conjuncture between black protest and electoral instability. But if the unemployed and blacks were the key collective political actors in the creation of the welfare state, it was nevertheless a development that turned out to have overwhelming importance for women.

The 1960s' expansion of social programmes occurred at a moment when major changes were occurring in the circumstances of women that in a sense thrust them into a close and multifaceted relationship with the welfare state. These changes in circumstances were profound because they were rooted in the transformation of major institutions. For one thing, the family was being transformed by rising rates of divorce and desertion and by the increasing numbers of unmarried women who bore children. For another, more and more women were becoming wage workers. These trends were partly related, since women who could no longer depend on the wages of male family heads were likely to seek employment. So, however, were many married women moving into the workforce, in an effort to maintain family income in the face of the overall decline in wage levels that began in 1973. Most of these new women workers were concentrated in low-paying and frequently irregular, temporary or part-time jobs in the enlarging service sector. Still, there were liberatory aspects of these developments, especially for better-educated women who experienced the loosening of the constraints of traditional marriage and expanding opportunities in the labour market as an opportunity to rise in the professions and business.

Because these intertwined changes in family patterns and labour market generated increased economic insecurity among women and children, they also led to increased reliance on welfare state income and service programmes. Some women raising children alone eked out a kind of livelihood on "welfare." Other women who worked irregularly or earned low wages, turned to income supports or services to supplement their earnings or to tide them over bouts of unemployment. Meanwhile, a startling proportion of the women entering the labour market turned to expanding welfare state programmes as a major source of employment. This was especially important for better-educated women; fully 50 per cent of the professional and managerial jobs held by women in the 1970s were in welfare state agencies.[3]

These developments peaked by the mid-1970s. During this brief period, the gradual expansion and improvement of the welfare state as a corollary of economic growth and democratic enlightenment was taken for granted, by experts and the broader public alike. Now, however, nothing is taken for granted. Criticism of welfare state programmes has mounted in the United States, and an emerging confidence in the stability and gradual evolution of the programmes has been replaced by the sense that a kind of historical watershed has been reached. Of course, something like this has occurred in most welfare states. But in the United States, welfare state politics have been especially heated, and the programmes have been subjected to a fierce and sustained assault. The nation known as the laggard in constructing the welfare state, seems to have become the leader in deconstructing it.

2   The Contemporary Assault

The roots of this attack on welfare state programmes are in the economic shocks of the 1970s and in the historic political mobilization of American business which it prompted. Indeed, it is not too much to say that for the first time in many decades, American business mobilized as a political class, with a degree of unity and on a scale not witnessed since the great mobilization of the 1890s when industrial and financial leaders pulled together to defeat what they perceived as the Populist-labour threat represented by the presidential campaign of Williams Jenning Bryan. Business leaders pulled together again in the 1970s, when they developed a political pro-gramme for the nation and set about implementing it with missionary zeal. The reorganization of the welfare state was high on their agenda.

This may seem like rhetorical hyperbole. After all, business interests have always paid a good deal of attention to government policies and have always worked to influence those policies – as lobbyists and campaign contributors, for example. Still, this was different. During the fat and easy years of "the American Century", business politics was the politics of fractionalized special interests who worked for favourable policies or rulings or contracts to increase the profitability of particular industries and firms, typically taking pains to pay off both sides of the aisle. The business political mobilization that began in the 1970s was different.

For one thing, the problems were different and much larger in scope. American corporate leaders were goaded to mobilize by worldwide economic changes which were producing sweeping and disturbing problems for American investors. In-tensifying competition from Europe and Japan – and later from newly-industri-alizing countries – was devastating the car, steel, electronics, and machine tools industries. Meanwhile, commodity prices of Third World suppliers were rising, as dramatized by the series of oil price shocks of the 1970s. And, perhaps because of the protections yielded by an expanded welfare state, the standard American macro-economic strategies to stabilize prices were not working well – as was revealed by the failure of the Nixon administration's efforts to dampen wage increases by allowing unemployment to rise. By the early 1970s, the consequences of these developments were evident in the shrinking profit margins of non-financial corporations and in the widespread sense of increasing economic uncertainty among business leaders.

Similar problems in other Western industrial nations prompted diverse business and governmental responses, including emphasis on increased capital investment, innovations in technology and in the organization of production, and in active labour market policies. The response of American business leaders, however, was distinctive. They set about trying to shore up profits by lowering wage costs, reducing public expenditures, and dismantling government regulations which were perceived as restraining business operations. To that end, top corporate executives organized new vehicles to promote the business outlook and programme, beginning with the creation of the Conference Board in the early 1970s. Exasperated by what they perceived as the radicalization of the universities, they poured hundreds of millions of dollars into the creation of new business-oriented think tanks, as well as into the expansion of existing conservative research institutions to provide the intellectual foundations for the business programme. Moreover, business executives became political organizers, mobilizing their stockholders and business partners, working to revive trade associations and such near-dormant organizations as the US Chamber of Commerce, and also working to raise the funds that made possible the modernization of the Republican Party and its centralization under conservative leadership.[4]

The results of this business mobilization could be seen first in the workplace, in hardened employer resistance to union wage and workplace demands and in escalated union-busting activities. Indeed, the 1970s saw the revival of a very American institution, the union-busting business. These businesses had prospered from the late nineteeth century up to the 1930s, providing private armies of thugs for hire to break strikes, such as the famed Pinkertons. All told, the men under arms in such firms more or less matched the men under arms in the American army. In the 1970s, when union-busting became a profitable speciality again, it was not thugs to which employers turned, but lawyers and public relations experts hired to use litigation and advertising to defeat new union drives or decertify old unions.[5] By the late 1970s, business influence in politics was clearly on the rise as well, especially in the Congress which began to roll back regulatory controls and to legislate significant increases in military spending – while defeating virtually all of the Carter initiatives on social spending, and also defeating a long-promised and much-heralded reform of labour law that would have redressed some of the pernicious features of the Taft-Hartley Act.

It was after the election of 1980, however, that the real fruits of business mobilization were gathered. A Republican regime backed by a virtually unanimous business community proceeded to slash taxes on business and on the better-off, in effect depleting the federal treasury of US$ 750 billion over the period of the first Reagan term, while raising taxes on workers through a large increase in 1983 in social security payroll taxes. The tax legislation of 1986 changed the method of taxation, but did not significantly alter the new class distribution of the tax burden; and recent Bush efforts to cut the capital gains tax would further reduce taxes on the truly rich. Meanwhile, rapidly-increasing military expenditures, which reached US$ 300 billion annually by the end of the 1980s, have to be understood – whatever else they also may be – as a major subsidy to defence industries habituated to "cost-plus" contracting. The deregulation campaign that had begun under Carter accelerated, largely through emasculation of the regulatory agencies which were stripped of funds and (in a pattern resembling the regulatory politics of the progressive period) staffed by representatives of the regulated industries. The campaign against unions also escalated, both in the visible and dramatic form of a President personally taking on and destroying the air controllers' union, and in the less visible but perhaps more devastating form of a series of appointments to the National Labour Relations Board so hostile to organized labour as to provoke a number of union leaders to call for the abolition of a Board that had been established as a concession to labour in the 1930s.

Finally, and most germane to our argument here, the new Republican administration began a campaign against welfare state programmes, with mixed success. Early efforts to cut old-age pensions were quickly reversed when virtually unanimous opposition in the Congress revealed the influence of the organized aged. This, together with the Medicare programme – which underwrites a portion of the health care costs of the elderly – are far and away the largest of the transfer programmes; and they were successfully defended. Other programmes – particularly programmes for the poor and the unemployed – did not fare so well, however. Funds for housing programmes were slashed by 75 per cent, bringing the construction of publicly-subsidized housing to a virtual standstill.[6] Unemployment benefits were sharply reduced, largely by changes *in formulae* that were not well understood, with the result that during the relatively high unemployment years of the mid-1980s, only 25-30 per cent of the unemployed received any benefits at all – the lowest coverage since the programme was first introduced in the 1930s. And the means-tested programmes which mainly provide aid to poor women and children were badly mangled, partly because they were associated with the minority poor and public support for them was thus weaker, but also because the efforts to cut them were persistent. The means-tested programmes, which accounted for only 10 per cent of the federal budget, absorbed 40 per cent of the budget cuts made by the end of the first year of the Reagan administration. And after January 1981, the regulated minimum wage level was not raised, although consumer prices rose by 39 per cent by the end of the decade so that the real legal minimum fell to the level of 1955.[7] Measured another way, in the 1960s and 1970s, earnings at the minimum wage lifted a family of three over the poverty line. By 1989, when 70 per cent of minimum wage workers were women, a family depending on the minimum wage lived at a level 30 per cent below the poverty line.[8]

Additional cuts planned for subsequent years were for the most part resisted by the Congress, although administrative practices introduced by the Reagan administration nevertheless resulted in millions of people being denied benefits. The use of bureaucratic obstacles to discourage utilization is in fact an old problem in the means-tested programmes, but it appears to have worsened as a result of new and often confusing requirements for demonstrating eligibility, and perhaps also as a result of the increasing stigmatization of users in a hostile political climate. For example, a study conducted by the Social Security Administration in December 1986 and May 1987 found that 84 per cent of those suspended by the Supplemental Security Income programme (for the impoverished aged and disabled) should have received payments.[9] Other studies report that overall participation rates in the programme range from 50 to 64 per cent. And a series of studies of the food stamp programme – by the Urban Institute, the Congressional Budget Office, and the General Accounting Office – found that only one third to one half of all eligible persons were receiving food stamp benefits.[10] In addition, an Urban Institute study found that between 20 and 25 per cent of the families eligible for the AFDC programme do not receive benefits[11] and that one third of those eligible for Medicaid, a health insurance programme specifically for the poor, are not receiving benefits.

3   The Impact of the Cutbacks

Not surprisingly, these changes in public policy taken together had a wide impact on the distribution of income and well-being in American society – partly as a simple and direct consequence of shifts in the incidence of taxation and benefits, and partly because changes in public policy contributed to a redistribution of power and income in the larger economy.[12] Indeed, the changes that have occurred over the past 10 years are so large as to constitute to our minds a reordering of the class structure. Consider, for example, the shifts in income inequality that have occurred. By the end of the decade, the income share of the poorest fifth of the population fell to 4.6 per cent, the lowest level since 1954; the income share of the next poorest fifth fell to 10.7 per cent, which was the lowest share on record, as was the 16.7-per-cent share of the middle fifth. By contrast, the share of the richest fifth rose to 44 per cent, its highest level ever.[13] Overall, the income ratio between the top fifth and the bottom fifth had widened to 9.6, from 7.2 in 1968, and from a postwar average of 8.2.

Or consider a related measure, the changes in levels of income within different *strata*. Between 1979 and 1988, the average income of the poorest fifth fell by over 6%, while the average income of the top fifth rose by 12%; and of the top-five-per-cent, by 16%.[14] Meanwhile, the income of the top-one-per-cent rose by an estimated 50%.

These broad income shifts have been accompanied by especially worsening straits among people at the very bottom of the class structure, those whose income leaves them below the official poverty line of approximately US$ 12,000 in 1989 for a family of four. In 1979, not an especially good year, 11.7 per cent of the population fell below the poverty line. By 1988, the fifth year of an economic boom, over 13 per cent, or some 32 million people, lived below the poverty line. Minorities were especially hard hit: among blacks, the poverty rate was three times the average; and among Hispanics, two and a half times.[15] The poor were also poorer. The average poor family reported an income nearly $5,000 below the poverty line in 1988. Children were especially numerous among the officially poor – fully 20 per cent of all children, or 12.5 million and three million more than in 1973, are poor – and by the end of the 1980s, more than half of these children were not even receiving subsidized health care.[16] Poverty increased most rapidly among full-time workers, rising almost by half over the decade. Of course, these numbers cannot convey the human experience of material misery and the cultural marginalization which accompanies it. Homeless people huddled beneath discarded newspapers for warmth, now occupy many of the public spaces in American cities; scores of beggars, often displaying gross deformities, harass passers-by on city streets, evoking medieval *tableaux*; criminal court judges in New York City conduct trials of people charged with the crime of sucking dollar tokens out of subway turnstile slots.

Income inequality, however measured, is not the whole of it. Shifts in electoral politics and in public policy have also had wide reverberations on power relations, and especially between labour and capital. On the one side, workers read the attack on unions by business and government and the stripping of income protections as a warning, evidence of their weakness and the risks they confront – especially in the context of the rising unemployment which prevailed in the early 1980s. That strikes fell to their lowest level in half a century in 1982, was evidence of the powerlessness experienced by workers and unions. Even at the end of the decade, when the unemployment level dipped to 5.5 per cent, the major unions were signing contracts with pay increases that lagged behind the rate of inflation – while they battled mightily to hold the line against employer efforts to reduce contractual health and pension benefits. Overall, average wage levels have slipped steadily downward since 1973.[17] Consistently, while the United States has been a leader in the creation of new jobs, it is also a leader in creating "junk jobs".[18] Some estimates indicate that fully 50 per cent of the jobs created since 1979 pay wages insufficient to maintain a family above the poverty level. And new cohorts of males entering the labour market in 1984 earned one third less than comparable cohorts a decade earlier; black cohorts earned one half less.

On the other side, business interests appear to have treated the changes in politics and policy of this period not only as a vindication of the business outlook on what was wrong with the American economy, but as a license for new and fantastic predatory manipulations in the marketplace. The rash of Wall Street "insider trading" scandals (when stock traders use information which is obtained illegally), is an example – although the elaboration of entirely legal forms of paper speculation is surely more important. And predatory business practices increasingly penetrate government programmes, as evidenced by repeated defence contracting scandals or by the federal "bailout" of the savings and loan banks at an estimated cost of at least US$ 100 billion. Polemical excoriation of government spending notwithstanding, businessmen were not above looting even the much-reduced funds that remained in federal low-cost housing programmes.

4   Conservative Explanations of the Assault: Why They Are Persuasive

A regime that gained control over government through electoral politics had, of course, to try to make explanations for its policies that find some acceptance with the electorate. Naturally, elections in the United States do not usually turn on specific public policies, which are generally overshadowed by the more salient questions of war and peace and overall economic prosperity. Moreover, for reasons deeply embedded in American electoral institutions, substantial proportions of those who were suffering the most dire consequences of these policies do not participate in contemporary elections.[19] Even so, the changes in public policy that were being implemented were dramatic, and their consequences were far-flung. From the start, a mobilized business community paid close heed to the problem of justifying its new policies, as evidenced by the efforts to fund and institutionalize a business-oriented intelligentsia. Accordingly, as new policy initiatives unfolded, so did a series of powerfully-mounted arguments about why the policy changes were both necessary and right.

4.1   Invoking Democracy

One explanation for the campaign against welfare state programmes was simply that democratic public opinion demanded it. Presumably, the voters had turned against "big government," as evidenced by the election of Ronald Reagan in 1980 and his re-election by a substantial margin in 1984. Thus the case was made that the regressive redistribution underway reflected public sentiment, or so Republican leaders claimed, and many Democrats seemed to agree. At first glance, this argument is not so unreasonable. After all, the United States is commonly said to be the land of "possessive individualism", and its people are presumably hostile to collectivist welfare state initiatives. More than that, the large role of segmented means-tested programmes in the US isolates and highlights the minority poor, thus activating not only the individualistic biases of Americans, but also their deep racism.

Nevertheless, the public opinion data tell a somewhat different story. For one thing, the exit polls of 1980 do not show that dissatisfaction with the welfare state caused voters to defect from Carter. Apparently Reagan did not expect this to be a winning issue either; except for a single speech to a group of bankers, he did not make proposals for welfare state cuts during the campaign and, indeed, promised to preserve "the safety net". Of course, he did assail "big government", but a large body of survey data shows this phrase to have diverse and changing meanings to respondents.[20] Mainly, Reagan campaigned on a platform promising to restore the international prestige and military pre-eminence of the United States and to set straight an economy plagued by stagflation; and these goals did meet with public approval. Exit polls make clear that voters turned against Carter precisely because of the poor overall performance of the economy in an election year (especially high unemployment), and because of the battering of American prestige associated with the Iranian hostage crisis.[21]

When Reagan ran in 1984, he again did not feature his opposition to welfare state policies. Indeed, by this time he was publicly claiming to be the champion of the social security programme. In any case, the election turned on economic trends, and specifically on the economic upturn which had produced a stunning increase in real personal income of 8.5 per cent during the election year. And in 1988, George Bush, Reagan's appointed successor, ran as the "kinder, gentler" candidate who would improve education, protect the environment, and do something about the homeless.

In other words, there is not much reason to consider the elections of the 1980s as referenda on the American welfare state. Public opinion data add weight to this assessment. Although public support for general economic security policies is not as high in the United States as it is in some European welfare states,[22] large majorities nevertheless support a number of such objectives (seeing to it that everyone who wants a job can have one, to health care for the sick, and to decent standards of living for the old); and surveys show steadily enlarging support over the decade both for general principles of the welfare state and for particular programmes, including even the beleaguered means-tested programmes popularly known as "welfare".[23]

4.2 *Welfare Hurts More than it Helps*

Naturally, the conservative campaign also tried to shape the public opinion it claimed as its mandate. This was done not by attacking the broad security goals of the welfare state. To the contrary, there rapidly developed a kind of tacit acceptance of the fact that public opinion supported those goals. Instead, the argument focused on programme effectiveness. The means-tested programmes in particular were accused of producing perverse effects by creating disincentives to work effort and stable social life, thus presumably increasing underlying poverty and social pathology. The palpable evidence of worsening poverty and associated evidence of social and personal disorganization, was said to be the result precisely of mistaken efforts to ameliorate these conditions.

Of course, this basic argument is familiar from a long history of punitive poor-law reform. Nevertheless, it was resurrected in the 1980s, as in Reagan's well-known anecdotes about the miscreant poor. However, it was not only politicians who took up this theme. It was also the basis of a series of much-heralded and much-publicized books, some of them paid for by business-funded think tanks.[24] In addition, the view that welfare causes poverty, marital breakdown, illegitimacy, intergenerational poverty, and other ills has continued to dominate American research on the welfare state – no matter its apparent illogic, since a number of these problems increased even as the means-tested programmes were shrinking.[25]

5 *Neo-Laissez-faire*: The Imperatives of a Global Economy

The more powerful argument against the welfare state did not focus on democratic public opinion, however, or on the perverse effects of the programmes on the poor. Rather, the "hegemonic" argument which stifled or scattered opposition asserted that the basic Reagan package of slashed taxes and reduced government spending was an inevitable response to the new imperatives generated by global economic restructuring. Presumably, intensifying competition from Western Europe, Japan, the newly-industrialized countries of Southeast Asia, and of emerging low-wage producers in Latin America, demands new policies to meet the challenge. What new policies? Apparently, new distributional policies. To make the US lean and tough for the competitive fight, the entrepreneurial spirit of businessmen has to be unfettered by minimizing government regulation and slashing taxes so as to enlarge profits and, hence, investment. Meanwhile, workers and citizens have to become lean and tough, too: hence, lower wages and fewer work protections, as well as cutbacks in the programmes that provide social services or economic security – not only because the cutbacks are the inevitable consequence of slashed taxes (and increased defence expenditures), but also because the cutbacks will force increased work effort. This argument effectively makes it appear that the policies associated with the business political mobilization have nothing to do with politics at all. Instead, the business programme is presented as the inevitable spelling out in policy of a series of adaptations demanded by international market developments. This argument is the more forceful, of course, because it emanates from a well-funded and coordinated propaganda campaign and because it draws heavily on a view of the "naturalness" of the market that has always figured largely in traditional American ideology. Still, these are only suppositions. In a sense, the power of *neo-laissez-faire* propaganda to carry public opinion has not really been tested, simply because the public has not been exposed to counter-interpretations. What there is of an ideological opposition in the Democratic Party, has been virtually silent on these issues.[26]

But there are reasons that go beyond deliberate propaganda efforts which explain the credibility of the *neo-laissez-faire* interpretation. One is the palpable evidence in recent American experience of the reality and scale of international competition. Foreign products have indeed penetrated and even taken over huge markets in areas like cars and electronics. And a noticeable percentage – an estimated 10 per cent – of American workers now work for foreign firms, and state and local governments compete with much fanfare to attract new foreign investments. Moreover, the *neo-laissez-faire* argument gains adherents because it is not entirely dismal. It is persuasive, perhaps becoming "hegemonic", because it promises a solution that speaks to the interests and hopes of ordinary Americans. Lean and tough policies will presumably slow down foreign penetration of the American economy and, ultimately, perhaps even generate renewed economic growth and the improved jobs and public benefits that growth will make possible.

So far, however, the results have been far from clear. To be sure, the United States is well into the sixth year of an economic boom; and profit levels are high. But the evidence suggests that what is going on is the rush for short-term profits rather than the rejuvenation of the American economy. Indicators that speak to longer-term economic prospects, are not cheering. Productivity growth remains sluggish, at about half the level of the 1947-1973 period, and technological advance in the United States is lagging. Consistently, corporate spending on research and development is falling behind the rate of inflation, a fact that becomes more ominous in light of the prospect of sharply-reduced military spending on research and development.[27] Meanwhile, unconstrained by trade barriers, tax laws, and local content laws through which most of Europe and Japan have restrained capital flight, American corporations are investing more and more overseas – not only in operations that take advantage of low-wage labour, but in high technology research and production as well. Finally, there is evidence that the programme cuts made in the 1980s – justified because they would help spur economic growth – may be producing perverse effects. One is the erosion of the national government's capacities to regulate its own activities and expenditures. The General Accounting Office, in a recent review of the results of the Reagan administration's efforts to both "privatize" many government activities and reduce federal agency budgets, reports that cuts fell disproportionately on oversight and enforcement functions – which are, in any case, more difficult to exercise with private contractors. The resulting losses are estimated in the range of US$ 300 billion (including the costs of bailing out the savings and loan institutions mentioned earlier).[28] Meanwhile, estimates of the costs of dealing with the hazards created by weapons plants that have been pouring radioactive materials into their surroundings, run at more than US$ 100 billion. And some corporate leaders are even beginning to worry about the "makings of a national disaster" through the creation of "a Third World within our own country". What these leaders have in mind is the creation of a large population of impoverished minorities without the skills necessary even for low-level jobs in an advanced service economy.[29]

The "hegemonic" *neo-laissez-faire* argument asserts that contemporary market conditions require the rollback of the welfare state. In fact, there is sound reason and some evidence for thinking that it is not only markets which pattern and limit welfare state possibilities, but that welfare states pattern and delimit market possibilities. In the American case, a limited welfare state may be helping to free investors, and the conservative regime with which they are allied, to respond to international competition by wresting short-term profits instead of pursuing longer-term growth. By contrast, in the handful of countries which have the several interrelated institutions of vigorous welfare states – strong unions, comprehensive transfer programmes, and a large public sector – these institutions in turn seem to have the effect in the contemporary period of constraining both investor and government responses to global competition.[30] In nations where public and private unions are formidable, and where income protection programmes are more generous, the American corporate option of shoring up profits by slashing wages and public expenditures is, in effect, politically precluded. This is not entirely hypothetical. There is accumulating evidence that strong unions, as well as left-wing parties in government, not only block the adoption of the American strategy of short-term profit-seeking, but also create the stable environment which encourages longer-term investment and hence higher rates of growth. Thus, Garrett and Lange maintain that union centralization and scope, when matched by strong leftist role in government, is a source of long-term economic growth.[31] The reasoning is that this combination of conditions makes it possible to restrain wage demands in favour of the collective gains yielded by higher rates of reinvestment, guided and guarded by leftist control of government.[32]

All of this suggests the possibility of trouble ahead in the United States. If the business political mobilization fails to fulfil its hegemonic promise of economic success in an international economy, such public tolerance as there has been for eroding public programmes, may evaporate.

6 The Rout of the Experts

These portents of political trouble for the American business agenda remain, however, hazy and uncertain. In the meantime, support for the welfare state among liberal and leftist intellectuals seems to have evaporated in the face of the multifaceted business assault. What may be especially important, at least in the short run, is the erosion of liberal support. For one thing, liberal intellectuals are far more influential because they are connected with large and influential institutions. For another, liberals had been firmer supporters of the welfare state in the past, for they viewed it as evidence of the gradual and progressive adaptation by government to the morally-legitimate claims of citizens in an affluent and democratic society.

The liberal establishment – lodged in the universities, research institutes, and in government bureaucracies – is tied closely to welfare state agencies which provide a good portion of its funding and rationale. During the 1970s and 1980s, this establishment devoted itself to studies which examined the conservative charges about the pernicious effects of the means-tested programmes on the work effort and social behaviour of the poor. To its credit, it produced an enormous body of empirical research that helped to undermine these arguments. Even so, the influence of the conservative assault was considerable: for it in effect set the agenda for the liberal establishment, turning it from the investigation of the roots of poverty and social disorganization in larger social and economic processes, in favour of narrow questions about the bearing of the means-tested programmes on these problems.[33] In this sense, although the substance of their charges were largely disproved, the conservatives succeeded in defining the issues.

Notwithstanding the successes of the liberal establishment in puncturing this particular line of conservative attack, their confidence in state intervention did not revive – as demonstrated by the recent turn to "underclass" research. This vigorous and well-funded endeavour is, of course, a variant of the older "culture of poverty" perspective. It holds that poverty and social disorganization in the United States are significantly the result of distinctive anti-social attitudes and behaviours, rather than the result of institutional or structural arrangements. Thus, underclass research does not focus on the increase of irregular or low-wage employment, or on social programme cutbacks, but instead directs attention to the cultural patterns among the poor which make significant numbers of them into an "underclass". Of course, no reasonable analyst would deny the cultural effects of persistent poverty and social marginalization. This, however, is not what is meant by the underclass. Isabel Sawhill, who pioneered the use of the term (and also pioneered a kind of epidemiological research into underclass dynamics which consists of mapping indicators of social pathology so as to reveal their geographical incidence and spread, presumably through a "contagion" effect)[34] makes clear the thrust of the term:

> If the term is to be useful, the underclass must be distinguished from the poor ... [In] America today certain norms are widely held. First, children are expected to study hard and complete at least high school. Second, young people are expected to refrain from conceiving children until they have the personal and financial resources to support them ... Third, adults are expected to work at a steady job ... Fourth, everyone is expected to obey the laws. These are social obligations. Those who fulfil them are unlikely to be chronically poor. If they are poor despite having abided by the rules, society is much more likely to come to their rescue. This is ... the nature of the social contract. The problem is too many people who are not fulfilling their end of the bargain.[35]

In fact, the evidence for the existence of a cultural underclass apart from institutional conditions is not very persuasive. Perhaps the most publicized symptom is the rise of illegitimate births, especially to black women, and the correlative rise in female-headed households. But publicity aside, the rate of illegitimate births to black women has not increased – although the rate of legitimate births has declined, and declined very sharply among teenagers.[36] Nor do other indicators of the spread of an underclass culture among the poor fare much better, although of course there is indisputable evidence that traditional sexual norms and perhaps work norms are weakening throughout society.[37]

The shift in attitude among leftist intellectuals is quite another matter, and it is profoundly puzzling. After all, not so long ago, nearly everyone on the left agreed that welfare state programmes had to be understood in terms of class politics. The programmes originated in class conflict and, once established, had consequences for the power of workers, on the one side, and employers on the other. There was still a good deal to argue about, of course, including whether on balance the programmes helped workers more or capitalists more and, relatedly, about just which class forces should be credited or blamed for them. But for all of the wordy and often-heated disputes, one premise was not much disputed: the welfare state was somehow forged in the vortex of class conflict. Programmes which provided non-market income or services to the old or the unemployed or the ill, were either the achievements of the working class; or they were evidence of the machinations of the capitalist class who thus foisted reproduction costs onto the state; or, perhaps more reasonably, they were both. Explanations in the capitalist state genre made a similar albeit indirect argument, positing that welfare state programmes *legitimated* a class society, and thus could be understood as a stratagem to submerge or avert class conflict.

During the late 1960s and early 1970s, these debates flourished in part because the workings of class forces in American politics were, in fact, murky. On the one side, popular pressures for welfare state expansion came less from the obvious organs of the traditional working class than from the black movement. On the other side, the notion of the capitalist class as a political actor seemed hypothetical and strained. Real business interests were divided, their policies were often *ad hoc* – when they had policies at all. They did not look or act like an empirically observable class. What one could see instead were myriad special interests, most of them ready to buy influence from both sides of the aisle and without a programme that looked much beyond the short-run profitability of particular firms or industries. Certainly the politics that could be observed revealed a profusion of actors and events, thus nourishing disputes on the left about the role of classes in the historical development of the welfare state.

As the 1970s wore on, however, American capitalists did begin to look like a political class. Corporate leaders began to organize, they developed a political programme for the nation, then they set about implementing it with missionary zeal, and they placed the reorganization of the welfare state high on their agenda.

This was an historic moment. For the intellectual left, it was an opportunity to evaluate past debates about the welfare state. After years of theoretical dispute, the capitalist class had finally emerged from the empirical murk, as the unambiguous antagonist of welfare state programmes. Here was an opportunity to test theory and to learn from events something about the bearing of particular programmes on business interests, thus perhaps gaining a specificity which earlier debates had sorely lacked. Which sectors of capital were taking the initiative? What programmes were targeted, and for what sorts of changes? Who specifically mounted resistance, and to which sorts of changes? And what were the effects over time of programme cutbacks on income distribution, on class relations, and particularly on labour power?

However, the revelatory moment appears to have come too late. Discussions of the welfare state on the American left no longer focus much on class conflict. No matter the currents of the real world, the irresistable currents of intellectual fashion propelled a good many leftist intellectuals up and away into the esoteric realms of post-modernist discourse. For those who continued to investigate the class bases of public policy, moreover, the relentless attack on welfare state programmes was disorienting. Leftist critics who had argued that the programmes functioned to legitimate capitalist relations, clearly had some explaining to do. And the strident insistence that programmes lacked popular support, also undermined the confidence of those who had once insisted that the welfare state was a working class achievement. Overall, a profound sense that state provision is flawed – perhaps deeply and perhaps intractably – has engulfed the left. This, too, helps explain the weakness thus far, especially the ideological weakness, of opposition to the business attack on the American welfare state.

Notes

1 Arrighi, Hopkins and Wallerstein (1988).
2 Just how "distinctive" the American programmes in fact are, is debatable. Increasingly elaborate typologies of welfare states in recent work focus on significant variations among nations in overall expenditure levels and structure of programmes. See, for example, Heidenheimer, Heclo and Adams (1975); Esping-Andersen (1986).
3 Erie and Rein (1988).
4 Ferguson and Rogers (1986).
5 On the use of legal stratagems, see especially the data in Ferguson and Rogers (1986).
6 Housing subsidies for the better-off remained unscathed, however, because these take the form of tax expenditures. The better-off who owned their homes continued to be able to deduct property tax and interest expenditures from their taxable income.
7 A sharply-fought contest in the Congress did finally result in a modest increase in the fall of 1989, but only to US$ 4.25. If the minimum wage were to match the real value of the minimum in 1981, it would have been raised to US$ 4.79.
8 Center on Budget and Policy Priorities Report dated March 21, 1989.
9 *New York Times*, December 8, 1989: 20.
10 See, for example, United States General Accounting Office, December 8, 1988.
11 We ourselves suspect that this estimate is too low. Studies of a practice known as "churning" in AFDC, in which the inability or unwillingness of people to meet new administrative requirements becomes the occasion for at least temporary mass terminations, suggest the possibility that the percentage of eligible families denied aid at any given time may be considerably higher. So does

the recent emphasis on terminations as a sanction for not conforming to the requirements of training or job search programmes. And the State of Wisconsin has recently begun to terminate families from AFDC when children fail to attend school.

12 A series of studies attempt to sort out the direct impact of changes in tax and income transfer policies on income distribution. See, for example, Blank and Blinder, 1986; Danziger and Plotnick, 1986; Smeeding, 1977.

13 US Census Bureau, 'Annual Report on Poverty, October 1989', cited in Coalition on Human Needs, 'Insight/Action: A Report on Federal and State Policy Issues', November 1989. Washington, D.C.

14 Center for Budget and Policy Priorities, October 20, 1989.

15 *Dollars and Sense*, June 1989.

16 The child poverty rate among blacks climbed to 44 per cent; among Hispanics, to 38 per cent.

17 Reich, 1989. Reich also reports that the real average earnings of non-supervisory workers was at its lowest level since 1966. By contrast, workers in the securities industry had realized an income gain of 21 per cent from 1978-1987.

18 Esping-Andersen, 1990.

19 For an extended historical examination of the politics of non-voting in the United States, see Piven and Cloward, 1987.

20 It might be argued that voters understood that the tax cuts promised by the Reagan campaign implied reduced spending on government programmes. However, the exit polls show the election did not turn on promised tax cuts either.

21 Burnham, 1981.

22 Smith, 1987.

23 Lipset, 1985; Navarro, 1985; Shapiro, 1986.

24 See for example Anderson, 1978; Gilder, 1981; Murray, 1984; Mead, 1985. The Hoover Institution is, of course, one of the older conservative think tanks. Both Gilder and Murray were funded by a newer think tank, the Manhattan Institute.

25 For a more detailed review of the evidence for and against "perverse effects", see Piven and Cloward, 1987.

26 Offe, 1990, suggests a broadly similar bipartisan consensus with regard to the politics of welfare state issues in the German Federal Republic.

27 *International Herald Tribune*, January 24, 1990.

28 *New York Times*, December 19, 1989.

29 *New York Times*, September 25, 1989.

30 Esping-Anderson, 1986.

31 Garrett and Lange, 1986.

32 See also Garrett and Lange, 1989; Hicks, 1988; Hicks and Patterson, 1989; and Hicks, forthcoming, which attempts to synthesize a range of neo-pluralist and neo-Marxist works on the impact of social-democratic corporatist arrangements on growth. For a cross-national evaluation of the direct bearing of welfare state spending on economic growth, see Friedland and Sanders, 1985. See also Block, 1990.

33 See Piven and Cloward, 1987, for a discussion of this development.

34 See Ricketts and Sawhill, Winter 1988.

35 Sawhill, Isabell, Summer 1989. The term "underclass" was first used by Ken Auletta in a series of articles for the *New Yorker* in 1981. He also published a book with that title in 1982. Wilson also employs the concept and gives weight to underclass culture, but this is only part of an argument that stresses the ultimate importance of employment conditions in generating poverty. See Wilson, 1987.

36 For an extensive discussion of the data and its misrepresentation, see Piven and Cloward, 1987.

37 For a thorough evaluation of the evidence on the existence of an underclass, see Jencks, 1989.

References

Anderson, M. (1978) *Welfare: The Political Economy of Welfare Reform in the United States*. Stanford, California: The Hoover Institution.

Arrighi, G., Hopkins,T. K., Wallerstein, I. (1988) 1968: *The Great Rehearsal*. Paper prepared for XII Political Economy of the World System Conference, 'War and Revolution in the World System'. Emory University, Atlanta, March 24-26.

Auletta, K. in a series of articles for the *New Yorker* in 1981.

Blank, R., Blinder, A. (1986) in Danziger, Sh., Weinberg, D. H. (eds.) *Fighting Poverty: What Works and What Doesn't*. Cambridge, Mass.: Harvard University Press.

Block, F. (1990) *Postindustrial Possibilities*. University of California Press.

Burnham, W. D. (1981) 'The 1980 Earthquake: Realignment, Reaction, or What?', in Ferguson, Th., Rogers, J. (eds.) *The Hidden Election: Politics and Economics in the 1980 Presidential Campaign*. New York: Pantheon.

Center on Budget and Policy Priorities. March 21, 1989 *Making Work Pay: A New Agenda for Poverty Policies*. Washington, D.C.

Center on Budget and Policy Priorities. October 20, 1989 *Poverty Rate and Household Income Stagnate as Rich-Poor Gap Hits Post-War High*. Washington, D.C.

Danziger, Sh., Plotnick, R. D. (1986) 'Poverty and Policy: Lessons from the Last Two Decades', *Social Service Review* 60 (1).

Erie, S. P., Rein, M. (1988) 'Women and the Welfare State', in Mueller, C. (ed.) *The Politcs of the Gender Gap*. Sage.

Esping-Andersen, G. (1986) 'Power and Distributional Regimes', *Politics and Society*: 223-256.

Esping-Andersen, G. (1990) *Post-Industrial Cleavage Structures: A Comparison of Evolving Patterns of Social Stratification in Germany, Sweden, and the United States*. Paper prepared for the Conference on 'Popular Power in Post-Industrial Societies. Wagner Institute, City University of New York, February 1989.

Ferguson, Th., Rogers, J. (1986) *Right Turn*. New York: Pantheon.

Friedland, R., Sanders, J. (1985) 'The Public Economy and Economic Growth in Western Market Economies', *American Sociological Review* 50: 421-31.

Garrett, G., Lange, P. (1986) 'Performance in a Hostile World: Economic Growth in Capitalist Democracies', *World Politics* 38: 517-545.

Garrett, G., Lange, P. (1989) 'Government Partisanship and Economic Performance: When and How Does "Who Governs" Matter?', *Journal of Politics* 51: 676-93.

Gilder, G. (1981) *Wealth and Poverty*. New York, Basic Books.

Heidenheimer, A. J., Heclo, H., Adams, C. T. (1975) *Comparative Public Policy: The Politics of Choice in Europe and America*. New York: St. Martin Press.

Hicks, A. (1988) 'Social Democratic Corporatism and Economic Growth', *Journal of Politics* 50: 677-704.

Hicks, A. (Forthcoming) 'Unions, Social Democracy, Welfare and Democracy', *Research in Political Sociology* 5.

Hicks, A., Patterson, W. D. (1989) 'On the Robustness of the Left Corporatist Model of Economic Growth', *Journal of Politics* 51 (3).

Jencks, Ch. (1989) *Which Underclass is Growing? Recent Changes in Joblessness, Educational Attainment, Crime, Family Structure, and Welfare Dependency*. Paper prepared for a conference on William Julius Wilson's The Truly Disadvantaged. Northwestern University, October 19-21, 1989.

Lipset, S. M. (1985) 'The Elections, the Economy, and Public Opinion: 1984', *PS: The Journal of the American Political Science Association* 18 (1).

Mead, L. (1985) *Beyond Entitlement: The Social Obligations of Citizenship*. New York: The Free Press.

Murray, Ch. (1984) *Losing Ground: American Social Policy. 1950-1980*. New York: Basic Books.

Navarro, V. (1985) 'The 1984 Election and the New Deal: An Alternative Interpretation', *Social Policy* 15 (4).

Offe, C. (1990) *Smooth Consolidation in the West German Welfare State: Structural Change, Fiscal Policies, and Populist Politics*. Paper prepared for the Conference on 'Popular Power in Post-Industrial Societies'. Wagner Institute, City University of New York, February 1989.

Piven, F. F., Cloward, R. A. (1987) 'The Contemporary Relief Debate', in Block, F., Cloward, R.A., Ehrenreich, B., Piven, F.F. *The Mean Season: The Attack on the Welfare State*. New York: Pantheon.

Reich, R. (1989) 'As the World Turns', *New Republic*.

Ricketts, E., Sawhill, I. (1988) 'Defining and Measuring the Underclass', *Journal of Policy Analysis and Management* 7: 316-325.

Sawhill, I. (1989) 'The Underclass: An Overview', *Public Interest* 96.

Shapiro, R. Y. (1986) *The Dynamics of Public Opinion Toward Social Welfare Policy*. Paper delivered at the annual meeting of the American Political Science Foundation. Washington, D.C.

Smeeding, T. (1977) 'The Antipoverty Effectiveness of In Kind Transfers', *Journal of Human Resources* 12 (3).

Smith, Th. W. (1987) 'Public Opinion and the Welfare State', *Public Opinion Quarterly* 51: 402-421.

United States General Accounting Office, *Food Stamps: Reasons for Nonparticipation*, GAO/PEMD-89-5BR, December 8, 1988.

Wilson, W. J. (1987) *The Truly Disadvantaged*. Chicago: University of Chicago Press.

CHAPTER 5

The Interface between the Economy and the Welfare State: A Sociological Account

Jon Eivind Kolberg
Hannu Uusitalo

1   The Promise of the Welfare State

"The central problem of present-day politics is not the choice between 'totalitarianism', 'fascism', and 'democracy'. ... Nor is the formal ownership of the means of production – the crux of the debate between 'capitalism' and 'communism' – the central political issue. The real challenge is how to create institutions which ensure public welfare and popular participation within advanced industrial societies." Norman Furniss and Timothy Tilton, the authors of this formulation (1977: 46), saw the welfare state as the optimal answer to the challenge. They rejected the idea of self-regulated markets, although "liberal economics has generated a body of thought to show that a price system operating through free markets allocates resources efficiently and distributes goods justly". But they also rejected "the traditional socialist nostrum of nationalization". Instead, they perceived the welfare state as a search for a "middle road" between the waste and irrationality of unencumbered capitalism and the loss of liberty and individuality imposed by "totalitarianism". This middle road implies that politics is inserted into the social and economic order and is based on the values of equality, freedom, democracy, solidarity, security, and economic efficiency. However, the case of the welfare state is not to be made primarily because of its superior values, but because of the superiority of its social techniques as compared to those of liberal capitalism and state socialism. The idiosyncratic combination of budgetary planning, active labour market policy, social welfare legislation, progressive taxation, community planning, and democratic participation, permits the welfare state to avoid the major failings both of an unregulated capitalist economy and of excessive reliance upon the nationalization of industry (Furniss and Tilton, 1977: 28-39).

2   The Crisis of the Welfare State

This promise of the welfare state has met with a set of serious political challenges in the 1970s. The long economic recession, the end of "the golden age of capitalism", and the apparent failure of "Keynesian" economic policies, have led to a new and critical evaluation of the happy marriage between market and state intervention. Decreasing economic growth, increasing unemployment and simultaneous inflation, and growing social needs – together with declining prospects to finance them – were obvious signs of a crisis. In many eyes, the promise of the welfare state has failed. The question has been frequently raised of what is wrong with the relationship between the economy, society, and the welfare state. And what is more, the welfare state itself has been seen to be one, or even *the* main cause, of the problems of contemporary capitalism. This kind of a "crisis" claims that there is something fundamentally wrong with the relationship between the economy and the welfare state.

There are also theoretical reasons to intensify the study of the interface between the economy and the welfare state. The uncritical contemporary self-congratulation and celebration of Western capitalism has either tended to ignore the existence of the welfare state or, by implication, invites us to believe capitalism and the welfare state to be happily married forever. We maintain that their affiliation is more complex than ever, which is indicated by the many sociological theories about them – some of which we shall briefly mention here.

There is first the well-known "Keynesian" argument that the welfare state stabilizes the fluctuations of the capitalist economy by maintaining effective demand in situations of unemployment. Secondly, there is the human capital argument that welfare and efficiency can go hand in hand at even a higher level, because the welfare state represents true investment in human resources and thereby in economic production. Thirdly, there is the contention that the welfare state promotes the capitalist economy by reducing the intensity and structure of industrial conflicts, moving issues out of the orbit of the labour-capital relation and transforming conflicts into gradual rather than dichotomous issues. A fourth main model essentially goes beyond economic systems such as capitalism or socialism, seeing the welfare state as a response to the decline of social integration assumed to be the result of economic modernization. A fifth perspective regards the welfare state as the handmaiden of capitalism by sustaining capital accumulation and promoting the legitimacy of the capitalist social and political order. A sixth approach rejects this kind of Marxist functionalism and highlights the contradictions of the institutional symbiosis of capitalism and welfare state. Thus, neo-liberal attacks on the welfare state at both the theoretical and political level, have been depicted as the new class war. And lastly here, the neo-liberal argument itself regards the welfare state as a harmful and alien element in the body of the market economy, a decisive cause of imperfections and distortions.

The sheer magnitude of existing theories, the discrepancies between them, their uncertain empirical status, and their renewed political relevance – all are good reasons for more research on the interface between the economy and the welfare state. Furthermore, in a broader comparative context, it is important to keep in mind that the economic story of the West is a success story trailed by significant problems. Thus, to take the best-known example, from just 1970 to 1987 unemployment soared from less than 10 to more than 25 million people in the OECD area; and long-term unemployment, from 3.1 million individuals in 1980 to 9.4 million in 1985. It has become evident to almost all observers, irrespective of political or other leanings, that a lot has changed and that something is wrong with the interface between welfare state and economy.

3   The Ambition of the Chapter

It is only possible to address a small subset of all the questions that come to the fore once we begin to conceptualize the relationship between the economy and the welfare state. We will deal with two issues. The first of these is the question of the redistributive effects of the welfare state. The second problem is the postulated negative consequences of the welfare state on the volume of work. This chapter could be read as a sociological critique of the fashionable assumptions of neo-liberal thinking. As already indicated, this influential theory maintains that the market mechanism is distorted by the welfare state by compressing the stratificational order and thus damaging the motivation to work. The motivation to work is also impaired by taxation – in particular, by progressive taxation – and by the creation of alternative means of income through welfare state programmes authorizing what we could call "paid non-work". Thus, according to the neo-liberal argument, the welfare state promotes a decline in the supply of labour in the modern economy through a variety of mechanisms. Our critical confrontation with the neo-liberal ideas on the relationship between the economy and the welfare state, means that we tend to believe that capitalism, or should we say modern production, needs the welfare state. More precisely, the main thesis of this chapter is that the welfare state has become the main institutional vehicle of capitalist restructuration and that this is the baseline, and probably the root cause, of the crisis of the welfare state. This is not the same as to embrace the *reformist view*[1] that the marriage between welfare and efficiency, or between the welfare state and capitalism, is happy. Let us add to this that we are open but skeptical *vis-à-vis* what we could call the *independence hypothesis*, which maintains that the welfare state does not have any impact on economic growth because various effects largely cancel each other out. Yet the idea of countervailing effects, as opposed to unidirectional causation, is appealing. What we do want to sell, however, is the idea that we need to strengthen our efforts to conceptualize the interface of the welfare state and the economy. The last part of the chapter will indicate the direction we advocate.

4   The Impact of the Welfare State on Inequality and Poverty

It is interesting to note that both the neo-liberal hypothesis and the opposing reformist hypothesis share the assumption that the welfare state is, indeed, effective in its attempt to enforce equality. Are they right, or did the welfare state fail to achieve greater economic and social equality between citizens?

The Luxembourg Income Study (LIS) is an international research project which has established a data bank of coordinated household income data including about 10 industrialized countries, as well as facilitated reliable comparisons on income distributions (see Smeeding, Schmauss and Allegreza, 1985; Uusitalo, 1989). Figure 5.1, which is based on this data, shows that the more developed welfare states tend to have more equal income distributions. The Scandinavian welfare states, with Sweden in first place followed by Finland and Norway, have relatively equal income distributions.[2] Great Britain comes next – whereas such countries as New Zealand, Canada, Australia, the United States and Israel have wider income inequalities.

This is not only an incidence of correlation but also of causality. The welfare state does redistribute income through its cash transfers and taxes. Their combined effect is largest in the Scandinavian welfare states, with Sweden being ahead of Finland and Norway. Great Britain is in the middle; while in Israel and in North America, redistribution by the state is less significant. The major explanatory factor of cross-country variations in income inequality is the redistributive effect of the welfare state (Ringen and Uusitalo, 1992).

The conclusion is further strengthened by time series analysis. A study focusing on the development of income inequality in three Scandinavian countries between the mid-1960s and mid-1980s, points out that the major – if not the only – cause of these changes is the welfare state. Increased levels of cash transfers and direct taxation have reinforced income equality (Gustafsson and Uusitalo, 1990).

The promise of the welfare state has also included the elimination or reduction of poverty, at least in its harshest form. "To ask about poverty in the welfare state, is to question the elementary effectiveness of social policy" (Ringen, 1987: 141).

International comparisons of relative poverty levels have recently been presented by using LIS data, describing the situation around 1980. A strictly relative poverty line has been used: individuals are counted to be poor who live in families having equivalent income (disposable income per consumer unit) less than 50 per cent of the median equivalent income. Because relative poverty is an aspect of the income distribution, the results resemble although are not identical to those reported above and referring to income distribution. Norway and Sweden have low poverty rates while Finland has a somewhat higher rate close to the level of the Federal Republic of Germany. Great Britain and Switzerland display slightly higher poverty rates, while in countries outside Europe, poverty is even more common: in the United States as much as 17 per cent of the population have equivalent incomes below half

Figure 5.1: Income Inequality by the Size of the Welfare State in Nine Countries around 1980

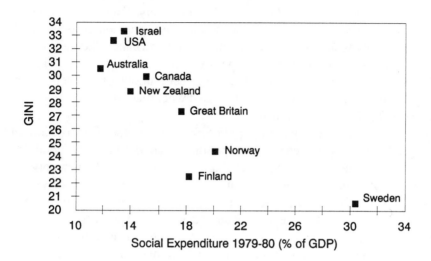

Source: Hingen and Uusitalo, 1992, Graphs 3.3 and 3.4.

of the median. The size of the welfare state – i.e. the GDP proportion of cash trans-fers – is an important factor explaining the cross-national variations in relative poverty rates. The bigger the welfare state, the smaller the relative poverty rate. This conclusion is further strengthened by a time series analysis of poverty in Finland and Sweden (Gustafsson and Uusitalo, 1990).

To some extent, to put it modestly, the welfare state has succeeded in its goal to promote equality – as both the neo-liberal and the reformist hypotheses have assumed. Has this distorted economic efficiency – as the neo-liberal hypothesis has claimed – or made it possible to use resources efficiently, as the reformists have argued? Or should we reconceptualize the problem?

5   Micro-economic Evidence

In economics, this question has been mainly examined at micro level. The be-havioural responses of the labour force to the welfare state have been in the foreground. An extensive and sophisticated body of studies has focused on the *disincentive effects* of cash benefits and taxes on savings and labour supply. These studies have been summarized by Stein Ringen (1987: 107-20, 224-32). The evidence first suggests little or no effect on household savings. Secondly, the increase of tax levels does not seem to decrease the supply of labour, possibly because income and substitution effects pull in opposite directions and more or less balance each other out.[3] In these respects, the neo-liberal hypothesis is not supported. However, there is ample evidence that the supply of labour is sensitive to changes in cash transfers and in progressivity of taxes. The higher the progression of taxation, the greater the decrease in labour supply. Transfers also seem to decrease labour supply. This is, of course, an intended behavioural response: the purpose of pensions, maternity and sickness allowance, and many other cash benefits is exactly to make exit from labour, temporary or permanent, possible. The neo-liberal hypothesis is right in its claim that the redistributions of the welfare state have impacts on labour supply; this is disclosed when the effects of progressive taxation and transfers are examined.

However, the decreasing labour supply effects of progressive taxation and transfers lead to the loss of economic output only if an array of other conditions are met. If there is unemployment, for example, the decreased labour supply may not cause loss of economic growth. Secondly, the studies referred to above have focused on the supply side only. Social policy may have effects on the demand side as well: cash transfers influence consumer demand, and public services create a demand for labour to produce services. Finally, the long-term effects on the supply of labour are neglected, and here the reformist hypothesis may be right. Greater economic and social equality may facilitate the mobilization of talent, and public educational services may improve the quality and productivity of the labour force.

Briefly stated, there is an obvious need to complement the micro-level view of disincentive studies by macro-level studies about the relationships between the economy and the welfare state. This will be done in two steps. As a first point, we will move to the macro level and summarize the results of the studies concerning the impact of the welfare state on economic performance. Second, we recognize the need to examine the complex interplay between the economy, the labour market, and the welfare state, and we will survey the various mechanisms of their linkages.

6   Macro-level Evidence

The literature on the impact of the welfare state on economic performance is, at least apparently, conflicting and inconclusive. The first reading of this body of research is that both the neo-liberal and the reformist hypotheses can be supported by empirical results. Some researchers have found that there is an inverse relationship between public sector size and economic growth, while others have exposed a positive relationship (see Saunders, 1986: 56).

One factor leading to conflicting results is the measure of the welfare state used. In most earlier studies, the commonly applied measure is the size of the public sector (as percentage of the GDP); while in later research, more subtle measures of particular aspects of the public sector are used. In one of the most recent and methodologically most advanced studies, Castles and Dowrick (1988) found that government revenues have no significant impact on economic growth – while social transfer payments have a positive effect, although not a large one.

Secondly, the results depend on the time period investigated. Saunders, for example, found an inverse relationship between public sector size and economic growth over the period from 1960 to 1973, but no statistically significant effect at all from 1975 to 1982. Obviously, other factors may strengthen or weaken the estimated relationship.

Thirdly, the sample of countries has a bearing on the results. Typically, the relationship between the public sector and economic growth has been studied among the Western advanced democracies. Often, the number of cases has been increased by pooling the data representing different periods. Korpi (1985: 108) and Castles and Dowrick (1988: 27) found, for example, that the results depended upon the inclusion or exclusion of Japan. Finally, the results differ depending on what other determinants of economic growth are accounted for when estimating the effect. Weede's results (1986) indicate a fairly strong negative impact of government spending, and particularly of social security transfers on economic performance over the period from 1960 to 1982. Castles and Dowrick (1988: 27), in a similar design, found, however, that no such effect remains if pre- and post-"oil shock" periods are accounted for.

What conclusions remain? First, the road is still open both to those who believe in the neo-liberal hypothesis and to the supporters of the reformist hypothesis. Both are wrong if you go to the extreme and argue that the welfare state is *the* determinant of economic performance. It is obvious that the size of the welfare state is just one of many potential determinants of economic performance – the significance of which, whether positive or negative, is easily exaggerated. Secondly, the relationship between the welfare state and economic performance is not necessarily constant over time. It may change depending on other determinants of growth. Thirdly, various elements of the welfare state may well have diverging impacts on the economy. Progressive taxation may lower the work effort and, under some conditions, lead to reductions in growth; ambitious employment policies or effective social, educational and health services may facilitate growth.

7 The Welfare State and the Labour Market

It is possible to argue that the comparative sociology of the welfare state has been preoccupied with the welfare state as a dependent variable. The main interest has been to pinpoint those independent variables that best explain variations in welfare state effort or differences in the institutional architecture of welfare states. These approaches are by all means legitimate. However, the welfare state should also be regarded as a very significant institution with some vital repercussions on other societal institutions – such as the labour market, the class structure, the relationship between the sexes, the normative structure, and the systems of distribution and redistribution. In other words, the welfare state should also be conceptualized as a major independent variable. To date, this has largely been the province of economics. Perhaps even more fundamentally, very strict designs where variables are declared as either independent or dependent, could be potentially misleading – because what characterizes the relationship between the family institution, the labour market, and the welfare state is co-variation, interactions, and multifarious impacts. As a rule, we use to speak about the welfare state *and* the economy, and the welfare state *and* the labour market, as if these institutions were two different things – as distinct and separate institutional categories or areas. Our point is that this way of conceptualization makes little sense today, because the line of demarcation between these institutions is becoming increasingly blurred. This implies that we need to explore *institutional complexes*. The concept of institutional complexes refers to how the family institution, the labour market, and welfare states are related to one another. The leading idea is that these three institutions (families, labour markets, and welfare states) are linked in specific configurations; that these configurations change over time; that they vary significantly across countries; and that these patterns have certain causes and effects. The importance of such institutional complexes becomes evident when we begin to consider how they have changed during the last 50 years.

8   From Functional Differentiation to Functional Integration

The modern welfare state was designed in such a way that a clear line of demarcation between the labour market and the welfare state should be maintained. The welfare state should not interfere with the clearing mechanism of the market. Thus, the welfare state was not supposed to have a role to play in employment policy, and the welfare state should only cater to those absolutely incapable of work; it was not supposed to induce anybody to leave work for welfare. The welfare state was, in addition to this, designed in the image of the adult male industrial worker. Its design took for granted, at least implicitly, that the traditional female role as caregiver and service worker in the family would remain dominant. For this reason, the idea that specific (welfare state) programmes were needed to ease the integration of working life and family obligations was absent.

This configuration has changed remarkably under advanced Western capitalism, and we will argue that these changes are of far-ranging importance. The result of these changes – Gøsta Esping-Andersen (1990) writes about them as silent revolutions – is that social policy, the family institution, and the welfare state have become interwoven and mutually interdependent institutions. We will highlight the general aspects of the transformation of the relationship between the family, the labour market, and the welfare state in terms of four major points.

The walls that once separated the labour market and the welfare state are crumbling. This is seen, for one thing, in the massive exodus of able-bodied older workers who are leaving the labour market for early retirement in Western capitalist nations. The programmes of early retirement have been upgraded both in the sense that the criteria of eligibility have been liberalized and that they provide vastly improved compensation levels. Moreover, the repertoire of early retirement programmes has been considerably extended in a majority of nations. That millions of older workers have been induced to leave the labour market on a permanent basis, via early retirement, has two very important consequences. One is that the finances of the welfare state are strained, because the "logic" of the welfare state is to maximize employment in order to maximize revenue and minimize expenditure. The other effect is that early retirement has come to serve as a vehicle for firm rationalization and restructuration. What we observe, then, is that the social collectivity, via the welfare state, helps to organize and finance firm competitiveness. Since the welfare state requires high rates of employment for optimal performance, a growing tension seems to emerge between this logic, on the one hand, and the capitalist firm's desire to minimize labour input – and stabilize or expand output – on the other hand.

The other major transformation also complicates the relationship between the market and the welfare state, contributing to something which is quite far from the ideal type of market. What we have in mind is, that modern welfare states are no longer systems of social provision only. They have, in many nations, become virtual employment machines and have constituted the only significant source of job growth over the past 25-30 years. Today, the Danish and Swedish welfare state employs about 25 per cent of the labour force. Again, the employment function of the modern welfare state is a remarkable departure from the theory of the labour market as a self-regulatory organism. The employment function of the welfare state underscores that its functions *vis-à-vis* the labour market are complex indeed. Thus, welfare states help to reduce labour supply through early retirement; yet at the same time, they also promote ordinary employment in education, health, and social services. The employment function of the modern welfare state means that a substantial part of the "labour market" is no market at all in the normal sense, but instead a true politically-organized system of collective production of goods. Welfare state employment, of course, is also organized around the labour contract, exchanging labour time for wages. Yet its logic is qualitatively different. The concept of productivity hardly exists; wages are to a certain degree politically determined; jobs are typically tenured; and employees normally enjoy substantially more autonomy, freedom, and authority over how they allocate their time and make their work/welfare choices (Esping-Andersen, 1990).

It is possible to argue that the third major change implies that a buffer has been inserted at the point of interface between the labour market and the family institution.

What we have in mind, is a series of welfare state programmes allowing working people to withdraw from the labour contract on a temporary basis – such as sickness insurance, maternity and parental leave, and leaves of absence to allow the fulfilment of caring *vis-à-vis* dependent family members. The proliferation of programmes promoting temporary absence from paid work is significant for several reasons. One is that the welfare states appear to play a not unimportant role in shaping behaviour within the work contract. In principle, the work contract stipulates the exchange of labour time for pay. This time is in principle "owned" by the employer, and the worker has little authority over the allocation of his/her time. Thus, the menu of programmes of temporary absence reduces the imperative of the market to the extent that the worker can exert more freedom of choice. The other significant aspect of these programmes is that, to a certain degree, they seek to make it as easy as possible for people to resolve the difficulties of harmonizing working life with family life, squaring the dilemmas of having children and working, and combining productive activity with meaningful and rewarding leisure (Esping-Andersen, 1990). Through this function, these programmes have promoted the colossal growth in female labour force participation in Western capitalist nations throughout the last 25 years.

We have argued above that the market economy has been transformed in a decisive way by the growth of early retirement, welfare state employment, and the proliferation of escape routes from the world of paid work through programmes for temporary absence. Yet the market is penetrated by additional crucial elements as well. We will argue that the combined effect of unemployment insurance, labour market policy, subsidies, and macro-economic policy has moved our Western capitalist economies even wider apart from the pure market.

9 International Variations

We have so far talked in general terms about the spectacular changes of the relationship between the family institution, labour markets and welfare states. However, preliminary empirical analyses indicate quite strongly that far-ranging international differences exist in the advanced Western capitalist world. These international differences have a certain structure, which invites us to conceptualize distinctive regime types. For one thing, the outflow of older workers below the age of 65 years varies tremendously in advanced Western capitalism. Thus, the labour force participation of older male workers is high in Scandinavia and very low in a comparative perspective in such countries as Germany, the Netherlands, Italy, and France. The same pattern holds, yet the range is even wider, when we examine female labour force participation.

We know, secondly, that the rates of unemployment vary extensively among advanced capitalist countries; and it is interesting indeed to observe that the corre-

Table 5.1: **Labour Force Participation Among Males 55-64 Years of Age in Selected Capitalist Countries; 1970, 1975 and 1985 (Percentages)**

	1970	1975	1985	Change 1970-1985
Australia	85.1	78.8	60.4	-24.7
Austria	63.6	63.9	46.1	-17.4
Belgium	78.6	73.5	–	–
Canada	84.2	79.4	70.2	-14.0
Denmark	86.5	86.0	64.7	-21.7
Finland	73.9	65.6	51.7	-22.2
France	75.4	68.9	50.1	-25.3
Germany	80.1	68.1	57.0	-23.1
Greece	74.5	73.9	67.7	-6.8
Iceland	–	90.4	–	–
Ireland	91.0	83.8	75.4	-15.6
Italy	48.2	42.4	38.6	-9.6
Japan	86.6	86.0	83.0	-3.6
Netherlands	81.4	72.2	47.0	-34.4
New Zealand	81.6	80.2	66.0	-15.6
Norway	83.7	84.1	78.4	-5.3
Portugal	83.5	78.3	66.4	-17.1
Spain	80.6	79.8	66.3	-14.3
Sweden	85.4	82.0	75.9	-9.5
Switzerland	91.2	90.2	–	–
United Kingdom	91.2	87.6	68.2	-23.0
United States	80.7	74.6	67.3	-13.4

Sources: OECD, 1989; ILO, 1990.

lation between early retirement and unemployment is very high, which is by no means self-evident.

Thirdly, some welfare states strongly encourage temporary absence from paid work, while others do not. Again, the Scandinavian countries (with the possible exception of Denmark) are extreme cases with high rates of paid non-work in terms of temporary absence. The continental European countries lie in the middle, and the Anglo-Saxon countries (except Britain) are very low in terms of temporary absence from paid work.

Table 5.2:   Labour Force Participation Among Women 55-64 Years of Age in Selected Capitalist Countries; 1970, 1975 and 1985 (Percentages)

	1970	1975	1985	Change 1970-1985
Australia	23.3	23.7	19.3	-4.0
Austria	24.1	25.4	14.9	-9.1
Belgium	13.8	14.3	–	-13.8
Canada	29.8	30.8	33.8	4.0
Denmark	33.7	34.6	41.3	7.6
Finland	45.2	43.1	46.2	1.0
France	40.0	35.9	31.0	-9.0
Germany	28.5	24.8	22.6	-5.9
Greece	19.9	23.2	26.3	6.4
Iceland	–	35.2	–	–
Ireland	21.3	20.9	17.9	-3.4
Italy	10.6	8.5	10.2	-0.4
Japan	44.4	43.7	45.3	0.9
Netherlands	15.6	14.2	12.3	-3.3
New Zealand	21.9	22.3	29.8	7.9
Norway	28.4	45.7	52.7	24.3
Portugal	14.6	32.3	31.7	17.1
Spain	13.3	23.0	19.9	6.6
Sweden	44.5	49.6	59.9	15.4
Switzerland	34.6	35.9	–	–
United Kingdom	39.2	40.1	34.7	-4.5
United States	42.2	40.7	41.7	-0.5

Sources: OECD, 1989; ILO, 1990.

Finally, welfare state dominance of the employment structure is very strong in Scandinavia and very low in both the United States, Canada, and the continental European nations.

Table 5.3: **Unemployment Rates; 1970, 1975, 1980 and 1985 in Selected Advanced Capitalist Countries (Percentage of Total Labour Force)**

	1970	1975	1980	1985	Difference 1970-1985
Australia	1.6	4.8	5.5	7.5	5.9
Austria	1.4	1.7	1.5	3.6	2.2
Belgium	1.8	4.2	7.7	12.0	10.2
Canada	5.6	6.9	7.2	7.5	1.9
Denmark	0.7	4.9	7.0	9.0	8.3
Finland	1.9	2.2	4.7	5.0	3.1
France	2.4	4.1	6.4	10.2	7.8
Germany	0.6	4.1	3.3	8.3	7.7
Greece	–	–	2.8	7.8	–
Iceland	–	–	1.0	0.8	–
Ireland	–	–	7.3	17.3	–
Italy	4.9	5.3	7.1	9.6	4.7
Japan	1.1	1.9	2.0	2.6	1.5
Netherlands	1.6	5.9	6.3	14.2	12.6
New Zealand	–	–	2.8	3.9	–
Norway	1.5	2.3	1.7	2.6	1.1
Portugal	–	–	7.8	9.2	–
Spain	–	–	12.3	21.8	–
Sweden	1.5	1.6	1.6	2.4	0.9
Switzerland	0.0	0.3	0.2	0.8	0.8
United Kingdom	3.1	4.1	6.1	11.7	8.6
United States	4.9	8.4	7.2	7.1	2.2

Sources: 1970 and 1975: Maddison, 1982; 1980 and 1985: OECD, 1987.
(Missing countries in Maddison are: Greece, Iceland, Ireland, and New Zealand.)

Table 5.4: Paid Absence from Work: Annual Hours Absent as Percentage of Hours Worked. 1980

	Sickness Absence	Total Absence	Sickness as Per Cent of Total
Denmark	3.9	8.8	44
Norway	3.2	7.0	46
Sweden	4.3	11.2	38
France	5.1	6.6	77
Germany	6.1	7.7	79
United States	1.3	–	–

Source: Esping-Andersen, 1990: 155.

Table 5.5: The Welfare State as Employer. The Public/Private Mix in Health, Education and Welfare Employment. Percentages, 1985

	HEW* Employment as Share of Total	Public Share Of HEW Total Employment	Public HEW as Share of Total Employment
Denmark	28	90	25
Norway	22	92	20
Sweden	26	93	25
Germany	11	58	7
Austria	10	61	6
Italy	12	85	11
Switzerland	12	58	7
France	15	75	11
United Kingdom	16	77	12
Netherlands	20	38	8
Australia	15	65	10
Canada	15	44	7
United States	17	45	8

* HEW = Health, Education and Welfare (ISIC 931, 933, 934).

Source: Kolberg, 1991.

The distributions on the four dimensions – early retirement, unemployment, temporary absence from paid work, and welfare state employment – suggest that we can speak of clusters of nations, or models if you like. There is a Scandinavian model (represented above all by Sweden and Norway) which is characterized by low scores on early retirement, low unemployment, high rates of absenteeism, and considerable welfare state employment. There is also a Continental European model which is typified by high rates of early retirement, high unemployment, medium to low temporary absence from paid work, and low welfare state employment. There is also a transatlantic Anglo-Saxon model, where early retirement falls in the middle, where unemployment is medium, where absenteeism is strikingly low, and where the welfare state is relatively small in terms of employment.

The international variations we have indicated along these dimensions cry for explanations. Why do they exist, and what consequences do they produce? These intriguing questions represent a formidable research agenda. As a starting point, we tend to believe that the four dimensions are not independent; that high levels of absenteeism are related to low rates of early retirement, low unemployment, and to a large and feminized social service labour market. The same logic applies to medium or low rates of absenteeism, high rates of early retirement and unemployment, and a small welfare state in terms of employment.

10 Implications

The results of both our approach and analyses challenge our understanding of social policy in several important respects. We will spell out eight implications for future research.

First, our conception of Western-style development, inspired by Parsons' famous AGIL formulation, should be reconsidered. One of Parsons' leading ideas is that modernization implies functional differentiation, i.e. the separation of functional areas such as politics and economy. However, what we see in the real (advanced capitalist) world is the opposite: namely, the functional integration of institutional areas such as labour markets and welfare states. Studies of welfare states and labour markets in terms of early retirement, welfare state employment, temporary absence from paid work, and unemployment, disclose interaction and an uneasy institutional symbiosis between these functional areas. What does this mean for sociological theories of social change?

Secondly, our analysis has implications for our conventional conceptions of social policy. These different conceptions – be it that the welfare state is the handmaiden of capitalism, or a working class project to promote redistribution, or a functional necessity due to social disintegration – all share one important idea: that social policy is a response to problems created in other areas. This notion is, of course, not totally out of hand. However, the development we have shown indicates that the functions of social policy are gradually more offensive. Intentionally or not, social policy has come to play a larger and larger role in the process of the restructuration of capitalist production.

Thirdly, our analysis of variations along the dimensions of early retirement, welfare state employment, temporary absence and unemployment, has revealed substantial divergence. This divergence should serve as a definite warning against mono-causal theories. Our theoretical work has to be guided and inspired by these empirical differences, since they cannot be accommodated within a unidimensional theoretical framework. One of our challenges is to explain the divergent patterns of welfare state/labour market relationships which we can observe. What is needed, among other things, is to explore to what extent the specific patterns of early retirement, unemployment, absenteeism, and welfare state employment can be traced to socio-economic forces inherent in modern economic production, and the extent to which they are induced by differences in social policy. What are the forces, and how exactly do they produce these impressive variations?

The fourth theoretical challenge has to do with the controversial neo-liberal claim that the welfare state distorts the market mechanism; in other words, that there exists a trade-off between efficiency and equality or – if you like – between capitalism and the welfare state. We have in the first part of this chapter referred to a synthesis of the research literature which concludes that the empirical status of the postulated "big trade-off" is uncertain. In addition, one of the challenges springing from the analysis consists in the reformulation of the efficiency/equality dilemma. Of course, we cannot rule out that the welfare state has a negative effect on the incentive to work and that there is an efficiency/welfare trade-off in this sense, and at the individual level. But the welfare state has other, and often neglected, effects as well. Thus, by providing decent escape routes from the labour market, the welfare state also contributes significantly to firm productivity and competitiveness. Also, by providing social services such as day care for children and home-help services, the welfare state creates improved possibilities for labour market participation, thus expanding the volume of work. Again, the welfare state seems to have a complex function, and this should be the basis for a respecification of the big trade-off in terms of the level and the meaning of efficiency.

Our results pose yet another challenge for the development of the macro-sociology of the welfare state. The analysis of the interconnections of early retirement, unemployment, welfare state employment, and temporary absence, indicates that it might be fruitful to expand research efforts beyond separate programmes and empirical distributions connected with one specific programme. The consideration of a wider entire menu of relevant programmes, appears to provide a more comprehensive understanding of the characteristics of each of them. However, we would like to see this hypothesis better substantiated.

The next remark relates to the consequences of the patterns we have disclosed. One of the first tasks in this connection will be to explore their impact upon the development of social stratification. Our hypothesis would be that the effects upon social stratification will become great. The Scandinavian model, with its high level of employment and its huge and highly-feminized social service sector (health, education and welfare), might produce new cleavages between the public sector and the private sector. This axis is also likely to become gender-specific. The indications for this development are intensified tension within the trade union movement and diversification according to gender in party preferences. Women in Scandinavia are already quite clearly more left-leaning than men. However, more research is needed on this new axis of political formation. The Continental pattern is likely to be different due to its particular welfare state/labour market profile. Here, new and intensified tensions may develop based on the distinction between insiders and outsiders in the labour market. The North American pattern is likely to deviate from this. Its employment record during the last 25 years is impressive indeed. But the quality of a considerable part of the job growth is hardly impressive, and one possible scenario depicts growing tensions between the incumbents of good and bad jobs.

The final point we would like to make, is that the interactions between the economy and the labour market on the one hand, and the welfare state on the other, is even wider than indicated in this chapter; and one task for future research would be to specify a wider set of intersections. One candidate for inclusion would certainly be labour market policy; and subsidies, as well as the effects of macro-economic policy, might also be considered.

Notes

1   Walter Korpi (1985: 97-100) has outlined three hypotheses on the impact of the welfare state on the economy: the first two are the *market liberal hypothesis*, corresponding to the neo-liberal argument; and the *reformist hypothesis*, which claims that the welfare state can be an irrigation system which supports economic efficiency and growth. Also, this could take place through different mechanisms. Social inequality, unless mitigated by the welfare state, leads to a waste of human capital, because lower classes do not have opportunities to utilize their talent. The welfare state can maintain the high and stable level of demand, diminishing the harmful effects of fluctuations. Thirdly, it may make the use of labour more efficient through effective labour market policies. The third hypothesis, which could be called the *independence hypothesis*, maintains that the welfare state does not have any impact on economic growth, because various effects largely cancel each other out.

2   Income inequality is measured by the Gini coefficient, which varies between 0 and 100. The higher the value of the coefficient, the greater the income inequality. The disposable incomes of households having different sizes and structures, are made comparable by using the so-called LIS equivalence scale. It means, for example, that a family of two adults and two children is assumed to need 2.5 times the income of a single adult in order to enjoy the same level of economic welfare, i.e. their incomes are equivalent if the family of four gets 2.5 times more income than a single-adult household. The distribution presented in Figure 5.1 is the distribution of disposable equivalent

income between individuals. Each member of the family is assigned the same income. This specification of income distribution is now widely regarded as the most important one, if the interest is in the welfare impact of incomes.

3　There is a substitution effect if increased taxation leads to a lower work effort. The income effect is opposite: increased taxation leads to greater work effort, because of the wish to maintain the previous (net) income level despite increased taxation.

References

Castles, F. G., Dowrick, S. (1988) *The Impact of Government Spending Levels on Medium-term Economic Growth in the OECD, 1960-1985*. Discussion Paper. Canberra: The Australian National University, Centre for Economic Policy Research.

Cutright, P. (1965) 'Political Structure, Economic Development, and National Social Security Programmes', *American Journal of Sociology* 70: 537-50.

Esping-Andersen, G. (1990) *The Three Worlds of Welfare Capitalism*. London: Polity Press.

Furniss, N., Tilton, T. (1977) *The Case of the Welfare State*. Bloomington and London: Indiana University Press.

Gustafsson, B., Uusitalo, H. (1990) 'The Welfare State and Poverty in Finland and Sweden from the Mid-1960s to the Mid-1980s', *The Review of Income and Wealth* (forthcoming).

ILO (International Labour Organization) (1990) *Retrospective Edition of the Yearbook of Labour Statistics on Population Censes, 1945-89*. Geneva: ILO.

Kolberg, J. E. (ed.) (1991) *The Welfare State as Employer*. New York: M. E. Sharpe, Inc.

Korpi, W. (1985) 'Economic Growth and the Welfare State: Leaky Bucket or Irrigation System?', *European Sociological Review* 1 (2): 97-118.

Maddison, A. (1982) *Phases of Capitalist Development*. Oxford: Oxford University Press.

OECD (1987) *Employment Outlook*. Paris: OECD.

OECD (1989) *Labour Force Statistics, 1967-1987*. Paris: OECD.

Ringen, S. (1987) *The Possibility of Politics. A Study in the Political Economy of the Welfare State*. Oxford: Clarendon Press.

Ringen, S., Uusitalo, H. (1992) 'Income Distribution and Redistribution in the Nordic Welfare States', in Kolberg, J. E. (ed.) *The Study of Welfare State Regimes*. New York: M. E. Sharpe.

Saunders, P. (1986) 'What Can We Learn from International Comparisons of Public Sector Size and Economic Performance?', *European Sociological Review* 2 (1): 52-60.

Smeeding, T., Schmauss, G., Allegreza, S. (1985) *An Introduction to LIS: Luxembourg Income Study Working Paper*. Luxembourg: LIS.

Uusitalo, H. (1984) 'Comparative Research on the Determinants of the Welfare State: the State of the Art', *European Journal of Political Research* 12: 403-22.

Uusitalo, H. (1989) *Income Distribution in Finland. The Effects of the Welfare State and the Structural Changes in Society on Income Distribution in Finland from 1966 to 1985*. Statistical Studies No. 148. Helsinki: Central Statistical Office of Finland.

Weede, E. (1986) 'Sectoral Reallocation, Distributional Coalitions, and the Welfare State as Determinants of Economic Growth Rates in Industrialized Democracies', *European Journal of Political Research* 14: 501-19.

CHAPTER 6

The Impact of Unemployment upon Welfare

Adrian Sinfield

In a society where unemployment is accepted, great material and social gaps develop, resulting in the mutual isolation and alienation of different groups. Any social order not based on full employment must imply a restriction of living conditions and a squandering of human resources. (Extract from the terms of reference for the Swedish Royal Commission on Long-term Employment, set up in March 1974)

The experience of market economies in the years since 1974 has only added greater weight to this view. Old lessons have had to be relearnt, generally at the expense of those already most vulnerable in our societies. At the start of the 1990s, many countries in Central and Eastern Europe are in danger of overlooking the importance of this evidence. As markets are given greater freedom, the impact of increased unemployment is bound to be very considerable, since employment is the main way by which most people obtain resources and achieve welfare for the greater part of their lifetimes. Whether directly or through employed members of their families, earnings are the major determinant of their standard of living. This chapter shows how increased unemployment reduces people's opportunities and ability to fare well and restricts society's own efforts to promote welfare and well-being for all members.

Unemployment is not "a kind of inevitable exhaust" of the "economic engine ... It is also a social process powered by the values we hold and the choices we make" (Liebow, 1970: 29). Any study of unemployment across different countries, or even over time within the same country, reveals this very clearly. The level and trend of economic activity in a country at any one time does not automatically determine the extent of unemployment, let alone the experience of those out-of-work. Employers employ a wide range of strategies to cope with any reduction in demand. They are influenced by past experience and established traditions, by judgements on the state of their competitors as well as future economic and business prospects both nationally and internationally, by expectations of trade union reaction and by their view of the potential supply of specific labour needs, and by many other factors. Besides mass redundancies bringing the closure of whole plants or branches, there are many other measures they may use to reduce the size of the workforce. These include selective pay-offs with schemes for voluntary redundancy and early retirement, increased short-time and work-sharing, reduced overtime, "natural wastage" and no new recruitment – combined with some labour-hoarding of those thought to be most difficult to replace when work picks up. Their decisions may be heavily influenced by the role of the state – both directly in its support to certain industries, enterprises or regions and indirectly in its policies of overall economic management.

The organization and distribution of work is accompanied by patterned variations in the allocation of reward, power and social honour. These institutionalized decisions significantly affect who are to be most vulnerable to unemployment and who are to be best protected from economic insecurity and job loss. Unemployment, therefore, must be considered first as a characteristic of society and the way it operates and only secondly as an experience of individuals who happen to be out-of-work at present.

"The essential tool of the sociological imagination and a feature of all classic work in social science", said C. Wright Mills, was the pursuit of the connection between "personal troubles" and "the public issues of social structure". The first illustration which he gave of this thesis, was unemployment. "Both the correct statement of the problem and the range of possible situations require us to consider the economic and political institutions of the society, and not merely the personal situation and character of a scatter of individuals" (1959: 8-9).

The differing patterns that have evolved over time as to how work is distributed, which work is paid and which unpaid, influence official and private perceptions of who and how many are without work and which of these people are regarded as "unemployed" rather than outside the labour force altogether – and so classified as retired, mothers, housewives, students or persons with disabilities. The problem is particularly acute in relation to women, especially married women and those with young children; their statistics of labour force participation, as well as unemployment, are subject to much ambiguity (Beechey, 1989). In those countries where the regular statistics of unemployment are based on administrative counts of benefit recipients rather than on household surveys, understanding of the scale, nature, and distribution of unemployment is likely to be particularly constrained by prior decisions about who should be entitled to benefits. In Britain, for example, "less than 20 per cent of women losing jobs actually show up in the official data because so few are eligible for benefits in their own right" (Unemployment Unit, 1990: 8). The gender insensitivity of the statistical measures reflects a more general neglect of the position of women in the labour force. Discussions of full employment and labour market measures to promote employment have often rested upon the presumption that mothers of school-age or younger children will remain outside the labour force in unpaid domestic work.

1   Trends in Unemployment Across Societies

After relatively low unemployment in the two decades after World War II, capitalist countries experienced rising unemployment from the late 1960s. By 1972, the unemployment rate for 15 OECD countries had reached 3.7 per cent. It had already begun to fall quite sharply when the dramatic increases in oil prices led to even sharper rises to 5.3 per cent by 1976. A slow recovery brought the average down to 5.1 per cent by 1979, but it leapt to 8.6 per cent in 1983 – an increase of two thirds in four years. By 1989, the total average had fallen to 6.2 per cent (OECD, 1990a, Table R 18: Standardized Unemployment Rates in Fifteen OECD Countries). However, the declining trend has halted and the rate in many countries began to rise again in 1990.

There have been marked differences between countries. In Table 6.1, the data have been standardized by the United States Bureau of Labor Statistics to take account of the different ways in which labour market statistics are defined and collected in the 10 countries. While Japan and Sweden have remained relatively low, the increase in unemployment has been greater elsewhere, but it is important to note that the relationship between these other countries has not remained constant. The Netherlands, the United Kingdom, France, and Australia have joined – and in some years have even overtaken – Canada and the United States as high unemployment countries. The contrast between these two groups of countries in the 1960s and the 1980s is marked.

"Both the supply and the demand for labour have been much more dynamic in North America compared with Western Europe, both during the recession and during the upswing ... Although the Western European labour force grew by 5.4 million between 1983 and 1988, only two fifths of the increase in North America, there were 1.5 million more unemployed West Europeans in 1988 than in 1982 while in North America unemployment fell by 4.3 million" (UNECE, 1989: 41). Within Western Europe there have long been marked variations. In 1988, unemployment rates varied from 18 per cent in Ireland to under 1 per cent in Switzerland. Rates were well below average in Austria, Finland. Norway and Sweden; and above average in Spain, France, Italy, Belgium and the Netherlands. Unemployment in the United Kingdom, which had risen from near average to well above average in the earlier 1980s, had fallen appreciably by 1988 – although by 1990, it was rising again.

The position of Sweden deserves particular attention. A 1989 OECD Economic Survey reported: "Labour market performance and policy in Sweden are distinctly different in several ways from performance and policy in other OECD countries.

**Table 6.1:   Unemployment Rates since 1960 Standardized to US
                Definitions**

Averages of	USA	Canada	Aus-tralia	Japan	France	Germany	Italy	Nether-lands	Sweden	UK
	%	%	%	%	%	%	%	%	%	%
1960-64	5.7	5.7	2.2	1.4	1.4	0.6	3.0	NA	1.6	2.5
1965-69	3.8	3.9	1.7	1.2	2.1	0.7	3.5	NA	1.8	2.8
1970-74	5.4	5.8	2.2	1.3	2.8	0.8	3.4	3.4	2.3	3.5
1975-79	7.0	7.6	5.6	2.1	5.0	3.3	4.0	5.1	1.9	5.7
1980-84	8.3	9.8	7.6	2.4	8.2	5.3	5.3	9.9	2.8	10.5
1984-89	6.2	8.8	7.6	2.6	10.3	6.4	7.4	9.7	2.0	9.7
1990 latest	5.7	8.4	–	2.9	9.5	5.1	6.8	–	1.6	6.4
Highest	9.7	11.8	10.0	2.9	10.7	7.2	7.9	12.3	3.5	11.8
Year(s)	1982	1983	1983	1987	1987	1985	1987/8	1983	1983	1983/4

Note: An attempt has been made to allow for the different ways in which countries define employ-
        ment and unemployment and collect these statistics (for details of the calculations see
        Sorrentino, 1981). It is based on a civilian labour force, excluding military personnel. For
        Italy, inclusion of those reported as unemployed but not actively seeking work in the past
        30 days would almost double the unemployment rate prior to 1986 and raise it to 11-12 since.
        In the Netherlands, the average for 1970-74 is based on data for the last two years only.

Source: Bureau of Labor Statistics, US Dept. of Labor, Nov. 1990 and earlier.

The objective of full employment has been given high priority, and several indicators show a significant amount of flexibility in the Swedish labour markets. As
a result, unemployment rates did not rise significantly after the two oil price shocks,
contrary to developments in most other OECD countries" (OECD, April 1989: 55).
The scale of this achievement merits emphasis. Successive external reviews of the
persisting low unemployment in Sweden have tended to underline the fragility of
the success; and yet unemployment has been kept low through a series of international crises.

     Many explanations have been put forward to explain the national differences
in unemployment including changes in technology, economic demand, labour

force supply and government policies; and among these, social security benefits. Changes in the structure of the international economy and its division of labour significantly increased the risk of unemployment in Western capitalist countries in the 1970s (Townsend, 1981: xii). However, reasons for the differences in unemployment levels, such as those shown in Table 6.1, have been in the last resort institutional and political. This has been demonstrated particularly clearly by Göran Therborn in his analysis of the experience of 16 countries. "The existence or non-existence of an institutionalized commitment to full employment is the basic explanation for the differential impact of the current crisis." This institutionalized commitment "involves: a) an explicit commitment to maintaining/ achieving full employment; b) the existence and use of countercyclical mechanisms and policies; c) the existence and use of specific mechanisms to adjust supply and demand in the labour market to the goal of full employment; d) a conscious decision not to use high unemployment as a means to secure other policy objectives". Therborn attributes the acceptance of the commitment to two very different sets of reasons: "an assertion of working class interests" by a "politically dominant labour movement" as in "Sweden and – with some qualification – Norway" and "a conservative concern with order and stability as being of equal importance to capital accumulation" as in Japan and Switzerland. In Austria, there was an unusual combination of both elements (Therborn, 1986: 23-24; Ashton, 1986; Kreisky Commission, 1989).

2 The Experience of Unemployment

The experience of unemployment has been much more varied than the literature based largely on case-studies of redundancies and plant shutdowns would suggest. As unemployment has risen in the last two decades, there has been growing support for a thesis on the "psychology of unemployment" which claimed that there was a dominant pattern or cycle of adjustment to being out-of-work. A general progression from an initial shock, followed by an active and optimistic search for work, led to increasing anxiety, stress and pessimism until eventually the unemployed fatalistically adapted to being out-of-work. Reference was often made to a detailed review of the literature on interwar unemployment by Eisenberg and Lazarsfeld (1938): in fact, they put forward their hypothesis very much more tentatively and with cautious qualifications.

This thesis has not been sustained by further research. Firstly, careful comparison of studies at different stages of the business cycle, has indicated the importance of both the level and the trend in economic activity which significantly affect chances of re-employment – and, consequently, the attitudes and behaviour of both those out-of-work and potential employers. (Review of the current literature indicates that far too little consideration has been given to earlier studies carried out under different labour market conditions.) The differential opportunities of return to work, combined with different amounts of and access to resources, may help to explain the varying responses to unemployment by occupation, area and time, as much as any psychological characteristics do.

Secondly, there are considerable differences between the situation of those paid off after many years of steady employment due to a factory, shipyard, or pit closure – the experience by far the most frequently studied – and those who generally compose the much greater part of the unemployed. These include those entering the labour force for the first time from school, those re-entering – such as mothers with young children, those close to retirement age accepting more or less willingly the opportunity to "volunteer" for redundancy when staff have to be cut back, and those workers who have never had much security even at times of high employment – such as unskilled building labourers and many service workers.

Thirdly, it should be added, case-studies and longitudinal studies provide much less evidence of unemployed people settling down and adjusting to prolonged unemployment than the responses in a single interview do. Contact with those who have just returned to work has been especially revealing of the ways in which people out-of-work have struggled to cope with unemployment, as well as of the reasons why they may present an apparently acquiescent or indifferent front to the visiting employed interviewer.

2.1 Unequal Distribution

Economists, politicians, and many others often speak of unemployment as "the price we have to pay" for past economic or industrial failings or present progress; or they ask "how much unemployment can the country stand? Strictly speaking, it is not 'the country' that is being asked to 'stand unemployment'. Unemployment does not, like air pollution or God's gentle rain, fall uniformly upon everyone ... It strikes from underneath, and it strikes particularly at those at the bottom of our society" (Liebow, 1970: 28).

Inequality in its incidence appears to be a general characteristic of unemployment, with manual workers more at risk than non-manual. The extent of inequality – among men, at least – is significantly greater in Britain, where the low-paid are more vulnerable to unemployment than in North America (Smee, 1980); and Western Europe seems more likely to resemble Britain. However, in all countries where the evidence is available, those most vulnerable to unemployment are already among the least secure: those in poorly-paid and low-status jobs; the very young and the very oldest in the labour force; ethnic, racial, or religious minorities; those with disabilities and handicaps – and generally, those with the least skills and living in the most depressed areas. In addition, the actual experience of unemployment may trap many at the bottom of society.

Table 6.2:   Male Unemployment in the Previous 12 Months, 1975-77 and 1983-84, Great Britain

	1975-77 %	1983-84 %
Socio-economic group		
Professionals, employers and managers	4	6
Intermediate and Junior non-manual	8	12
All non-manual	*6*	*8*
Skilled manual	9	17
Semi-skilled and unskilled manual	18	32
All manual	*12*	*22*
All males aged 18-64	10	17
Colour		
White	9	17
"Coloured"	17	27
Males aged 18-24	21	33
25-39	9	16
40-59	9	12
60-64	7	13

Source: General Household Survey 1975-77. CSO (1980), Tables 5, 18 and 19. 1983: CSO (1985), Table 4.26. 1984: CSO (1987), Table 4.26. Data *not* published for females. Respondents were asked if they had been out-of-work within the previous 12 months.

With the increase in unemployment in most countries, it was generally assumed that the unequal distribution of unemployment by occupation had been reduced. In Britain at least there is clear evidence that the opposite happened as is shown in Table 6.2. In the mid-1970s, 10 per cent of all men in the labour force had spent some time unemployed in the previous 12 months: by the mid-1980s, the percentage had risen to 17. Men in unskilled and semi-skilled work had been three times as likely as men in non-manual jobs to experience unemployment in the earlier period. As total unemployment increased, the risk became four times as great (the data are not available for women). Among unskilled men alone, the risk of unemployment at some time in the course of a year was 45 per cent: they "live in the shadow of unemployment" (Townsend, 1979: 601).

2.2 Prolonged Unemployment

Long-term unemployment increases as total unemployment rises. While the total out-of-work remains high, the proportion experiencing prolonged unemployment increases. In recent years, the growth in the problem – and the acceptance of it – has led to slippage in the definition of long-term unemployment. In the 1960s, the term was usually applied after six months out-of-work; and in some countries, after only two, three, or four months (Sinfield, 1968: 14). Since then, the term has come to be applied after a full year. This issue has become a particular problem in Western Europe: the higher level of unemployment has reflected more of those out-of-work suffering longer unemployment as much as it has reflected more people becoming unemployed (Kreisky Commission, 1989). In the UK during the relatively low unemployment years of the 1950s, those out-of-work for over a year averaged just 34,000 – 12 per cent of the registered unemployed: by 1987, the average had risen to 1.3 million – over 40 per cent of the claimant unemployed (see Table 6.3). When the overall rate falls, those who have most recently become unemployed are more likely to get back to work first; and so, the proportion "long out-of-work" tends to rise further. Although the extent of long-term unemployment varies across countries, this pattern appears in most of them (OECD, 1983; Sinfield, 1968).

The longer anyone is out-of-work, the more difficult it becomes for them to get back to work. The vivid metaphor of the Pilgrim Trust half a century ago, still catches the problem particularly well. The unemployed "are not simply units of employability who can, through the medium of the dole, be put into cold storage and taken out again immediately they are needed. While they are in cold storage, things are liable to happen to them" (Pilgrim Trust, 1938: 67). An increasing amount of evidence in recent years confirms the findings of research into the interwar recession with greater hardships and setbacks for those left long out-of-work and for their families. In many countries the level of public income support falls after a year

Table 6.3:   Long-term Unemployment, UK

	Average Number	Percentage of Official Unemployed
1950s	34,000	– 12% of registered unemployed
1960s	66,000	– 16% of registered unemployed
1987	1,260,000	– 42% of claimant unemployed
1989	713,000	– 39% of claimant unemployed

Note: Because of changes in definition and measurement the 1987 and 1989 figures are not strictly comparable with the earlier ones. On a comparable basis they would be at least 200,000 higher.

Source: Department of Employment.

– and may be cut again after that, so increasing financial hardship may result. Even without such a fall in income, the exhaustion of any savings tends to coincide with an increasing need to replace worn-out household equipment, clothing, bedding, and other necessities. This leads to a greater risk of poverty among the long-term unemployed – and very often increasing debt, especially when they are faced with the urgent need to replace clothing for growing children.

The accumulating impact of multiple rejections, combined with deepening poverty, affects the health and morale of those suffering prolonged unemployment and their families. Research carried out on 15 years of data in Edinburgh, found that the risk of parasuicide (deliberate self-harming, including attempted suicide) was 11 times greater among unemployed than employed men, and 19 times greater among men who had been out-of-work over a year (Platt and Kreitman, 1985).

The disadvantages of long-term unemployment are compounded by employers' responses. Particularly when there is a surplus of labour, they – along with both public and private employment agencies – tend to fall back on length of time out-of-work to choose between applicants for jobs. When unemployment is falling, there is a tendency to regard those who remain among the unemployed as at least "hard to employ", if not "unemployable". It is not unusual for employers to claim labour shortages with numbers of unemployed still high. It is argued that the unemployed have lost the ability or the will to work.

The number of unemployed who come to be regarded as "marginal", "hard to employ", "unemployable" or "workshy" appears to be very much a function of the level of demand for workers at any one time. In the relatively low unemployment years of the 1950s and the early 1960s in Britain, they were seen as a small group. With the higher unemployment of the 1980s, they were regarded as a much larger group. Those who had been sought as "essential manpower" under the stimulus of labour shortages became neglected and downgraded as "labour surplus" during recession.

2.3 Recurrent Unemployment

The risk of repeated unemployment has received less attention, as most national statistics only regularly collect data on the length of the current spell out-of-work. Longitudinal studies have revealed that unemployment is more concentrated than the number of spells might suggest. In Canada, seven out of ten people with any experience of unemployment between 1975 and 1982, were out-of-work more than once – and half of these, at least four times. Nearly half "of those who received unemployment benefits in Germany between 1976 and 1982 did so more than once", accounting for seven tenths of the total weeks of unemployment (OECD, 1985: 112). In Britain, over half the men who became unemployed in the autumn of 1978 had been out-of-work in the previous 12 months; and over three quarters had been unemployed in the previous five years (Moylan and Davies, 1980).

This reflects the greater vulnerability of certain groups, which is enhanced by the practice common in most countries of "last-in, first-out", with the most recently-recruited being the first to be laid off in any cutbacks. The problems of these people are increased in those countries where the level and/or duration of unemployment benefits are affected by employment and earnings over the past year, especially if there are no insurance contributions credited during spells out-of-work. Some may never regain their social and economic security; and for others, unemployment becomes an acute phase in a long period of chronic disadvantage.

2.4 Poverty

Unemployment was the major cause of the increase in poverty during the 1980s. A still-unpublished report of the European Commission in 1988, indicated the impact of increased unemployment on the numbers in poverty in the Community (*Guardian*, 24 November, 1988). In Britain, the unemployed have been shown to be "amongst the poorest of the poor". Study after study from both governmental and independent sources has revealed their particular vulnerability to poverty (Sinfield, 1981; Atkinson, 1989). The long-term effects of deprivation can make it more difficult for these people to return to work. Poorer health and higher mortality are revealed to be particular risks for both those out-of-work and their families (Bartley, 1988; Moser et al., 1987; Smith, 1987).

The link between poverty and unemployment is tightened by the unequal distribution of joblessness. Those with low-paid and marginal jobs not only have a greater risk of unemployment, but they also have less opportunity to build up their savings and poorer access to resources. They are less able, therefore, to protect themselves and their families against deprivation during unemployment. In consequence, they are particularly vulnerable to poverty – especially if unemployment becomes prolonged. The adequacy of the available benefits is therefore all the more important to them, and any cuts fall all the more heavily upon them.

3   Income Maintenance and Labour Market Policies

The recessions of the mid-1970s and the early 1980s revealed the inadequacies of income support for the unemployed; but they also led to major changes which left the most vulnerable unemployed even more poorly protected. It became evident that the expansion in public social security support which had occurred in many countries over the previous 50 years was by no means as generous for the unemployed as for other groups. Unemployment insurance tended to be a separate scheme with limited coverage (Lawson, 1985; Sinfield, 1983; Atkinson, 1989; Micklewright, 1991). Even where, as in Britain, it was integrated with other social insurance provision, benefits were almost invariably more limited in duration and subject to tighter controls and surveillance than those for the sick and those for persons with disabilities.

Unemployment insurance schemes in most countries were originally planned for and limited to the more generally secure and unionized industrial worker, with little if any support for those outside the traditional large production industries. In the last two decades, "unemployment has risen for young people, women, and a markedly enlarged marginal minority population – groups given scant attention when unemployment insurance programs were first designed" (Reubens, 1989: 22). Except in particular industries such as textiles, women were not recognized as established and regular members of the labour force. In 1933, an ILO report commented "in many trades no married women are accepted, and the woman who marries while in employment is discharged" (quoted in Sinfield, 1983: 454). In many jobs, the discrimination continued well into the postwar years.

In the 1960s and the early 1970s, "improvements in real benefit levels were the most important factor contributing to the increase in unemployment expenditures", according to an OECD survey of seven large countries (Reubens, 1989: 23). The improvements to the benefits, however, tended to reinforce already-existing distinctions between the more skilled, better-paid workers who were more likely to experience only short-term unemployment and the rest. Extended duration was often accompanied by tighter eligibility conditions which had the effect of limiting the improved benefits to those already most firmly established in the labour force.

Table 6.4: Unemployed Claimants by Benefit Status, May 1990, Great Britain

	UB only %	UB IS %	(All UB) %	IS only %	(All IS) %	No benefit %	N = 100%
Men	15.1	4.1	(19.2)	67.6	(71.7)	13.2	1,067
Women	24.6	1.1	(25.7)	52.8	(53.9)	21.4	366
Married	43.4	0.8	(44.2)	21.4	(22.2)	34.4	130
Other	14.3	1.3	(15.6)	70.1	(71.4)	14.3	236
All	17.5	3.4	(20.9)	63.8	(67.2)	15.3	1,432

Of those not receiving UB in above table

	Men %	Women %	All %
UB exhausted	44.6	23.3	39.5
Contribution Deficiency	37.0	48.4	39.7
Not yet Determined	10.7	16.3	12.0
Other	7.7	12.0	8.8
Total	100	100	100

UB = National Insurance Unemployment Benefit (contributory)
IS   = Income Support (means-tested)

Source: DSS, 1990.

As unemployment increased even further in the 1980s, "the tightening eligibility and payment criteria and slow or negative growth in the real value of benefits" helped to contain expenditure (Reubens, 1989: 24). The proportion of unemployed receiving unemployment insurance benefits at any one time fell. In Britain, for example, the contributory National Insurance Unemployment Benefit was intended as the first defence against unemployment; but the number receiving it at any one time actually fell as total unemployment rose (line UB in Figure 6.1). The fall as a proportion of unemployed claimants was even more marked (Figure 6.2). By May 1990, only one in five people among those officially classified as unemployed were receiving any unemployment insurance benefit – while nearly two thirds were totally dependent on the means-tested Income Support, the current form of means-tested public assistance (Table 6.4). Two fifths of those without the insurance benefit had not worked enough to gain an adequate contribution record, and these were especially likely to be young people who had yet to establish themselves in the labour force and women re-entering it after childbirth. A similar proportion, and even more among men, had simply been unemployed for too long and had therefore "exhausted" all the 12 months of insurance benefit to which they had been entitled. An increasing proportion of the unemployed and their families were forced to rely upon the more limited and restricted support of Income Support (IS in Figures 6.1 and 6.2 – for more detailed discussions of how benefits work in practice, see Micklewright, 1990; Atkinson, 1989).

**Figure 6.1: Unemployed Claimants by Benefit Types,
November 1979-1988**

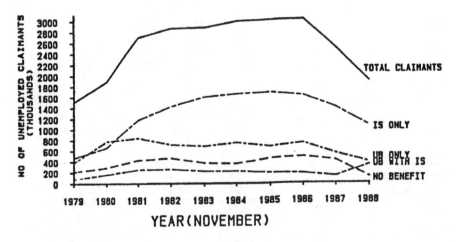

UB = National Insurance Unemployment Benefit (contributory)
IS = Income Support (means-tested)

Source: DSS, 1988.

Only in Belgium has prolonged unemployment been accepted as a social or external cost: elsewhere the exhaustion of benefits has generally increased the risk of poverty for the long-term unemployed. By contrast, some countries have extended the duration of benefits – though generally only for older workers –, introduced early retirement pensions, or made greater use of disability or invalidity pensions to reduce their labour supply.

Generally, however, the degree of support has been lessened with unchanged or even falling replacement ratios. This was confirmed in a United Nations Economic Commission for Europe study for 17 European countries, Canada and the United States. "A special analysis of Finland and the United Kingdom ... found a sharp decline over time in replacement ratios" when the comparison was made with potential current earnings rather than past earnings (quoted in Reubens, 1989: 27).

(The failure to allow for inflation and the persisting tendency to compare present benefit levels with past earnings – and to make no allowance for the increasing value of employee benefits and other in-work additions to resources – might itself be said to be indicative of the second-class treatment of the unemployed by researchers as well as administrators.)

A review of income support across Western Europe for the 40 years to 1985 found that, with the single exception of Sweden, "high unemployment and dualist tendencies in the economy have brought about a significant restructuring of unemployment benefits, involving the erosion of contributory insurance protection

Figure 6.2: Percentage Unemployed Claimants by Benefit Types, November 1979-1988

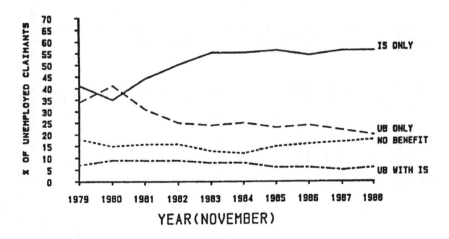

UB = National Insurance Unemployment Benefit (contributory)
IS = Income Support (means-tested)

Source: DSS, 1988.

Table 6.5: Public Spending on Labour Market Programmes in 1987 (in % of GDP)

	Employment services and administration (1)	Labour market training (adults) (2)	Special youth measures (3)	Direct job creation and employment subsidies (4)	Special measures for the disabled (5)	Subtotal: "active" measures (1-5)	Unemployment compensation (6)	Early retirement for labour market reasons (7)	Subtotal: income maintenance (6-7)	Grand total
Australia	0.11	0.03	0.08	0.10	–	0.32	1.21	–	1.21	1.53
Austria	-0.11	0.13	0.02	0.12	0.03	0.41	0.91	0.16	1.07	1.48
Belgium	0.17	0.08	–	0.69	0.16	1.10	2.42	0.83	3.25	4.35
Canada	0.21	0.22	0.12	0.02	–	0.57	1.68	–	1.68	2.24
Denmark	0.13	0.52	0.21	0.03	0.25	1.14	2.64	1.25	3.89	5.03
Finland	0.10	0.27	0.02	0.35	0.02	0.76	0.99	0.64	1.63	2.39
France	0.12	0.27	0.24	0.06	0.05	0.74	1.26	1.07	2.33	3.07
Germany	0.23	0.29	0.06	0.20	0.21	0.99	1.33	0.02	1.35	2.34
Greece	0.15	0.20	0.05	0.16	0.03	0.59	0.39	–	0.39	0.98
Ireland	0.17	0.56	0.40	0.32	–	1.45	3.66	–	3.66	5.12
Italy	0.08	0.01	0.37	–	–	0.46	0.49	0.32	0.81	1.27
Japan	0.03	0.03	–	0.10	0.01	0.17	0.42	–	0.42	0.59
Luxembourg	0.05	0.02	0.09	0.07	0.27	0.50	0.30	0.72	1.02	1.51
Netherlands	0.07	0.17	0.06	0.06	0.72	1.08	2.90	–	2.90	3.99
New Zealand	0.07	0.45	–	0.11	0.02	0.65	1.07	–	1.07	1.72
Norway	0.12	0.07	0.02	0.01	0.19	0.41	0.36	–	0.36	0.76
Portugal	0.08	0.22	0.08	0.14	0.04	0.56	0.38	–	0.38	0.94
Spain	0.08	0.10	0.19	0.38	0.01	0.76	2.50	0.04	2.54	3.30
Sweden	0.21	0.49	0.15	0.26	0.75	1.86	0.70	0.10	0.80	2.66
Switzerland	0.07	0.01	–	–	0.09	0.17	0.23	–	0.23	0.40
United Kingdom	0.16	0.11	0.27	0.31	0.04	0.89	1.66	0.02	1.68	2.57
United States	0.06	0.11	0.03	0.01	0.03	0.24	0.59	–	0.59	0.83

Note: For Denmark and France, the figures refer to 1986. For Australia, Canada. Sweden, Japan, New Zealand, the United Kingdom and the United States, the figures refer to fiscal years covering part of 1987.

Source: OECD Secretariat. April 1989, Table 24, p. 81.

and greatly increased reliance on inferior forms of means-tested assistance and on family support". It concluded that "passive compensation is not only excessively expensive but reinforces divisions and conflicts in society with those most vulnerable to unemployment most likely to suffer ... unless [it is] accompanied by efficient and equitable active employment policies" (Lawson, 1985: see also Micklewright, 1991, for a discussion of the policy implications for income maintenance strategies).

3.1 Labour Market Policies

Most countries have developed a wide range of special labour market measures in response to high unemployment (OECD, 1990b). These include training, retraining, rehabilitation, schemes to help the unemployed move to a job, and subsidies to encourage employers to create new employment or to take on people who have disabilities or are long-term unemployed. The wide variation in total expenditure on such measures among countries and the different mix of programmes is shown in Table 6.5. Five of the 22 countries spent over 1% of Gross Domestic Product in 1987, while seven spent under 0.5%. The table also compares this with spending on income maintenance measures, including early retirement for labour market reasons – revealing an even greater variation in total spending and in the allocation of resources across the different programmes. For example, Sweden and the United Kingdom – with similar totals – show marked differences on most items, a fact which cannot simply be explained by the very different levels of unemployment at the time.

Analyses of the experience of different countries underline the importance of the broader policy context for the impact of specific schemes (Brown and King, 1988). Even though the details of two programmes may be very similar, their outcome and reception are likely to be very different when one forms part of an expansionist strategy of employment creation and the other is linked to schemes to reduce real wages and trade union power and to limit public expenditure. Equally, measures to help the older worker or the long-term unemployed are likely to be much more effective when unemployment is kept low. This may appear obvious, but many schemes have been introduced with insufficient attention to the ways in which unemployment remaining persistently high undermines their potential success (Finn, 1988).

4   The Significance of the Policy Response – A Case-study

The social construction of unemployment which shapes public and governmental responses to the issue, is much influenced by the dominant explanations of present levels and trends in unemployment. This is brought out clearly by a comparison of policies in Britain over two decades. During the mid-1960s, it was widely believed that there was insufficient mobility (e.g. NEDC, 1963). In consequence, the then

Labour government introduced a range of measures aimed to encourage what was called "redeployment" by reducing employers', workers' and their trade unions' resistance to the higher level of unemployment which would result from increased mobility. These included the right to notice, state redundancy payments, and an earnings-related supplement to National Insurance Unemployment Benefit for the first six months of unemployment.

While support for the long-term unemployed was limited and measures of control were introduced for others, especially among the unskilled, the overall strategy stands in sharp contrast to the policies of the Conservative administrations of the last decade. David Ashton has analysed the series of explanations for unemployment which have shaped employment policy and measures for the unemployed since 1979 (1989: 20-21). "An initial belief that the increase in unemployment was just part of the business cycle" could not be maintained as unemployment continued to rise. At first this "was blamed on the previous government"; then it was presented as "the result of the international situation over which Britain had no control"; the particularly high rate of youth unemployment was attributed to the institutional rigidity of high wages and the thesis that workers were "pricing themselves out of jobs" became a more general theme of ministerial statements on the economy and still-rising unemployment (see, for example, Department of Employment, 1988a and b).

Both strategies set out to change attitudes, as well as policies, towards unemployment. The Labour government in the mid-1960s sought to gain the support of workers, encouraging them to risk job mobility by protecting them against the rigours of unemployment. Two decades later, the Conservative government reversed these policies, including specifically limiting and even abolishing the measures introduced in the 1960s.

Since 1979, benefits for the unemployed in the UK have undergone significant changes. Atkinson and Micklewright identified 36 changes in the social security system affecting the unemployed between the return of the Conservatives to power in 1979 and October 1988 and painstakingly modeled the impact on the incomes of the unemployed. They concluded "the total effect is that the unemployed covered in our analysis would have received £510 million more than under the present policy". The difference was equivalent to "around 7 per cent of the predicted total benefit expenditure for the unemployed" (Atkinson and Micklewright, 1988; reprinted in Atkinson, 1989: 143, 145).

The significance of the changes has been much greater than is revealed by calculation of the aggregate financial loss alone. First, the cuts have been larger for those on the lowest incomes, thus increasing and deepening poverty with a marked fall in replacement ratios (the differences between incomes in and out-of-work). Second, the conditions under which benefits are obtained, the form and degree of scrutiny have also changed. These have included an extension of the maximum period of disqualification from benefit from the six weeks set out in the original legislation of 1911, to 13 weeks in 1986, and then 26 weeks in 1988. There have also been increased scrutiny and surveillance of the unemployed accompanied by additional checks on their search for work and significant reduction of the right to refuse employment which is unsuitable because of its pay and conditions. Third, employment policies have been changed to reinforce the direction of the social security measures. These include limitations on employment protection rights established over the last two decades, reminiscent of the Fair Wages Resolution protecting public service workers, cuts in minimum wage protection for adult workers, and removal of the public subsidy to the state redundancy payments scheme.

Particular attention has been directed to changing the attitudes of young people. Entitlement to means-tested benefits, except in exceptional circumstances, has been abolished in the first two years after the minimum school-leaving age of 16; and the level of benefits has been reduced for single people between the ages of 18 and 25. The protection under the limited minimum wage legislation has been totally removed for those under 21; while special employment measures have been introduced for young workers with subsidies confined to jobs paying very low wages.

Overall, therefore, there has been a move away from benefit and other policies based on a recognition of the external causes of unemployment and a consequent public responsibility for compensation. Instead, most cuts and innovations have been premised on the individual's own responsibility for becoming or continuing to be unemployed. This has been specifically linked with an emphasis on the "culture of dependency" which government Ministers argue perpetuates unemployment. In terms reminiscent of the Poor Law Commissioners of 1832-34 who produced the report which led to the 1834 New Poor Law founded on "less eligibility" – a report described by the economic historian Richard Tawney as "brilliant, influential and wildly unhistorical" – they have blamed the unemployed and current policies for persisting unemployment (Levy, 1988).

The effect of the policy changes has been to lower the status of the problem of unemployment as a policy priority and, at the same time, delegitimize the claims of unemployed people to state support and assistance. Rather than doing more for those out-of-work, the government seeks to gain more support to do more to them – to make the unemployed change their behaviour by reducing or limiting benefits and by making these more conditional on work-tests etc. Poverty, or at least low income, becomes considered – however regrettably – as a necessary spur to work for those who should be doing more to help themselves and not as a condition from which all citizens should be protected. At the same time, the need for the government itself to take other means to tackle unemployment, is reduced. The responsibilities of the state become more narrowly defined "by retrenching the state's commitment to the provision of citizenship rights offsetting the impact of market relations upon the population" (Brown and King, 1988: 89).

5   The Wider Impact

A society with unemployment remaining high for many years is qualitatively different from one which provides adequate opportunities for all who want work. The unemployed bear a heavier burden as unemployment increases and becomes more prolonged, but a recession affects many more people than those currently out-of-work (Kreisky Commission, 1989: 9; Sinfield, 1984). Particularly vulnerable are those groups whose resources and ability to participate in society have been reduced. High unemployment also has wider implications affecting the distribution of resources, power and opportunity among different groups and classes in society.

The shift in the balance of power between the employer and the worker, between the employing and the working classes, is perhaps the most significant. The higher the unemployment, the more the balance tilts in favour of the employer and "hiring requirements tend to rise – the definition of an 'acceptable' worker is tightened up" (Reynolds, 1951: 73).Those with least bargaining power in the labour market, including ethnic and religious minorities, become even more vulnerable to exclusion and deprivation. The risk of low pay and poor working conditions is increased.

This is not to say that the maintenance of high employment is sufficient to avoid such problems; but the experience of the last two decades confirms that it is a necessary requirement. In country after country, it has become evident that many basic social policies depend upon unemployment being kept at a low level for their success. For example, any recession is a major obstacle to attempts to reduce or prevent poverty – not simply amongst the unemployed but amongst the disabled, single parents, and even older people. Equal opportunity programmes and reha-bilitation services also experience particular difficulties. Traditionally, success in many health and personal social services has required restoring people to a "normal" life in the "community" after a particular crisis – whether it be due to some physical injury, an illness, a breakdown or a period in prison. What this has really meant is getting people back into a job – for most men and women, the main source of a regular income and status in society, a daily routine, and a range of social con-tacts. With unemployment persistingly high, such rehabilitative measures are threatened. Unemployment may not have contributed at all to the initial problem but it may inhibit its solution and eventually worsen it.

The double pressures placed on public social services by increasing needs and diminishing real resources (or at least a public or political reluctance to provide them) have become exacerbated by the high cost of unemployment in extra spend-ing on benefits for the unemployed, and even more by the heavy loss of direct taxes and other revenue which they would have provided in work. In Britain in 1984-85, the revenue loss to central government per average unemployed greatly exceeded the cost of the direct spending in benefits to those out-of-work (see Table 6.6). While this lost revenue is rarely taken into account publicly in Treasury calculations, it

Table 6.6: Direct Exchequer Costs of Unemployment, 1984-85, United Kingdom

Benefits	£ 7.44 billion (37.4%)
Lost Income Tax	£ 5.69 billion (28.6%)
Lost NI contributions	£ 5.20 billion (26.1%)
Lost indirect taxes	£ 1.58 billion (7.9%)
Total	£ 19.91 billion (100.0%)
or	£ 6,300 per claimant unemployed

Source: Fraser and Sinfield, 1985.

adds considerably to any fiscal crisis – a point well recognized in a Swedish saying: "this country is not rich enough to afford unemployment" (quoted in the Kreisky Commission, 1989).

The costs of unemployment become added to all the other factors creating greater demands on welfare state provision. It is not simply that the increased number of unemployed are competing with a rising number of retired and other groups in need at a time when escalating health costs and rising expectations of public provision among the population at large are already making heavier demands upon state services. Higher unemployment also means increased needs among many other groups besides the unemployed themselves, including those in work and others outside the labour force. Under the increased pressures, standards in many public services fall; and those who can afford it turn to alternative forms of provision outside the state. They may purchase these services privately or support demands for increased provision by their employers.

Resource problems become intensified when, as in many countries, this alternative provision is supported and subsidized by tax concessions leading to a reduction in state revenues. These less visible subsidies further squeeze public expenditure to the benefit of the better-off (Sinfield, 1986). They become one more factor leading to the widening of inequalities in resources, power and security under the pressure of increased unemployment. "The more secure are the 'ins', the greater the penalty for being an 'out' " (Kerr, 1954: 105). It is significant that Sweden has been particularly successful in limiting segmentation and even reducing it in recent years when unemployment has been falling. Against trends frequently regarded as inevitable elsewhere, reduced unemployment has been accompanied by no increase in the proportion of long-term unemployed, a faster fall in youth than adult unemployment, a drop in part-time employment, and a marked fall in the number and proportion of discouraged workers (OECD, April 1989, Table 19).

In many countries, the importance of at least sustained low unemployment – if not genuine full employment – as crucial to preventive strategies in social policy and integral to welfare promotion policies has not been adequately recognized. The point is brought out very clearly in the conclusion to what is still one of the most comprehensive comparative studies of measures to help the most vulnerable groups in the labour market. "The maintenance of overall unemployment at two per cent or less for years at a time may be the single most important factor in minimizing the number of hard to employ and motivating a programme to seek the residual group who might appear unemployable ... at four per cent unemployment" (Reubens, 1970: 384).

At the beginning of the 1990s in many countries, the reference to four per cent as high unemployment may seem unbelievable – so far have perceptions and expectations been changed by the experiences of the last decade and a half. In late 1980, I wrote: "We need sustained full employment because it provides the essential basis for many other policies: a more effective attack on low pay and dirty jobs; positive programmes to counter discrimination in work ...; and a strengthening of workers' and citizens' rights to a healthy and safe environment in and out-of-work" (1981: 155). The experience of daily observation, as well as research, in the intervening years has only served to strengthen my belief in the social value of sustained low unemployment as one of the prerequisites for democratic citizenship.

Those who argue for the necessity of unemployment to maintain industrial discipline and work incentives and to reduce dependency are seldom aware of the full costs of unemployment. In part, it is because the effort and technical expertise which are devoted to counting unemployment are not also directed to measuring the social, economic and psychological impact on those who experience it as well as the costs for society at large. Even more, in my view, it is due to the fact that the burden falls unequally. This helps to create a vicious spiral which exacerbates the problems and reduces the chance of wider social recognition of the harmful impact of unemployment. The more unequally it falls, the more likely it is that more of the cost has to be borne privately by already poorer and weaker groups on the margins of society. While the burden of unemployment is made less visible, the state and behaviour of the victims seem to reinforce the view of the better-off that there exists some culture or underclass of dependency which can only be overcome by tougher measures of restricted benefits and tighter controls. This, in turn, reinforces public and administrative views about their undeserving nature. Insofar as the ultimate test of any democracy is the quality of life that it enables all its members to enjoy, the responsibility is all the greater to identify, examine, and respond to the problems created by unemployment.

Note

I am particularly grateful to Jochen Clasen, David Taylor, and Dorothy Sinfield for their comments and assistance.

References

Ashton, D.N. (1986) *Unemployment under Capitalism: The Sociology of British and American Labour Markets*. London: Harvester Wheatsheaf.

Ashton, D.N. (1989) 'Unemployment', in Brown, Ph., Sparks, R. (eds.) *Beyond Thatcherism: Social Policy, Politics and Society*. Milton Keynes: Open University Press.

Atkinson, A.B. (1989) *Poverty & Social Security*. London: Harvester Wheatsheaf.

Atkinson, A.B., Micklewright, J. (1988) *Turning the Screw: Benefits for the Unemployed 1979-1988*. London: S.T.I.C.E.R.D. – reprinted as chapter 8 of Atkinson (1989).

Bartley, M. (1988) 'Unemployment and Health: Selection and Causation – A False Antithesis', *Sociology of Health and Illness* 10 (1): 41-67.

Beechey, V. (1989) 'Women's Employment in France and Britain: Some Problems of Comparison', *Work, Employment and Society* 3 (2) September: 369-378.

Brown, A., King, D. (1988) 'Economic Change and Labour Market Policy: Corporatist and Dualist Tendencies in Britain and Sweden', *West European Politics* 11 (3) July: 75-91.

Cook, D. (1989) *Rich Law, Poor Law*. Milton Keynes: Open University Press.

CSO (1980) Central Statistical Office *Social Trends* 1980. London: HMSO.

CSO (1985) Central Statistical Office *Social Trends* 1985. London: HMSO.

CSO (1987) Central Statistical Office *Social Trends* 1987. London: HMSO.

D.E. (1988a) Department of Employment *Training for Employment*. Cm 316, London: HMSO, February.

D.E. (1988b) Department of Employment *Employment for the1990s*. London: HMSO, December.

D.S.S (1988) Department of Social Security *Unemployment Benefit Summary Statistics*. Newcastle: D.S.S, November.

D.S.S (1990) Department of Social Security *Unemployment Benefit Summary Statistics*. Newcastle: D.S.S, November.

Eisenberg, Ph., Lazarsfeld, P. F. (1938) 'The Psychological Effects of Unemployment', *Psychological Bulletin*: 358-90.

Finn, D. (1988) 'Training and Employment Schemes for the Long-term Unemployed: British Government Policy for the 1990s', *Work, Employment and Society* 2 (4) December: 521-534.

Fraser, N., Sinfield, A. (1985) 'Can We Afford High Unemployment?', *Unemployment Unit Bulletin*, July.

Kerr, C. (1954) 'The Balkanization of Labour Markets', in Bakke, E.W. (ed.) *Labour Mobility and Economic Opportunity*. New York: John Wiley.

Kreisky Commission (1989) Commission on Employment Issues in Europe: *A Programme for Full Employment in the 1990s*. Oxford: Pergamon Press.

Lawson, R. (1985) *Income Support during Unemployment: Comparisons in Western Europe*. Report for the European Institute of Social Security, Colloquium on "Balanced Development of Long-Term Benefits". Nürnberg, October.

Levy, D. (1988) 'Moore's American Cure for Britain's "Dependency" Habit', *The Listener* 18 February: 4-5.

Liebow, E. (1970) 'No Man Can Live With the Terrible Knowledge That He Is Not Needed', *New York Times Magazine*, 5 April.

Micklewright, J. (1990) *Why Do Less Than a Quarter of the Unemployed in Britain Receive Unemployment Insurance?* Taxation, Incentives and the Distribution of Income. Discussion Paper TID1/147. London, London School of Economics, September.

Micklewright, J. (1991) 'The Reform of Unemployment Compensation: Choices for East and West', *European Economic Review*, 1990 Conference Proceedings.

Mills, C. W. (1959) *The Sociological Imagination*. New York: Oxford University Press.

Moser, K.A., Goldblatt, P.O., Fox, A.J., Jones, D.R. (1987) 'Unemployment and Mortality 1981-83: Follow-up of the 1981 Census Sample', *British Medical Journal* 294: 86-90.

Moylan, S., Davies, B. (1980) 'The Disadvantages of the Unemployed', *Employment Gazette*, August: 930-831.

NEDC (1963) National Economic Development Council: *Conditions Favourable to Faster Growth*. London: HMSO.

OECD (1983) 'Long-term Unemployment in OECD Countries', Chapter V, *Employment Outlook*. Paris: OECD, September: 53-71.

OECD (1985) 'Moving In and Out of Unemployment: The Incidence and Patterns of Recurrent Unemployment in Selected OECD Countries', Chapter VI, *Employment Outlook*. Paris: OECD, September: 99-114.

OECD (April 1989) *Sweden, Economic Surveys*. Paris: OECD.

OECD (1990a) *Employment Outlook*, No. 47, June. Paris: OECD.

OECD (1990b) *Labour Market Policies for the 1990s*. Paris: OECD.

Pilgrim Trust (1938) *Men Without Work*. Cambridge: Cambridge University Press.

Platt, S., Kreitman, N. (1985) 'Parasuicide and Unemployment Amongst Men in Edinburgh 1968-1982', *Psychological Medicine* 15: 113-123.

Reubens, B. G. (1970) *The Hard-to-Employ: European Programs*. New York: Columbia University Press.

Reubens, B. G. (1989) 'Unemployment Insurance in the United States and Europe, 1973-83', *Monthly Labor Review* April: 22-31.

Reynolds, L. G. (1951) *The Structure of Labor Markets*. New York: Harper.

Showler, B., Sinfield, A. (eds.) (1981) *The Workless State*. Oxford: Martin Robertson.

Sinfield, A. (1968) *The Long-Term Unemployed*. Paris: OECD.

Sinfield, A. (1981) *What Unemployment Means*. Oxford: Martin Robertson.

Sinfield, A. (1983) 'Unemployment', pp. 415-471 in Kohler, P. A., Zacher, H. F. (eds.) *Beiträge zu Geschichte und aktueller Situation der Sozialversicherung*. Berlin: Duncker and Humbolt.

Sinfield, A. (1984) 'The Wider Impact of Unemployment', pp. 33-66 in OECD *High Unemployment: A Challenge for Income Support Policies*. Paris: OECD.

Sinfield, A. (1986) 'Poverty, Privilege and Welfare', pp. 108-123 in Bean, Ph., Whynes, D. (eds.), *Barbara Wootton: Social Science and Public Policy*. London: Tavistock.

Smee, C. (1980) 'Unemployment and Poverty: Some Comparisons with Canada and the United States', presented to the SSRC Research Workshop in Employment and Unemployment. London: June.

Smith, R. (1987) *Unemployment and Health*. Oxford: Oxford University Press.

Sorrentino, Constance (1981) 'Unemployment in International Perspective', Showler, B., Sinfield, A. (eds.), op.cit.

Therborn, G. (1986) *Why Some Peoples are More Unemployed Than Others: The Strange Paradox of Growth and Unemployment*. London: Verso.

Townsend, P. (1979) *Poverty in the United Kingdom*. London: Allen Lane.

Townsend, P. (1981) 'Foreword', Showler, B., Sinfield, A. (eds.), op.cit.

UNECE (1989) United Nations Economic Commission for Europe: *Economic Survey of Europe*. New York: UN.

Unemployment Unit (1990) *Working Brief*. London, Unemployment Unit, November.

Part II

THE CHANCES OF SOCIAL POLICY
IN POST-TOTALITARIAN EUROPE

CHAPTER 7

Social Policy in Spain: From Dictatorship to Democracy (1939-1982)

Ana M. Guillén

1   Introduction

The political history of Spain during the present century has been full of upheavals and traumatic episodes. Over the last 100 years, Spain has been ruled by five politi-cal regimes of very varied ideological tendencies and duration: the Restoration Monarchy (1876-1923), the Dictatorship of Primo de Rivera (1923-1930), the Second Republic (1931-1936), the Francoist Dictatorship (1939-1975), and liberal democracy. All these regime changes would lead one to expect radical discontinuities in the process of construction of the welfare state during the twentieth century – at least as regards the philosophy that informs social policy, as well as the macro-insti-tutional design for the provision of public social services and benefits. However, every political shift has been characterized by the preservation of the previously existing institutional design and by the expressed will of policy-makers to enlarge it and make it more efficient. From its very beginnings, the Spanish welfare state system has been based on the provision of public services for workers (especially industrial workers) and their dependants, not for citizens in general; and it has been organized, up to the present, along very similar institutional lines. The system can be characterized throughout its history as a mixed one, financed mainly out of the contributions of employers and workers, and highly fragmented in both organiza-tional and managerial terms. Although approaching universal coverage at the present date, the Spanish welfare state has been built in an incremental and piecemeal way, despite the broader context of uneven political development.

Of all the political regime shifts that have taken place during the present cen-tury, the period of transition to democracy (1975-1982)[1] appears, at least at first sight, as the most likely occasion for thorough reform. Given the transformations that took place within socio-political institutions, the opportunity for open debate was unprecedented – as were the possibilities to express demands on the part of interest groups and the population in general. Moreover, there was a widespread aspiration both among politicians and the public to "belong to Europe" in terms of modernization and development. As regards social policy, the Spanish situation was thought of as not having reached European standards, neither in terms of public expenditure nor in coverage – especially considering that the most admired model was the social-democratic one, exemplified by Sweden.

Yet, as will be argued below, the most salient feature of social policy during the period of transition was its high degree of continuity with that of the previous regime. During the transition period, a debate among politicians, civil servants, intellectuals, and interest groups took place on the future and reorganization of the welfare system. While this debate did not lead to actual significant reforms in the transition years, it can be argued that it paved the way for the reforms that took place during the 1980s,[2] under the rule of the Socialist Party. Yet these latest reforms are not an exception to the rule of incremental change: the bases of the Francoist welfare state were preserved and a better organization of the system was sought; but, as in the previous cases, no radical changes took place.

The aim of this chapter is to assess the significance of the changes that occurred in the domain of social policy during the Spanish transition to democracy. At least three indicators may be used for this purpose: first, the existence or absence of reforms in the macro-institutional design[3] and in the organization of the welfare system; second, changes in social expenditure and expansion of coverage; and third, changes in the character of the decision-making process in social policy. As noted above, no significant changes of the first type were implemented; but institutional rearrangements of a lesser scope did take place. An intensification of public expenditure and coverage rates can be ascertained. Whether this increase was due to the change of regime or was part of a trend initiated before that was either difficult or inconvenient to control, is also a matter for discussion. Changes in the decision-making process did take place due to the advent of democracy for new social actors were able to participate in it.

The first section of this chapter will consider how the welfare system was built under Francoism and it will evaluate the results achieved. The next section will single out indicators of change during the period of transition. Attention will be paid mainly to the provisions that are included in the so-called national social security system (*Seguridad Social*, NSS system), that is, pensions (including all benefits in cash), health care, and social services for the elderly and persons with disabilities. Lastly, the third section of this chapter will offer an interpretation of the evolution of social policy during the transition period. The question of what is to be expected in social policy matters in the context of democratic transitions has not, as yet, been taken up by the literature on these subjects. Hence, it is impossible to contrast the Spanish case with the findings of any theoretical construct. Thus, an attempt is made in this study to build a list of possible causal factors, with special attention to the socio-economic and political precedents of the transition and to its character (*"ruptura"* versus *"reforma"*).

2   Social Policy under Francoism: From Social Insurance to Social Security[4]

During the first third of the twentieth century – that is, from the introduction of the first legislation concerning labour accidents to the outbreak of the Civil War in 1936 – most social policy measures in Spain were voluntary, stimulated by the state through subsidies, and, in all cases, directed to industrial workers with low incomes. The main institution for social provision, the National Institute of Insurance (*Instituto Nacional de Previsión*, INP) was created in 1908 and lasted until 1978. Its aim was that of promoting social insurance among low-income workers, who were to receive a public economic incentive when they decided to join the insurance system. The basic principle informing the new institution was defined as "subsidized freedom". The INP could delegate its managerial competences to private entities which led to an incipient fragmentation of the system that would significantly increase during the Francoist regime.

Two important conferences on social insurance were held in 1917 and 1922 in which it was decided that compulsory insurance should be applied to the coverage of all social risks. However, it was also concluded that the different insurance schemes were to be introduced independently from each other at several stages, and that they should remain directed to low-income workers. The coordination of insurance schemes – rather than their unification under a single system – was also seen as desirable. In the period ranging from the early 1920s to the mid-1930s (including the dictatorship of Primo de Rivera and the Second Republic), little advancement took place in actual social provisions – with the exception of the statement by the Republican constitution that it was the responsibility of the state to create a system of social insurance against illness, labour accidents, unemployment, old age, disability and maternity. This first statement of the role of the state as social provider represents a turning point towards public provision in the sense that it was not questioned thereafter. Republican policy-makers did attempt to establish a unified system of social insurance, but the legislation was not submitted to Parliament until shortly before the outbreak of the Civil War.

On balance, the Francoist regime was to inherit an institutional framework based on the provision of services and benefits for low-income workers and consequently covering a very small proportion of the population.[5] During the previous period, only three social risks had been the object of compulsory insurance programmes: namely, old age (1919), maternity (1926) and labour accidents (1932), leaving the rest of the contingencies to private provision only partially subsidized by the state.[6] The system had therefore reached a very low level of development. However, a broad consensus had been reached on two crucial issues: one regarding the desirability of compulsory social insurance, and the other concerning state responsibility in providing benefits in case of short-term labour market absence or illness.

The Francoist regime (1939-1975) can be divided into two different periods from the point of view of economic, political, and social conditions. The first period lasts until the end of the 1950s, and the second one finishes with the demise of Franco in 1975. This chronological division is also useful for studying social policy, since it coincides with the switch from the system of social insurance – which reached its peak during the 1940s and 1950s – to the system of social security, which began in the mid-1960s. Important measures towards the amelioration of the NSS system were introduced during the latter phase of the Francoist regime.

2.1 The Forging of a Social Insurance System

The first period (1939-1958) was characterized by state intervention and autarchy in economic terms and the organization of society along corporatist lines through the introduction of vertical unions of compulsory membership. During these two decades collective bargaining was non-existent and the state was in charge of fixing salaries. Social policy was in the hands of Falangist politicians for the whole period, although some of the top spots of the INP remained in the domain of Social Catholicism – as had been the case traditionally. The Labour Ministry was for 15 years (1941-1957) headed by a convinced Falangist, Girón de Velasco. Girón had an extremely strong personality and enjoyed great independence of decision. His thorough understanding with Franco remained untouched until the death of the latter, and at this early time of the regime and despite the youth of the Minister – he was 29 when he gained office – Franco entirely relied on him as regards social policy matters. Despite the poor state of the economy, the introduction of social insurance programmes by the state – together with labour policies aimed at granting secure jobs – were used by the regime as a trade-off mechanism for gaining political legitimacy. Some of the law proposals included in the Republican project for a unified system of social insurance were passed and implemented hastily during the 1940s with very slight changes in the legal texts.

The principles on which social policy was to be based under the Francoist regime were established as early as 1938 in the Labour Charter (*Fuero del Trabajo*), which was turned into a "fundamental" law of the regime a decade later.[7] This legal document stipulated that workers were to be protected when in misfortune but was very ambiguous about the means through which this was to be done. It declared the desirability of introducing a "total insurance scheme" without specifying whether this meant a total coverage of risks, a unified insurance system, or a mere coordination of the different schemes. Furthermore, health insurance was absent from the list of various schemes that should exist. In addition, the document announced the amelioration of still non-existent schemes, such as those for invalidity and unemployment. Other fundamental laws insisted on the guaranteeing of social insurance to the workers, this time establishing explicitly that the state was in charge of doing so (*Fuero de los Españoles*, 1945), and even expressed the right of all Spaniards to the benefits and assistance of social security (*Ley de Principios del Movimiento Nacional*, 1958).[8] Even though a universal social security system was never achieved before the end of the regime, all these laws prevailed in force, despite the contradiction that they entailed by referring to workers in some cases and to all citizens in others.

Although they were introduced in a disorganized and contradictory way, the actual social reforms that took place during the first Francoist period are very important, because most of their provisions were incorporated in the Basic Law of Social Security in 1963. As regards old-age pensions, an old-age subsidy (*Subsidio de Vejez e Invalidez*) was introduced in 1939 following the Labour Charter recommendations to pay special attention to retirement pensions. This scheme substituted the compulsory programme created two decades earlier. It established fixed-quantity pensions for low-income workers over 65, and also for those with disabilities over 60 and was to be financed by the employers and the state. This old-age subsidy was turned into the Old Age and Invalidity Insurance Programme (*Seguro de Vejez e Invalidez*, SOVI) in 1947, roughly maintaining the same characteristics. The consideration of disability as "premature old age" is present in both schemes, which led to an equivalent level of protection for both contingencies until the reform of the 1960s. In the mid-1950s, a new provision for old widows was introduced, and the condition of low income for access to the system was eliminated.

The growth and development of the SOVI was slowed down by the introduction of a very peculiar institution in the Spanish social insurance system; namely, mutual aid associations (*mutualidades laborales*, ML). The MLs could include workers of an industrial or services branch at a national or provincial level, or even the workers of a single firm. Their creation was induced by the state who controlled, supervised, and coordinated them. It was precisely when the SOVI was created in 1947 that mutual societies providing basically the same benefits,[9] started to increase their activity under the protection of the Labour Ministry. The process of development of mutual associations ended up by creating a double, concurrential structure in the management of social provision, for they coexisted with national insurance programmes.[10] From 1960 onwards, autonomous workers could also join the mutual societies system. This peculiar institution had an obscure origin serving as a complementary system to social insurance. Eventually, it came to grow to such an extent, and to gain so much political support, that the reform of the 1960s – which tried to introduce a full-fledged social security system – divided management between the MLs and the National Institute of Insurance (Rull Sabater, 1971: 117). In 1949, the administrative and technical aspects of the several national insurance programmes were unified and partially coordinated with the MLs.

Compulsory health insurance was introduced in 1942 (*Seguro Obligatorio de Enfermedad*, SOE). The SOE was conceived in a very limited way, both in terms of the population coverage and range of services (in kind and cash) that it provided. The programme was directed at low-income industrial workers and their dependants. In 1946, eight million people had joined the system, which meant a coverage of 30 per cent of the Spanish population. By 1960, 13 million – that is, 44 per cent of the total population – were covered (Barea, 1988: 262-263). Affiliates had a right to very restricted health care including only primary care, free pharmaceuticals out of a closed list, and temporarily limited hospitalization for surgery. Specialist care and clinical hospitalization were to become included among the services of the SOE step by step from the 1950s onwards. From the mid-1940s, primary health care centres and hospitals began to be built, following the directives of a national plan passed by the government in 1945 (*Plan Nacional de Instalaciones*). Financing was tripartite (employers, workers, and the state), and the services were to be provided either directly by the National Institute of Insurance or indirectly by collaborating private entities, and other entities to which services were contracted out (*conciertos*). In 1947, some occupational illnesses began to be insured, but it was not until 1963 that the programme was extended to all of them.

Activity in the field of family policy began as early as 1937 with the creation of the *Subsidio Familiar* for dependent workers. This programme did not establish wage restrictions. In 1942, another programme was created, the *Plus Familiar*, which was managed independently in each firm by a committee of workers and financed by the employers. Rather than an insurance programme, the *Plus Familiar* was a complement to salaries. Unemployment insurance (*Seguro Nacional de Desempleo*) was established much later, in 1961 – although a very limited previous scheme directed to unemployment caused by the introduction of technological innovations that had been authorized by the government was in place since 1954. The 1961 programme was directed at the affiliates of the retirement and illness insurance schemes, imposing wage restrictions on the beneficiaries in this indirect way.

In sum, during the first two decades of Francoism, the social insurance system that was built offered a restricted array of services and benefits to a small proportion of the population. National insurance schemes coexisted with the mutual associations organization, leading to duplications, difficulties for management, and squandering of resources. From the supply side, the model established was a contributive one, based on the fees of employers and workers.[11]

2.2 Attempts at Building a System of Social Security

The second Francoist period, ranging from the late 1950s to the mid-1970s, was a time of unprecedented material well-being in Spain. In these years, life became much easier and more pleasant for many Spaniards, compared to the harsh post-war period. The poor condition of the economy during the 1950s, plagued by disequilibria and low performance, resulted in the renunciation of the autarchy model in economic policy. The economy was opened to international competition, and a package of measures was devised for its adjustment. The Stabilization Plan (*Plan de Estabilización*) of 1959 included the relaxation of official price controls and was accompanied by the introduction of a qualified system of collective bargaining. The outcomes of these new policies were the introduction of new instruments of production, the restructuring of existing manpower patterns, and an increase in productivity. Full employment was attained, although partly through the emigration of a considerable proportion of the labour force to other European countries. Legislation impeding the dismissal of workers was maintained, fostering consequently a situation of security and stability. The new economic conditions enhanced the introduction of "limited pluralism" in the political and interest representation systems (Linz, 1981: 387).

In the 1960s and early 1970s, Spain was not an exception to the general behaviour of Western countries that used the increase of production of goods and services in an important proportion to foster social welfare. Almost 90 per cent of public expenditure growth was due to the expansion of social protection (Barea, 1988: 263). Two were the main reforms that took place in the social policy sphere: the 1963 Basic Law of Social Security (*Ley de Bases de la Seguridad Social*, LB), which can be considered as a turning point in social policy, and the 1972 reform (*Ley de Financiación y Perfeccionamiento*, LFP).

At the end of the 1950s, two plans had been elaborated for the creation of a national social security system. The first was the one elaborated by the administrative council of the INP, including four different proposals that were submitted to the Labour Minister in 1959, and the second was presented by the Social Council of the Syndical Organization.[12] Neither of these plans was successful; and it was not until 1963 that the reform establishing a social security system was passed, and not until 1967 that it began to be implemented.

The LB unified the previously existing programmes into a single institution, the NSS system. However, the organization of the system was kept along occupational lines, and its financing continued to be based on the contributions of the affiliates. State transfers continued to be very scant, despite the declared intention of the LB to increase them. The 1963 reform led to the consolidation of a highly fragmented system, consisting of a general scheme for dependent workers and several special schemes for other professional categories. Special schemes had already started to be created in the mid-1950s: as, for example, those for students, peasants, seamen, and home workers. These special schemes were included as such in the new NSS system, which continued to grow thereafter by the same means of establishing special schemes for different labour collectives. Velarde (1990: 47-49) lists 13 kinds of schemes within the present NSS system that vary according to requirements for affiliation, services received, and financing mechanisms. Even within the general scheme, several "concealed" schemes that bear peculiarities can be found. This reflects the long-lasting corporatist character of the system, despite the enlargement of coverage that has taken place until the present date. The LB also confirmed the division of management between the NSS system and the MLs, thus consolidating the polarization of the system between two broad institutional frameworks.

Despite the low level of benefits, the NSS system accumulated high levels of reserves (savings and surpluses). Part of this unnecessary accumulation of capital was deviated until 1970 to low-return investments – as, for example, in the acquisition of bonds issued by the National Institute of Industry (Infante, 1975: 54-58). In addition, many special schemes were not able to be financed out of the contributions of their members, and resources were transferred to them from the general scheme or from public funding.

Other social policy measures undertaken during the second period of Francoism included the creation in 1963 of a non-contributive pension programme for people over the age of 70. At the end of the decade the so-called "complementary social services" for the old and persons with disabilities were introduced and integrated into the system of provision of the NSS system.[13]

The 1972 reform was designed to expand social protection – especially in retirement, unemployment, and temporary labour incapacity benefits. The improvement was achieved through the linking of member contributions to real incomes that was to be introduced by stages. This procedure substituted the one in place since 1963 that linked member contributions to a scale of professional categories. The formula to calculate benefits, which was related to contributions, remained untouched. As a consequence, expenditure on benefits increased significantly over the next years.[14]

The final result of the activities of the Francoist regime in the field of social policy, was the construction of a welfare system organized along corporatist lines, with significant dissimilarities among the varied professional categories and a highly fragmented management. The total number of contributors in 1975 was slightly over 10 million, whereas the number of beneficiaries of pensions amounted to 3.5 million. On the other hand, 29 million people (80.9% of the total population) were protected by the health care system (Fundación FOESSA, 1983: 805, 809). In short, the system had attained a rather high level of coverage but was also peculiar and chaotic in organizational and managerial terms.

3   Developments in Social Policy During the Spanish Transition[15]

From the beginning of the 1970s a generalized wish was felt in Spain for improving the social security system and catching up with the levels of expenditure of

Western European countries. More specifically, the goal became the achievement of a system of social protection that would group all citizens, would cover all contingencies, and would become a real instrument of redistribution. The proliferation of publications on comparative studies or on the possibilities of harmonization among different European systems, and the 1972 reform, which adjusted contributions to the social security system to real salaries to follow the European model, are evidence of this aspiration.

The feeling of backwardness was grounded in reality, at least in quantitative terms. First, public expenditures in 1975 only amounted to 24.7 per cent of the GDP, while the average figure for the rest of the OECD countries was 40.2 per cent (Tanzi, 1988: 101). Second, the level of social expenditure as a percentage of GDP in Spain and other European countries is shown in Table 1 of the Appendix. In 1975, social expenditure in Spain (12.1%) was much lower than in other EEC countries, reaching only to about half of their level (with the exception of Portugal and Greece, which are not included in the table). Last, Table 2 offers a comparison between state transfers to social security as a percentage of GNP in Spain and the average in OECD countries. Data for 1975 show that the OECD average was more than 28 times the figure for Spain (12.1 and 0.43%, respectively).

Yet the wish for a more advanced model of social security during the transition years was confronted by economic crisis and the questioning of welfare models in other countries that Spanish policy-makers were seeking to emulate. Due in part to this situation, the Spanish system showed a high degree of incapacity to accommodate to the economic and social changes that took place between 1975 and 1982. A certain dose of dynamism was still present in this period by the implementation of successive stages of the 1972 reform. However, attempts at readaptation to the new conditions were hampered by disagreements over decisions about conflicting issues – such as universalism versus professionalism, expansion of protection versus restriction in expenditure, and public management versus private management (Gonzalo González et al., 1985: 96).

In 1978, the democratic Constitution introduced the principle of universal extension of coverage of social security to all Spaniards (Articles 41, 43 and 49). Nevertheless, new special schemes continued to be created for specific categories of citizens. In particular, schemes were created between 1977 and 1979 for members of Parliament, football players, and clergymen. All these population groups were classified with the bizarre expression "similar to workers", in order to justify their inclusion into the system as opposed to other groups of citizens still lacking public social protection.

A broad, though superficial, *debate* on social security matters opened timidly at the beginning of the 1970s, and was intensified from the middle of the decade onwards. The proliferation of publications on the social security system – such as textbooks, handbooks, and studies on particular aspects of social provision – on the one hand, and the elaboration of reform proposals on the part of the bureaucracy on the other hand, reflect the increased interest in the details of public social policy and the possibilities for its amelioration. The massive preliminary studies for the White Book of the Social Security, as well as the publication of a summary of them in the White Book itself in 1977, started a series of proposals for reform on the part of the bureaucracy. These books were always named after a colour; as for example the Red Book (1980), the Green Book (1981), and the Yellow Book (1982). All these studies had a significant impact among the political parties and interest groups that used the information contained in them to build their own proposals for reform.[16]

The sense that reform was urgent, was also reflected in the opinions of political parties and interest groups. In general, their views coincided in the need for change, oscillating from cautiousness to radical proposals. The opinions of the parties, unions, and employers' organizations are relevant because the transition to democracy brought about the upsurge of a different path to take decisions in the domain of social policy. These decisions had remained almost exclusively in the hands of bureaucrats during the Francoist regime, but the advent of democracy meant the participation of interest groups in the debate on the future of the welfare system. Whether this participation led to actual reforms or not, does not make the change in the *character of the decision-making process* less relevant.

The socialist union, UGT, initially had a very critical opinion on the situation of the NSS system and was in favour of radical changes. However, as time went by, the UGT proposals became increasingly moderate, so that in 1982 it was ready to accept a gradual improvement of the welfare system leading to universal coverage and an expansion both of the services and the benefits provided. On the contrary, the communist union, CCOO, was in 1982 more prone to support a rationalization and amelioration of the inherited welfare system than to introduce radical modifications in it, which may be due to its worry for the conditions of formal workers *vis-à-vis* the entire population.

The main employers' organization, CEOE, maintained a very cautious position at the beginning of the transition, supporting a period of study in order to single out priorities before actual decisions were taken. This position shifted to a more radical one by 1982, when the CEOE was in favour of the increase of private provision and private management in the welfare system (Gonzalo González et al., 1985: 39-42).

Political parties shared the general opinion about the need for urgent change and coincided to a large extent on the diagnosis of the problems of the NSS system. From the programmes of the parties for the electoral campaigns, it can be deduced that the right-wing parties, especially AP, were in favour of the incorporation of private initiative in the management of the system and viewed the amelioration of the financing mechanisms as a priority. The Communist and Socialist parties regarded the expansion of public social provision as fundamental. The party in office, the centrist UCD, was both cautious and vague in its proposals for change. The government continuously insisted on the need for reform in the domains of services and benefits, management, and financing, as well as on the desirability to approach the European models. Reform proposals were elaborated, but their implementation was always postponed (Gonzalo González et al., 1985: 43-48).

The *specific measures* that were introduced during the transition period can be characterized as occasional, trivial, and isolated from one another – and even contradictory in many cases. As regards the *organization of the system*, one of the most important innovations was the creation of four independent institutes in 1978, each devoted to the management of a broad area of social policy: INSALUD for health care, INSS for economic benefits related to retirement or compulsory loss of income, INSERSO for social services directed to old age and disability contingencies, and INEM specialized in unemployment situations. These new institutes were curiously introduced at the same time as the democratic constitution was being discussed and meant the liquidation of the old managing institute of social policy, the 70-years-old INP.

The idea of creating a national institute of employment responded to a deep need for a specific answer to the problem of unemployment, for it was perceived by the population as one of the crucial issues of the time.[17] The institute was supposed to enable the state to pursue an integral policy of employment by unifying all the agencies in charge of the different aspects of employment.

The decree of 22 December 1978 creating the four social institutes, contemplated the participation of unions and employers in the "control and surveillance of the management of the social security, health care and employment schemes" and created specific institutions within the various social institutes in which participation was to take place. This participation, intensively fought for by interest groups and already an old claim, came to be more theoretical than real and effective.

It was also in 1978 that a general treasury office was created for the NSS system which helped to improve its economic and financial management. In turn, the elaboration process of the Social Security annual budget was defined in different stages that were to conclude with parliamentary approval. In general, the inspection and control of the system was ameliorated through several measures. This should have led to a significant improvement of the management and planning aspects, but it also entailed some negative unintended consequences – such as an increase in administrative rigidity (interference of public agencies such as the Minister of Finance, and other tutelage ministries) leading to a loss of autonomy, and to dehumanization in the rendering of services to users (Gonzalo González et al., 1985: 99).

Changes in the organization of the system also entailed the creation of a Ministry of Health and Social Security in 1977, which could have led to an attenuation of the professional character of the NSS system – for its dependence to the Labour Ministry came to a halt. However, in 1981 both ministries were unified again and converted into a single institution – namely, the Ministry of Labour, Health, and Social Security – and at the end of the same year, a second split took place, this time leading to the creation of a Ministry of Labour and Social Security and a Ministry of Health and Consumption. These changes account for the existence of a climate of insecurity.

Finally, public action regarding the protective activity of the system was in general of scant relevance. Some restrictive measures were undertaken in order to lower expenditure. The most noteworthy among these was perhaps the introduction of a ticket on pharmaceutical consumption and a 15%-reduction of the payments for temporal incapacity for work. In terms of the extension of benefits, some examples were the creation of a subsidy for long-term unemployed bearing family burdens, and the revision of the general normative for unemployment to make the programme more nimble. From 1976 onwards, other measures to alleviate the growth of unemployment were set up: several programmes for early retirement were introduced, and different procedures were created to ease the payment of employers' contributions. From 1977, an emphasis was placed on the increase of the lower pensions at the expense of the higher ones.

During the period of transition, *coverage* rates augmented in all the different programmes of the NSS system, although in 1982 14.4 per cent of the Spanish population was still excluded from the system (Fundación FOESSA, 1983: 811). Coverage rates for unemployment were an exception to the general expansionary rule: they only rose slightly until 1980 when a downward trend was initiated. From 1975 to 1981, the unemployed population enjoying subsidies was on average 36.6 per cent, consequently maintaining a low level of coverage and leading to an increase in the absolute number of unemployed lacking protection (Desdentado Bonete and Cruz Roche, 1983: 318).

Another indicator that has been defined in order to assess the existence of change in social policy during the Spanish transition is that of the evolution of *expenditure* in social provision. Expenditure on social protection in 1981 was one-and-a-half times higher than in 1975 (see Table 1, Appendix). The differentials in comparative terms with other OECD countries were narrowed without totally closing the gap. Tables 3 and 5 (see Appendix) show that in 1975 expenditure on health was closer to the OECD average than expenditure on retirement pensions. However, by the end of the transition period, in 1982, the situation was the opposite – for expenditure on pensions grew more than that on health.

The number of pensioners rose by 31.6 per cent between 1976 and 1982, while the contributors only increased by 0.04 per cent. Such a high increase was only partly due to the expansion in the amount of retirement pensions (16.5%); the upward trend in disability pensions was much more significant, amounting to an increase of 42.2 per cent (see Table 4, Appendix). The latter figure may be explained by the use of disability pensions as a substitute for unemployment insurance, and thus may be understood as a way to ease the impact of the crisis on the working population. In addition, unemployment rose from 2.62 per cent of the active population in 1974 to 14.35 per cent in 1981, and the beneficiaries of the unemployment subsidy in 1981 were nine times those of 1974 (Desdentado Bonete and Cruz Roche, 1983: 318). Expenditure on unemployment benefits (in 1970 constant *pesetas*) multiplied by 13 between 1974 and 1981 (Fuentes Quintana et al., 1983: 102).

This situation made a more intense participation of the state in the *financing* of the system inescapable. Public funding was also necessary in order to alleviate the pressure on the employers and to foster the creation of jobs. Measures were also taken to facilitate the payment of contributions on the part of firms such as the introduction of the possibility of fractionate payments and moratoria. The collection procedure was also ameliorated after the 1977 taxation reform through the submission of pensions to direct tax on income (IRPF). State transfers to social security increased more than four times during the period of transition, but they remained much lower than the average of the other OECD countries (see Table 2).

To sum up, during the transition period the welfare system maintained its occupational character and its fragmentation, although some innovations with regard to organizational aspects were introduced – leading in particular to improvements in management. The very change of regime allowed for the participation in public affairs of new social and political actors (such as free unions and employers' organizations, and political parties). The emergence of such new actors had a double impact on social policy issues. On the one hand, societal actors' demands and opinions fuelled the incipient debate on the reform of the Spanish welfare system. On the other hand, the existence of these new actors and the democratic continuation of the already-existing tradition of informal bargaining set the bases for a slight change in the social policy decision-making process, as the inclusion of social security issues in the so-called social concertation shows (see below).

In general, the measures taken in order to improve the existing welfare system were scant and contradictory. Some of them were introduced in order to reduce costs, but most of them resulted from the impact of the economic crisis. Increases in coverage and, especially, in expenditure were significant, and the rise of state transfers was also important. However, no radical reform took place either in the direction of universal coverage of citizens, total financing from public revenues, total public provision of services, or in the direction of private management and/ or provision of services.

4   Social Policy During the Transition to Democracy: An Interpretation

The fact that the political transition to democracy in Spain coincided with the oil shocks of the 1970s makes it difficult to ascertain to which extent decisions in the area of social policy are linked to, or even caused by, the political process itself, or are due to conjunctural events such as the international economic crisis. In order to reach some clarifying answer to the questions of why the Francoist social security system was kept with minor institutional modifications, and why a significant increase in social expenditure and public funding took place, three sets of possible causal factors may be considered. The first of them can be labelled as the "inheritance of Francoism" and includes some of the long-lasting political and economic characteristics of the old regime that may affect social policy directly or indirectly. The second set of factors can be derived from the "kind of political process" through which democratization was achieved. Last but not least, a third set of factors regarding contextual aspects of the transition may be considered, the most important being the advent of the economic crises. This last group includes factors that are alien to the political process but that nevertheless have a clear influence on either decision or non-decision processes.

4.1 The Francoist Inheritance

First of all, the idea that the transition does not begin with Franco's death has to be underlined, for it suggests at least one very important issue: capitalist development was a favourable condition for the installation and consolidation of liberal democracy, but it also meant that the capitalist institutions on which to root a social security system did not have to be created from the scratch. This circumstance, together with the existence of a wealthy economic environment due to growth during the 1960s, favoured the permanence of the social security system. Although *per capita* income in 1964 was less than US$ 700, by 1973 Spain had become the world's 10th-ranking industrial power with over US$ 2000 *per capita* income, a figure comparable to that of Japan in 1970 (Gunther, 1980: 56-57).

On the other hand, the inheritance of a regressive and inefficient taxation system hindered the amelioration of the social system during the transition.[18] During the last 15 years of Francoism, the government was incapable of introducing increased taxation; and all reform projects were met by Franco's personal opposition. Consequently, the taxation system could not take advantage of the wealth of the economy and did not suffice to foster a more redistributive social policy. Despite the 1977 reform which allowed for fast public-sector growth, fiscal pressure remained low in Spain throughout the transition: in 1981, Spain still ranked 20th (only before Turkey) among OECD countries. Including social security fees, fiscal pressure amounted only to 23.4 per cent of GNP (IV Jornadas de Economía de la Salud, 1985: 27).

As far as social policy is concerned, the institutional system that was created under Francoism provided services and benefits, even if not high-quality ones, to the bulk of the population. This circumstance had contradictory effects when the introduction of reform was at stake during the transition period. On the one hand, it meant that reform or expansion of the system was not as urgent in the short run. It meant, as well, that the space for reform was constrained: the size of the social security system was very large already both in administrative and coverage terms, and this made it difficult for the democratic government to undertake a radical reorganization. On the other hand, the existence of a large system implied that the population was accustomed to making use of state-financed and state-run institutions and aspired to an expansion and amelioration of these with the advent of democracy.[19]

The absence of a standardized accounting system of social security revenues and expenditures impeding proper comparisons with other European systems, and the lack of knowledge of available resources for social policy at the end of Francoism, also hindered reform and planning. In particular, information on human and material resources for health care were not available until the early 1980s, when "health maps" were produced and published. Another unfavourable element for the introduction of reform was that the Franco regime and its institutions had not been completely delegitimized, either among the political élites or among the population in general. This led to a situation of great uncertainty and ambiguity that advised caution when decisions were needed.[20]

Conversely, changes in civil society that had taken place during the 1960s and 1970s meant the birth of an incipient tradition of attaining agreements through either formal or informal negotiation processes among interest groups and among these and the state apparatus (Pérez Díaz, 1990). This tradition was greatly reinforced during the transition period, fostering a certain type of consensual decision-making (especially on macro-economic issues), and a better knowledge of the positions of the administration and the interest groups in social policy matters.

4.2 The Character of the Political Process of Democratization

The so-called "reform path" through which the Spanish transition to democracy was achieved entailed, on the one hand, the reaching of a consensus among political and social forces and their inescapable participation in processes of decision and, on the other hand, the continuity of the bureaucratic apparatus of the state.

The first implication, that of the need for consensus, slowed down processes of decision-making and reform because every opinion had to be taken into account and agreements were not easily reached. Furthermore, the demands for self-determination or at least autonomy on the part of the historical nationalities, and the need to negotiate the process of decentralization regarding very varied competencies – among which social policy was a relevant one – were a decisive factor for postponing reform.

As mentioned above, a new tradition of "pactism" was invented shortly before this moment and incorporated in the emerging political culture. Social pacts began to be reached from 1977 onwards, when the Moncloa Pacts were celebrated.[21] The following series of social pacts can be mainly understood as a tool for an income policy, through which unions tended to accept some kind of wage restraint as a means for coping with the economic crisis. Those same Moncloa Pacts included among the compensations unions and workers were to get, the governmental commitment to set up a progressive tax system and an expansion in social security coverage. As regards the employers' side, the government compromised to moderate the contributions of firms to social security.

Unions' proposals to the Social Pacts' Committees suggest that they had a very clear idea of what kind of public welfare system they wanted to see functioning: the two main unions clearly stated their adherence to a social-democratic model and also accepted the need to postpone its achievement or, at least, that it be completed in a piecemeal way.[22] In 1981, the National Employment Agreement (*Acuerdo Nacional de Empleo*, ANE) guaranteed the institutional participation of unions in the national Institutes of Social Security. This had been an old aspiration of the unions. Actual participation did not start until 1982, and the scarcity of technical experts both within the unions and employers' organizations reduced this institutional participation to a formality. In general, social concertation in Spain has been more successful in attaining wage control and union responsibility (stabilization of the economic and political systems) than in improving the welfare system and the participation of the workers in it.

The second implication of the reform path was that of the continuity of the bureaucratic apparatus of the state. A distinction between "regime" and "state" may be useful at this point. "A regime can be defined as the formal and informal organization of the centre of political power and of its relations with the broader society. A regime determines who has access to political power and how those in power deal with those who are not. The state, in contrast, is a (normally) more permanent structure of domination and coordination including crucially a coercive apparatus and the means to administer a society and extract resources from it" (Fishman, 1989: 9-10). A state may remain in place even when regimes come and go, as has happened at many points in the history of Spain. The period of transition constituted no exception to this rule, for the regime change took place step by step while the state remained in place. The preservation of the institutional framework of Francoism in social security matters, as well as the expansion of the system in terms of coverage and expenditure, is consistent with continuity in the state apparatus: no radical reform was introduced in the organization or philosophy of the system, but civil servants and professionals were able to increase their power through the expansion of the existing system.

4.3 Contextual Aspects of the Transition

The first and most important contextual factor constraining the decision process during the transition was the economic crisis of the 1970s. This unfortunate coincidence can be considered as the main source of strains both for policy-making and for policy implementation. The economic crisis had a greater impact in Spain than in other OECD countries,[23] both due to the high dependence of the Spanish industry on oil imports and because of the delay of adjustment measures to cope with it. Spanish policy-makers were convinced for a long time that an expansion in the public sector could be borne by existing economic conditions. This perception matched with the need for reaching a political consensus on any crucial decision, may explain why the first regulatory measures for the economy were agreed upon by the political parties in the Moncloa Pacts, even as late as the end of 1977.

As a consequence, the economic crisis brought about dramatic increases in unemployment and inflation that surpassed those of other OECD countries. Unemployment had already grown slightly during the 1960s and early 1970s, but since 1974 (3.0%) the upward trend rapidly accelerated: reaching 11.2 per cent in 1980 and peaking at 21.4 per cent in 1985, when it started to decrease slowly again (OECD, 1988: 39). Unemployment growth was not only due to the impact of the crisis on the production structure but also to the return of the migrants of the last decade from other European countries, and to the incorporation of the cohorts of the baby boom of the 1960s to the active population. Another reason for the rise in unemployment were the intense inherited rigidities of the labour market, which remained almost untouched during the transition – thus obstructing the necessary adjustment to the new conditions. Inflation rates reached a maximum in 1977 (24.5%) and did not recover the level of the early 1970s until 1984 (11.3%) (OECD, 1988b: 83).

The economic crisis had the effect of increasing public social expenditure on unemployment benefits and on pensions as well, because of the introduction of early retirement programmes. Difficulties in terms of competitiveness led a considerable number of industrial firms to engage in illegal ("black") economic activities in order to avoid the payment of social security fees, with the result of a quick socio-economic dualization. The flourishing of informal activities was tolerated by public authorities because they served to dampen social unrest: many of the unemployed could find a job in this kind of activities. Thus, the state could be relieved of part of the burden of social provision. Under these circumstances, radical reform towards universal coverage could have led to the consolidation of fraud, something politicians wanted to avoid because it meant the impossibility of gathering part of the resources while having to increase services provided.

It is in periods of crisis when changes are needed most, that they are also harder to implement. The period of transition to democracy in Spain can be considered as a phase of instability and uncertainty in all social, political, and economic domains within the country. Generalized economic instability abroad also had to be faced. The appearance of a phenomenon that can be labelled as the "fears of transition" also increased the tendency towards cautiousness. Fear above all of the army's reactions, of the ghost of the *coup d'état*, was shared by political élites and interest groups, especially unions. This may explain the lack of radicalization, as well as the caution with which demands were placed and the fear among policy-makers of taking wrong decisions that could destabilize the political or social situation. All these "fears", matched with the high level of uncertainty, halted the introduction of extensive reform in social policy. Conversely, the fear of radicalization of social demands among political élites, along with the need for legitimation of the new regime and the new political class, had the opposite effect of fostering a moderate expansion of the welfare state – together with the general desire to approach European levels in social policy.

5   Conclusions

During the first 20 years of the Francoist regime (1939-1975), a set of social insurance programmes was established, directed mainly at low-income industrial workers and their dependants and highly fragmented in organizational terms because of the fact of being managed by two broad institutions: the different national insurance schemes and a complex of workers' mutual aid associations. During the 1960s, an ample reform was implemented, leading to the establishment of a social security system: the NSS system, which incorporated the existing insurance programmes into a single institution. The new NSS system continued to be organized along professional lines, for it was divided into a general scheme for dependent workers and an array of special schemes for different labour categories. The fragmentation of management was consolidated, and the system remained financed by the contributions of employers and workers, along with a very low proportion of state transfers. By the end of the regime, three quarters of the population were covered, and the level of benefits was increased by a reform in 1972.

Three indicators have been used in order to assess the significance of the changes that took place during the subsequent period of transition to democracy (1975-1982). The consideration of the first one – namely, reforms in the macro-institutional design – leads to the conclusion that no major changes were introduced. The system continued to be predicated on the same principles, remaining an example of the mixed type of welfare system and continuing to be organized along professional lines and to be financed out of contributions, although a significant increase of state transfers did occur. Coverage also increased, but universalism failed to be reached. Some reforms did take place as regards the institutional organization of the system, leading to an improvement of management.

Social expenditure, defined as the second indicator of change, underwent a significant increase during the transition years, partly due to the expansionary thrust imposed on the system by the 1972 reform, and partly derived from the consequences in terms of unemployment and social needs connected with the economic crisis. The third and last indicator, that of possible changes in the character of the decision-making process in social policy, shows that an incipient change took place. Decisions in the social policy area were taken almost exclusively by politicians and bureaucrats during the Francoist period; but the birth of informal collective negotiation processes in the last years of the authoritarian regime, and especially the advent of democracy that allowed for the consolidation of a tradition of collective decision-making, led to the inclusion of such social groups as unions and employers' organizations in the decision-making process.

From the consideration of all these indicators, it may be deduced that the most salient feature of social policy during the Spanish transition to democracy was its high degree of continuity with processes in the last years of the authoritarian regime. This continuity may be accounted for by three different sets of causal factors: namely, the long-lasting political and socio-economic characteristics of the old regime, the type of transition to democracy, and the contextual aspects of the transition (especially its coincidence with the economic crisis of the 1970s).

The existence of a regressive and inefficient taxation system, the already large size of the welfare system, the lack of knowledge about the existing available resources for social policy: all these were factors inherited from Francoism that hampered the introduction of reforms. Besides, the wealthy state of the economy at the end of the Francoist regime could have entailed the existence of favourable conditions for reform, but the advent of the economic crisis reversed the situation. The impact of the economic crisis was one of the main sources of strains in arriving at decisions in the area of social policy, for it led to the emergence of new social needs that had to be urgently met at the same time as the establishment of cost containment measures was convenient. The economic crisis also added to the general atmosphere of instability and uncertainty in the political and social domains.

The "reformist" character of the process of transition to democracy entailed, in the first place, the need for consensus – which slowed down processes of reform because agreements were not easily reached. In the second place, the continuity of the bureaucratic apparatus of the previous regime also hindered the introduction of radical reform. Finally, the actual establishment of a democratic regime permitted the participation of new social actors in the decision-making process, thus changing its character and also leading to the introduction of measures aimed at the improvement of the existing welfare system: social demands could now be expressed; and they had to be met, at least partially, in order to legitimate and consolidate the new regime.

Notes

1　In 1982, democracy was consolidated in the sense that the new political institutions were in place and no reversal of the democratization process was viewed as possible by Spanish society.

2　The main reforms took place in 1985 in the case of pensions; and in the following year, in the case of health.

3　The macro-institutional design of a welfare system may be defined primarily in terms of three dimensions: (1) whether the services are provided by the private market, the state, or a combination of the two; (2) how the system is financed; and (3) the political principle that defines who is to be covered (citizens, workers).

4　General information on the process of the construction of the Spanish welfare state and the main reforms it underwent, has been drawn from the historical records contained in *Libro Blanco* (1977: 17-79), Infante (1975: 45-50), Rull Sabater (11-25), and Velarde (1990: 40-7).

5　The last restrictions on the salary and employment qualifications for inclusion in the public system, were removed only in the early 1970s. This is evidence of the durability of the principles upon which the system was predicated (*Libro Blanco*, 1977: 30).

6　In 1925, out of a population of 22 million, only 400,000 people were protected by private mutual aid societies (*Libro Blanco*, 1977: 21).

7　The so-called "fundamental" laws of the authoritarian regime were supposed to play a similar role to that of a constitution in a democratic regime, in the sense of being the basic and most important pieces of legislation.

8　*Fuero del Trabajo* (Title X, Articles 1 and 2); *Fuero de los Españoles* (Chapter 3, Article 28); *Ley de Principios del Movimiento Nacional* (Principle IX). See *Leyes Políticas de España* (1958).

9　At the beginning, mutual associations provided benefits for retirement, disability, long illness, widows, and orphans (González Catalá and Vicente Merino, 1985: 37). The 1963 reform reduced their competences to the provision of mainly retirement and disability benefits.

10　In 1949, the administrative and technical aspects of the several national insurance programmes were unified and an attempt was made at partial coordination with the mutual societies system.

11　State contributions to the national insurance programmes fell to 4.3 per cent in 1940 – from their previous level of 24.04 per cent in 1935 – and remained at an average level of 3.7 per cent from 1946 onwards (Infante, 1975: 46).

12　It is not surprising that a reform of the social insurance system was regarded as urgent at this moment, for the degree of fragmentation of the management of social provision had become unbearable. The administration of the different programmes was in the hands of private insurance companies (labour accidents and entities collaborating with the health insurance programme), the numerous mutual societies, all firms obliged to participate in the family aid programme (*Plus Familiar*), and the public entities that were in charge of the national insurance programmes (Rull Sabater, 1974: 19).

13　Aside from the Social Security system, Francoist policy-makers were very keen on housing policies that were in part used as a device to combat unemployment. Activity in this field had already taken place during the first period of the regime, but it was at the end of the 1950s when a Housing Ministry (*Ministerio de la Vivienda*) was established and housing policies intensified – especially cheap state-financed lodgings (Medhurst, 1973: 156-157).

14　See de Pereda Mateos and Desdentado Bonete (1973: 23-81) for a detailed analysis of the modifications brought about by the 1972 reform.

15　The information included in this section follows closely the excellent work of Gonzalo González et al. (1985). Details have also been drawn from Velarde (1990) and Rodríguez Cabrero (1989).

16　An analysis of the proposals of these publications, as well as an exhaustive list of the studies of the social security system elaborated by academics, can be found in Velarde (1990).

17　In February 1979, a public survey sponsored by the newspaper *El País* showed that 50 per cent of those interviewed regarded unemployment as the most important problem of society.

18　For data on the extent of regressiveness of the Francoist tax system, see Gunther (1980: 60).

19 Information on the opinion of the Spanish population about the social security system and the revisions that should be carried out within it, can be found in Alvira Martín and García López (1982) and also in Fundación FOESSA (1983: 812-817). State intervention in the provision of social services and benefits was also viewed as desirable by the population because ideological alternatives – namely the liberal, anarchist and social-catholic traditions – had withered away long before the period of transition (Pérez Díaz, 1990).

20 From a series of interviews with government leaders carried out in 1976, Coser (1976) deduces that the regime was willing to make concessions to the opposition but continuing to safeguard its prerogatives. The regime was not ready yet to grant full democratic rights, and future developments seemed to be dependent on the balance between government and opposition.

21 In fact, the Moncloa pacts cannot be exactly characterized as "social pacts", because they were reached among parliamentary parties and the government. However, their contents were accepted both by employers' organizations and trade unions as binding.

22 See "Seguridad Social (Documentos)" on the proposals made by the main unions (UGT, CCOO) and the employers' organization (CEOE) regarding social security at the beginning of the 1980s.

23 While inflation grew on average 10.7 per cent in the OECD countries between 1974 and 1981, the increase in Spain was 17.8 per cent. The figures for unemployment were 5.3 per cent and 8.4 per cent, respectively (Fuentes Quintana et al., 1983: 25).

References

Alvira Martín, F., García López, J. (1983) 'La Seguridad Social y los españoles', *Papeles de Economía Española* 12/13: 32-35.

Barea, J. (1988) 'La asistencia sanitaria pública', *Economistas* 35: 262-266.

Chouraqui, J.C. (1988) 'La evolución del gasto público: una perspectiva internacional', *Papeles de Economía Española* 37: 116-125.

Coser, L. (1976) 'Spain on the Eve', *Dissent*: 338-384.

de Pereda Mateos, A., Desdentado Bonete, A. (1974) 'Estudio del texto refundido de la Ley General de la Seguridad Social', in *Ley General de la Seguridad Social. Texto Refundido:* 17-101. Madrid: Ministerio de Trabajo.

Desdentado Bonete, A., Cruz Roche, I. (1983) 'Las prestaciones de desempleo ante la crisis', *Papeles de Economía Española* 12/13: 317-335.

Fishman, R. (1989) 'Rethinking State and Regime: Southern Europe's Transition to Democracy'. Mimeo.

Fuentes Quintana, E. et al. (1983) 'Estrategia para un tratamiento de los problemas de la Seguridad Social', *Papeles de Economía Española* 12/13: 20-107.

Fundación FOESSA (1983) *Informe Sociológico sobre el cambio social en España 1975-1982. IV Informe FOESSA*. Madrid: Euramérica.

González Catalá, V.T., Vicente Merino, A. (1985) *Análisis económico-financiero del sistema español de Seguridad Social 1964-1985*. Madrid: Ministerio de Trabajo y Seguridad Social.

Gonzalo González, B. et al. (1985) *Evolución y tendencias de la Seguridad Social durante la crisis económica*. Madrid: Ministerio de Trabajo y Seguridad Social.

Gunther, R. (1980) *Public Policy in a No-Party State. Spanish Planning and Budgeting in the Twilight of the Franquist Era*. Berkeley: University of California Press.

Infante, A. (ed.) (1975) *Cambio social y crisis sanitaria*. Madrid: Ayuso.

IV Jornadas de Economía de la Salud. Aspectos económicos de la reforma sanitaria (1985). Sevilla: Junta de Andalucía, Consejería de Salud y Consumo.

Leyes políticas de España (1958). Madrid: Instituto de Estudios Políticos.

Libro Blanco de la Seguridad Social (1977). Madrid: Ministerio de Trabajo.

Linz, J.J. (1981) 'A Century of Politics and Interests in Spain', pp. 365-415 in Berger, S. (ed.) *Organizing Interests in Western Europe*. New York: Cambridge University Press.

Medhurst, K.N. (1973) *Government in Spain. The Executive at Work*. Oxford: Pergamon Press.
OECD (1988 a) *Reforming Public Pensions*. Paris: OECD.
OECD (1988 b) *Historical Statistics 1960-1986*. Paris: OECD.
OECD (1987) *Financing and Delivering Health Care*. Paris: OECD.
Pérez Díaz, V. (1990) 'The Emergence of Democratic Spain and the "Invention" of a Democratic Tradition', *Estudios, Working Papers* 1. Madrid: Centro de Estudios Avanzados del Instituto Juan March.
Rodríguez Cabrero, G. (1989) 'Orígenes y evolución del Estado de Bienestar español en su perspectiva histórica. Una visión general', *Política y sociedad*, Winter: 79-87.
Rull Sabater, A. (1974) *Instituciones y economía de la Seguridad Social Española*. Madrid: Confederación Española de Cajas de Ahorros.
Rull Sabater, A. (1971) *La Seguridad Social en España*. Madrid: Euramérica.
'Seguridad Social (Documentos)' (1982) *Papeles de Economía Española*, Special Issue.
Tanzi, V. 'Tendencias generales del gasto público en los países industriales', *Papeles de Economía Española* 37: 100-116.
Velarde, J. (1990) *El tercer viraje de la Seguridad Social en España*. Madrid: Instituto de Estudios Económicos.

Appendix: Tables

**Table 1:   Expenditure on Social Protection, 1970-1981
(as a Percentage of GNP)**

Countries	1970	1975	1980	1981
West Germany	21.5	28.0	28.7	29.5
Belgium	18.5	24.5	27.6	30.2
Denmark	19.6	25.8	28.7	29.3
France	19.6	22.9	25.9	27.2
Britain	15.9	19.5	21.4	23.5
Netherlands	28.8	28.1	30.5	31.7
Ireland	13.2	19.4	22.0	–
Italy	–	22.4	22.8	24.7
Luxembourg	16.4	22.4	27.6	27.1
Spain	9.5	12.1	17.2	17.7
Average	*17.2*	*20.1*	*25.2*	*24.8*

Source: Velarde, 1990: 109.

Table 2:   State Transfers to Social Security, 1967-1982

Year	State Transfers/GNP (Spain)	State Transfers/GNP (OECD Average)	State Transfers in constant pta. (1967=100)
1967	0.21	–	100.00
1968	0.23	–	115.67
1969	0.42	–	237.79
1970	0.43	9.0	255.49
1971	0.45	9.4	274.98
1972	0.48	9.4	320.11
1973	0.47	9.8	341.79
1974	0.67	10.5	523.68
1975	0.43	12.1	337.06
1976	0.40	12.1	325.34
1977	0.40	12.0	325.74
1978	0.97	12.1	814.90
1979	1.17	12.5	989.70
1980	1.12	12.8	947.22
1981	1.33	13.3	1,112.87
1982	1.82	14.1	1,542.89

Sources: González Catalá and Vicente Merino, 1985: 260. Chouraqui, 1988: 117-118.

Table 3:   Public Expenditure in Retirement Pensions, 1967-1982 (Percentage of GDP)

Country	1967	1975	1982
France	8.2	10.1	12.3
West Germany	11.2	12.6	12.5
Italy	7.5	10.4	13.8
UK	5.1	6.0	7.1
Belgium	–	10.5	12.6
Denmark	5.5	7.4	9.3
Greece	5.2	4.8	9.0
Ireland	2.9	4.2	5.3
Netherlands	6.4	8.9	11.3
Portugal	1.5	4.1	7.3
Spain	2.4	4.3	8.2
Average	*5.6*	*7.6*	*9.9*

Source: *Reforming Public Pensions*, OECD, 1988a: 138-141.

Table 4:   Pensions in the Social Security System, 1976-1982

	1976	1979	1982	1982 (Δ%)
Number of Contributors	10,341,092	10,502,384	10,720,054	0.04
Number of Pensions	3,592,005	4,015,098	4,728,878	31.6
Number of Retirement Pensions	1,959,012	2,133,515	2,281,594	16.5
Number of Disability Pensions	713,113	974,093	1,119,855	42.2

Source: Fundación FOESSA, 1983: 805, 824.

**Table 5:   Public and Total Health Expenditures, 1965-1982
            (Percentage of GDP)**

Country	1965		1975		1982	
	PH/TH	TH/GDP	PH/TH	TH/GDP	PH/TH	TH/GDP
Belgium	75.3	3.9	80.9	5.4	92.3	6.1
Denmark	85.9	4.8	91.9	6.5	85.6	6.9
France	68.1	5.3	72.2	7.6	71.1	9.3
West Germany	70.9	5.1	80.2	7.8	78.7	8.1
Greece	71.1	3.1	61.6	4.0	84.4	4.4
Ireland	76.2	4.4	82.5	7.7	93.6	8.1
Italy	87.8	4.6	86.1	6.7	84.6	7.2
Netherlands	68.7	4.4	76.5	7.7	80.2	8.6
Portugal	–	–	58.9	6.4	71.1	5.7
Spain	52.6	2.7	70.4	5.1	72.4	6.3
Mean	*67.6*	*4.8*	*76.2*	*7.0*	*79.0*	*7.5*

Note: PH = Public Health Expenditure
         TH = Total Health Expenditure

Source: *Financing and Delivering Health Care*, OECD, 1987: 55.

CHAPTER 8

Labour and the Legacy of the Past[1]

Vladimir Shubkin

1 The Stalinist Labour Relations' Regime

Vast and rapid changes occurring in the Soviet Union and Eastern European countries have given rise to a continuous debate on Stalinism and its roots, and on the
crisis of socialist ideas and theories. They have urged the revision of numerous
theories and concepts that only yesterday seemed unshakable. In this sense, we
can speak of the crisis of the doctrine of socialism.

Here, we shall dwell on one aspect of this doctrine which is essential for a better
understanding of the current problems of *perestroika*, and of labour relations in
particular.

In their analysis, neither Karl Marx nor Friedrich Engels paid much attention
to factors that stimulate intensive and conscientious labour – to ensure efficient
production – under socialism. It is common knowledge that in a capitalist economy,
these factors are provided by the mechanisms of market relations and competition.
However, Marx implied that these mechanisms were not compatible with communism (Marx and Engels, 1960-62: 18) and Lenin only echoed Marx when he
proclaimed that " ... (f)or hundreds of years, freedom of trade was the hallmark
of economic wisdom, for millions of people. Such freedom ... is simply a cover
for capitalist lies, violence and exploitation, as well as other freedoms proclaimed
by the bourgeoisie. Down with obsolete social networks, down with obsolete
economic ties, the obsolete freedom of labour, obsolete laws, and obsolete habits.
Let us build a new society" (Lenin, 1958-65: 108).

Attempts to build a new society guided by these negations during the period of
"military communism", led to disorganization and economic collapse. Claims that
the socialist economy would be guided by the principle of distribution according
to work could change nothing. Thus, the problem of distinguishing between
complex and simple labour turned out to be insurmountable, since a single criterion
– for example working hours – did not take into account all the aspects of labour:

such as labour expenses or the results of different categories of workers. This meant that the distribution according to work could not be achieved. Instead, the result was total equalization, a fading interest in intensive and productive work, and the fall in labour productivity – and hence in the compulsion to work, which contributed to violations of the law, and to the reinforcement of anti-democratic principles of leadership.

The conceptual doctrinal utopias were supplemented by grave errors and fantasies on the part of the revolutionary leaders. Let us point out some. Starting with the October Revolution, the Bolsheviks set extraordinary goals. They regarded the country as an outpost of the world revolution which was to break out soon. Thus, Grigory Zinoviev in the Politburo's report to the 13th Party Congress in 1924, said: "At the time of the Brest Peace Treaty, Vladimir Illyich [Lenin] considered that the victory of the proletarian revolution was a matter of some months. There was a time when we in the Central Committee were daily expecting the revolution in Germany and Austria. We thought that if we seized power, we would open the way for revolutions in other countries".[2] Thus, the primary aims were to keep and promote power, along with the task of organizing the army for self-defence and of assisting the revolutionary movements in Europe and Asia. There was also the task of organizing production, transportation, and distribution. And the main thing was to make workers and peasants work and produce all that the state and the army needed for solving these aims. How could that be accomplished?

For Marx, the alternative was either economic or non-economic compulsion to work. The latter – i.e. violence and outright force – was most appealing to the revolutionaries. Such was the practice to which non-professionals usually resorted when confronted with such complicated and demanding tasks as economic management. On this, there were no conflicts within the group in power. Both the politics of "military communism" and Trotsky's economic programme appealed to the majority. That programme was in fact a programme of converting the country into a system of concentration camps where everyone should consider himself "a soldier of labour". "If an order is given to somebody to send him someplace, he must follow it; otherwise he would become a deserter and should be punished."[3]

Such declarations are not devoid of logic. When all state property, and when the production and distribution of all material elements of production were centrally planned, a crucial question arose: how to organize the labour force? Could the workers be allowed to choose a place of residence, a profession, and a job? Then major mismatches would arise. Raw materials and equipment would be sent northwards, while the manpower would prefer to move southwards. A new plant would be planned in Siberia, while people would prefer to stay in Moldavia and the like. In this logic, the answer to the above dilemma was self-evident: the compulsory distribution of the labour force, the registration of the workers in one – and only one – enterprise, so as to tie the worker, as it were, to the means of production. This was the logic of the creators of a tremendous, all-embracing system of total compulsion. The system needed a special commanding and punitive apparatus, for which the former specialists and managers of production were not suitable. They could be allowed to work only in some sectors of the national economy, and only under strict control. The system was in need of other, new, kinds of people, and they turned up. They made up the new bureaucracy; semi-literates, brought up in the army with its merciless methods of command and direct compulsion that allowed commanders to send their subordinates to death. Mistrustful of anything new or unusual, these people strived for increasing their power and aspired to "violently destroy the old world, woe betide the bourgeoisie".

Their main aim was the immediate transition to communist production and distribution. "Military communism" was temporary, or a certain stage to them. Many communist leaders considered it a kind of panacea. The political system which was established during the first years of the Soviet state, served these ideas. Uncontrolled power was concentrated in the hands of a single person.

The question arises: is it possible to build up structures having one clever and kind leader in mind? And if he is not kind, if people mean nothing to him, what will happen then? And what will happen if he is not clever, and people will suffer tremendously because of his decisions? Does this not mean that there were some grave errors in the very construction of the political mechanism? As a result, it could function only as it did under Stalin.

It might be that, when elaborating the political mechanism, one should start with the acknowledgement that human nature is not perfect, and that society should be able to protect itself against the unlimited power of any leader who might be stupid or vicious, mercenary or schizophrenic. Society should have sufficient methods of control. Only then can it start to solve other problems.

George Plehanov pointed to the grave errors in the arrangement of the Party from its very birth at the beginning of this century. He strongly objected to the over-centralized Party, and to the Central Committee's capture of extraordinary power and its right to dissolve any local group. He argued: "Just imagine that the Central Committee acquires this disputable right of 'dissolving'. Then, in view of the next congress, the Central Committee would dissolve all the opposition groups or would fill them with its own obedient followers. In this way, it would provide for a majority and have a congress that would approve of any good or bad action, and would applaud any plan or project. There would be neither a majority nor a minority in the Party then. The dreams of the Persian Shahs would come true ...". Plehanov regarded himself as a centralist and stood for the creation of a strong organization, but he did not want the centre to set up the whole party (Plehanov, 1926: 90, 92).

This danger increased by many times when the Party gained political control, and concentrated huge economic and political power. The calamity has been aggravated, since this political pattern, once accepted, has been reproduced at all levels; at the state level, in the *Komsomol*, in the trade unions, and even in pioneer groups. The result was a unity of hierarchical structures – nomenclature – that has used its energy to suppress any independent activity, as well as all initiative. Violence has become the main instrument of economic and political management.

The doctrinal dreams of the revolutionary leaders, and their craving for violence was fully embodied in Stalin's totalitarian state. Stalin was the first to see the fantastic possibilities of the type of power he brought to life. He also found both the means of power (the apparatus) and the methods (violence and terror).

At the same time, the trade unions turned into state organizations, and stopped to be the representatives and protectors of working people. Now, the workers and employees were left alone confronted by the powerful force of compulsion. They could not protect their own economic rights. The trade unions became an appendix to the administrative bodies that were used to exert pressure, and to increase the productivity of labour.

As for spiritual life, the situation was even more dramatic. A violent onslaught upon religion – first of all upon the Orthodox Christian Church, but also upon Catholicism, Islam, Buddhism – did not take the form of disputes. It took a much simpler and radical form: clergymen were arrested and imprisoned; churches and monasteries were closed, blown up, or burned down. The authorities attempted to replace the spiritual vacuum by various forms of paganism; by the cult of the leader, and by vulgar Marxism with a touch of religion. The propagandists became ministers of religion, the only true and compulsory religion for all.

By 1928, the countryside, with 26 million peasant households, remained the last and main stronghold of this nation's independence. Therefore, Stalin's collectivization probably became the decisive blow. When the most industrious and self-sufficient peasants were deprived of their property, sent to Siberia, killed, or left to die of hunger, nothing was left to prevent the punitive system of management from taking over the country.

The devastation of the peasantry and of religion meant all at once the uprooting of the national culture and of morality as well as the blossoming of violence. It helped to train the apparatus for future purges. The newly-trained were ready to follow any order, to do anything. That was exactly what Stalin needed and intended to have.

Some of the systems' creators, and its future victims, were aware of the implications. Nikolai Buharin, for instance, came to understand that the worst things possible were "... the deep changes in the mentality of those communists who took part in the purges ... Those who remained sane turned into professional bureaucrats. For them, terror and violence were the normal methods of rule: obedience to any order became the primary virtue" (*Conquest*, 1974: 31).

In order to eliminate the New Economic Policy (NEP), Stalin resorted to the most brutal methods and to mass genocide, causing the death and boundless sufferings of millions of people. Only during collectivization, the direct and indirect losses amounted to 10-13 million people (including those who died of hunger, or in the purges, and as a result of the decrease in fertility ensuing thereafter). According to Western experts, no less than 5.5 million people in the Ukraine died of hunger during that period in time. Millions of people perished in the 1930s, in the years of the "great terror". It has been estimated that the population loss in the years from 1926-1939 was between 16 to 26 million people (Anderson and Silver, 1985: 531). In cities and towns, a violent attack on small craftsmen and proprietors practically destroyed the service sector. All this explains the low productivity of forced labour – and hence, stagnation – and the increase in social tensions and conflicts between nationalities.

Development may enhance the role of spiritual and moral values; but it can also turn into the opposite, when moral values are violently discarded. The peoples of the Soviet Union have gone through the latter experience.

The structure of the biological/socio-spiritual layers had previously been in the form of a pyramid, with biological being at the bottom and spiritual being at the top. This pyramid was not only beheaded: "social man" was eliminated. Any kind of independent social activity was strictly prohibited. In the first post-revolutionary years some communists desperately called for preserving democracy within the party if democracy outside it was impossible. Very soon, their voices ceased forever.

The majority of the population was doomed to purely biological existence. Incredible hardship and suffering in trying to satisfy the vital needs (food, clothing, housing) squeezed out any mention of human rights and self-esteem. "Biological man" became the character of the time.

The system of labour relations under Stalin was based upon the slave labour of millions of GULAG-prisoners, and upon state feudalism in industry and agriculture. Workers and farmers (*kolkhozniks*) were registered at enterprises and collective farms, and were not allowed to leave them of their own free will. Imprisonment was the main type of punishment for any violation of the labour regulation: such as coming late, or truancy. The whole population was registered at some location, and each individual could not change his/her place of residence. *Kolkhozniks* could not even temporarily leave their place of residence without a special permit from the local authorities.

Several generations of Soviet people lived in a atmosphere that transmitted violence and increased alienation from labour, which was regarded as some alien and hateful force that the enslaved people had to withstand. Such attitudes stimulated vandalism and the meaningless damaging of goods created by human labour. Long before 1917, a Russian saying stated that, "No one can profit from righteous effort". Now it became evident that by honest and righteous effort it was impossible to provide for one's family. Theft became a form of labour relations.

Anyone could steal anything anywhere, both in state enterprises and at the collective farms. In spite of rigorous regulations – and armies of watchmen, supervisors, and militiamen – stealing grew yearly and was regarded with approval by the public. This trend became the hallmark of labour relations in the Soviet Union.

The persisting unwillingness of people in the USSR (and in some Eastern European countries) to work in industry and in agriculture, can be explained only by the continuous attacks on the work ethic in the Soviet state. The legacy of the proletarian revolution should be taken into account in the analysis of the transition to market relations and the change to organic economic stimuli to work.

One must also keep in mind that the epoch of world communism was not over in 1949 when the Communist International was officially dissolved. In some form, it persisted until 1985. The doctrine of the world revolution continued to have an impact on the problems of work stimuli and social policies in the USSR. In spite of the huge gap in the economic potential between the USSR and the US, and between the East and the West, the maintenance of nuclear parity exhausted the material resources of the country. In fact, the vital needs of the people were sacrificed to maintain the arms race. This led to the decrease in living standards, to the total disintegration of the entire social fabric, and to paradoxes in the area of labour relations. Official ideology claimed that the socialist principle of payment according to work was fulfilled in the country. In fact, the situation was exactly the reverse. Many industrial enterprises – in fact, whole branches of the national economy – were in a way drawn into a permanent slowdown. The existing system, as if intentionally, prevented people from normal labour – and it succeeded.

At a certain stage of historical development, the situation could only lead to a revolution against the totalitarian regime and to its collapse. In the different countries of Eastern Europe, the force of the explosion turned out to be in proportion to the volume of pressure exerted and to the level of social tensions.

2   Challenges for the Future

An extremely complicated task for the Soviet Union now, is to manage the transition from economic compulsion to economic stimuli to work. It implies that the structure of labour relations will be turned upside down. Otherwise, it will be impossible to satisfy the vital needs of the population and to wake it up to economic, social, and civil life.

Let us dwell upon two aspects of the transition from non-economic compulsion to market-economic relations: the development of a mixed economy, and the spiritual and moral renaissance of the nation.

Only free labour can be efficient and productive. It means a complete and consistent elimination of state monopoly and the free development of all forms of property. Only then will the alienation of peasants and workers from work, and from decision-making, cease. Only then will men of science, men of letters, and artists stop being the employees of the state and instead become its free partners.

A worker must own the goods and services he produces and be in charge of them. He is the one to decide what to produce, how to do it, where to sell, and at what price. Naturally, he is to pay taxes to the state that provides environmental protection and control, and health care. All types of property should be made equal. Raw materials should be sold at the same price to anyone. Otherwise, it is impossible to achieve market competition. We need a mixed economy: state, cooperative, and private enterprises, as well as joint ventures.

Nowadays, professionals write a lot on the necessity to change property relations to increase labour productivity. The problem of the relationship between the different types of property and the development of democracy, is sometimes ignored. Pluralism in politics gains momentum when it is based upon interest. And interest, in turn, is based upon property. That is why, when independent farmers grow in number, the political scene is sure to change; from then on, political parties representing them will emerge. The same is true of the cooperative movement, of industrial workers, and of white-collar employees, i.e. of all social layers of Soviet society.

Economic independence is the core of democracy. If a person is not his/her own master, he/she cannot have a feeling of being someone. But when one becomes master of one's own fate, and of one's own property, one is sure to acquire this feeling. Then, the platform of political leaders will be analysed and evaluated by one's own interests and aims.

However, it would be a mistake to limit the problem of the transition from non-economic labour relations based upon direct violence and brutal force to a change in the forms of property alone. Moral and spiritual aspects are no less important. The violent rupture of ties with one's own spiritual heritage, the attempt to twist or falsify them which are so typical of periods of revolutionary transformations, come close to a national catastrophe. The period of recovery can be long and painful, since the loss of self-esteem and self-conscience cannot be regained soon. Meanwhile, years of official propaganda, of attacks on the past as well as on the present, could only create a vacuum which must be filled.

One of the traditional patterns of analysis in the search for the roots of Stalinism goes back to the time of Ivan the Terrible. It is easy to say that violence has always persisted in the history of this country. The Russians cannot have it any other way. However, in my opinion, this thesis requires better substantiation in terms of systematic cross-national historical evidence.

As for the growth of bitterness and violence in this population, it must be regretfully admitted that we lead the world top on that score. What are the roots of this trend? It is not easy to find the answer. However, when we speak about Russia, we must bear in mind that the thin layer of Christian moral values helped, for centuries, to preserve morals, conquering "the beast" in the human being. When this layer was destroyed ardently and with enthusiasm, when the cult of violence won, and when everything sacred was desecrated, there was not much human left.

Moreover, the problem of re-education was fast and intense. One of the teaching methods was the schizophrenic idea of being surrounded by enemies, be it through fratricidal civil war, during the great purge, or through the unbearable brutality and injustice of World War II. During these experiences, a man was treated like an insect that could be done away with at any moment. Only bitterness could grow from this cult of violence and terror.

Recently, a demarcation line began to separate Soviet social scientists. Some prioritize economic change. Others regard political changes in the direction of democracy to be most important. A third group insists that moral values make up the core of the problem.

Some argue that the main thing is to have a good and conscientious leader. Nothing else matters. It cannot be denied that much depends upon the moral standards of the leader. In particular, this becomes true in a strictly centralized system where the attitudes of the leader can shape the attitude and moral standards of the whole society. But it is a mistake to think that it is the best one who gains power. Such an idea can be harmful for society.

Another trend which recently has grown noticeably is to reject the importance of economic stimuli. It is sometimes said that if the vital human needs are satisfied in this country, it will become evident how little material incentives matter. It is not by chance that these notions persist. In a way, they reflect the current state of society at large. Low wages and empty shops have helped to make workers indifferent to the small wage increase they can actually get. When the market will be filled with goods, the material stimuli will work with an intensity one cannot imagine today.

At the same time, the problem cannot be oversimplified and reduced to material values and interests alone. People are not indifferent to the type of society they live in, i.e. to its aims – and to what they and their children can expect for the future. As has been mentioned already, civil and social ideals can be based upon moral values only. In this sense, they provide the foundation for the organization of work, for discipline, and the quality of labour – and they become an important stimulus for the latter. However, violence and compulsion can eliminate this stimulus.

To become active and conscientious workers and citizens, people need to regain faith in social and political institutions and believe that they function in the interest of the nation, and not against it. An individual cannot secure his/her sovereignty, the right to self-fulfilment, and self-development unless his/her rights are guaranteed and protected against violence – either from the authorities or from a party, be it at the state or at the local level.

In the history of this country, waves of violence, starting with the Civil War of 1918, have always created an atmosphere of violence so intense that it has been dangerous, not only for ourselves, but for all mankind. It is this experience of violence transmitted over generations, and not the political naivety of (temporary) unofficial leaders, that presents a threat for the whole society. Ideological facets may differ, but all of them are dreadful because of the suicidal brutality towards people and towards nature. This is the terrible legacy of the past that we have inherited. The sooner we get rid of it, the more reason we shall have to believe that society is on its way to recovery and to regaining normal stimuli to life and to work.

Notes

1 This chapter was prepared within the framework of the *All Academic Programme "Man, Science, Society"*.
2 Report to the XIIIth. Congress of RKP(bO): 40.
3 Report to the IXth. Congress of RKP(bO): 94.

References

Anderson, B. A., Silver, B. D. (1985) 'Demographic Analysis and Population Catastrophes in the USSR', *Slavic Review* 44 (Fall).
Conquest, R. (1974) *The Great Terror*. Florence: Aurora Edizione.
Lenin, V. I. (1958-65) *Polnoe Sobranie* (Complete Works). Moscow: Gospolitizdat, Vol. 41.
Marx, K., Engels, F. (1960-62) *Sobranie* (Collected Works). Moscow: Gospolitizdat, Vol. 19.
Marx, K., Engels, F. (1960-62) *Sobranie* (Collected Works). Moscow: Gospolitizdat, Vol. 23.
Plehanov, G. V. (1926) *Collected Works*. Moscow-Leningrad, Vol. XIII.
IX. Congress of RKP(bO) (1960) *Report*. Moscow: Politizdat Publishers.
XIII. Congress of RKP(bO) (1963) *Report*. Moscow: Politizdat Publishers.

CHAPTER 9

Perestroika in Light of Public Opinion 1991

Tatiana Zaslavskaya

1   The Present Stage of Perestroika

Five years ago, a new stage in the development of the USSR began. It has been referred to as *perestroika*. By the extent to which it has pervaded public life, by the depth and historic significance of the reforms being instituted, perestroika may doubtlessly be compared with the October Revolution of 1917. The main objective of perestroika was to turn our society away from the blind alley of so-called "real socialism" to the broad way of development trodden by other countries – in other words, to return Soviet society to the general values of humane civilization.

Five years of perestroika have clearly demonstrated that not only the system of the economic control, as it was previously believed, but the entire politico-social system of society should be dismantled. It has also clearly demonstrated that the key to this dismantling lies, first of all, in the political sphere. Indeed, whatever radical new laws the Supreme Soviets of the USSR might pass, the ruling class – State and Party nomenclature – would always prevent their coming into effect. Therefore, only a radical restructuring of the whole sphere of political power might really open a way to new forms of economic activity.

The most striking feature of the present stage of perestroika is the spontaneous and uncontrollable transition of the "reform initiated from above" into a "revolution from below". This transition manifests itself by two main facts: firstly, in the intensifying processes of redistribution of economic wealth and political power; and secondly, in that the initiative of changes has clearly gone over from the narrow circle of political leaders to the increasingly activated masses. *As a result, social processes, which have earlier run according to scenarios of the Communist Party leadership, more and more frequently break loose, assuming unexpected, sometimes even dangerous forms. The originally slow pace of events is piling up on one another like ice blocks during a violent ice drift, thus making the steering of perestroika more and more complicated.*

The other important feature of the situation is that the economic, political, and social relations that were historically welded into a single (though quite inefficient) system are now disintegrating, while the new social system, which has to replace the old one, is only just being formed. As a consequence, a multitude of complicated social problems arise. Thus, the volume of national income and of buying power have been decreasing. Daily goods are getting more and more scarce, and there are exasperatingly long queues. Redundancies in industry, administrative apparatus, and army lead to both structural and regional unemployment. As a result, more than 90 per cent of the population appears to be extremely worried and are now unsure of their future.

The main factor that has aroused this feeling of insecurity, is the fall in the standard of living for the majority of the population. Our Centre for Public Opinion Studies regularly asks people what problem they consider to be the most acute. In 1988, answering this question, people named first of all the scarcity of food and industrial goods in shops. Two years later – that is in 1990 – this problem was indicated by only 12 per cent of respondents; while the problem of inflation and prices and income cuts was nominated by 34 per cent and came to the forefront, reflecting insufficiency in people's means of living. This conclusion is proved by the fact that, two years ago, the statements, "We never have enough money" and "We just have enough for bare necessities" were choosen by one third of all respondents. But now the share of such answers has risen to one half. Less than one fifth of those surveyed believe that "such people as themselves have favourable conditions to increase their incomes".

Perestroika processes affect not only the lower strata of society, but also its upper, privileged layers: because it is sweeping away many of their socio-economic and political privileges. This concerns first of all high-ranking officials of the Party and State apparatus, ideologists and teachers of Marxism-Leninism, persons in the military-industrial complex, those engaged in retail trade, dealers in the "moonlight" economy, and some others. Perestroika is threatening to reduce their political influence, to diminish their incomes, to deteriorate their way of life, and to lower their social prestige.

Naturally enough, this stimulates those behaviours which tend to slow down social changes undesirable for influential groups – and the forms of behaviour hindering perestroika are highly diverse. They range from concealment of day-to-day goods from the people to organization of political strikes and to fomenting violent inter-ethnic conflicts. The main result of such forms and behaviour, is the growing disruption of the economy, the mounting fatigue and exasperation of the population, and sprees of different forms of crime. *Thus, the five-year experience of perestroika has clearly shown that to wake up the indifferent "hibernating" people is not enough at all. Not less important (and much more difficult) is to regulate the behaviour of those who have been "awakened" but who have neither time nor possibility to orient themselves within the new reality.*

It is quite clear that, in order to control the radical transformation of society, one should have the reliable knowledge of public opinion about this complex and dangerous process. Let me begin with public opinion on the acute political questions.

2   Public Opinion on Political Changes

The political aspect of perestroika means the transition of Soviet society from the totalitarian regime based on the monopolist power of the Communist Party, to the democratic system of management. To fulfil this aim, it is necessary, first, to transform the unitary state – the USSR – into a free confederation of politically independent and sovereign republics; second, to transform the CPSU (i.e. Communist Party of the Soviet Union) from a ruling to a parliamentary type of party and to introduce a multi-party system; third, to create in our country a civilized legal state with thorougly separated legislative, executive, and judicial powers.

It is quite apparent that these tasks may be realized only under condition of a sincere support of the people. But one of the peculiar features of the present situation in the USSR, is the very low confidence of the population in the institutions of political power. As a matter of fact, five years of perestroika and *glasnost* have exerted a tremendous influence on public consciousness. The difficult but glorious 70-year historical road trodden by Soviet society, now appears to the people in the most critical light. They faint about the cruel terror, mass repressions, and enormous number of human victims on one side of the scales; and about the technological backwardness plus the extreme poverty of their society on the other side – which could not keep the scales balanced. Hence the insistently arising question of who is to be blamed. As our polls have shown, the people's answer is that the guilty were the Communist Party and the Soviet Government, who chose and led the wrong way. Therefore, it is not suprising that only less than 20 per cent of all people express complete confidence in the Soviet Goverment, while more than one fourth of them has no confidence in it.

However, the most important shift in social consciousness is a precipitous fall in the social prestige of the Communist Party. In the poll conducted some months ago, 81 per cent of those surveyed stated that the prestige of the CPSU dropped; and only 6 per cent said that it rose. Only 14 per cent of the population reported to have complete confidence in the CPSU, whereas 42 per cent had no confidence at all. The lack of confidence in the Communist Party is associated with the fact that people hold it responsible for the present social crises. When asked who is the first to be blamed for the distressing social situation, 94 per cent indicated the Communist Party of the USSR. About two thirds of the respondents believe that "the Party has lost the initiative, the events getting out of its control" (49%) and that it "hinders the process of democratic reforms" (14%). More than one half of those polled in August 1990 consider that the CPSU should not play the ruling role in Societ society.

The loss of confidence in political institutions is an extremely important factor hindering perestroika in economic relations. Indeed, to take the country out of the economic crisis, drastic, often unpopular measures are needed. But the leadership may take such steps only if it enjoys the people's confidence. If there is no such confidence, any steps leading to the lowering of the people's standard of living may result – and really do result – in strikes, riots, blockades and other forms of extremist behaviour.

The other very painful spot for political life in the USSR is without a doubt, inter-ethnic conflict. The situation in this sphere is rapidly becoming more and more complex. The surveys conducted within the last two years showed that different nationalities held fundamentally different opinions of what the optimal organization of national relations should be. Thus, the majority of Russians were striving to retain the unitary state with a common economy and a centralized political authority. The dominant orientations of the Baltic peoples were the complete independence of the republics and political secession from the Soviet Union. Similar moods existed in the Western Ukraine and in Moldavia, while most of Armenians would like to stay in the Soviet Union provided that the economic and cultural independence of their constituent republic would be significantly increased.

The opinions of various peoples about the principles of settlement of inter-eth-nic conflicts, were also widely divergent. In one of the polls, we asked the question, "What should be taken primarily into consideration in settling inter-ethnic conflicts?" In reply, the population of the Russian Federation rated above all the interests of the Soviet state. The citizens of the Baltic Republics stressed the interests of the native population; the Armenians, the historical rights of nations to control certain territories; and the Ukrainians, the necessity of reaching the compromise of interests.

However, the last few years have brought about radical changes in the situation. Indeed, the Supreme Soviets of all the republics of the USSR declared their sovereignty and political independence. It means that radically new relations are to be developed and fixed into the new Union Treaty. The necessity for the conclusion of such a new Treaty was noted by 56 per cent of the respondents. But only one third of them believed that it would be possible to keep all the republics in the USSR. The much more probable situation would be the plurality of approaches and decisions of different republics. Thus, some of them might unite in close federation; others, desiring more independence, might become members of a con-federation; while a third group could be members of a free association of completely independent states. Right now, the public opinion on these problems is deeply polarized. For example, 45 per cent of those polled support the possibility of secession of certain republics from the USSR, while 39 per cent held a completely opposite view. Thus, the inter-ethnic relations will remain a difficult and painful problem for many years.

3   Public Opinion on Economic Reform

The main problem of planned economy, I believe, is the absence of adequate incentives for workers and employees to work efficiently. The radical changing of this situation is the first and main aim of the necessary economic reform. The programme of such a reform worked out by Academician Shatalin's group, and being intensively discussed in the USSR, includes such radical measures as (a) getting rid of state ownership of the means of production, (b) demonopolization of the economy, (c) instituting private property, (d) encouraging of all kinds of enterpreneurial activities, (e) development of market relations and competition, and (f) providing strong economic incentives for intensive and effective functioning of all branches of the economy.

In practice, however, the realization of economic reforms appeared to be one of the most complicated elements of perestroika. The passing of the necessary laws in the Supreme Soviet of the USSR, and especially their practical implementation, were hampered by the resistance of an unexpectedly wide circle of both open and hidden opponents. Many such opponents maintain that the Soviet people are not yet prepared to adopt private ownership of production or market relations. And it will take a long time to get them prepared.

To check this very important statement, our Centre conducted some polls about the economic reform. They showed that the idea of variety of forms of ownership, which has been widely discussed by the mass media, has penetrated the public consciousness rather deeply and is now shared by most of the people. Thus, 70 per cent of the respondents approved setting up enterprises that would belong to or would be leased by those engaged in them. Almost the same part of the population supports joint ventures with foreign companies; 45 per cent approve incorporated enterprises; and more than one third, purely foreign firms acting in the USSR.

People's attitudes towards private ownership are not so straightforward. To the direct question of what their reaction would be to enterprises owned by individuals, only one fourth of the respondents answered "positive", while two fifths answered "negative". But to a more specific question as to which branches of economy should require or at least admit private enterprises, over three quarters named such spheres as agriculture and agricultural production processing; 60 per cent, light industry; almost one half, medical service and school education. About half of the population believe that the emergence of private enterprises will improve the economic situation in the country. And only 10 per cent were convinced that it would mean the rejection of socialist achievements and therefore could not be allowed. These data make an important argument for admitting Shatalin's programme of an accelerated privatization of the means of production and the decisive introduction of the market economy.

The general attitude of the respondents towards entrepreneurship is also rather positive, especially with respect to agriculture. The various forms of land ownership transferred to peasants, are endorsed by almost four fifths of the population, with those supporting the plans to give peasants the inherited ownership of land being 54 per cent. About one third believe that peasants should be given the right to buy and sell land, as well as to have hired workers.

A no less important and interesting question is, how widespread among the respondents are orientations for their own involvement in entrepreneurship. It is generally believed that the entrepreneurial "vein" of the Russian people is as good as dead, that nowadays "nobody in the USSR wishes anything", and only very few people are ready to work hard in order to achieve a higher standard of living. An attempt to check this statement has yielded an entirely unexpected result, which has refuted the common belief. It has turned out that almost one third of the respondents would not mind starting their own business. In rural areas, the picture is even better: nearly two fifths would like to work on their own farms; and another 14 per cent would not mind thinking about it at a later time, now assuming a wait-and-see attitude.

It goes without saying that far from all the people who generally approved private farms are ready to become independent farmers themselves. Eight per cent responded that they cannot do it only because there was no appropriate law (which had not yet been adopted at the time of the poll). But the remaining respondents have expressed their distrust of the state, which always used to annul its own earlier decisions. The results of these surveys have been intensively discussed and used in drafting Soviet laws on land ownership.

4   Public Opinion on Social Shifts

The major social issues of Soviet society are as follows: a too-deep differentation of socio-economic status of various social groups; extremely poor living conditions for a significant part of the population; and the fact that the people have completely lost their faith in the justice of the socialist system. Let me take, for example, public opinion about the income distribution system. Less than 3 per cent of the respondents consider it to be just; 45 per cent, only partially just; and 53 per cent, completely unjust. These data strongly manifest that the people are alienated from the social system, which appeared to be incapable of securing even the most elementary conditions of their daily life.

In this situation, the government cannot count upon serious support by the people. In order to surmount their alienation, it has to satisfy to a much higher degree the people's need for social justice. This can be done, firstly, by a purposeful shaping of a new system of employment relations, based on a labour market, but including the necessary social guarantees for the population. And secondly, by taking steps to increase protection against inflation and poverty of the poorest groups – such as the unemployed, pensioners, persons with disabilities, the aged and the ailing. A relatively rapid and resolute transition from an administrative to a market-oriented economy will almost inevitably give rise to unemployment. And those first found to be redundant will be women with children, single mothers, persons with disabilities and elderly workers. The threat of at least temporary unemployment, as well as a forced degradation to a lower-paid, less-skilled and less interesting job, is now keenly felt by a significant part of the respondents.

An acute problem is also the deepening of a socio-economic differentation within society. Thus, in 1989, the widening income brackets were noted by two thirds of the respondents. Under the conditions of a diminishing living standard, levelling views have become more widespread. Many people believe that, once the society has hard times, all groups have to suffer equally. Hence there is a disapproving attitude towards a rapid growth of incomes of those linked to new forms of the economy, along with demands to withdraw all socio-economic privileges of the élite groups. There is also a positive attitude towards various forms of food rationing (about 60 per cent support the introduction of food ration cards) and the approval of the progressive income taxation system, and so on.

The studies that have been done so far show that about one third of the population hold the levelling views, two fifths approve of the income distribution according to labour input, and only about one quarter believe that it is just to encourage efficient business activities. In the years to come, an increasingly larger part of individual incomes will be formed on market and business principles which are considered by most people to be unjust. This might become yet another factor for growing social tensions.

Summing up, I would like to note that, historically, the radical transformation of economic and social relations in the USSR has no alternative. It should be realized and it will be realized. The real question is, in what time and at what social price should it be done? I believe that one of the main conditions for perestroika's success is the confidence of the people in its very idea. The trouble is, that the public consciousness of the Soviet people is at present rather marginal; it is unstable, morbidly sensitive and explosive. Many people are tired of the total deficit of goods and disappointed with the results of five years of perestroika. Thus, being asked about these results, they nominated first of all the increasing uncertainty of people about their future (more than 40%), the crisis of inter-ethnic relations (37%), the dismantling of the whole system of management (32%), and the economic crisis (29%). They consider that the most probable changes in the national economy in the next year will be a further rise in these problems (83%). No more optimistic are the forecasts for political changes: 74 per cent of respondents expect a further growth of political tensions. My point of view is that the social pessimism of practically all groups within the population is a direct consequence of the uncertain and therefore ineffective policy of perestroika's leaders, including Mikhail Gorbachov. Verbally, they are making a revolution, but actually, they are afraid of any profound social changes.

One of the recent examples of such behaviour on Gorbachov's part was connected with the programme of economic reform. The radical variant of this programme was approved by the Supreme Soviet of the Russian Federation and by many People's Deputies of the USSR. But Mikhail Gorbachov, who previously had also preferred this variant of the programme, unexpectedly torpedoed it at the session of the Supreme Soviet. Naturally, this does not add to his popularity. In the last two or three months, the rating of Gorbachov was lowering, while Yeltsin was becoming more popular. Thus, in August 1990, we asked people whose position they supported to a greater extent – Gorbachov's or Yeltsin's. Fifty-two per cent of those surveyed answered that they supported Yeltsin more; and only 21 per cent, Gorbachov. Sixty-nine per cent of the respondents evaluated the results of the first six months of Gorbachov's activity in the economy as president of the USSR as bad or as very bad. In the sphere of inter-ethnic relations, this percentage was 62. So, the situation is becoming critical.

The only decision which can really stabilize the situation is getting rid of doubts and uncertainty and beginning a practical realization of Shatalin's programme aimed at radical democratization of social, economic and political life. Of course, in this case, society will have a rather hard time; but nowadays it already has it, and the situation is worsening. Thus, society has to choose between hard times with a hope for better times, and hard times without such hope. A great many people understand this choice and support the radical transition of the national economy. The number of supporters of Shatalin's programme, among those surveyed, is three times larger than the number of its opponents. And the supporters of this programme are ready to bear some difficulties in order "to earn" the chance to live better and happier then they are doing now. I am sure that this readiness should be utilized.

Chapter 10

Economy, Policy and Welfare in Transition

Jan Hartl
Jiri Vecerník

1 Introduction

There is a wealth of literature dealing with the general character of the Eastern European "socialist" countries. A smaller part is devoted to empirical analyses and to the assessment of their economic performance. The major part deals with the political and ideological features of these societies, while social policy remains in the background. We shall try to show some of the roots of the present dilemmas, and the future prospects of social welfare in Eastern Europe, with the Czechoslovak experience in mind. We believe that Czechoslovakia, once characterized as a "desperately sterile, entropic society" (Brooks, 1990), can serve as a good case in the study of the transition towards a new type of society in Eastern Europe – due to its rich historical past, to the turmoil of current reforms, and to the challenge of the present revolution.

In a way we are reinventing our historical past – flying backward with an attempt to preserve dignity (cf. Enquist, 1984). The past with a "democratic, developed society, in which Masaryk fused nationalism and social reform", thus introducing "the tradition of democratic humanism, a heritage for which no other East European country had an equivalent" (Griffith, 1967: 18, 20) may have a motivating power. The task of reconstituting civil society in our modern and diversified world, however, poses a whole set of unprecedented problems. This is exactly a situation which may enhance the danger of short-term approaches – and of simplistic, narrow-minded solutions.

We are left with an imperfect society, with the remnants of "the sterility of dogmatism, the inertia of the ideological economy, and the monopoly of power" (Djilas, 1969: 262). The obstacles to growth which have piled up in the recent past are looming today as large as they did 20 years ago. Certainly we have the idea of a market economy, the newly-found respect for the laws of supply and demand,

and the total downgrading of central planning. And the transition takes place under conditions where we talk much more of contraction of social programmes than of their expansion (Miller, 1988: 371).

2   The Revolving Reality: On Continuity and Change

Revolutionary movements in a majority of Eastern European countries have entirely changed the political scene. The changes of a formerly rigid political system are quite obvious – although we know only the first steps of a very immature democracy. The progress in the economic sphere is rather slow and full of tensions, heavily loaded with the legacy of the former state-centralist practice and of the still prevalent centralist psychology. The former centralist, rigid, monolithic system undoubtedly killed human initiative, violated essential rights, and thus destroyed both civil society and the economy. The heritage of the past is not only manifested in a rundown institutional societal base and in the social-psychological sphere: namely, in historically fixed and routinized patterns of behaviour which express the general decay of social norms and values such as solidarity, cooperativeness, help, care, social concern, devotion, morality or initiative. It would be far too easy to dismiss this legacy with a light heart as something which violated basic human rights and expectations, as something unnatural and, in a way, "non-existent". The period of state socialism represents an indisputable social fact – a historical gap which is difficult to surmount. Obviously, there are no immediate and easy solutions. And they are definitely not as simple as one may be tempted to believe when reading the daily newspaper. The Czechoslovak transition is oriented by three forces: 1) the example and practice of developed Western countries, with the USA on the one side and Scandinavia on the other; 2) a nostalgic memory of our own prosperous capitalist democratic system; 3) the state-centralist, institutional, as well as social-psychological barriers to social change: to inequality, promotion, the individualist ethos, etc. We often speak of an unprecedented transition, of unexpected difficulties, of an immense challenge. With a bit of scepticism, we might as well point to the fact that the new phenomena of democracy, pluralism, liberation, etc. may in fact be a revitalization of historical concepts, an adoption of foreign experience and the result of large-scale European cultural transfers.

The continuity of social development was already disrupted 40 years ago. The present quest for radical social change imposes a whole series of questions: how much can we rely on common sense, and how much on science, in this unprecedented situation? Are we really constructing a new type of social reality? What are the overall strategy and the principles upon which we can rely? With our social experience, how do we cope with such dilemmas as individualism vs. collectivism, or autonomy vs. social control, in a given historical context? What material, human, and social resources are available? How do we discern the elements of ideology and reality? Most probably, we shall try to find the answers to these questions for years; and for years, we will be puzzled by the phenomena of general social paralysis.

The real problem is not whether we are sufficiently critical towards the past. The crucial concepts are those relating to the future. Our first experiences are controversial – fraught with irrational, time-consuming disputes, hidden personal ambitions, and the pure power game. When trying to be objective, we have to acknowledge that even "neutral" notions such as prosperity, efficiency, and even social security have their specific historical connotations. And we must admit that our "scientific" knowledge of these phenomena is far from being comprehensive, in spite of the abundant empirical evidence on the last 20 years barely utilized up to now. Therefore, a thorough analysis of the *ancien régime* is vital not only for a deeper understanding, but also for practical steps towards social change.

The revolution of November 1989 has completely changed our political scene. It gave rise to new forms of political life and brought about a whole wave of euphoria, hopes, and expectations in the social sphere in general. It put an end to the routinized schedule of political obedience and to private passive resistance. However, the euphoria is only a temporary phenomenon. And the expectations are to be met in a complex process of political struggle and economic reform.

It would be rather short-sighted to expect that the pure expression of beliefs and attitudes of people, together with the removal of the main political obstacles, would be sufficient to reshape our social reality. In one opinion, there are two interrelated obstacles to this progress:

1) The so-called "socialist revolution" of the late 1940s disrupted continuous social and economic development and finally created a tremendous developmental gap. The impasse of history which was often presented as an "organic unity of social- ist virtues and achievements of the scientific and technological revolution" (R. Richta) in fact meant the wholesale exploitation of social potentials and re- sources. The introduction of totalitarian socialist elements into political, economic, and cultural life resulted in general stagnation. The disrupted continuity of social development damaged the social transfer of values, norms, and motives; and it diluted social networks, community ties, family relations, and private initiative.

   Although the social discontinuity is obvious, we rarely fully admit the fact that even such economic terms as "market", "private ownership and property", "efficiency" and others are linked to a social and cultural tradition, that they have their own social content and meaning. In fact, they require a stable normative system as well as a continuity in cultural transfers.

2) It cannot be pretended that there is no heritage of "real socialism". Nor would it be fair to state that the socialist practice was harmful to all groups of the population. And it brought about something that we may call an ideological consensus. Everything that seems rather strange today – the consent of people,

the adoption of the *status quo* (with only scarce reservations *ad quem*), the proliferation of mediocrity and hypocrisy, the loss of a long-range horizon for social action and of the motives of people – all that may serve as an indication of a new quality of social reality. These results of "real socialism" should be taken as social facts in a Durkheimian sense. At least two generations of people with their everyday conceptions of life, and with their systems of instrumental and terminal values, were confronted with direct control in all spheres of their life. This control hid the existence of a strong verticality of social positions and of limited access to social promotion. All official slogans, however, heralded the exact opposite. Skidders represented a significant group in our socio-political past, while moonlighters could serve as an example of a desperate quest for a better economic future.

In this context, we should note that the sphere of social policy was presented as a primary concern for "socialism" and as a real achievement leading towards a new kind of just society. In fact, this "primary concern" represented a restful, comfortable, and indolent conception of social security, and sometimes even a system of overprotection. The ideal of social equality, which was probably valued as high as in Scandinavia (cf. Logue, 1987), resulted in a shabby egalitarian system with a high degree of general uniformity. And even the positive aspects of the welfare system were flawed.

Social policy at any given time reflects its broader social context. This context represents an interwoven net of social, cultural, and economic standards and possibilities consisting of human values, the heritage of the past, and the attitudes, beliefs, and interests of previous generations. And in a certain sense, our evaluation of the present reflects not only our history and our current potential, but also our conception about the future. Social policy thus expresses an existing standard of economic development and follows the path of the social and cultural history of the nation, acting as a strong agent on the political scene, which tries to balance controversial social interests and to mitigate social conflict.

We may point to a long history of social policy in pre-war Czechoslovakia. Social policy soon became a hot topic in our social thinking. Early scholarly works on social policy appeared around the turn of the century, and many others followed – especially during the 1920s. The main principles of our social policy were theoretically expressed during that 10-year period, and some of the principles were already implemented during the 1930s. It can be proved that at this time the Czechoslovak approach served as an example for other countries, e.g. Sweden or France. One example is the idea spelt out as early as 1919, which described welfare pluralism as a mixture of state, corporate, and private organizations and institutional networks of both a formal and informal character (Engliš, 1921).

The real achievements, measures, and solutions in social policy were always a subject of political struggle. As early as in 1923, one of our scholars complained that "a lot of things in the sphere of social policy which actually should be purely social or economic topics, in reality represent a very sensitive *politicum* that makes things uneasy and lengthy and is harmful to both the worker and the industry as a whole" (Verunáč, 1923). Although the theoretical approach at that time could serve as a leading example, the practical results were controversial and corresponded to the political situation. The system generally aimed at mitigating social inequality. The real benefits were, however, limited to some social and occupational groups. Still, within the social consciousness, this past remains an ideal, a reminder of an emerging and rapidly-lost welfare state.

After the war, there was a period which promised to fulfil the pre-war ideas of a welfare state. After the communist *coup d'état,* welfare was declared to be the centrepiece in the strategy of social and economic development. The system of general national insurance was introduced in 1948, together with universal maternity benefits. There was a striking development in female employment which paved the way for gender emancipation. In the first stage of socialist development there was an unprecedented expansion of the public sector – not only in production, but also in social services and social care in general. Some of the social-political solutions were rather short-sighted, though progressive at the time of their introduction. In retrospective, we would probably point out that economic growth was extensive, and that our welfare system required growing public expenditures. The remarkable growth of the number and the capacity of crèches and kindergartens did not in reality help the family, but rather only the extensive growth in employment – which further decreased the productivity of labour. Moreover, considering the economic results, the system was very expensive. Thus one could expect the inevitable deterioration of the whole system in some time. With a little license, we might say that the welfare system at that time had more of an ideological and political than a practical and human significance.

The system did not prove to be dynamic enough. Given the substantial intervention into traditional family and social life, social benefits and services were soon considered as simple and undisputable rights of the citizens, and an obvious obligation of the state. The postwar enthusiasm was slowly fading away, putting the traditional socialist concepts of equality and emancipation into a light of scepticism. The welfare system, providing a certain level of security, further contributed to income levelling. It is not necessary today to repeat all the well-known problems of bureaucratic management, of the neglect of our traditional democratic principles, and the trends towards the general uniformity of society. Neither the disorganized production, nor distribution and redistribution, had any development potential. They did not have stimulating and motivating effects and finally resulted in the prodigious passivity and resignation of the majority of the population.

The situation in the 1950s brought about significant social, economic, and political changes. In the political sphere, the well-known Stalinist principles crippled democratic rules and killed the debates on any broader socio-political and socio-economic topic. The change in structure of our economic system, relying on the key role of heavy industry and stifling the well-developed sector of light industry, caused a high demand for labour. The labour pool was the agrarian population, other groups of self-employed, and women. The orientation of the national budget towards military industry – fuelled by the cold war – strengthened the tendency to neglect social affairs. The official interpretation at that time stated that all social problems are automatically going to be solved by socialist development.

The late 1950s marked the start of a long chain of well-intended – and always unsuccessful – economic reforms. The sorely needed economic reforms gradually disappeared and buried the hopes for social change. For example, the Czechoslovak welfare system never adjusted its benefits to the level of inflation or to the rise of wages. In spite of the general uniformity within society, there was an unexpected diversity in the different benefits for different groups of the population – which were the result of unclear criteria and of the unqualified, purely voluntaristic approach of the state bureaucracy. The amounts of benefits were redefined from time to time – more or less incidentally – through temporary social and political pressures.

Can we really present the general levelling as a success on the road towards social equality? And can we believe that stagnation is social security? Empirical studies show that we are far from both equality and security. What is left is a crippled social body which only slowly is finding the strength to recover.

We often heard about shifting from "social equality" towards "functional differentiation". It was presented as a dilemma of the so-called intensification of economic and social processes. But this concept was just another ideological construct – this time, the concept of "social justice" was temporarily substituted by "ability", "achievement", "meritocracy", etc. It was often pretended that the welfare system is a real success of socialist development and that it represents the crucial interest of the state administration. In fact, it always was a residual category and it played the role of passive spectator. Rigid government institutions rejected even the slightest criticism. With a critical appraisal of our present situation, we must admit that we have not advanced much. Even now, we are playing around with the rather ideological constructs of "ability" and "achievement", hoping that using these words will bring us closer to the West and to "Europe". To dare to speak of social policy, or even of social justice, is seen as a traditional "leftist" deviation – tolerable perhaps in the case of a scholar, but suicide in the case of a politician.

Political transformation is the prerequisite for substantial social change. There are obvious economic barriers to an open market. There is a feeling that the principles of the market are quite natural and that when the market starts functioning, somehow many of the problems of social life will spontaneously cease to exist.

Some sociologists point out, though, that the restoration of the market is not only an economic, but also a complicated socio-cultural problem. The simple solutions of the past – economic matters first and all the rest later – have possibly no great chance to succeed. Certainly there are also rigid social barriers to be overcome, especially in terms of the people's motivation. With our social experience, we can hardly count on the discredited concepts of statism or on the belief that societal reforms will be enacted by the state under the "protective enclosure of institutions" (M. Weber).

3 The Standard of Living Reconsidered: The Shift Towards a Market Economy

In each modern social system, the standard of living of a household depends on three, more or less closely interrelated, areas. One of them is participation in the formal economy, the second is the social redistribution of resources, and the third is the authentic economic activity of the household or family. We should also mention a fourth area, the informal economy, though it has a rather ambiguous character. Until now, this sector operated on the boundary between the formal economy (from which it derived the means of production, materials, and often labour time as well) and the family economy (from which it derived above all human capital, labour time, and motivation).

During the communist period, all three/four sectors have undergone substantial change. The communist system was based on the centrally-planned allocation of labour and the remuneration of work (as concerns the formal economy), on the universality of protection by the paternalistic state (as concerns social welfare), and on relieving the family from household duties. The essential attributes of the communist system were summarized in the notion of "social security", defined as the main advantage of socialist society. It was assumed that only this type of social security represents genuine social progress – which guarantees social equality, emancipation, and space for individual development.

Social security guarantees undoubtedly represented the objective of the labour movement. Socialism was an idea of an alternative (perfect) society with a functioning economy (without crises and failures), and universal social welfare for everyone (without unemployment and injustice). The commitment to so-called social security under real socialism, however, concealed only the strong centralization of political and economic power, as well as the bureaucratic control of individuals. Civil society was swallowed by the system, and this inevitably produced the decline of economic efficiency and the deterioration of social welfare. At present, attempts to conserve acquired social securities contradict efforts aiming at economic prosperity. At the same time, only economic prosperity can ensure social welfare, even in a limited way.

Let us sum up prerequisites of social security in the former system:

1) The bureaucratic system of employment and work implied a policy of full employment, grounded in both the right and the obligation to work. Everything was centrally controlled: from the selection of future workers through qualification and training to their allocation, which involved (to varying degrees, depending on the occupation and the region) the duty to stay in the job. Bureaucratic control also meant the specification of qualification requirements for every job or position, detailed wage tariffs, and rules for the classification of employees.

2) The paternalistic state pretended to assure "optimal conditions" of work and life to everybody, assisting each citizen from cradle to grave. Hence, the massive social intervention into economic policy. The welfare policy was monopolized by the state, producing a centralized and uniform system of benefits, allowances, and pensions. The paternalistic role of the state mixed up the economic and social criteria of distribution. For instance, wage policy, which should be economically based, also fulfilled social functions (following the principle of distribution according to need). The state housing policy, presented as if it were imbued with social concerns, functioned in reality as an economic device for the allocation of the labour force between regions and economic branches.

3) The ideology of the "liberation of the household" implied the full employment of women, presumably promoting their emancipation and the abolition of the differences between men and women. Fragmentary, individualized, and ineffective housework was supposed to be replaced by an integrated, large-scale and highly productive service sector. It was presumed that, in the end, household duties would be removed from the home, and that family housing would be substituted by "hotel-type" housing. The family should be relieved from domestic obligations in order to devote the time to work, to society, and to the (ideologically commanded) education of children. This idea was very soon identified as illusory, but new apartments continued to be built with minimal space for home activities. The same was true for household equipment, which was absolutely neglected.

The ideological model in reality entirely failed, not only economically (to liberate work in the interest of higher efficiency and immediate usefulness for society), but also socially (to secure decent material and social well-being for everybody). What were the real effects of this development?

In the case of work, the right to work was converted – by means of administrative and economic pressure – into the obligation to work, which resulted in indifference towards one's results. Employment and wage policy simultaneously created apparent labour shortage and hidden unemployment. The brutally introduced and extreme employment of women led to, instead of their emancipation, their overwork and exploitation. On the one side, cheap labour supported the technological deterioration of industry and services and also helped the expansion of a useless bureaucratic system. On the other side, the efficiency of employment was low and constantly declining. Bureaucratic control over qualification prerequisites only hid a real misuse of human capital. All wage reforms (aiming at "strengthening the motivational capacity of the wage"), conserved only income levelling.

The paternalist policy of the state negatively affected the motivation for work and, hence, economic performance. It also brought about increasing differences between the active and the non-active population. The policy of social security produced the erosion of the long-term foundation of social security. The differences between families with a different number of children, have further increased. The housing shortage remained constant. Large social, regional, and generational inequalities prevailed in the cost of housing, including the price of new housing.

The liberation of the family from the household duties remained an ideological assumption. Whereas in the West a large service sector has emerged, in socialist Czechoslovakia the service sector was developed only in the first period, and then remained on the same low level. On top of this, an absurd policy of centralization concentrated the service sector (in order to strengthen its "working class character") and limited access to the services. Moreover – because in the services, "women serve women" – it was impossible to harmonize working hours and non-working time.

The excessive overloading of the family by material problems has broken its educational, cultural, and socialization functions. The family was overburdened in the economic area, where it could have been substituted. Simultaneously, in the educational and spiritual areas where the family cannot be replaced, "society" tried to replace it. A large part of the households were not able to get sufficient economic means despite full employment and great time sacrifices. The spiritual functions remained a no-man's land, an area of improvisations and many problems.

The transition means great hopes and big difficulties. The political debates concentrate on the questions of privatization, price liberalization, and other "macro ventures". The problems of the labour market, of the standard of living, of income inequalities and social transfers, are rather secondary to political and economic leaders, even though they are of top importance to the people. The social sciences are not well prepared either to explain the problems which can be expected. Until now, economics and the sociology of inequality were not only neglected, but even intentionally oppressed. The complexity of problems is multiplied by the unprecedented task of restoring the mechanisms of the market in societies where the moral and value systems do not correspond to the market model.

Let us enumerate the main directions of these unprecedented changes:
1) In the area of the *formal economy*, a very difficult transition from the "powerful producer" to the "powerful consumer" is to be accomplished. The centralized

allocation of jobs should stop, and a labour market should emerge. Instead of a uniform wage system, a plurality of earning schedules will soon appear, entailing a considerably increased differentiation. This will produce adverse reactions of workers used up to now to the strict control of incomes and to income limits. Therefore, "securities" which have been until now in the hands of the producers, will be transferred to the consumers as a result of an increased market value of money. At the beginning, most of the consumers will be rather poor and they will not be able to utilize the possibilities of the market.

2) The *social sphere* was officially designated as the main target area. In reality, it will most probably remain a residual one. But now, for the first time, the standard minimal requirements are being met. The minimum wage is being introduced. The valorization of social pension and family benefits is being proposed. We start to talk of a social "safety net" which should protect individuals and families throughout the entire life cycle. And only now do we start to consider means-tested benefits and decentralized social institutions. But just when the new welfare system is discussed, we are threatened by the curtailment of the state budget. The "social net" will face a critical scarcity of resources. We must be prepared for its possible collapse, since absolute poverty will exceed relative poverty, and social measures conceived for a small percentage of households or exceptional individual cases will have to cover large segments of the population.

3) *Family economics* represents a somewhat hidden, though particularly important factor of economic transition. In the past, this sector counterbalanced the shortcomings of the formal economy and represented a considerable source of wealth – if not (for many households) the main instrument for survival. These functions will become more important with growing inflation. Households expect serious financial problems in the near future and will seek different strategies to cope with them. The transitional process will certainly require active strategies on the part of the household, flexible economic behaviour, a diversity of forms of employment, and a mix of activities in the public and private sector. The results of our survey suggest, however, that the households will lean strongly towards passive strategies, expressed in the willingness to economize and to restrict expenses for a limited period of time, while expecting the solution to come "from above" as an automatic outcome of governmental policy (see the Appendix).

Considering the actual state of things, what are the urgently necessary changes to transform the distribution system and to make it transparent?

- *To eliminate the still preserved intermingling of economic and social criteria of distribution.* No effective redistributive policy is possible when state redistribution is omnipresent. No effective social policy is achievable when social aspects are considered as an attribute of all economic decisions. (But even more: the very term "social" is politically biased because, since the 1950s the aim of social justice was replaced by the preservation of political power at any price.)

- *To establish a labour market and abolish purely bureaucratic ways of allocating and rewarding labour.* Its creation, connected with the liberalization of wage arrangements, will bring about new rules of earning differentiation. The role of demographic factors will be reduced and that of the characteristics of the job and of the necessary qualification will increase.
- *To consider the family as an important economic unit,* which affects the economic process in an active way – not only in terms of consumption, but also as producer and mediator of labour force distribution. Socio-economics and social psychology should be taken into account in the economic reform.
- *To acknowledge economic consciousness* as an important factor of the economic situation, both limiting and enhancing the possibility of desirable change. The "objective laws" in Marx's tradition should not only be replaced by Smith's "invisible hand". They should first of all take into account the value context, the normative expectations, the existing and prospective cleavages in the social structure, and the subjective functions of social inequality and social conflict.

4   The Prospect of Pluralism: Self-realization and Security

The past centralization of all social functions clearly underestimated the vital importance of such institutions as the local community and the neighbourhood, of semiformal and informal associations, and also of the family. The family lost some of its functions, but it had to develop a whole range of new social roles within the grey economy, in the general use of time and leisure, and in the network of social relations. The state attempted to take over the provision of care and satisfy the needs of the whole population. This patriarchal function of the state went beyond its economic limits; and moreover, it did not meet the expectations people had. It offered basic security and presented it as a generous state gift, but it deprived the individual of the feeling of responsibility for his/her own life. It hardly offered any choice, narrowed social space, limited individuality, and crippled private initiative. A general levelling of the society left no hope for efficient change and offered no motivating or stimulating potential.

Rapid industrial progress drove the informal sector into the formal sector of professional activities (Robertson, 1982). The formal systems of social security undermined, however, the existing system of social networks. In such a situation, "one of the most attractive possibilities is to decentralize the whole system of delivery service by putting it in the hands of local authorities, who would be completely autonomous" (Andersen, 1984: 137). This is undoubtedly a tempting road towards new forms of social organization and social welfare.

The pluralistic character of our future society could be accompanied by a flexible strategy of welfare, fully acknowledging the existence of the state, the cooperative and the private sectors even in social services. The former welfare system was mainly composed of benefits, loans and supports. The whole sphere of social services has been neglected. In a way, we are trying to establish "a welfare state with greater choices, autonomy, and cooperativeness, where the (legal) informal economy is an important avenue of experimentation and modeling for flexibility, self-help, and solidarity. It is the arena in which a new type of economy and society can be constructed on a smaller scale with less bureaucracy and more self-determination" (Miller, 1988: 372-373).

We believe that the welfare system should be clear and transparent to people, and that even the system of financing social security should be understandable – in other words, that the welfare system should have a subjective meaning to people. In our country, this subjective meaning was already lost in the 1950s, together with the reform of income taxes. The taxes were no longer a source for covering the expenses of pensions, health insurance, and public consumption, but were a simple duty without any destination or recipient. On the other hand, the anonymous, impersonal system of welfare was given by the state as a gift, "free of charge".

The former type of "directive central planning with binding quantitative plan targets and input limitations, with a growing network of material balances, and with strictly-controlled prices" (Hardt, 1982: 9), as well as the system of general social uniformity, is hopefully over – lost in the annals of history. The remnants, however, will survive and, at least in the first phase of the transition, they will influence a new type of social relations. The tradition of state centralism is very strong, and the political leaders are tempted to "cut short" the thorny way to pluralism and democracy by a tough centralist approach. On the other hand, the comfortable concept of an average living standard for an average work effort may put a barrier to economic inequality and functional differentiation. The process of privatization in our complex situation can hardly be just and generally approved. There was a strong debate on "cleaning of dirty money" in the privatization process. Perhaps in an exaggerated way, the debate revealed that the advantages obtained in the totalitarian past could be legitimized and capitalized.

There is no alternative to a pluralistic society. The former bureaucratic, monolithic state apparatus was completely discredited and meant no future for the people. The process of decentralization is inescapable. However, there is still alive in the minds of the people and in the practice of social institutions and organizations, of economic enterprises, and of political parties and movements, the tradition of a strong hierarchy and vertical positions, of onedimensional communication and responsibility. Almost everybody expects directives "from above", from some kind of authority – at least as a sign of approval. Spontaneous, authentic, autonomous human initiative is limited; and a general mistrust towards everything and everybody is prevailing, especially in smaller towns and in the countryside. The revolutionary atmosphere of solidarity, harmony, and concord is slowly fading away. Evidently, a reawakened conscience could not slide back into totalitarianism again, but it could quite well finish with our traditional escapism, heralded by the good soldier Svejk.

The new future opens new possibilities, new chances for an exchange of ideas, and chances for a much more diversified social space. Political liberty, as well as cultural activity, will be expressed through a plurality of views, attitudes, and interests. There is a general belief in economic individualism which is seen as juxtaposed to rigid statism. It is not quite sure if this plea for individualism also includes increasing inequality, widening social distances, and the creation of social barriers. Public opinion surveys rather point to a prevailing tendency to egalitarianism, although the recent results show a considerable variance, indicating a possible redefinition of traditional "socialist" concepts. And it is completely unclear how much differentiation and diversity, in spite of their willingness to share in the costs, may be tolerated by the people in the sphere of social services and social care.

Egalitarianism was undoubtedly controversial, yet it represented a source of social security for the majority of the population. Equality for a long time was the only highly appreciated social value. In this way, egalitarianism was consensual and solidaristic (Einhorn, 1987: 218). It is not easy to predict how much the desire for pluralism and individualism is a reaction to the former totalitarian system, and how much it is a real retreat from the values of collectivism and equality.

Together with Svetlik, we may sum up three strategies of the transition towards a new type of Eastern European democratic society:
1) decentralization;
2) de-etatization;
3) marketization.
But even these strategies show no easy solution. For example "decentralization is not a guarantee for de-etatization ... Instead of having one centralized state bureaucracy which would control the welfare system, tens or even hundreds of them were developed at the local level" (Svetlik, 1988: 333).

Existing welfare mixes in the West are the result of social tradition, of the existing balance between supply and demand, of a wide social field of individual choice, and of a developed network of formal institutions and of semiformal and informal associations. The role of the state in the welfare mix is clearly dominant, all other forms are merely complementary. In our situation, the formal, semiformal, and informal systems are to be formed anew or at least have to be revitalized. The whole process of social and economic transition provides a chance to introduce a system of welfare policy into all sectors of the national economy and at the macro, meso, and micro levels of social organization. This is also a chance to overcome the historical gap and to preserve the sense of social security.

References

Andersen, B. R. (1984) *Rationality and Irrationality of the Nordic Welfare State*. Daedalus, 113, No.1: 109.
Brooks, J. (1990) 'The Cleansing Edge of Laughter', *The Independent* 20 (1).
Djilas, M. (1969) *The Imperfect Society: Beyond the New Class*. New York: Harcourt-Brace.
Einhorn, E. S.(1987) 'Economic Policy and Social Needs: The Recent Scandinavian Experience', *Scandinavian Studies* 59: 203.
Engliš, K. (1921) *Sociální politika*. Praha: F. Topič.
Enquist, P. O. (1984) *The Art of Flying Backward with Dignity*. Daedalus, 113, No.1: 61.
Griffith, W. E. (1967) *Communism in Europe, Vol. II*. Cambridge, Mass: MIT Press.
Hardt, J. P. (1981) 'East European Economies in Crisis' in *East European Economic Assessment*. Washington: Joint Economic Committee U.S. Congress.
Logue, J. (1987) 'And We Dreamed of a New and Just Society', *Scandinavian Studies* 59: 129.
Masaryk, T. G. (1988) *Otzka socilni*. Praha: Jan Laichter.
Miller, S.M. (1988) 'Evolving Welfare State Mixes' in Evers, A., Wintersberger, H. (eds.) *Shifts in the Welfare Mix*. Vienna: European Centre for Social Welfare Policy and Research.
Nagorski, Z. Jr. (1974) *The Psychology of East-West Trade: Illusions and Opportunities*. New York: Mason and Lipscomb.
Pesek, B. P. (1965) *Gross National Product of Czechoslovakia in Monetary Terms, 1946-1958*. Chicago: University of Chicago Press.
Robertson, J. (1982) *What Comes after the Welfare State*. Futures, February 1982.
Svetlik, I. (1988) 'Yugoslavia: Three Ways of Welfare System Restructuring' in Evers, Wintersberger (eds.) *op.cit.*: 331ff.
Vecerník, Jiri (1989) *Economic Base of the Life Style Differentiation*. Paper for the meeting Working Group in the Correlates and Consequences of Social Stratification. Prague, December 1989.
Verunáč, V. (1923) *Delnické otázka a nás prumysl*. Praha: Masarykova akademie práce.
Weber, M. (1948) *From Max Weber: Essays in Sociology*. London: Routledge and Kegan Paul.

Appendix

Table 1:   Household Strategies for Solving Financial Problems

Variant	1	2	3	4	5	6	7	8	9	10
1) Higher Income	24.7	12.6	14.3	9.4	7.4	6.4	6.7	6.8	5.1	6.4
2) Better Job	14.0	19.1	12.9	14.2	9.3	8.6	7.1	7.9	4.8	2.3
3) Work Abroad	5.5	4.3	5.4	6.1	5.0	7.8	7.1	7.3	13.8	37.8
4) Extra Income	6.2	10.1	14.7	15.5	14.7	11.6	8.8	7.3	6.5	4.5
5) Private Firm	4.8	4.2	4.2	6.4	8.2	9.1	11.1	12.1	26.3	14.2
6) Rent Rooms	1.5	2.3	3.7	5.6	8.4	11.5	15.7	22.7	15.1	13.5
7) Sell Goods	1.8	4.2	7.2	9.8	13.6	15.7	17.8	15.8	10.8	5.1
8) Sell Fruits	2.7	4.7	9.0	9.8	12.5	14.8	14.9	11.7	10.3	9.8
9) Work at Home	9.4	24.0	16.3	14.5	12.2	7.5	6.4	4.8	2.9	2.0
10) Economize	32.2	16.2	13.2	9.0	8.5	6.2	3.9	3.5	3.3	3.9

The Rank Order columns are headed 1 through 10.

Answers to the question "Imagine your family is facing a series of financial troubles due to external factors. Please rank possible solutions according to your likely decision, to the extent they would be acceptable to your family."
1)   To get a higher income from your present job.
2)   To find a better-paid job.
3)   To work abroad.
4)   To get a supplementary job, extra income.
5)   To found a private firm.
6)   To rent rooms, weekend house.
7)   To sell home-made goods.
8)   To sell produced fruits, vegetables, or flowers.
9)   To make, produce, or repair things at home at maximal extent.
10) To economize.

Chapter 11

The Changing Face of Civil Society in Eastern Europe

Lena Kolarska-Bobinska

The transition from the socialist system to a market economy implies the necessity of changing the organizing principles of society. This applies, among other things, to those principles on the basis of which people join public, political, and economic life. The organization and management of socio-economic life commanded from above is to be replaced by entrepreneurial initiatives from below; by the self-organization of groups, of interests and of capital; and by a system of self-help of the citizens. Central management in every sphere is to be replaced by the self-government of local autonomous units.

In brief, it is frequently assumed that while under real socialism, civil society persisted on the margins and in the shadow of the omnipotent state – or even outright in opposition to it – the abolition of the communist rule and a change of the system will see a reversal of this situation. The organization of public life from below, democratic elections, and the freedom of association are to fill the gap left by a state in retreat from many fields. The nature of a civil society and its former functions of protest and self-defence, shaped mainly in conflict with an overwhelming adversary like the state, must now be modified. As has been pointed out by many authors, not all grass-roots initiatives were based on contestation and self-defence (Wertenstein-Zulawski, 1989; Modzelewski, 1989; Frentzel-Zagorska, 1989), but all of them emerged in a landscape dominated by the state.

The transition to a market economy and democracy requires not only a modification of the character and orientation of the existing islands of social activity. It requires different principles of the organization of the entire social order. And here the question arises: will society, after the removal of those barriers which once restricted its activity, avail itself of the freedom and the numerous new opportunities provided by the market economy and democracy to build a new social order? Will a civil society, once repressed and restricted, fully develop in the process of self-organization and self-government? The success of the whole process of change depends on how far Polish society (on which I concentrate my attention) will join that process, accept the rules of the game, and begin to behave in accordance with them. The question under consideration is also justified in the light of many contradictory sociological observations which address the situation during the first half of 1990.

On the other hand, and striking even to those who participate, there is little enthusiasm, joy, and willingness to act and participate in undertakings which could considerably speed up the changes. This is particularly felt by the generation which so actively and so enthusiastically joined "Solidarity" in 1980. The younger generation, which knows of the strikes of August 1980 mainly from reports, is not active either; but it does not feel surprised by this fact. Sociologists have recorded numerous instances of lack of social participation, of passivity, apathy, and even mutual dislike and hostility. Solidarity's trade union wing now has some 2.5 million members, as compared with 10 million in 1981. The small turnout during the first "almost" democratic elections in June 1989 surprised many: it amounted to 64 per cent of those entitled to vote. The level of participation during the May 1990 (self-government) elections was even smaller, 42 per cent. The freedom to form political parties did not promote a rapid growth in membership, nor did it make society politically active. The fragility of those organizations resembles that of many new associations which practically do not exist (Wesolowski, 1990). There are many reasons for this state of affairs. They vary in character: many still-existing barriers, the passivity learned under the old system, fatigue with the hardships of everyday life. In this chapter, I shall concentrate on two points:

1) The perceived role of the state. The definition of the situation as a new one – and in particular, the perception of the role of the state in the organization of economic and societal life – may essentially contribute to the emergence of entrepreneurial activity at the grass-roots level.

2) The features of the transformation process which, while eliminating some existing causes and manifestations of anomy, produce new ones equally conducive to that psychosocial condition.

The definition of the situation is essential because action largely depends on the way in which the actor perceives his situation, and hence on how he defines the world around him and his own social identity and role. The state plays a key role in that definition for several reasons. On the one hand, various authors resorted to the concept of the state to define that of civil society. The latter was autonomous vs. the state, but the state appeared in the definitions of civil society to stress its distinctive character. The state was always the point of reference. On the other hand, the reliance on the state has been usually treated in the literature of the subject as an essential feature of "socialist consciousness", i.e. the result of the long domination of the communist political system. Passivity and learned helplessness were the consequences. I do not want to engage here in a debate on definitions. My intention is merely to demonstrate that, in the analysis of the future of civil society in Poland, the perception of society and its political élites, of the role of the state, of its functions and its scope of action, is of key importance.

In the second part of the chapter, I shall discuss some causes and manifestations of social anomy, because it essentially affects one's personal life in order to cooperate with others and to form or join organizations of various kinds. Undoubtedly, different factors condition one's participation in societal, political, and economic life. Similarly, there exist various forms and degrees of participation. New economic rules may be (a) disregarded either by ignoring them, or by rejecting them; (b) people may adjust to them if they directly interfere with their life; or else (c) the new rules of the game may be used for the attainment of various goals. The behaviour of the first type was observed in industry during 1990 when most enterprises instead of changing their behaviour did nothing in the hope that former conditions would return. The behaviour of the second type might consist, for instance, in the modification of consumer habits and lifestyle under the impact of price rises; or the change of job caused by dismissals from work and the necessity of occupational retraining. Such behaviour, even though it is enforced by the external situation and mainly consists in adjustment, significantly contributes to the building of a new social order. The behaviour belonging to the third type consists in the active participation in various social and political groups and organizations, in seeking better jobs, and in participating in new economic undertakings. These three forms of (non-)participation are well documented in the relevant literature. I shall not analyse each of them but shall concentrate on some basic factors contributing to the formation of civil society.

The programme of the first non-communist government was to promote a market economy and a democratic system. I shall accordingly analyse social activity from the point of view of society's participation in those new efforts. I am particularly interested in the occurrence, during the period of change, of some contradictory tendencies: anomy and integration; hopes for a better future and apathy; consensus on many values and unwillingness to take part in their realization; the sense of danger threatening many interests, and the weakness of their defence; the decomposition of the old group identities and formation of new ones.

1   State's (Statal) Society or Civil Society?

The change of the role of the state is crucial in the transition from socialism to an order based on market economy and pluralism. This is why the withdrawal of the state from the economy and other fields in Poland has been made one of the axes which organize the governmental programme of transition to market economy. This is taking place at a time when the living standards of many groups are drastically falling, the sphere of poverty widens, and the danger of unemployment becomes very real. The economic reform, which in its initial period (the duration of which can hardly be estimated) will adversely affect many spheres of life, is being carried out in Poland 10 years after the beginning of the economic crisis. Hence, living standards have not risen for 10 years, while economic problems have intensified.

The attitude of the population towards the state and its protective functions is thus ambivalent: on the one hand, the universally-accepted government, for many "the cabinet of the last hope", claims that these functions must be limited; but, on the other hand, the situation calls for their intensification. This ambivalence must be examined in light of society's attitude towards the state, which has lasted for years. Until recently, the overlapping of the political, economic, and social spheres resulted in a basic paradox: on the one hand, society has developed different attitudes towards the different spheres of the state's activity; on the other, it has shifted its attitudes from one sphere to another.

The former was expressed through the acceptance of the state's welfare activities and the simultaneous rejection of its efforts to control political and economic behaviour. As Pawel Kuczynski argues: "The ambivalent attitude towards the state is expressed, on the one hand, by demands put upon it, and on the other, by resistance to the all-encompassing monopoly of the state. In other words, the slow change of the attitude towards the state is reflected in the belief that the state should secure and take care of the social security and standard of the individual" (Kuczynski, 1986). I am of the opinion that, under communist rule, the competitive market was for many people a means of attaining freedom – the highest value. It was also a means of setting a limit to the undeserved privileges of many former party officials (of the Polish United Workers Party); of basing pay on clear and measurable factors and not on arbitrary administrative decisions; and of making ability rather than political merits the starting point of careers. Thus the market was perceived as a means of limiting the political and economic functions of the state. The rather hesitant acceptance of the social consequences produced by the market, was a result of treating social benefits as something valuable or as one's due.

The tendency to reduce state control over the economy for political and efficiency reasons, was accompanied by the fear that the welfare state would completely withdraw from the economy. This feeling was reinforced by deteriorating living conditions.

Moreover, the expectation of the various benefits provided by the state was combined with a reluctant attitude towards the latter. Koralewicz (1987) writes about the "unfriendly" world of institutions. In the research project "Poles 84", the belief that well-being and earnings depend on the decisions made at the top was combined with a negative assessment of that fact ("Polacy 84", 1986). At present, the attitude towards the state should change gradually because that state is finally "ours".

But what if the state, on which millions of people depend in one way or the other, begins to be friendly – but at the same time firmly disclaims its various earlier duties? What if, at the time when it should play an essential role in the planning of societal life, it urges the citizens to organize self-help and charitable activities?

The comparison of the propaganda slogans about the state's withdrawal with the facts of the matter leads to curious results. First of all, it is emphasized by the critics of the government programme that the state has withdrawn from various subsidies but continues to play the key role in setting limits to salaries and wages. The number of Ministers and their deputies in the new cabinet – one of the indicators of centralization – has not declined. Also, some representatives of the government have sought through the mass media to reassure the public that, while the state has withdrawn from the economy, it will return to its former function as the mediator or even as the main regulator in case of grave disturbances. Can one then rely upon the state or not? What is its true role now? It is the state which is carrying out the stabilization plan and the reforms. Hence, the state is perceived as the authority of change. The state raises and lowers taxes and interest rates, and declares that it will block the further price rise of bread if that becomes too high. Hence it is the state, and not the invisible hand of the market, which – people think – raises prices, or at least influences them. Many examples confirm people in their belief that the state continues to be present in various spheres of daily life. On the other hand, it has withdrawn from many others. People can hardly grasp the logic of those decisions.

At the same time, people continue to expect protection from the state. At the end of 1990, nearly one year after the beginning of the implementation of market reforms, 66 per cent of the Polish people accepted the introduction of state control over prices (22% were against) and 80 per cent accepted the statement that "the state should help more people that are helpless" (Kolarska-Bobinska, 1991). While in October 1988, 25 per cent of the respondents considered it likely that they would lose their jobs, in 1990 that percentage rose to 49. In the opinion of 74 per cent of the respondents, it is the government's duty to secure new jobs to all those discharged; and 87 per cent of them think that the state should secure opportunities for retraining (Public Opinion Research Center, 1989a). All respondents had a clear opinion on that matter – there were exceptionally few hazy answers (such as "it is hard to say").

The clash between the declarations made by the state authorities on the one hand, and social expectations and the existence of old as well as quite new practices on the other, produces a complex situation. One might risk the hypothesis that, in some time, there would emerge a new perception about the "unfriendliness" of institutions. It would not be related any more to the rejection of the political and economic activities of the state, but to the non-acceptable way in which it performs its protective functions. Perhaps that change of perception will

be conducive to the emergence of civil society which, in the field of social welfare, would resemble in many respects the ones in Western Europe. The gap
observed after the withdrawal of the state from many of its functions, will have
to be filled by the actions of a self-organizing society. Assistance extended by
members of one's family or one's neighbours will prove insufficient. But the
essential question is whether people will define the present situation as entirely
new and requiring new thinking and new behaviour or will treat it as a prolonga-
tion of the earlier situation under economically unfavourable circumstances. Will
they treat it as a change in the role of the state, or merely as its increased op-
pressiveness and "unfriendliness"? And, as in previous years, will the negative
attitudes towards one of the spheres of the activity of the state shift to other
spheres – for instance, from the social to the political? For the time being, there
are no well-grounded answers to these questions.

2   Anomy and Social Optimism

Several sociologists have pointed out that social anomy was one of the fundamental features of Polish society in the 1980s. They mention the sense of "temporari-
ness", apathy, pessimism, loneliness, lack of sense in life, and the weakening of
the acceptance of values, all of this observable after the events in August 1980
(Nowak, 1984; Wertenstein-Zulawski, 1989; Szafraniec, 1989).

The clash between widely-accepted values and the socio-political corset imposed
by the system which prevented their realization, resulted in a specific dissonance
between accepted and realized values, the values of the private and of the public
sphere. In line with Merton, Nowak has pointed out that one of the causes of anomy
in Polish society was that societally-accepted goals became unattainable for a large
part of society through accepted means and norms (Nowak, op. cit.). The blocking
of the attainment of life goals was accompanied by a strong feeling that little could
be achieved in a society whose functioning was chaotic and hardly predictable,
and dominated by the feeling that one's actions do not make sense.

If social anomy in Poland was linked to the blocking of possibilities related to
the attainment of goals and values; to the feeling of a lack of influence upon one's
own situation and that of one's country; to a lack of sense in life; to a pessimistic
vision of the future; and to restrictions imposed on the expression of one's opinions;
on opportunities for action, and on associating with others – then it may be said
that now many elements of the situation which favoured anomy have vanished.
First of all, the political system is no longer the rejected group of "them", but an
accepted government which shares its values with society. Society does not only
have confidence in the government but also links to it its great hopes for the improvement of the situation of the country. That confidence is – to some degree –
blind, because only 14 per cent of the population declared in 1989 that they knew

what the economic programme of the cabinet was, while 75 per cent thought that the cabinet works well (Public Opinion Research Center, 1989b). The legislative proposals submitted by the cabinet were accepted even by those who do not know what they are about (Sulek, 30 November 1989). The government also called for self-help, self-organization, formation of groups, and the reconstruction of the social tissue by strong human bonds. At the same time, the government was gradually removing the barriers which restrict freedom of action.

But while many factors conducive to anomy have disappeared, new ones are emerging which strengthen that condition. Anomy now is not a derivative of the restrictions imposed by a non-accepted socio-political system. At present, the conditions producing anomy come closer to those described by Durkheim (Durkheim, 1964). Its causes are to be sought mainly in the violent social changes which cause a "disturbance in collective order" (op. cit.: 179). The joy caused by the change and the dislike of the old system cannot neutralize the numerous consequences caused by change. People are uncertain whether they face a revolution related to the emergence of a new, "capitalist" value system, or the restoration of the pre-war one. It would be a simplification to say that the present situation is so entirely new that it gives rise to a completely new state of anomy. Many structures, situations, and behaviour patterns have not changed or are changing very slowly. My point, however, is to indicate several new factors which may influence the state of anomy and the mental condition of Poles in the early 1990s and hence may influence the emergence of civil society.

1) First of all, the changes now taking place will result in a modification of the existing social structure: some individuals and groups will find the transition to the new socio-economic order advantageous, while others will find it disadvantageous. Durkheim's description fits the present situation very well: the "declassation" which suddenly pushes down certain individuals to a position lower than that they had so far, means that they must reduce their requirements, restrict their needs, and learn greater restraint (Durkheim, 1964: 186). This will not take place in a short time because it requires time to adjust to the new, imposed situation; and the very prospect of that seems unbearable to many. But people who gain as a result of the change lose their bearings, too. The downward movement of entire social groups on the ladder of wealth, power, and prestige must develop in them the sense of discomfort, depression, and loss of the right course. It can also develop various tensions in individuals and social groups.

The declassation which will affect many groups must be considered against the background of financial – or more broadly, material – aspirations. In the 1980s, there was in Poland a strong sense of non-satisfaction of many aspirations aroused by the policy pursued in the 1970s. The economic crisis resulted in an unfavourable perception of one's own earnings. While in 1973, 30 per cent of the respondents in Warsaw believed their earnings to be just and right (Reszke, 1977), in 1987 only

7 per cent were satisfied with their incomes (Domanski, 1989). Some 90 per cent of the respondents thought that their remuneration was below what they deserved. For comparison, it may be added that 60 per cent of Americans believed their incomes to be satisfactory, while 36 per cent of them assessed them as too low (op. cit.). The important point is that the fall in the material standards in Poland in 1990, takes place in a situation marked by a very strong discrepancy between earnings and aspirations. The tensions caused by that fact have not manifested themselves so far because of the high level of political legitimation of the cabinet which carries out the reform. But they nevertheless exist and influence the psychosocial condition and the moods of the Polish people.

A poor economic situation favours anomy not only because of a decline of living standards. It also absorbs much time, attention, and effort earlier needed for purchasing commodities and now spent on the protection of falling living standards.

This fact divides people instead of bringing them closer to one another. The crisis increases the need for self-help and self-organization but, at the same time, breeds centrifugal tendencies which atomize society. Moreover, it makes social consciousness more economy-oriented and favours the neglect of values of a higher order – among them, the sense of social solidarity.

2) Every change in the politico-economic order requires changes in the system of values; but the passage from the socialist formation to that based on pluralism and market economy, must be based on a genuine revolution of values. Many values change their position in the hierarchy while others are replaced by their opposites. The praise of social equality and restraint in consumption is driven out by the eulogy both of getting rich and of inequalities as the basic stimuli for economic activity; the former approval of being "average" is replaced by the striving to get ahead and to prove oneself better than others; the norms of group solidarity are dislodged by the spirit of competition and the struggle for improving one's own condition; the carefree attitude towards one's job and one's future has to switch to self-reliance; the lack of commodities on the market is replaced by the lack of money with which everything can be bought; the search of institutions for employees is replaced by the search of prospective employees for jobs.

Some of the new values, norms and behaviour patterns related to them have been present for some time in Polish society. However, they pertained more to the individual than to the public sphere. In Poland the learned helplessness at one's workplace and the inability to act independently in public life were accompanied by prudence, entrepreneurship, and self-reliance in taking care of one's own interests and those of one's family (Marody, 1989). Now, those values should come to the surface from the cosy corners of privacy and should begin to control public behaviour, thus being to the advantage not only of individuals but also of the institutions which employ them. This requires a certain essential change which will not be easy to attain: a re-evaluation of people's attitudes towards the law and state institutions. A journalist recently exhorted people to pay for rides in municipal buses and trams. In the past, she claimed, we used to steal free rides to protest against the non-accepted political system (Berberyusz, 1990). Now that we have "our government", we must change those attitudes.

Without discussing this problem in greater detail here, I merely want to stress the sense of confusion caused in individuals by the revolution of values. It might be claimed that in the 1980s, a large percentage of Polish people accepted certain values which underpin the market economy. But the verbal acceptance of the transition to the laws of the market economy, and the actual adjustment to the specifically Polish form of the initial stage of that process, are two different things.

3) The sense of confusion and chaos is intensified by the changing system of legal norms. It might be argued that this system does not change quickly enough from the point of view of the requirements of reform. But it creates in many people the impression that human actions are not regulated. "All that is not prohibited is allowed", is one of the main principles in the initial stage of the Polish reform. The sense of chaos, or rather growing anarchy, is intensified by the liberalization of political life. Polish society for many years lived in an atmosphere of suppressed conflicts and apparent uniformity of opinions. It was not accustomed to an open play of interests. The abolition of political barriers favours the manifestation and activation of many, often greatly diversified, interests which are in open conflict with each other. Plurality and diversity may appear as a manifestation of chaos; and concern for group interests, as a manifestation of anarchy.

4) January 1990 witnessed the beginning of an essential change in the system of rules which regulate economic activity. Legal barriers have been replaced, although not fully, by economic ones. Decisions based on calculation, and not on coercion and restrictions, are to determine the behaviour of organizations and individuals. Market barriers can, on the one hand, appear to many as a lack of the regulation of behaviour patterns. On the other, however, they mean a corset much tighter than the legal regulations which were circumvented, twisted by interpretations, and modified by exceptions, etc. Many people begin to notice that their goals will never be attained because of barriers created by the economic system and the financial situation.

Social activity is mobilized when the goal to be attained does not seem very distant and unrealistic. The conviction that it can be attained by one's own effort, and that one's needs and aspirations can thus be satisfied, is an important motivating power of human action. In Poland in the first half of 1990, many people, instead of perceiving opportunities for various actions and for an improvement of their situation in the democratic system based on the market economy, saw that they would never attain their former living standard. At the same time, however, surveys of public opinion indicated that people believe that the government programme will improve the situation of the country. In my opinion, the explanation of this apparent contradiction is to be found in the fact that people differently assess the impact of the reform upon the economy and its influence upon their personal situation: its impact upon the national economy as a whole is perceived as much more favourable than its influence on one's personal situation. It may be supposed that today only a small group sees a change for themselves in the transition to the market economy. For many, that change rather means a restriction of their individual chances. Moreover, it is an essential source of uncertainty: the future seems obscure and unpredictable.

5) The state of anomy does not affect all social groups to the same degree. This process, and its intensity, is different in the case of young and old people; in the case of groups which have profited from the change; and of those which are vulnerable and weak; in the case of those groups which have always been in favour of the market economy; and those which supported egalitarian principles. It is worth quoting in this connection the changes in the mood of the various social groups. As has been said, the political change in 1989 significantly increased the number of those who were optimistic about the future. But optimism increased in particular in the groups of professionals from the humanities (Public Opinion Research Center, 1990). That group was also marked by a decrease in stress. One of the reasons is that the position of this group of people improved considerably in 1989, especially in the political arena. They were the authors of the reforms and of many solutions leading to market economy and democracy. It is striking to note that, to the contrary, engineers showed signs of declining optimism and rising stress. In the 1980s, this group was one of the stronger advocates of economic reform. It seems that their psychological condition was affected by the unstable situation of enterprises and the disastrous state of the national economy which constitutes the context of their professional work. Even though the owners of private firms always formed the group with the highest level of satisfaction, their optimism did not rise and even slightly declined, in spite of opportunities for further activity. The ratio of those who do not expect anything good for them from the future ranges from 20 to 50 per cent in the various social groups (op. cit.).

The state of anomy favours social disintegration and is an essential barrier to social participation and to the undertaking of self-organizing actions starting from the grass roots. The question arises whether civil society can develop in a situation of anomy.

To answer this question, one must take into account the issue which I have not discussed so far: namely, group interests. One might advance the hypothesis that, in the future, the defence and representation of group interests will play a more essential role in the self-organization of society than shared values. At present, "the advocates of change more frequently group themselves around common values, whereas interests are more often the force which integrates opponents of changes" (Adamski et al., 1990: 6). One of the causes of this is that there are no groups which would perceive their own interest in the change. I do think, however, that this is mainly due to the fluidity of the ever-changing situation and the unclear character of the future socio-economic order. The following quotation illustrates the uncertainty: "One cow can bring a loss of one million zlotys in a day ... " The peasants are furious: there are not people wise enough to cope with big economics. But uncertainty is the worst of all things: is one to sell one's product or try to wait out the situation? Is one to lose or to try to break even? In the meantime, people say that one thing is certain today: they have lived long enough to see the day when nothing is profitable for the farmer" (Wilczak, *Polityka*, 20 January 1990). Such a drastically unclear and variable situation is, of course, transient; but uncertainty will accompany the changes until the emergence of a new social order. That new order will also form the foundation for the formation of interests.

I think that the interests of the various groups, which even now have a certain organizational base, will in time crystallize and become institutionalized. New groups and new interests will also emerge. Many of them will be responses to direct threats. Others will develop in connection with growing problems and new issues that will require quick solutions. This is why, although in Poland politics change more quickly than does the economy, economic interests will consolidate and become structured more quickly than political interests will. To a greater extent political interests tend to organize themselves around commonly shared values; whereas economic interests are interpreted as a state or situation which does, or can, bring advantages to an individual or a group. If we classify the motives of new initiatives, as Evers and Wintersberger did, into self-defensive ones and those expressing the need for greater autonomy, responsibility, and participation, then the former will dominate in Poland (Evers and Wintersberger, 1988). This may happen also because the state, when withdrawing from many services, encourages society to take over some of its duties. This gives rise to a paradoxical situation: civil society may develop neither in opposition to the state and its structures, nor parallel to them, but due to the initiative and inspiration of the state itself.

What was to rise from the bottom as a spontaneous phenomenon, is inspired from the top – as is also the economic reform. But appeals from the top cannot replace grass-roots motivation. Yet the state of anomy described above does not suggest that integration and self-organization may come quickly – the less so since self-organization and self-help are mainly specific to the middle class (op. cit.), which has not yet developed in Poland. This is why during the *interregnum* – after the withdrawal of the state from many spheres and before the formation of a new network of organizations and initiatives – a vacuum may develop. This vacuum itself will have an adverse effect on the development of civil society in Poland. More and more people will feel themselves pushed out of the mainstream of change rather than drawn in by the opportunities the economic and political reforms represent.

References

Adamski, W., Jasiewicz, K., Rychard, A. (eds.) (1986) *Polacy 84. Dynamika Konfliktu i Konsensusu* (Poles 84. Dynamics of Conflict and Consensus). Warsaw: University of Warsaw.

Adamski, W. et al. (1990) *Polacy 90 w Europie* (Poles 90 in Europe). An outline of a research project. Unpublished manuscript.

Berberyusz, E. (1990) 'Czyje jest MZK' (Whose Municipal Transport?) and 'We wlasnym domu' (In Our Own House), *Gazeta Wyborcza*, January.

Domanski, H. (1989) *Od czego zaleza aspiracje zarobkowe* (On What Do Aspirations in the Sphere of Earnings Depend?). Unpublished manuscript. The Polish Academy of Sciences, Institute of Philosophy and Sociology.

Durkheim, E. (1964) 'Typy samobójstw' w: J. Szacki/E.Durkheim, Warszawa.

Evers, A., Wintersberger, H. (eds.) (1988) *Shifts in the Welfare Mix*. Vienna: European Centre for Social Welfare Policy and Research.

Frentzel-Zagorska, J. (1989) *Civil Society in Poland and Hungary*. Unpublished manuscript.

Kolarska-Bobinska, L. (1989) 'Poczucie niesprawiedliwosci, konfliktu i preferowany lad w gospodarce' (The Sense of Injustice and Conflict, and the Preferred Order in the Economy), in Adamski, W., Jasiewicz, K., Kolarska-Bobinska, L., Rychard, A. and Wnuk-Lipinski, E. (1989) *Polacy 88. Dynamika konfliktu a szanse reform* (Poles 88. The Dynamics of Conflict and the Chances of Reforms). Warsaw: University of Warsaw.

Kolarska-Bobinska, L. (1990) 'The Socialist Welfare State in Transition: the State, the Market and the Enterprise in Poland', in Deacon, B., Szalai, J. (eds.) *Social Policy in the New Eastern Europe*. Aldershot: Avebury.

Kolarska-Bobinska, L. (1991) 'Ustroj ekonomiczny a interesy grupove' (Economic System and Group Interests), in Adamski, W. et al. (1991) *Polacy 90. Konflikt a zmiana* (Conflict and Change). Warsaw: IFIS PAN ISP PAN.

Koralewicz, J. (1987) 'Obrez spolenenskwa i pomicie dyskomportu psychicinego' (The Picture of Society and the Psychological Comfort), in Wunk-Lipinski, E. *Nierownoscii ...?* (Unequalities and Disabilities in Social Consciousness). Warsaw: Polish Academy of Science.

Kuczynski, P. (1986) 'Swiadomosc polityczna robotnikow: pomiedzy modernizacja a "normalizacja" (Political Consciousness of Workers: Between Modernization and "Normalization"), in Morawski, W. (ed.) *Gospodarka i spoleczentwo* (Economy and Society). Warsaw: University of Warsaw.

Marody, M. (1989) *Postrzeganie polityki a partycypacja polityczna spoleczenstwa polskiego* (Perception of Politics and Political Participation of Polish Society). Unpublished manuscript.

Modzelewski, W. (1989) *Nowa generacja ruchow spolecznych i stowarzyszen w Polsce* (The New Generation of Social Movements and Associations in Poland). Unpublished manuscript.

Nowak, S. (1984) 'Spolecenstwo polskie czasu kryzysu w swietle teorii anomii' (Polish Society at the Time of Crisis in the Light of the Theory of Anomy), *Polska 2000* (Poland 2000).

Public Opinion Research Center (1989a) *Public Opinion on Unemployment*.

Public Opinion Research Center (1989b) *Opinions about the Economic Policy of Prime Minister Mazowiecki's Cabinet*.

Public Opinion Research Center (1990) *Serwis Informacyjny* 1.

Reszke, I. (1977) *Nastepstwa rozbieznosci miedzy poziomami zarobkow i kwalifikacji* (Consequences of Discrepancies Between Earnings and Qualifications). Wroclaw: Ossolineum.

Szafraniec, K. (1989) 'Anomia jako teoria tlumaczaca antropologiczny wymiar kryzysu spolecznego w Polsce' (Anomy as a Theory Which Explains the Anthropological Dimension of the Crisis in Poland), in Kolarska-Bobinska, L. (ed.) *Sisyphus*, Vol. VI.

Sulek, A. (1990) *Opinie i nastroje spoleczenstwa polskiego na przelomie 1989/1990 r.* (Opinions and Moods of Polish Society at the Turn of 1989). An expert report for the Solidarity Parliamentary Group, January 1990.

Wertenstein-Zulawski, J. (1989) 'Anomie and Youth Movements. Crisis and Change in the Social System in Poland', in Kolarska-Bobinska, L. (ed.) *Sisyphus*, Vol. VI.

Weslowski, W. (1990) Transition from Authoritarianism to Democracy: Poland's Case. Social Research (summer).

Wilczak, J. (1990) Wielkie czekanie (The Big Waiting), *Polityka*, 20 January.

CHAPTER 12

Social Policy between Negative and Positive Equality: The Yugoslavian Case

Veljko Rus

1 Introduction: Cultural or Economic Determinism?

Marxists are perhaps right when they criticize cultural determinism as an explanatory paradigm of capitalist societies. It seems that capitalist societies are mainly the product of the market economy and not the outcome of Protestant ethics. Therefore, economic determinism is a much better explanatory paradigm for the rise of capitalist societies than is cultural determinism.

For socialist societies, we might say the opposite: they are more the outcome of ideological projects than the outcome of capital concentration or class conflicts. Cultural determinism is for these cases a more appropriate explanatory paradigm than economic or social determinism.

Following the above statements, we would try to analyse the relationship between the economy and welfare politics in Yugoslavia by describing those socialist projects which have directly influenced them.

2 Negative Utopia

Socialism was conceived by Marxists as the antithesis to capitalism, as an anti-capitalist and not as a post-capitalist social order. Equality, as the dominant value of all socialist movements, was also defined in a negative way: as the abolishment of class privilege through the abolition of private ownership. Such a negative concept of equality has the following implications for social policy:
1) It is defined as class- or block-related equality, not as equality among individuals (Rae, 1981).
2) It is defined as final equality or equality of results, and not as equality of opportunities or as initial equality (Coleman, 1983).

3) It is defined as redistribution of goods or services; not as the redistribution of tasks or roles (Ferge, 1980).

These three attributes have determined the frame of value orientation for all socialist movements which have been based on Marxist ideology. They primarily tried to abolish class or group inequalities, and ignored inequalities among individuals.

Priority of equality of outcome over equality of opportunity forces intragenerational equalization and ignores inter-generational mobility. Because of this orientation, individual occupational (or circular) mobility was disregarded. This might be proved by comparative East-West studies which show slightly lower circular mobility in the Eastern European countries as compared to Western European ones (O'Connor, 1979; Wesolowski and Mach, 1986).

Finally, distributive justice oriented towards consumer equalization did not pay enough attention to equalization of work roles and therefore generates something that was characterized by Marx as a kind of "vulgar socialism".

Such a negative concept of equality also has political consequences creating increasing ghettoization of the working class. Before World War II, ghettoization of the working class was typical for social-democratic movements as well (Esping-Andersen, 1987).

3   Positive Utopia

After World War I, Social Democrats and Leninists tried to develop a positive concept of equality. Social Democrats based it on the inclusive concept of "social citizenship"; Leninists, on work status. However, with this transition from exclusive class politics based on the negative concept of equality to inclusive populist politics based on the positive concept of equality, social-democratic movements have brought about new contradictions between private economy and public social policy, between economic efficiency and social equality, and between economic liberalism and social paternalism (Rein, 1987).

Leninists, on the other hand, have accused the social democrats that their inclusive social policy means nothing more than "socialization of the costs of reproducing labour power, the legitimation of an exploiting economic order, and the acceptance of the negative by-products of capitalist growth" (Esping-Andersen, 1985: 244). Hence, for the Leninists, the abolishment of capitalist society, is the "condition *sine qua non*" of any socialist solidarity. This Leninist position is perfectly compatible with the concept of negative equality, i.e. with the abolishment of class privilege; but it is not compatible with their positive concept of equality based on work status.

First, according to Leninists, work contribution should be the measure for reward. On the other hand, it is also true that this kind of distributive justice is nothing more than a "bourgeois right" – as Marx said in the Gotha Programme. Any kind of meritocratic justice, whether formulated in a soft or hard way, is not compatible with the socialist concept of justice.

Secondly, it is almost impossible to operationalize this criterion, since it is not clear how work contribution in a non-market economy should be objectively measured; it certainly should not be evaluated in subjective terms. According to Marx, "right can never be on a higher level than the economic structure of society and the cultural level conditioned thereby" (Marx, 1970: 19).

Thirdly, even greater difficulties are connected with the positive definition of justice to be achieved in communist society. It was defined by Marx in the *German Ideology* with the slogan, "from each according to his ability and to each according to his needs". This equation generates at least three *additional* difficulties:
1) It could not be realized in a society with scarce resources.
2) It is not a relevant criterion of justice for a society in which scarcity would eventually disappear.
3) There is an unacceptable gap between the meritocratic definition of justice (correlation between work contribution and reward), and the communist definition of justice which is based only on reward according to one's needs.

Since socialist society is defined as a period of transition from a capitalist to a communist society, such *contradictions* in the definition of justice of these two societies certainly create numerous paradoxes.

4 Unqualified Egalitarianism

In the Eastern countries, socialist justice has never been clearly defined due to the difficulties mentioned above. Early on, justice was connected with the negative concept of equality; while in recent times, it has almost disappeared from the ideological vocabulary of these countries.

The qualitative notion of just equality was reduced to a quantitative one. Instead of optimal equality, maximal equality became the dominant value in Eastern European countries. Such an uncontrolled transition from relative equality towards absolute equality (Rae, 1981) actually means unlimited solidarity in which "everybody contributes for all and all for everybody" (Pusic, 1987). Hence, there is no (cor)relation between equality and justice; there is also no discussion about just inequality or unjust equality. Socialist equality is understood as maximum equality for a maximum number of individuals. Rawls would qualify this concept of equality as a kind of "unqualified egalitarianism" (Rawls, 1971).

Unqualified egalitarianism also means the absence of a value hierarchy. Equality as the highest value is not defined in relation to liberty, brotherhood, solidarity, etc. There is no "lexical order" as in Rawl's theory of justice; therefore, the other values do not *explain* what is just (in)equality.

The reality in Eastern European countries demonstrates the opposite logic. A relatively high level of (economic) equality became meaningless and valueless in the absence of (political) freedom. Recent history has therefore proved the validity of Rawl's "lexical order".

5   Reduction of Equality to Economic Equality

If we try to summarize the discussion about the ideological base of socialist societies, we might conclude that no positive concept of just equality was developed there, although all of them treated equality as the highest value and as the main basis of legitimation.

We should look for the reasons for this deficiency in the writings of Marx and Engels. Engels, for instance, wrote in *Anti-Dühring* that any effort on the part of a social movement to do more than abolish existing classes, would lead towards absurd projects (Engels, 1974). This statement could be *logically connected to* Marx's thesis, according to which the given level of equality is a function of the existing productive forces. Marx expected that the abolition of class inequalities would entail the disappearance of social and political inequalities, too (Marx, 1979). We here again meet economic determinism. A socialist society should become an egalitarian society through the implementation of the negative concept of equality, which should be achieved by the abolition of private ownership as the source of class privilege.

The analysis of documents from the postwar congresses of the Yugoslav Communist Party also reveals that equality as a positive concept is mentioned very seldom. In the official documents of all eight congresses after 1945, equality was mentioned only 10 times (Pesic, 1987); and even in these cases, it is reduced to economic equality. Notions like unjust equality or just inequality are never mentioned in these documents.

6   Abolition of Private Ownership, Cooperation and Solidarity

The transformation of competitive relations among workers into cooperative relations among them, was postulated to be the most important consequence of the abolition of private ownership. The dominance of cooperative relations should create overall solidarity among employees and the feeling of mutual responsibility. Such expectations have not only been cherished by Marx, but also by Durkheim – and later even supported by some experimental studies (Berkowitz, 1963). According to Durkheim's hypothesis, the abolition of "external inequalities" would automatically create a "normal division of labour and workers' solidarity". His hypothesis even influences contemporary social scientists. Morton Deutsch (1985), for instance, suggests that in cooperative relations solidarity would prevail; while in competitive relations, reciprocity would be the main type of interpersonal relationship. These differences should have implications for social policy. In cooperative relations, we might expect the prevalence of equalization as a criterion for redistributive solidaristic justice; while in competitive relations, we might expect reciprocal relations and commutative justice.

Deutsch's contingence theory of distributive justice might be questioned by the recent reinterpretation of Durkheim's basic hypothesis about the division of labour, and about solidarity as its outcome. As stressed by Alexander (1986), Durkheim in his later writings modified his basic theory in "On the Division of Social Labour". He later believed that solidarity was not the automatic outcome of a normal or spontaneous division of labour. The abolition of external inequalities and the establishment of a natural division of labour, is a necessary but not sufficient condition for solidarity. Human solidarity cannot be born without a new moral community. With this statement, Durkheim made a break with socio-economic determinism. He replaced it by a combination of historical determinism and moral voluntarism.

If we follow this way of thinking, we should stop to see the abolition of private ownership as the panacea for social problems. We should accept the hypothesis that poverty is not only the outcome of exploitation established through private ownership, and that solidarity – as a positive notion of equality – cannot be established solely through the "normal" division of labour. The existence of today's "underclasses" typifies that poverty does not only have structural socio-economic roots, but also cultural roots. And we also see that class privilege was not abolished in the Eastern countries alongside the demise of private ownership. In these countries, we have observed the opposite phenomenon: the "reification" of political privileges.

7 The Main Strategic Dilemma: Elimination of Class Privileges or De-marginalization

The basic dilemma of socialist social policy might be defined in terms of the following question: should social policy abolish class discrimination, or should it prevent marginalization caused by the division of labour? Socialist social policies have not been able to offer a clear answer to this question because they have not clearly differentiated between unprivileged groups and marginalized groups. As we see from Table 12.1, there is a substantial difference between these two social groups. There is no equilibrium between contribution and reward in the cases of privileged and unprivileged groups; while with marginal and central groups, the equilibrium between contribution and reward exists. From the meritocratic point of view (which demands a high correlation between work contribution and reward), groups A and D are the outcome of a just differentiation; while B and C are the outcome of unjust discrimination.

**Table 12.1: Classification of Groups According to their Contribution
and Reward**

		Reward	
		High	Low
Contribution	High	A – Central Groups	B – Unprivileged
	Low	C – Privileged Groups	D – Marginal Groups

What are the implications for socialist social policy if it accepts the "bourgeois" or meritocratic principle defined by Marx in the Gotha programme? Should inequality arising from discrimination be abolished, and the inequality arising from differentiation be accepted? Such an option would mean that functionalist criteria are accepted. According to these criteria, functional differentiation is a benign and necessary condition for the social order. What about the poor, then? If we try to decrease the distance between A and D, do we not at the same time prevent functional differentiation – which is an unavoidable feature of modernization?

Those who are willing to accept a cognitive distinction between differentiation and discrimination might choose different or even opposite solutions. Offe (1984) would prefer a complete break between work contribution and reward, between the job one is doing and the wage one is getting; while Ferge (1980) would prefer the de-differentiation of jobs as a condition for a greater equalization of wages. Both solutions create new difficulties. If the "social wage" is established, the meritocratic criteria of distributive justice are offended. If we abolish the criteria of meritocratic distributive justice, then we are compelled to specify new general criteria for distributive justice in order to avoid disorder and anarchy. On the other hand, if we introduce job de-differentiation, we would certainly be able to avoid the above difficulty. However, in this case, we should be able to answer another question: how to promote the process of modernization which is based on the differentiation of roles?

At the institutional level, these two alternatives have even graver implications. Offe's suggestion implies a break between economy and welfare policy, while Ferge's suggestion leads to the subordination of economic policy to social engineering.

8   The Disordered Relationship Between Economy and Welfare Policy

The domination of negative equality, operationalized as the abolishment of class privilege, has transformed social problems into political issues and brought about the complete domination of politics over economic and social regulation. Welfare issues have been subordinated to general developmental policy and have become an instrument of politics. Because of the domination of politics, a *confused* relationship exists between general politics, on the one hand, and economic and social policies on the other. Between the last two, there is neither mutual exclusion nor mutual penetration (in the sense of Luhmann's system theory). Both are mutually substitutive components of general developmental policy.

Since the goals of economic and social policy were subordinated to general developmental goals, mutual goal displacements were frequent. Solidarity, as a typical value of social policy, was frequently implemented in the economy; enterprises in debt were maintained by money taken from social programmes. The Yugoslav government, for instance, uses a greater part of the GNP for the support of inefficient investment and for the "socialization" of debts than for the whole educational system (Sefer, 1987). In Yugoslavia, this *protection* of incompetent management is called "social policy for management" and it is very similar to Kornai's "soft budget constraint". Actually, this kind of solidarity is only one part of a much broader system of employee protection. High protection of employees generates immobility of labour – and, consequently, high youth unemployment. "Work and production are subordinated to social policy", and social policy is reduced to "negative social security" (Pesic, 1987). Instead of a welfare system, a kind of meta-economic workfare system is created in which value and instrumental rationality (Flam, 1987) substitute each other in unpredictable ways.

The above-mentioned disordered relationship bears no relation to the integrated welfare state described by Mishra (1984). The integrated type of welfare state of Sweden or of Austria is based on the previously-mentioned functional differentiation and on institutional separation. It may produce a kind of equilibrium between private initiative and public responsibility, because the separation between "public" and "private" welfare systems is already established (Rawls, 1971).

9 Market and Plan as Sources of Social (In)equality

The thesis that private ownership generated through the market is a source of exploitation, domination, and social inequality, leads to the conclusion that not only private ownership, but also the market should be abolished and substituted by a *state* plan. It seems that such an assumption needs specification. We should ask the question of whether the labour market or some other factor outside it are the source of social inequality.

In connection with this question, the information of Lester Thurow (1981) might be highly relevant. He shows that wage differences among white employed men in the USA do not exceed the ratio of 1:5 and that the steadily increasing educational level of employees does not increase wage differentials. On the other hand, income differentials among those who do not participate in the labour market are much greater. The ratio is 1:27, which means that among them inequalities are five times greater than among employed white people in the USA.

Meanwhile there is increasing evidence of inequalities in those societies in which a *state* plan has been the main regulator of income distribution. Szelényi and Manchin (1987), for instance, show that in Hungary the lowest decile of the population has five times less income than the average income in the country, and that the top decile has the double of the average income.

Social inequalities also exist in other areas of distribution. They are most visible in the housing sector, where a highly-elaborated system of privilege has developed.

Taking into account the above findings, we could agree with Szelényi and Manchin that it is not important whether the market, the plan, or a combination of both are used as the main regulator of distribution. In all cases, it might be observed that they reproduce those social inequalities which already exist. Therefore, with the introduction of the market into a previously-planned society, bureaucratic privileges do not disappear but rather are "commodified".

Charles (1985), focusing on social policy in Western countries, has suggested the same conclusion. He argues that reciprocal interactions exist between social stratification and the implementation of social policy. According to him, social stratification determines social policy and is at "the same time influenced by it" (Charles, 1985: 200). This statement might be fully supported by Yugoslavian experience, although in this country the market and the plan have been implemented simultaneously. Yugoslavia has extremely high regional differences (2% unemployment in Slovenia and 40% in Kosovo) and high wage differences for similar jobs in different industrial branches (1:8), etc. The only exception is the levelled wage system within enterprises, where wage differentials usually do not exceed the ratio of 1:3.

Undesirable side effects of the market and the plan have motivated the Yugoslav government to establish a third regulative mechanism of distributive justice: the system of social contracts institutionalized through SCIs (Self-management Communities of Interest). The function of the SCIs was to create on all levels of social services yearly contracts between "users" and "providers". The contracts between them had to specify yearly programmes for the providers of services and budgets for the users. At the beginning, these contractual relations in the fields of social services were well received, because they were seen as a substitute for bureaucratic paternalism and for profit-making market activity. But when it became clear that they were mainly the instrument for coalition formation between professionals and political élites, they were abolished. These coalitions have created lower financial reliability, greater dependence of the professionals on the local political élites, and lower influence of the clients. Perhaps they could function in a more desirable way if they were the complement to, instead of a substitute for, the plan and the market (Svetlik, 1989).

Svetlik's assumption is, however, not the only message we would like to draw from the above description of the SCIs. Our main conclusion is that social equality should not be the main *criterion for the regulation of social policy*. The main criterion for this should be the allocation of public goods.

From this point of view, the main theoretical problem is the definition of public goods. There are numerous definitions of public goods. I would prefer to take into account those developed by Samuelson and Barr. According to Samuelson (1968: 387), "Public goods are goods in the case of which each individual's consumption leads to no subtraction from any other individual's consumption". According to Barr, public goods "exhibit three characteristics: non-rivalry in consumption, non-excludability, and non-rejectability" (Barr, 1987: 83). Both definitions tell us that the major characteristic of public goods is their indivisibility and non-exclusive use. As such, they cannot be allocated and distributed through the market – not because of any ideological reason, but simply because their essential nature is incompatible with market allocation.

10 Institutional or Non-institutional Solidarity?

Solidarity is ideologically the most powerful, yet at the same time the least well-defined, value in socialist social policy. In ancient Roman law, it meant the collective or mutual obligation of a group of people to repay the debt of each member of the group in cases of strained circumstances. Social security programmes, which mutually protect citizens against industrial and urban risks, seem to have a similar function in contemporary society.

However, in Marxist theories, solidarity is a much broader concept. It is conceived as a synonym for medieval charity, for altruistic behaviour, and as an instrument of social integration. Pusic (1987) thinks that one of the main weaknesses in Marxist theory is the ambiguous meaning of solidarity. At times, it is treated as an emotional, *philanthropic* value; at other times, as a consciously accepted obligation. Pusic also thinks that the same might be said of Durkheim's notion of organic solidarity.

As already noted, Durkheim later modified his early theory. According to his later understanding, solidarity is not the automatic outcome of the "normal" division of labour (Alexander, 1986). We found no such correction in social-democratic or in Marxist theories.

Nedeljkovic made an excellent statement referring to the function of solidarity in Yugoslav social policy: "Solidarity became an empty value, and an instrument of redistribution, which in a non-transparent way reproduces exploitation" (Nedeljkovic, 1987: 140). Nozick (1974) would say that this ambiguous concept of solidarity serves to legitimize the expropriation and redistribution of goods and services which have been legally obtained through the market and/or through personal effort.

Social-democratic theories of the welfare state interpret solidarity in a similarly ambiguous way. However, Social Democrats are more explicit than Marxists. Esping-Andersen, for instance (1985: 245), argues that "universal solidarity should marginalize the market". He also stresses that the residual concept of the welfare state is the most dangerous for Social Democrats, because it offers the opportunity for a majority of workers to secure their welfare through the market and not through the welfare state. And *vice versa*: where social democrats are able to establish universal solidarity based on social citizenship, liberal advocates of the market will be delegitimized.

Since the social-democratic paradigm is expressed by the slogan "Politics Against the Market", the above statements are perfectly compatible with it. However, they in fact mean that the processes of employee equalization are assured by the institutionalization of solidarity. Equalization through the institutionalization of solidarity might be found everywhere: in Yugoslavia, in other Eastern European countries, as well as in Western European countries. It seems that societal communities (Ferris, 1985) had been *endangered* by institutionalized solidarity two centuries ago in a much less visible way than by market mechanisms. Zijderveld (1986), for instance, thinks that the kind of institutionalized solidarity which is promoted by contemporary welfare states takes over vital functions of social communities and produces a kind of immoralism. According to him, the welfare state is so far-developed in the Netherlands that immorality has become one of the dominant features of social relationships.

Summarizing the above statements, we would like to say that institutionalized solidarity seems to be a key value by which modern (welfare) states are invading and destroying collectivities of (civil) society. Its effect is perhaps to some extent different in the West than in the East. In the West, it generates helplessness; in the East, powerlessness. However, in all countries, welfare states are in the name of solidarity destroying those social networks which are the "infrastructure" of the "community" as a meta-reciprocal collectivity.

If we try to protect societies against "imperialistic" welfare state interventions, we should make a clear distinction between institutional and non-institutional solidarity.

I would suggest that we should accept the late Durkheimian concept of solidarity as a product of a new moral entity, and not as the automatic outcome of the division of labour. If such an assumption is accepted, institutionalized solidarity should be recognized as a *contradictio in adjecto*: solidarity namely cannot be based on legal obligations, but only on moral obligations which are typical for social communities such as family, friendship, neighbourhood, etc.

If we accept this perspective, we will be able to establish a clear distinction between the "social state" and the "welfare society". *The function of the social state should be the promotion of negative freedom and negative equality; while on the other hand, the promotion of positive freedom and positive equality should be the function of a welfare society.* Such a functional division between state and society might at the same time limit state imperialism – which is the more dangerous, the more smoothly it is promoted. At the same time, such a division might facilitate the revitalization of societies by returning to them the care for the promotion of positive freedom and positive equality.

References

Alexander, J. (1986) 'Rethinking Durkheim's Intellectual Development', *International Sociology* 1 (1): 91-107 and 1 (2): 189-201.

Barr, N. (1987) *The Economics of the Welfare State.* London: Weidenfeld and Nicholson.

Berkowitz, L. (1963) 'Responsibility and Dependence', *Journal of Abnormal and Social Psychology* 5: 429-436.

Charles, A. (1985) 'Public Policy and Social Stratification', *Philosophy and Social Criticism* 11 (2): 1-7.

Coleman, J.S. (1983) 'Equality of Opportunity and Equality of Results', in Letwin, W. (ed.) *Against Equality.* London: MacMillan Press.

Deutsch, M. (1985) *Distributive Justice.* New Haven: Yale University Press.

Engels, F. (1974) 'Anti Duehring', in Marx, K., Engels, F., *Collected Works*, Vol. 31. Beograd: Prosveta.

Esping-Andersen, G. (1985) *Politics Against Markets.* New Jersey: Princeton University Press.

Esping-Andersen, G. (1987) 'Decommodification and Solidarity in the Welfare-State', in Rein, M. et al. (eds.) *Stagnation and Renewal in Social Policy.* New York: M.E. Sharpe.

Ferge, Z. (1980) *A Society in the Making; Hungarian Social and Societal Policy 1945-1975,* New York: M.E. Sharpe.

Ferris, J. (1985) 'Citizenship and the Crisis of Welfare State', in Bean, Ph., Ferris, J., Whynes, D. (eds.) *In Defence of Welfare.* London: Tavistock Publications.

Flam, H. (1987) 'Market Configurations; Toward a Framework for Socio-Economic Studies', *International Sociology* 2 (2): 107-129.

Marx, K. (1970) *Selected Works,* Vol. 3. Moscow.

Marx, K. (1979) 'Kritika Gotskog programmea' (Critique of the Gotha Programme), in Marx, K., Engels, F., *Collected Works*, Vol. 3. Beograd: Prosveta.

Mishra, R. (1984) *The Welfare State in Crisis.* Sussex: Wheatesheaf Books.

Nedeljkovic, I. (1987) 'Vrednostna opredeljena socialne politike jesu vrednostna' (Value Orientations in Social Policy are Value Based). *Socialna Politika,* Socialna situacija i vrendnostna opredeljenja u socialnoj politici. Beograd.

Nozick, R. (1974) *Anarchy, State and Utopia.* New York: Basic Books.

Offe, C. (1984) *Contradictions of the Welfare State.* London: Hutchinson.

O'Connor, W. (1979) *Socialism, Politics and Equality.* New York: Columbia University Press.

Pesic, V. (1987) 'Koncepcija drustvene jednakosti i socialna politika' (The Concept of Social Policy and Social Equality), *Socioloski pregled* 21 (1-2): 59-64.

Pusic, E. (1987) 'Solidarnost, humanost i smoupravljanje' (Solidarity, Humanism and Self-Management), Socialna situacija i vrednostna opredeljenja u socialnoj politici. *Socialna politika.* Beograd.

Rae, D. et al. (1981) *Equality.* Cambridge: Harvard University Press.

Rawls, J. (1971) *A Theory of Justice.* Cambridge: The Belknap Press of Harvard University Press.

Rein, M., Esping-Andersen G., Rainwater, L. (eds.) (1987) *Stagnation and Renewal in Social Policy.* New York: M.E. Sharpe.

Svetlik, I. (1989) 'Prestrukturiranje druzbenih dejavnosti' (The Restructuring of Social Services), *IB revija za planiranje* 8-9.

Szelényi, I., Manchin, R. (1987) 'Social Policy Under State Socialism', in Rein, M. et al. *op. cit.*

Sefer, B. (1987) 'Socialno stanje i sistem vrednostnih opredeljenja u socialnoj politici' (Social conditions and the value-system of social policy), *Socialna politika*. Beograd.

Thurow, L. (1981) *Equity, Efficiency, Social Justice and Redistribution*. Paris: OECD.

Zijderveld, A. (1986) 'The Ethos of Welfare State', *International Sociology* 1 (4): 443-457.

Wesolowski,W., Mach, B. (1986) 'Unfulfilled Systemic Functions of Social Mobility', *International Sociology* 1 (1): 29-35 and 1 (2): 173-187.

CHAPTER 13

Social Policy Regimes and Social Structure
Hypotheses about the Prospects of Social Policy in Central and Eastern Europe

Zsuzsa Ferge

It is a sociological truism to affirm that social institutions, including the welfare system, of any given society, are shaped by the interaction of its social and political relationships, its dominant ideologies, its historical legacies, and its political system. Nonetheless, the implications of this "truism" have only recently been analysed in depth in the case of the welfare systems of market societies; and they have not been scrutinized in the ex-socialist countries neither in the last 40 years, nor nowadays.

Analyses of this type would be very much needed, though, in these rapidly-changing societies. Their welfare system is at a crossroad. The former, "socialist" model is rejected in a wholesale way, and the future seems to be open. The alternatives and the possible outcomes could be visualized more clearly if the social forces having moulded the past were better understood, and if one could make projections about the possible impact of the newly emerging class structure, of new class coalitions, and of new political alignments.

1   Types of Welfare Systems

In describing the past and prospective welfare systems of Hungary, I shall use some of the concepts recently worked out by Gøsta Esping-Andersen (1990). On the basis of the complex impact of the various social, political, and ideological forces on welfare systems, he has defined several "regime types", permeated by the three most influential political ideologies of the last 150 years.

Briefly recapitulated, in the first type – the "liberal" welfare state (e.g. the United States) – means-tested assistance, or other income maintenance programmes on a modest scale and heavily targeted towards the poor, predominate. The second, "conservative-corporatist" regime type (e.g. Austria and Germany) is based on a historically-evolved statist-corporatist legacy. Because of conservative traditions, status differentials are keenly preserved. Usually, it is strongly influenced by the Church – which implies a conservative commitment towards the traditional family and the traditional role of women. The third and smallest "cluster" is composed of the "liberal-socialist" Scandinavian countries in which "the principle of universalism and decommodification of social rights were extended also to the new middle classes". Because of the emphasis on rights and on the promotion of individual autonomy, the model is a fusion of liberalism and socialism.

In what follows, an attempt is made to identify the successive welfare systems of Hungary. Our main concern is with the recent past, and especially with the foreseeable future. In both cases, we try to indicate the social and political forces which have shaped welfare systems – and more specifically, those classes (or social groups) and class coalitions – which may explain future prospects. While most of the evidence used here relates to Hungary, many trends seem to follow a not-too-different path in the other former socialist countries.[1]

The difficulty is obviously that the Central and Eastern European countries in the last 50 years have undergone two instances of radical, systemic social change. In both cases – after World War II, and around 1990 – systemic change meant a radical break with the past and a deliberate rejection of the legacy of the past. The radical transformation of the foundations of the structural and structuring relationships of society, has since then reached probably unprecedented proportions. The social implications of these moves are hard to analyse because we are too close to, and too involved in, the momentous changes. Under these conditions, a detached and cool view is impossible to achieve. Only a first, tentative attempt can be undertaken – with more hunches than proofs.

1.1   Types of Hungarian Welfare Systems

1.1.1 The Legacy from Pre-war Hungary

Using the former labels, before World War II, Hungary belonged to the group of countries with a conservative, statist, corporatist welfare system. Despite two historical attempts (in 1848 and in 1917), the country did not undergo a successful bourgeois revolution. The capitalist system started to grow vigorously, with powerful state support, in the last third of the nineteenth century, amidst the survival of strong feudal institutions – large feudal-type land estates primarily. The other major conservative power was the Catholic Church (one of the largest landowners, too), which could withstand all attempts to separate state and church.

The great estates were operated with very cheap, mostly landless labour. The landowners rejected practically all welfare programmes on behalf of the labourers or of the poorer smallholders, because they objected both to the emancipation of labour and to paying for the programmes that could have benefited them. Thus, the largest social group – the rural poor – had only a very small, selective, means-tested programme for health care and no programmes for assistance in cash, let alone social insurance schemes.

State bureaucracy was, however, important both numerically and socially. The nobility, true to the conservative spirit, disdained business and entrepreneurship. If the land did not offer a suitable living to many of them,[2] they found refuge with the state as civil servants. They were therefore particularly keen on maintaining and strengthening the separate, privileged, corporatist, hierarchical state welfare system devised specifically for civil servants long before the advent of social insurance.

The working class remained numerically comparatively feeble, but it profited from its relatively late emergence: it had built up, practically from its inception in the late nineteenth century, a relatively modern labour movement with relatively strong trade unions as well as a by-and-large modern social-democratic party. Due to the interplay of a strong, corporatist state, and a traditional, "ghetto-type" labour movement, Hungary adopted a Bismarckian social insurance system already in the 1880s.

Insurance schemes remained limited to industrial workers up to World War II, covering less than one third of the population and offering relatively modest benefits. However, the acceptance of an unemployment benefit scheme was blocked by employers. Therefore, the number of the urban poor was relatively high, especially in the early 1920s, and during the years after the world crisis of the early 1930s. They were more concentrated and more visible than the rural poor. Nevertheless, relief programmes instituted on behalf of the poor followed the spirit of the early Poor Laws and remained largely inadequate. They offered mainly workfare instead of welfare, they remained entirely discretionary, and the provisions were less than modest. The state did little outside of rudimentary legislation. The responsibility of fund-raising and service delivery was shifted mostly to the church and private charity.[3]

The capitalist class, as well as the market-related segments of the middle class (i.e. freelance professionals, employees in the private sector) were at the end of the nineteenth century to a large extent originally composed of immigrants (mostly Germans), and Jews. While they formed part of the ruling class, they were less valued – or less supported – by the state than either the landed nobility or the civil servants. For welfare provisions, the richest *stratum* relied entirely on the market, while the middle *strata* built up their own segmented and hierarchical private insurance schemes.

On the whole, the pre-war welfare system presented in a pronounced way all the characteristics of the continental European conservative-corporatist-statist model. However, it combined (on the surface) conservatism with some elements of traditional liberalism: it rejected the concept of social rights in a wholesale way;

it adopted only stigmatizing practices of poor relief; and it accommodated market solutions, if only for one part of the upper and middle class. Liberalism is not a very apt descriptor, though. State intervention in the economy remained stronger, the market was less powerful, and civil and political rights were far more limited than in a truly liberal system. The configuration described above really reflects the dual social structure of the time, with the coexistence of a more feudal rural structure and a more capitalist urban one.

1.1.2 The "Socialist" Welfare System

The period following World War II has been rich in turns and twists which cannot be analysed here in detail. Right after the war, there was a chance to complete the "bourgeois revolution" in a non-bloody way, with strong liberal and social-democratic influences. This chance was missed when, from 1948 on, the communist party performed its "coup d'état". With this move, they prevented the consolidation of the liberal and socialist tendencies into a new system.

A genuinely new chapter started in 1949. The communist party undertook the construction of a "new society" by completely abolishing the former social, economic, and political order; by severing all continuity with the past; and by "creating" a series of new institutions in all walks of life.[4]

The break with the past also took place in social policy. With the exception of social insurance and of occupational welfare offered at the workplace, all welfare institutions were abolished. The negative consequences are clear. Social assistance and all forms of social work were stopped in 1950, when over half of the population was still in absolute poverty (Ferge, 1987). Means-tested access to health services was abrogated at a time when two thirds of the population were not yet entitled to use the state health system. (Since they could not pay the market prices, they had to go without medical help – unless the general practitioner took pity of them.) The termination of private insurance schemes left many without any provision at all. The prohibition of voluntary, church, or lay help – and especially of all grass-roots, self-help movements – not only reduced the resources of social policy, but it also fatally damaged the "natural" bonds, the forces of social integration.

Nonetheless, the break with the past had also many positive elements. They may be forgotten or, worse, denied by the new passion of wiping out the past 40 years – in the same way as the first communist rulers tried to wipe out the previous decades. I still think that there were gains, at least as far as principles go. I am still convinced that it was salutary to get rid of the feudal privileges and of the hierarchies consolidating status differences built into the welfare system. It was a gain to eradicate the humiliating practices of assistance, depriving the "beneficiaries" not only of social but also of political rights.

Also, the advancement was not limited to the realm of principles. While it is hard to find signs of genuine improvement in the early 1950s, the scene changed after the crisis of 1956. From the early or mid-1960s on, in Hungary, and also in some other Central and Eastern European countries, very real improvements could be observed (for Poland, see Ksiezopolski, 1990). Massive pre-war and postwar poverty was mitigated by (admittedly artificial) full employment, increasing wages, and a rapidly-expanding social security system. These same institutions, together with the absence of private ownership and the containment of wage differentials, have considerably diminished many inequalities. In the last two decades, elements of existential security have become firmly established.

Although it is considered a political impropriety nowadays to recognize the merits of state socialism, the wholesale rejection of the past is not as popular as the new élite would like to believe. It is, for instance, clear that the erstwhile poor peasants have appreciated access on the basic citizens' rights to the national health service, or the extension of the pension system to them – even though the pensions were modest. They have always known that even a small holding of two to five acres would not have enabled them to buy decent health or pension insurance. Public surveys have invariably reported, from the late 1970s on, that while the majority have approved of social services, satisfaction was always greater and criticism less harsh among the poorer, less well-educated groups than among others (Angelusz et al., 1986).

I believe that social policy could be more successful than most other subsystems because – despite all endeavours to sever continuity with the past and to annihilate all traditional arrangements – the organic link with the past was not completely destroyed in this case.

In the economy or in politics, basic institutions have been artificially invented by "existing socialism" on ideological grounds and forced on the societies in question in a ruthless and anti-democratic way, without any home traditions or popular support. Both in the economy and in politics, new institutions had to prove that (existing) socialism was formed as a direct negation of everything belonging to capitalism.

In the *economy,* for instance, private property has been replaced by a "no-man's land" with regard to ownership (banning individual or group self-interest as well as accountability to democratically-constituted control groups); the market has been replaced by central planning and by centrally-directed agents pursuing centrally-defined targets. This move – to use Polanyi's categories – banned both formal economic rationality (the rationality which makes capitalism tick because of the market being responsive to solvent needs) and substantive rationality (the ability of the economy to be responsive to human needs in general).

In *politics*, all traditional and historically-evolved forms of political life were replaced by the artificially-invented party-state and its organs – all copied from the Soviet model. Parliament without parties, local authorities without local autonomy, government without power, press without freedom – all were artificial constructions imposed on society. As a result, politics ceased to function as politics, as the field in which different interests could meet and compromise. In this sense, while politics was essentially about retaining power – and in this it was similar to politics in general – it lost its ability to act politically according to the inner rationality of politics.

In *social policy*, the story is somewhat different. The large systems – a unified social insurance scheme and public health service – were neither artificial constructions nor institutions forced upon society from above, by the will of the dictators. Welfare institutions had a long home tradition and a long history of social struggles. They were developed from the 1960s on in line with the age-old requests of the workers' movements – full employment included. Also in this case, the institutions did not attempt to negate capitalist solutions. On the contrary, in the last three decades they followed by and large the evolution in the Western countries, in line with ILO recommendations and conventions. Entitlements were expanded; universal or near-universal solutions were introduced; in the case of social insurance, the "insurance" principle was increasingly enriched by solidaristic elements, without giving up the "earnings-related" schemes meant to accommodate the better-off groups.[5]

Following the regime types of Esping-Andersen, the welfare system of state socialist countries at the end of the 1980s was *formally* quite close to the social democratic model.

Despite the formal resemblance, the welfare subsystem was not – similarly to politics or the economy – a subsystem with relative autonomy, and a rationality of its own. The domination of politics completely annulled its autonomy. The way in which existential security operated, did not serve the emancipation but rather the totalitarian control of the citizens: the condition of gaining this security was to accept state employment.[6] Social policy could not follow its own "rationality" (i.e. the socially efficient coverage of needs), partly again because of the political structure which did not allow for the expression of needs, and partly because of its paralysing relationship with the economy (Ferge, 1989). In the absence of democratic participation and control, the original legitimation of these systems has been slowly undermined. Part of the tragic inadequacies of these systems – the absence of indexation of benefits despite a high rate of inflation, the endemic shortages in the health service, and so on – are clearly related to the absence of democratic politics.

Some details may reveal convincingly that the similarities with the social-democratic model were really no more than formal.

Existential security based on artificial full employment was not only ephemeral, but also easy to destroy. Even while it lasted, it was detrimental both to the economy – in which it conserved the obsolete jobs – and to the "surplus-workers", in whose case it conserved their unskilled, lowly status. Also, the relationship between work and welfare was ideologically overloaded. In the Swedish model, this relationship has always been very strong, but it has never become so ideological as to deny basic social rights to those who eventually failed to integrate into the labour market. This, however, was common practice in state socialist countries. Those who did not work (for whatever reason) were denied even the most elementary help. (One of the most outrageous rules of the Hungarian social assistance scheme for families with children, introduced as late as 1974, was to deny the benefit unless *both* parents were employed, and to withdraw it if the *child* happened to fail in his/her duty, i.e. if he/she did not attend school regularly.)

While the socialist system rejected the former, quasi-feudal status hierarchies, it rapidly introduced new status privileges (such as separate, high-standard hospitals and holiday homes for the ruling élite, privileged pension rules for the party bureaucracy, and so forth).

Most importantly, the concept of citizenship – as well as the evolution of rights experienced in most capitalist societies – was absent from the Central and Eastern European model of socialism. In the "normal" course of development of bourgeois societies, the acquisition of civil and political rights paved the way to social, cultural, and economic rights (Marshall, 1965). The totalitarian systems of state socialism did not recognize civil and political rights. But in the absence of these, social provisions – even if they were of adequate standard and even if they were popular – could not become rights. They have remained gifts, charity of the party-state, reinforcing the subordination of "subjects". Also, in the absence of political rights, solidarities could not be built up. Partly because of the absence of rights, and partly because of the "community-centred" ideology denying the importance of the individual, social policy in these countries could not assume any politically emancipating function and could not promote the autonomy of individuals.

In short, despite formal similarities, the liberal and emancipating dimension of the Scandinavian model was entirely absent from the state-socialist model of welfare. It had even less in common with the other regime types in Europe. If one wants to label the state socialist welfare system, it could be described as an anti-liberal, statist, hierarchical, socialist mix, with conservative elements thrown in.

1.2 The Current Alternatives

All three great ideological systems are represented in the parties constituting the present Hungarian Parliament, elected after the collapse of the state-socialist system.[7] However, the self-assigned ideological labels of the parties are not good predictors of their social welfare programmes. On the one hand, their self-identification does not necessarily coincide with their real, often-shifting political orientation. In fact, one should rather talk about orientations, because the plurality of often-conflicting views characterizes almost each party. On the other hand, the parties have not managed as yet to elaborate any well-defined programmes of social policy.

1.2.1 The Governing Parties

The core concept used by the governing parties – especially the single biggest party, the Hungarian Democratic Forum – in order to describe their global social project, is the "social market economy". It is implied rather than made explicit that their social policy orientation follows from this programme. However, the core concept itself is not as clear as one might wish. It is widely known (at least in Germany) that the meaning and the substance of the "social market economy" has been continuously changing since its inception in the late 1940s. While originally a liberal economic programme, it has become essentially conservative. Also, in the view of many analysts, the prosperous economy has failed to fulfil many of its social promises (Bartholomaeus, 1985).

The social policy corresponding to this (essentially German) model can be described on the basis of the government's three-year programme of "national renewal" published in the Fall of 1990 ("A nemzeti ..."), of various public statements by politicians, and of the decisions and actions of the government.

In the programme, the government has recognized "the right of each citizen to a socially-accepted minimal level of livelihood", which is an important step forward. (Unfortunately, the realization of this declared intention is jeopardized because the right is not enacted, and the budget does not foresee the necessary funds.) The church is destined to have a prominent role both in forging the values and in performing services in the realm of social policy.[8] The family is also "to be strengthened", which means that caring duties are meant to be shifted back to the family. The employment of women is not seen in a favourable light; and therefore, child care institutions seem to get less support than before. Targeting help to the truly needy is seen as both necessary and just, and is accompanied by a slight distaste for universal benefits. (In the case of family allowance, for instance, made universal only in April 1990, there are already propositions to transform it into a means-tested benefit.) Indeed, in all former socialist countries, one can observe an unusually strong resistance to the idea of entitlements to social benefits.

It is worth mentioning, that while there are frequent allusions to the recommendations of the World Bank whenever the government wants to justify a cut or a withdrawal in welfare benefits, no reference has been made to the Bank's view about assistance. In fact, the World Bank has suggested that "providing a secure safety net for the unemployed and the poor implies creating entitlements – that is, establishing minimum standards of financial support that are transparent, normative, and widely known, ... with the right to a formal appeal process" (World Bank, 1990).

Statism is one of the leading motifs of the government programme. While public initiatives are praised – and many of them have indeed started – the government is maintaining in many respects the role of central state organs. The democratic mechanisms of participation and control are still missing. Also, while many responsibilities are shifted to local authorities, there are no matching funds allotted to them. (In Hungary, this has clear political reasons. The central government, elected in the Spring of 1990, is conservative. The local authorities, elected six months later, are predominantly independent or opposition.)

All in all, the government is in favour of a modest, rather conservative, residual social policy. One of the leading government experts in social policy, Member of Parliament of the governing party, has recently made explicit this opinion in an interview: "I interpret the concept of social policy in a narrower sense than what is generally accepted. I understand by social policy help given to the needy by the government, by local authorities, by society (through its associations or foundations), or by private persons. The needy are those who have gotten into a hopeless situation for some reason ..." (Hogyan kössünk ..., 1991).

1.2.2 The Liberals

The largest opposition party, the Association of the Free Democrats, is clearly of two minds as far as social policy is concerned. There is a wing representing economic (neo)liberalism, and a wing with a social-liberal / social-democratic outlook. In the programme already elaborated in 1989, the chapters on social welfare were worked out mostly by the social- liberal / social-democratic wing. Therefore this programme emphasized much more strongly than any other programme the importance of social citizenship, and of social rights. They were also favourable to many universal programmes, on grounds of the integrative role of such programmes. They advocated programmes of positive discrimination in favour of the marginalized, most deprived groups. The economic liberals have also had their say, though, in this programme. Therefore, they advocated (along with universal rights) a strong market sector in many welfare services, social insurance included. Also, because of their deep belief in the emancipating virtues of the market, they have often expressed their preference for a social policy catering only to the "truly needy".

There is no clear demarcation line between "conservative" and "liberal" social policies. In fact, there are many similarities in the social programmes of the governing and of the opposition parties. As already shown, a "minimal social policy" has an appeal for both sides. Market solutions are certainly essential for the liberals; but the conservatives, as in pre-war times, can well accept them, too. (Private health and pension schemes, as well as private schools, are already lawfully operating.)

The rejection of former social achievements is also a shared ground. The governing and the opposition parties alike have, for instance, accepted the inevitability of mass unemployment in the interests of profitability and restructuring. Despite a new and correct Employment Act (February 1991) building up the institutions and mechanisms of active labour market policies, their real impact is as yet insignificant. The reform of social insurance, implying the "cleansing" of the system of its non-insurance-based (i.e. solidaristic) elements, is also an objective pursued by both parties. The curtailment of occupational welfare (with the exception of fringe benefits for the upper echelons) is accepted on both sides. And no party dares confess to the citizens that some social benefits – like, for instance, the very generous and very popular child care grant scheme of the former system – will have to be seriously trimmed, because no private firm will guarantee a job to an absentee mother for three years.[9]

1.2.3 The Socialists

The third parliamentary force, the Socialist Party, is trying to transform itself into a social-democratic party. It has to face, though, two grave handicaps which are distorting its political position, social welfare programmes included.[10]

On the one hand, as the inheritor of the former ruling party, its legitimacy is continuously questioned. As a consequence, it has lost its self-confidence. Instead of being able to look ahead, it has to prove constantly that it is no more identical with its former self. It cannot endorse or proclaim programmes which are, if only remotely, reminiscent of solutions or slogans of the party-state (popular as they might be with the electorate). Worse still – since, as already shown, the welfare regime of state socialism had (even if only formally) many socialist or social-democratic elements – the present socialists have to repudiate it. They cannot formulate a policy of full employment; they have to join the chorus condemning the past, etc. One characteristic symbol of this defensive policy is that – while most Western socialist or social-democratic parties stand openly for the combination of the values of freedom, equality, solidarity, and justice – Hungarian socialists entirely dropped "equality" from their vocabulary.

The other burden afflicting the socialists is their recent past. There is one important continuity with the past they can and have to endorse, and that is their link with the reform wing of the former state party which has paved the way for the bloodless revolution from the 1980s on. (The majority of the socialist MPs have been among the reformers.) But it was the last socialist reform government which started the liberal reforms, not only in the economy but also in social policy. It is factually true, and has been criticized at the time by sociologists, that the last socialist government introduced – with Bolshevik methods, i.e. in a non-democratic way – a series of neo-liberal reforms in social policy. They were the first to implement high (almost market-level) user charges in case of many social services, including school meals or shelters for the homeless. They started to talk about the "cleansing" of social insurance. They were the first to condemn "expensive" universalism and to praise the merits of means-testing. They had already accepted the necessity of unemployment. Reform-minded economists belonging to, or cooperating with, this party, have requested – long before the programme of the Free Democrats was drawn up – the claims for marketization and privatization in health, education and insurance.

The present government, while rejecting and ridiculing most deeds of the former system, is happily continuing the liberal trend in social policy started by the last government. Therefore, it has a false ring if the socialists oppose cuts or liberal solutions in social policy. Whenever they dare to do this, they are immediately reminded that "it is easy to talk in opposition – why did not they follow their own recipe while in power".

Because of these predicaments of the Socialist Party, there are no advocates of a genuine socialist or social-democratic social policy project in the political arena. In other words, social policy is the weakest point of the Socialist Party. It might sound paradoxical, but the Socialist Party has a much easier task in propagating a social-democratic line in economics or in politics. In these fields, the social-democratic line radically differs from state socialist ideology and practice. One could say that the present situation of social policy is tragic because it was not bad enough in the bad old days ...

2   The Changing Social Structure

Under conditions of political democracy, there may not be any direct relationship between social structure and welfare regimes; but the indirect ties between the two may always be uncovered. Former state socialist societies seem to be an exception to this rule. In my assumption, the reason is that, instead of a living structure, they had a stifled or repressed one. This problem is obviously connected with their defective mechanisms of integration assuring social reproduction.[11]

2.1 The Non-System and the Repressed Structure

In recent decades, the problems of the integration of society – more specifically, "system integration" and "social integration" – have become a major theme in sociology (Habermas and Luhmann, 1971; Offe, 1972).

System integration refers to the relatively well-established reproduction of society. It can be achieved if the institutions or mechanisms which relate in a systemic way the various units or subsystems in a society – such as the market or communications – are functioning. Despite relatively smooth system integration, societies may show a high level of social anomies – destructive signs of social disintegration. In the approach of Habermas, system-integrative mechanisms cannot assure the genuine integration of society, cannot supersede "normative integration achieved through group identities". There is a need for mechanisms of social integration, which may be generated by norms and values based on consensus.

In the former socialist countries, as described above, the institutions and mechanisms of system integration have been created artificially. Therefore they could not become real mechanisms. System-integrative mechanisms functioned more or less normally only as long as they could be upheld by direct commands and coercion. But the simulation of integrative mechanisms could not replace the real ones – sooner or later, they had to collapse. At the same time, social integrations – which make life in any society humanly acceptable – have been either deliberately destroyed from above or fundamentally disrupted by the adverse conditions. In all probability, former socialist countries show a much higher level of social disintegration and anomy than Western democracies – although the latter are also in bad shape.

In short, the various types of mechanisms which may integrate a system and assure its reproduction, were either simulated and doomed to failure or were deliberately destroyed. That is why these societies may be described as *pseudo-systems* or *non-systems*.

Under these conditions, the structuring forces of society could not function normally, either. When they are operating relatively freely and spontaneously, they shape the social basis and assure the dynamics – of system-integrative mechanisms at the macro level, and socially integrative ones on all levels. If their spontaneous operation is hindered, the macro and micro structures – the groups which are vital in creating a social space – cannot develop, either. That is why I propose to describe these societies as having a *"repressed structure"*.

In case of this "repressed structure", the duality of the ruling élite and the rest of society was perceptible; but it was hard to discern other real social groups. I do not imply that society has become classless or homogeneous. The studies on social stratification carried on in Hungary, in Poland, and in Czechoslovakia from the early 1960s on, have convincingly shown that there were deep and clustering inequalities, as well as distinct strata. These were generated by well-known factors – power, knowledge, ownership, gender, ethnic affiliation, and so forth. However, the central power forced these factors to operate in such a way as to prevent the formation of "real" groups. By "real" groups, I mean groups which acquire a certain stability, which realize their own identity, which are capable of recognizing the nature of their relationship with other groups and hence of identifying their interests. Without such real groups, a social structure cannot become a dynamic entity and structural forces cannot acquire a political dimension.

This *modus operandi* of power is quite understandable. "Real" groups are not acceptable for a totalitarian logic, because they may oppose the unique, single "truth" and therefore endanger the *status quo*. In fact, whenever such a group threatened to emerge, the central power crushed it. When it did not follow this route, like in case of *Solidarnosc* in Poland, this meant – whether anybody was aware of this or not – that the system had given up its identity and was inevitably heading towards its demise. With regard to group or class formation, state socialist systems were "classless" societies, even if not in the sense which was given to this term by Stalinist orthodoxy.

2.2 The Structuring Forces or Relationships

With the change of the system, totalitarian political repression – and with it, the repressed structure – have come to an end. The vigorous action of the structuring factors had started. But we are only at the beginning of this process, and it is hard to foresee what "real" groups will emerge in some time. That is why a closer look of at least some of these factors, or structuring relationships, may be instructive.

2.2.1 Power

The restructuring, or pluralization of the monolithic power structure started with the separation of the legislative, the administrative, and the judiciary; with the emergence of a free press; and with the separation of central and local power. However, the groups generated by other structuring forces (such as knowledge, ownership, gender, etc.), which would operate as pressure or support groups and would influence the orientation of power, are still in an embryonic state. It is especially painful that the eternally oppressed groups – i.e. the workers, the women, the poor – have no political voice or political representation.

2.2.2 Ownership

In state socialist countries, state ownership was the dominant form of property. Thereby, central power appropriated control over the majority of assets in society. Hence, the structuring function of ownership consisted of the strengthening of the monolithic power structure. In other words, power and ownership did not operate as different factors but defined exactly the same dividing lines. One could not speak of a "political" and a "propertied" class – the two were identical. The pluralization of ownership relations already started within the "repressed structure" – with the slow acceptance of small private property and the growth of the second economy.

At present, one can observe the amazingly rapid ascendance of a new "middle" (and maybe "upper") class, which owns its existence and position to the market, to entrepreneurship, and to economic capital, and which is forging for itself a distinct identity. The wonder is not that this group has emerged. Its ascendance was ideologically prepared by the liberal reformers for at least five years; and practically prepared by the second economy. The surprising thing is that apparently this is the first group to constitute itself as a real group, recognizing its own place, role, and interests.

This may be explained, perhaps, by the recruitment of this class. It now seems that the members – and especially the best-positioned members of the new manager and entrepreneurial class – are predominantly those (political and economic) managers and technocrats who because of the political change had to leave the commanding posts of politics and the economy. Those having worked in the grey or black economy have a much smaller chance to accede to high new positions –

despite a widespread belief to the contrary. Many of them seem to lack not only the necessary physical or financial capital for successful entrepreneurship, but also the symbolic and the social (relational) capital – which is very much needed now. It may be added that, in Hungary, the "self-made man" was a rare phenomenon even at the (first) dawn of capitalism. Ninety per cent of the economic élite from before 1945 have been recruited from the upper ten per cent of society (Lengyel, 1989).

The social position of the propertied and entrepreneurial class will certainly be different from what it was before the war. It may be stronger and higher for various reasons:

- In all probability, the dual structure will not be restored. The members of the former landed upper class may be able to resurrect some of the symbols of nobility, but it is hardly likely that they would be able to reclaim the big estates. The attempts in this direction would not only clash with the interests of the peasants, but also with those of foreign and home capital.
- The supremacy of the entrepreneurial class will be indirectly strengthened by the weakness of the working class. It seems that the revival of a "real" working class may take a very long time. On the one hand, there are too many divisive tendencies. The threat of unemployment, the rivalry of the new workers' organizations, and the division of the workers by party politics, are all tendencies which are now gaining in intensity. The former segmentation of the labour market is also amplified because of a recent sectorial division. There is a strong, well-paying new private sector operating partly with foreign capital; a more and more impoverished state sector with strictly-regulated low wages; and the world of the insecure, ephemeral small ventures. Workers are, of course, competing for entry into the first group.
- The entrepreneurial class may be further reinforced if the best-qualified professionals, hitherto in state employment, desert the state – because the state had first disowned them. The pay and status of this segment of the middle classes is at present so low that an increasing number may choose either emigration, or the search for a better livelihood in the market sector (private medicine, private teaching, etc.). The hopeless deterioration of the state-financed middle class corresponds so well with the interests of the market-related middle class, that one cannot escape suspicion about the intentionality of the process.

The big unknown in the process of the changing property relations is the fate of the rural population. The question of landownership is still pending. The most vocal – though a minority – proposal in Parliament (that of the Smallholders' Party) wants to reinstate the state of affairs of 1949: giving back the land to those who were then owners or to their descendants (the majority of whom now live in towns). In this case, a large segment of the rural population will become hopelessly impoverished – especially all those who have been working in agriculture in the last decades, but whose family never owned land. If the milder plan for compensation is adopted (giving land back only to those who will cultivate it), the rural population will be restructured in a less polarized way. The emergence of a rural middle class is likely, all the more so because its contours have already appeared in the second economy.

2.2.3 Knowledge

The structuring role of symbolic capital – or knowledge – is undergoing a deep change, too. The relationship between power and knowledge was a sore and sensitive issue in the former system. Symbolic capital, always an important differentiating factor, could not be as easily expropriated as real (material) capital. For a short while after the socialist revolutions this did not seem to matter: because many intellectuals (the "owners of symbolic capital") spontaneously adhered to the very appealing socialist ideology. This honeymoon did not last long, though. And when the members of the "intelligentsia" started to ask irksome questions, and formulate their heterodoxies (Bourdieu, 1977), they have become dangerous for the totalitarian power. They hampered the total submission and ideological homogenization of the majority.

The first reaction of power was the project of their physical annihilation – implemented on a large scale in the Soviet Union from the late 1920s on. It turned out, however, that knowledge was killed together with its owner; and this created difficulties both in international competition and in the execution of domestic plans. The Central and Eastern European socialist countries came into being when this experience was already acquired. Therefore, they tried to work out mechanisms by which they could secure the collaboration of the intellectuals and prevent their disturbing impact: the dissemination of heterodoxies. (One of the techniques was to assure relatively good working and living conditions for the scholars enclosed in the ghetto-like institutes of the Academies of Sciences. The scholars could work there, but they had no opportunity to "corrupt", for instance, the university students.)

However, the isolation of the "knowers" could never be perfect. Also, there always appeared new members of this dangerous breed. Therefore, the relationship between the owners of power and of knowledge has remained, up to the collapse of the system, fraught with tensions.

Konrád and Szelényi (1978) may be right in saying that in the last decades many intellectuals have accepted positions in the power structure and have themselves become members of the ruling class. It seems to me, though, that under the conditions of the totalitarian system, access to the ruling class implied that one had to renounce to the very essence of "being intellectual", to the right to limitless doubt. This price may be required from most civil servants under any political regime. But in the state socialist systems, the newly-acceding rulers, as (former) intellectuals, had to know – even if they did not make it explicit – that they were joining an illegitimate power structure. Therefore, they had to distance themselves from this role; and hence they had to become either cynical or schizophrenic – or again they had to impose narrow boundaries on their own thinking.[12]

The social divisions created by the unequal distribution of knowledge then coincided, at least to a large extent, with the partitioning produced by power and (the control over) ownership. In all probability, this situation will change. One can expect that symbolic capital will become, similarly to other forms of capital, a relatively autonomous structuring factor. The outcome of the new differentiation is uncertain. Only some informed guesses can be formulated.

One of the hunches is that the former state-employed white-collars will split at least into three groups of the new middle class, with markedly different positions and interests.

- If the current trend of "statism" continues, professional bureaucrats (civil servants) are likely to become a rather privileged order. The government is already trying to win them over by relatively high salaries. The immediate reason for this is that otherwise – if they get only the average salary of those in state employment – they would leave the state bureaucracy for the more lucrative private sphere. (The state bureaucracy has already been decimated by the passion of the new governing parties to "cleanse public life" of all those who held even a minor position in the former system; consequently, the state apparatus would break down if the spontaneous exodus continued.) However, the state will not be able, despite all its efforts, to compete financially with the private sector. Hence – presumably – it will rediscover all the hierarchical status symbols and special privileges of the pre-war state bureaucracy (like, for instance, the corporative, privileged insurance system of civil servants).[13]

  The members of the new bureaucracy will probably be more self-assured than their predecessors. Under the new conditions, they ought not to define themselves any more as intellectuals having betrayed their vocation. As servants of a legitimate political order, they can give up the right to limitless doubt without qualms and without the unconscious, but self-imposed, self-distortion.
- The members of the newly-emerging "free professions" (or freelancers) will be recruited to a large extent from former state employees. Many of them will not have property, but they will all depend on the market. Their interests will be similar to those of the entrepreneurs, because only a smoothly-working market can assure the solvent demand they need. At the same time, however, part of their income will come from the state, through (partly or fully) state-financed private institutions. Therefore, they have to have good relationships with the state bureaucracy, both in order to boost the norms paid by the state and to multiply the opportunities for private undertakings financed partly by public funds.
- The third group will consist of intellectuals working in the public human service sector. If the present tendencies prevail, this group will become a "residue".

Part of its members will be the fanatics from their professional group, ideologically committed to the non-market sector. Many others will stay there either because there are no other opportunities at the place where they live, or because they are not good enough for anything else.

This part of the middle class is usually self-confident and strong in mature parliamentary democracies. The public sector (even if welfare pluralism is accepted) is legitimate. Their social position, including their remuneration, is similar to, and sometimes even better than, that of the professional bureaucrats. The reason is not only that the flawless functioning of public services has a legitimating function for the existing power. Public opinion may also play a role. It is well-known from surveys on occupational prestige that the public always rates higher the professional who offers personal services than the remote and uncontrollable bureaucrat. In a well-functioning democracy, this opinion may play a role – among others – in case of remunerations. As a result, this group is an integral and equal segment of the middle classes; demonstrating, among other things, that knowledge *per se* – that is, without any power position – is valued by the community.

In present-day Hungary, the situation is different. Because of the political conflict between the central and local governments, the central state is not concerned with decent remuneration of the intellectuals employed by local authorities. Simultaneously, liberalism on the rise is inimical to a welfare sector financed, let alone run, by the state (be it central or local). A further significant deterioration of the situation of this group, is therefore a distinct possibility entailing the continuing decay of public welfare services. (This will act as a "self-fulfilling prophecy", proving the necessity of private solutions.)

Another, more optimistic scenario is not excluded, though. It may be, even if the chances for victory are slim, that the members of the group in question use the new opportunities of a free system to fend for their own interests. In this case, the pluralization of society will be better promoted.

3 Structural Forces and Social Policy

3.1 The Legacy

As regards the social and political forces shaping the welfare system, and their representation in political decision-making, the pre-war formula is clear enough. While many details are awaiting historical research, one may affirm quite confidently that the political role of the working class was weak; and that of the rural poor, practically non-existent. The fraction of the middle class linked to the state (primarily civil servants) carried a significant weight. Neither could the ruling power neglect the market-related middle-class. However, in social matters, the decisive force was the coalition of the upper classes of the dual (partly feudal, partly capitalist) structure: the landlords, and the capitalists or employers.

One may still use class terms for the intermediary, non-consolidated period of the first postwar years. Social-democratic and liberal ideas prevailed – having their social basis in the working class, the former rural poor, and the professional middle classes. The landed upper class formally disappeared after the land reform. The state bureaucracy (after having served the fascist regime) was subdued. The same applies to the capitalist upper and middle class, but for different reasons.

3.2 The Recent Past

The period following the communist takeover in 1949 cannot be described any more in easy class terms. The essence of the totalitarian system was, even in the late Kádár period – which was a phase of mild dictatorship – that the power élite had an exclusive role in shaping politics. It successfully curbed and throttled all "natural" social forces and interests, even formally squeezing them out of decision-making.

It would be in vain, under these conditions, to look for the interplay of plural social forces. The political will (shaping everything, social policy included) was fuelled, as regards its ideology, by simplified socialist dogmas – and as regards its practice, by the passion for conserving the power structure. The declared objective of this ideology was to serve the interests of the working class. And in fact, at least in the case of social policy, the ideologically-motivated steps could simultaneously serve the aim of consolidating the power structure and meeting the interests of a majority.

It is impossible, though, to talk about the political support of the majority (or of the working class, or any other group). The problem is not only that policy-makers were not taking into account the opinions – and were not interested in the participation or support – of any social group. Politics could not have been shaped by the interplay of social forces: because the social relationships generating social dynamism were stifled, because the social structure itself was repressed.

3.3 The Present

The present is very blurred. I mentioned earlier that the map of social forces and that of political parties do not fully overlap, even in mature democracies. In the new democracies of Eastern and Central Europe, the situation is more complicated because both maps are very unclear. The political profile of the newly-emerged parties has not yet settled down: it is both unusually mixed and shifting. And the former repressed structure is also in flux: the "real", structurally-important groups will take a long time to develop.

Still, the previously discussed hunches about the future structuring of society may help to formulate guesses about potential alliances and class coalitions, and therefore about the future of social policy.

The state bureaucracy, and possibly the Church, are eminently interested in the reconstruction of something akin to the pre-war *conservative-hierarchized-corporatist* welfare regime. This implies minimal benefits, the absence of social rights, the strengthening of the puritan work ethic excluding from help the undeserving poor, an exalted role for private and church charity, an important welfare load shifted to the family with, in its centre, a traditional role for women, and hierarchically built corporative welfare institutions.

If the state expands the advantages of this system to the state-employed intelligentsia, they may also join the supporters. The model may have some appeal for the upper layers of the skilled workers, too – partly because of nostalgia for the past, and partly because they may hope to profit from the advantages of a hierarchical corporatist system.

The potential supporters of the conservative model are numerically not large, but their parliamentary-political strength is overwhelming.

The *liberal* welfare model – characterized by a minimal benefit level, but with entitlements, by a large market sector, by weak centralizing attempts, and by numerous grass-roots movements for self-defence – has hardly any home tradition. Its appeal is spreading, though, due to the impact of the neo-liberal ideology still on the rise and of some influential international bodies representing this ideology (mainly the IMF).

The social basis of the liberal welfare model consists essentially of the rising market-related middle and upper class, which is at present – as already mentioned – the most articulate and politically best-organized social force. This social basis may be enlarged by the better-off segments of pensioners and workers. They may indeed accept this model, on the strength of the argument forcefully presented to them that private insurance schemes may produce the immediate improvement of the health and pension systems.

Again, the numerical force of all these groups together is not too considerable. Still, the liberal model may count on relatively strong parliamentary support, with the majority of the opposition parties and a minority in the government coalition.

No doubt, the liberal opposition – now playing an important role in the local governments – should be interested in a welfare policy which is offering something to all the local citizens, and which therefore has an integrating force. But since in all probability the local authorities will be underfinanced, they may be forced to opt for the liberal solution (and in this will be supported by the better-off citizens).

The social basis of the *liberal, social-democratic model* might be stronger numerically than that of the former regimes. Regarding their objective interests, the majority of workers, small-holders, members of cooperatives (if the cooperatives survive reprivatization in some renewed form), small pensioners, a majority of women, and most of the poor could be among the supporters. Intellectuals who are committed to social solidarity and who oppose inequalities and injustices which limit freedom, are usually committed to this model.

The political, parliamentary support for this welfare regime is extremely weak, though. The socialists are a minority, and – as mentioned already – very much on the defensive. They do not dare to present "socialist" programmes, and they do not dare to submit the other programmes to a socialist critique. They are not even using the non-ideological, economically-based arguments in favour of non-market solutions in welfare services (Barr, 1987a, 1990). Because of their delegitimated status, they are unable to forge alliances with other parliamentary forces – for instance, with the social liberals of the liberal parties. Also, the organizations of "civil society" – trade unions and other pressure groups – are either in ruins or as yet unformed. Consequently, the institutions of collective bargaining – whether bipartite or tripartite – are not yet strong enough to have a genuine impact on government or on parliament.

While the political chances of a liberal, social-democratic welfare model are extremely thin, the political supporters of the conservative and the liberal model may easily form a coalition. In short, this means that the welfare regime of the coming years will consist, more likely than not, of a minimal safety net – along with corporatist, private, and semi-private solutions.

The rapid transformation, implying a very significant deterioration of the welfare benefit system, may be slowed down by two factors. One is that the organized political forces supporting the interests of the groups with rapidly-deteriorating conditions, will strengthen more rapidly than before. The other possibility is that the governing parties will realize the political risk of the uncompensated losses of large masses. The risk is not only the erosion of the political support for the present government, but also the utter desperation of large groups conducive to spontaneous outbreaks of violence. In this case, not only the present government but also the hardly-won, as yet fragile democracy will be in jeopardy.

If these dangers are realized in time, the safety net might yet be modified. Such a modification may not necessarily squeeze out or may not mortally injure the universal systems, which – if decentralized and democratized – could regain the support of the citizens.

I am convinced that, at present, this is the most one can hope for, both for the unprivileged groups and social peace at large. However, the chances of such an outcome are slim both because of the strength of the dominant new ideologies, and the gap between the yet unformed social groups and the already-existing parliamentary parties.

Notes

1) UNICEF has recently launched a project on the changing social situation in ex-socialist countries, with a special focus on children's well-being. The documents presented, and the discussions having taken place at these meetings, support the assumptions about converging trends (Cornia, 1991).

2) Because of the Trianon treaty in 1919, when two thirds of the area of the country were allocated to the neighbouring countries, many landowners lost their land. Also, many of the younger siblings had to find a living outside agriculture. In other cases, land was lost because of mismanagement.

3) This system cannot be described, though, in the terms of the subsidiarity principle. This principle – as followed, for instance, in Germany – defines a wide range of responsibilities which have to be financed by the state. However, state agencies (whether central or local) are allowed to deliver a service only in the absence of other social actors – the Churches, the Red Cross, or some other voluntary agency – willing to perform the function. In pre-war Hungary, the obligations of the state were not fixed, and no clear principle was followed in the implementation of welfare "pluralism".

4) The original plan was even more radical than the outcome. In the initial blueprint, for instance, even the family was sentenced to death as the hothouse of conservative relationships and of the transmission of privileges. The plan had to be given up – not only because the family proved to be too resistant, but because the revolutionary power soon became concerned with its own stability and became "conservative" in many respects. It then realized the importance of family stability.

5) The will to please better-off groups, combined with a eugenically-minded population policy, led to the introduction of an earnings-related child care leave which is almost unique in Europe.

6) No doubt, social control is almost always a hidden dimension of welfare provisions and (usually stable, full-time) employment is a condition of access to social insurance. The difference is, on the one hand, the extent of control. For instance, in order to apply for a passport, in Hungary one had to secure the recommendation and permission of one's employer. On the other hand, in Hungary one was more or less forced to take up employment in the state sector.

7) There are three conservative parties, two liberal parties, and one socialist party.

8) The views of the Catholic Church on the role of women, and especially on birth control, are forcefully presented and are gaining ground in the politics of both Poland and Hungary.

9) Parental leave was longer and better paid in most former socialist countries than in Western Europe. In Hungary, 20 or 24 weeks of fully-paid maternity leave was followed by two years of parental care allowance paid at a rate of about 70 per cent of former earnings, and then by one year as a flat-rate benefit. The employer had to preserve the job of the parent on leave. In the European Community, in 9 out of 12 countries the maternity leave was between 14 and 16 weeks at the end of the 1980s; and parental leave was everywhere either shorter, or unpaid, without a job guarantee (Commission,1990).

10) The various parties which label themselves social-democratic did not get enough votes to get into Parliament. They are torn by inner quarrels and petty jealousies. In fact, the socialist system killed social democracy – one of the biggest parties after the war – more effectively than any other political movement.

11) The issues treated in the following short section constitute an attempt to deal conceptually with the basic sociological issues of state-socialist societies. Despite some preliminary work they need further theoretical clarification and empirical support.

12) Incidentally, I think that we encounter here one of the less visible but most tragic features of "existing socialism". This is the problem of the self-imposed and ideologically-justified bounderies on one's own thinking, producing a repressed and distorted self. Although for the most varied reasons, (almost) nobody could be his/her "natural" self, whether he/she realized it at the time or not.

13) It may be interesting to mention the recent government proposal to Parliament about the new state decorations. One of the proposed decorations was founded by Maria Theresia for services to the nation, and another by Horthy for cultural excellence. Both are *closed orders* with 100 and 60 decorated persons, respectively. They clearly follow a feudal, and not a bourgeois, logic.

References

Angelusz, R., Nagy, L. G., Tardos, R. (1986) *A szociálpolitikai közvéleménykutatások eredményei.* Kézirat.
Barr, N. (1987a) *The Economics of the Welfare State.* London: Weidenfeld and Nicholson.
Barr, N. (1990) *Economic Theory and The Welfare State: A Survey and Reinterpretation.* Welfare State Programme directed by Atkinson, A.B., Le Grand, J., Hills, J., No. 54. Suntory Toyota International Centre for Economics and Related Disciplines.
Bartholomaeus, I. (1985) 'Soziale Marktwirtschaft', in Klees, B., Motz, H. (eds.) *Sozialreader. Beiträge zur Wirtschafts-und Sozialpolitik nach der "Wende".* Steinweg.
Bourdieu, P. (1977) *Outline of a Theory of Practice.* Cambridge.
Castles, F.G., Mitchell, D. (1990) *Three Worlds of Capitalism or Four?* The Australian National University, Discussion Paper No. 21. October 1990.
Esping-Andersen, G. (1990) *The Three Worlds of Welfare Capitalism.* Princeton: University Press.
Ferge, Zs. (1987) 'The Trends and Functions of Social Policy in Hungary', in Jallade, J.-P. (ed.) *The Crisis of Redistribution in European Welfare States.* Trentham Books.
Ferge, Zs. (1989) 'Social Policy and the Economy', in Bulmer, M., Lewis, J., Piachaud, D. (eds.) *The Goals of Social Policy.* London, Boston, Sidney, Wellington: Unwin Hyman.
Ferge, Zs. (1990) 'The Fourth Road: The Future for Hungarian Social Policy', in Deacon, B., Szalai, J. (eds.) *Social Policy in the New Eastern Europe.* Aldershot: Avebury.
Fordulat és Reform. (Change and Reform) *Medvetánc,* 1987/2. sz. Melléklete.
Garde d'enfants dans la Communauté Européenne, 1985-90. Commission des Communautés Européennes, Service Information Femmes, 1990.
Habermas, J., Luhmann, N. (1971) *Theorie der Gesellschaft oder Sozialtechnologie?* Frankfurt am Main: Suhrkamp Verlag.
Habermas, J. (1987) *Theorie des kommunikativen Handels.* Frankfurt am Main: Suhrkamp Verlag.
Hogyan kössünk szociális hálót? (How to Weave a Safety Net?) Interview with Gyula Fekete and Ottilia Solt, *Társadalmi Szemle,* 1 (1991).
Konrád, G., Szelényi, I. (1978) *Az értelmiség utja az osztályhatalomhoz.* (The March of Intellectuals to Power). In English: Harcourt and Brace.
Ksiezopolski, M. (1990) 'Is Social Policy a Problem in a Socialist Country?' in Deacon, B., Szalai, J. (eds.) *Social Policy in the New Eastern Europe.* Aldershot: Avebury.
Leibfried, St. (1992) 'Towards a European Welfare State?' (*In this volume*).
Lengyel, G. (1989) *Vállalkozók, bankárok, kereskedôk.* (Entrepreneurs, Bankers, Tradesmen). Magvetô Kiadó.
Marshall, T.H. (1950) *Citizenship and Social Class.* Cambridge: University Press.
Offe, C. (1972) *Strukturprobleme des kapitalistischen Staates.* Frankfurt am Main: Suhrkamp Verlag.
(A) Nemzeti Megújhodás Programja (The Programme of National Renewal). (1990) Budapest.
(A) Rendszerváltás Programja (The Programme for the Change of the System). (1989) Szabad Demokraták Szövetsége (Alliance of Free Democrats).
Titmuss, R.M. (1974) *Social Policy. An Introduction.* Allen and Unwin.
Titmuss, R.M. (1987) 'Developing Social Policy in Conditions of Rapid Change', in Abel-Smith, B., Titmuss, K. (eds.) *The Philosophy of Welfare. Selected Writings of Richard M. Titmuss.* Allen and Unwin.
The World Bank (1990) *Social Policy and Distributive System.* Manuscript, quoted with the permission of the World Bank, Mission Aide-memoire.

Part III

EUROPEAN FUTURES

CHAPTER 14

Social Policy, Economic Organization and the Search for a Third Way[1]

Anthony B. Atkinson

Introduction

The central theme of this paper is the close interrelation between the form of economic organization and the role of social policy. The role and functioning of social policy depends on the structure of economic organization. Conversely, the legitimacy and effective operation of the economic organization depends on a supporting system of social policy. In the first section of the paper, this interdependence is developed with regard to two "pure types" of economic organization – a centralized socialist economy and a market capitalist economy – and with respect to the income maintenance (social security) function of social policy.

The idea of a market capitalist economy enters frequently in the current debate about the development of Eastern Europe, but this debate too often appears to neglect the difference between the pure type and the reality. The second section of the paper sets out some of the reasons why the reality is different – notably, the existence of large-scale unemployment and the segmentation of the economy – and their implications for the effectiveness of social security. It is also important to remember that economic organization has to develop and evolve according to changing circumstances – such as the role of the family, the economic position of women, the extent of self-employment, and the degree of international interdependence.

The problems in reality with market-based economies, and the changing circumstances, have led to interest in a third way, or a form of economic and social organization different from both market capitalism and centralized socialism. What is less frequently discussed, is the relation between such a third way and radical reforms of social policy – such as the introduction of a basic income guarantee. It is on this that I concentrate in Section 3, where it is argued – following the work of James Meade – that the two aspects have to be seen in conjunction.

How far a third way is relevant to the developments in Eastern Europe, is a controversial question, but the experience of Western countries certainly contains important lessons, as is discussed briefly in the concluding comments.

1   "Pure Types" of Economic Organization and Social Policy

In this section, I describe two pure type forms of economic organization, labelled respectively centralized socialist and market capitalist. My purpose in doing so is not to contribute to an analysis of their economic properties, but rather to consider their relation to social policy – specifically, that of income maintenance. In both cases, the economy is assumed to be industrialized, with the basic unit of economic organization being the enterprise. They are described as pure types to emphasize that they do not necessarily correspond to actual economic organizations in East or West.

1.1   Centralized Socialism

In the pure type centralized socialist economy, employment is obligatory and guaranteed. There is full participation in the labour force of both men and women. Apart from industrial misconduct, the worker has security of tenure; and an enterprise cannot make workers redundant. The enterprise is owned and directed by the state, and the value added not paid to workers accrues to the state in the form of taxation or return on capital. The level of wages is assumed to be determined by the enterprise subject to state controls, providing both a lower limit in the form of a minimum wage and an upper limit in terms of the required return on capital and required taxes. There is no bankruptcy. Enterprises which make a loss while paying the minimum wage are subsidized by the state.

Income maintenance in this centralized socialist economy is closely tied to the enterprise. A minimum income at the minimum wage level is assured to all in the labour force by the guarantee of employment. There is no call for unemployment benefit or public assistance for those able to work. The enterprise provides the natural basis for other elements of income support such as the payment of sickness and permanent invalidity benefit to those unable to continue to work. For those with children, there is state provision of child care, along with the payment of child benefit. Pensions are paid to the retired through the enterprise where the worker was last employed, i.e. former workers continue to be paid by the enterprise.

1.2   Market Capitalism

In contrast, in the pure type of market capitalist system, there is no guaranteed association of workers with enterprises. The hallmark of this system is freedom of contract – on both sides of the market. A worker is free to work or not, as well as to choose his or her place of employment; and an employer is free to engage any worker or to terminate any contract. The value added in excess of wages is paid either in interest to bond-holders or in dividends to share-holders. An enterprise may belong to a wider holding company. The existence of an enterprise may be terminated either on account of bankruptcy or as a result of the decision by the holding company. Unlike the state-controlled system, there are no national boundaries, and enterprises may be owned by foreign shareholders.

Unlike the centralized socialist economy, the enterprise plays only a limited role in income maintenance; instead, the market capitalist economy is typically accompanied by a system of "social insurance". As was perceived by Bismarck, social insurance is a necessary complement of industrialized production. Once engaged in the industrial economy, a worker is protected against the risk of unemployment, or sickness, or industrial accident, by insurance which covers the whole sector (and hence does not depend on the fortunes of a particular enterprise). Provision for old age is made through pension schemes, linked to the record of employment and to contributions by both employees and employers. Such pensions may be paid by the enterprise as part of the employment contract, but it is the social insurance scheme which ensures full coverage of those in employment. For those who are unable to enter the industrial economy, or who fail to meet the contribution conditions of social insurance, there is a safety net provision in the form of social assistance, providing for both short-term and long-term contingencies. This safety net has long been recognized as an essential accompaniment of the freeing of the labour market.

We have therefore two pure-type systems, in both of which there are social security provisions intended to assure at least a minimum level of income support. In one case – centralized socialism – these provisions are based on the enterprise; in the other – market capitalism – they are based on social insurance supported by a safety net of social assistance.

2 Western Reality and Future Trends

In reality, the situation is less clear-cut – certainly for market capitalism, on which I concentrate in view of its topical relevance. If we take economies of Western Europe – such as the United Kingdom, France and West Germany (deliberately excluding Scandinavia) – as examples as to how the pure-type market capitalism may operate in practice, we find that there are significant divergences from the picture described above. In the first part of this section, I consider some of the most serious as far as they impinge on social policy.

2.1 Unemployment

The single most important fact – given the experience of the 1970s and 1980s – is the existence of wide-scale unemployment. Here a sense of historical perspective is necessary. The major challenge facing the Western European economies after the postwar reconstruction was whether monetary and fiscal policy would be sufficient to ensure full employment. The objective of full employment was generally agreed to be a fundamental measure of economic performance. What was uncertain was whether this could be achieved by Keynesian fiscal measures, or whether more extensive state intervention would be necessary. By the 1960s it appeared that there had been a considerable degree of success – at least on the European side of the Atlantic. Whereas Beveridge had in 1942 drawn up his proposals for social security on the assumption of 8 per cent unemployment (Beveridge, 1942: 164), the unemployment rate in Great Britain in fact averaged 1.7 per cent between 1948 and 1968 (British Labour Statistics, Historical Abstract 1886-1968, Table 165).

It is since the 1970s that the performance has worsened in Western Europe. Britain has had rates of unemployment for much of the 1980s which have exceeded Beveridge's prediction. According to the ILO definition of unemployment, there were in Great Britain in 1986 2.97 million people without jobs who were available for work and had recently sought work, or 11.1 per cent of the labour force (*Employment Gazette*, January 1988: 29). Of these, nearly one half had been unemployed for more than 12 months. These rates would have been widely regarded as unacceptable in the 1960s.[2]

There has been a great deal of debate about the reasons for the rise in un-employment and the extent to which it could have been avoided by government action. To the extent that government policy is effective, the role played by public opinion and electoral behaviour has to be examined. Here, there has been a definite shift in the way in which the objective of full employment is viewed in many Western countries. As Gordon (1988) has noted in the United States, a useful barometer is provided by the successive editions of Samuelson's introductory textbook *Economics*. In the 1970 edition, he described "full employment as a condition where 96 per cent of the labour force are employed, rather than where only 94 or 95 per cent are employed" (1970: 801). By the 12th edition in 1985, Samuelson (and Nordhaus) were reporting that "modern mainstream macro economics says that there is a natural rate of unemployment – today around 6 per cent" (1985: 766). The use in the economics profession of the term "natural" is symptomatic of the way in which high unemployment has come to be accepted and is no longer regarded as electorally disastrous for a government.

2.2 Segmentation

A second major source of concern is the segmentation of the economy. This segmentation takes a variety of forms, but has been conveniently summarized in terms of a "dual labour market". There is a "primary" sector offering relatively high wages, good working conditions, stable employment, and – typically – a career structure with internal promotion. This sector may also be associated with a high degree of union organization. Alongside this sector is the secondary labour market, offering jobs which are lower paid, often on temporary contracts or with a short expected duration, with no prospects, and often without union protection. This secondary sector may produce the same product as the primary sector; indeed, a single enterprise may offer both kinds of employment (as where temporary workers are taken on to meet short-term increases in demand). In certain situations, the secondary sector may consist of self-employed persons acting as subcontractors.

Such segmentation might not be a matter for concern if it were the result of individual choice. Self-employment or part-time work may indeed appeal to individual workers; their growth in Western economies may reflect an increased preference for flexibility, particularly with rising labour force participation by women. There may be a move away from a situation in which the norm is full-time work for the entire career; the breakdown of regular employment may be part of a longer-term trend. However, there can be little doubt that this is not the full explanation. Access to the primary sector is rationed, and the segmentation of the economy corresponds to a pattern of relative advantage and disadvantage. In France, one speaks of "la France à deux vitesses". There can be little doubt, too, that recruitment to the primary sector is more difficult for women returning to the labour force and for ethnic minorities. Segmentation serves to reinforce existing inequalities.

2.3 Problems for Social Policy

These features of the reality of market capitalism – large-scale long-term unemployment and segmentation – pose major questions for the relation between economic organization and social policy. The institution of social insurance is complementary to the primary sector, with its regular, formal employment relationship; it is less well-designed to provide for those in the secondary sector. Workers in the secondary sector may, for example, be precluded from claiming social insurance since they do not satisfy the contribution conditions related to length or regularity of employment. Workers may lose entitlement because the employers fail to make contributions or to keep records. Social insurance typically does not provide adequately for those who wish to work part-time. The self-employed are less fully covered. Over the lifetime as a whole, periods of unemployment or of secondary sector employment may leave a shadow on the contribution record which reduces the amount of pension to which the person is entitled on retirement. Where state pension schemes exist to provide for those not covered by their employers, the benefit provisions are typically less generous.

Mass unemployment places a strain on social insurance for which it was not intended. A scheme conceived on the same lines as private insurance (and in some cases, run by trade unions as such) may be able to provide adequate benefits in the case of limited business-cycle fluctuations where durations of unemployment are typically short. But widespread, and long-term, unemployment is a different matter. Social insurance in most countries is of limited duration and can provide no help to the long-term unemployed. Social insurance cannot provide for those unable to find employment on entry to the labour force; nor is it well-suited to financing periods of retraining. It is for these kinds of reasons that many unemployed workers in Western economies are not in receipt of unemployment insurance (Atkinson and Micklewright, 1990).

The limitations of social insurance in economies with substantial secondary sector employment and which suffer from large-scale long-term unemployment, place an additional burden on the social assistance system – a burden to which it has not proved equal. Social assistance is intended to provide a safety net; but the experience of Western economies with means-tested assistance, casts serious doubt on its effectiveness.

First, there is the problem of incomplete take-up. A sizeable minority of those eligible for social assistance, and who are informed of their eligibility, fail to claim the benefit to which they are entitled. As a result, they fall below the safety net level, and this is one of the major causes of the persistence of poverty in Western countries. Among the explanations of incomplete take-up is that social assistance is perceived as stigmatizing and demeaning. This is not without reason, in that a major concern in the administration of social assistance has historically been the maintenance of work incentives via the principle of "less eligibility" of those in receipt of assistance. The problem of incomplete take-up has its roots in the economic function of assistance.

The second problem is that there have always been pressures to keep down the levels of assistance. The history of the determination of the postwar benefit levels (see Veit-Wilson, 1989; and Atkinson, 1990) shows clearly the role played by considerations of work incentives, as just discussed, and of the budgetary cost. The containment of budgetary cost, and hence of the necessary tax rates, becomes increasingly predominant with the increased internationalization of the economy. The location decisions of firms and workers cause countries to compete to cut taxes. But it is also for domestic political reasons that the position of the disadvantaged has low priority. The determination of benefit levels in a democratic society is a matter for public choice, and one of the consequences of the political process may be that benefits are set at a level which is regarded as unacceptably low according to other criteria.

Thirdly, the social assistance safety net is based on the family or household as the unit of receipt. The income test is applied to the total income of the family or household. There is a liability on relatives to support other family members. These features of social assistance appear increasingly inappropriate and unenforceable as family ties weaken and change. The move to the formal independence within marriage of men and women, exemplified by the adoption of independent taxation and by separate pension rights, calls into question the continued reliance on family-based social assistance.

This account of the function of social policy in Western capitalist economies has been little more than a sketch, designed to highlight some of the most important departures from the "pure type" which underlies much of the debate. In considering these departures, attention has been drawn at several points to the role of the political process – for example, in influencing the employment policy or the degree of generosity of benefits. The operation of the democratic process may be as important, when assessing economic and social performance, as the working of the market.

3   A Third Way?

In the debate about the "return to Europe" of Eastern European countries, one finds discussion of a possible "third way" between market capitalism and centralized socialism. Such a possibility is canvassed by some and rejected vigorously by others. But whatever the merits for Eastern Europe, there is in my view a good case for examining the possibilities of such an intermediate system for Western Europe, in view of the manifest problems with its economic system and with its supporting social policy.

The debate about the third way is usually cast in terms of economic organization; there is however a parallel in the field of social policy, and the main point of this section is that the two should be seen in conjunction.

3.1   Basic Incomes

Beginning with the field of social policy, there has been greatly increased interest in recent years in the introduction of a basic income scheme to replace, on the one side, social insurance and, on the other, social assistance (see, for example, for the UK, Parker, 1989). Such a basic income would be a radical change in the basis on which social security operates. A basic income would be divorced from employment status and employment attachment. It would require no test of availability to work or past contributions. Those excluded from social insurance, such as new entrants to the labour force, would be covered.

The attraction of such a basic income is that it would provide a genuine safety net. The payment of a basic income to all, without test of means, would assure a minimum income without problems of non-take-up. There would be no question of recipients being "less eligible": everyone would be in receipt of the basic income. It would provide a floor on which private pension and other provisions could be built.

Moreover, the basic income scheme would be consistent with a development of the economy away from a situation in which the norm is full-time work for an entire working life and in which those unable to participate to this degree are penalized by the social security system. It would faciliate part-time work, in the sense both of people working for part of each week and of people leaving the paid labour force for part of their lives. It would be paid on an individual basis and thus would not depend on family structures or living arrangements.

The major problem with the basic income is that a high rate of tax would be necessary to finance basic incomes at a level sufficient even to replace the existing transfers. The scheme in its full form would replace all existing transfers and all income tax allowances, so that income tax would become payable on all income, the rate of tax usually being assumed to be constant. It may be seen that, if a tax rate of 20 per cent is required to finance other government spending, a basic income equal to 40 per cent of the average income would involve a tax rate of 60 per cent.[3]

The basic income scheme runs therefore into the same problem as the determination of benefit levels at present. If a basic income scheme were to be introduced, there would be the same political pressure to reduce the level of the basic income as we have noted in the case of current social assistance. If, for instance, political considerations limited the maximum conceivable tax rate to 40 per cent, this would mean that the basic income would be limited to 20 per cent of the average income – which does not appear generous. Adequacy of benefits would again be called into question by the compromises of the political process.

3.2 Labour-Capital Partnerships

One approach to resolving this difficulty is to consider the reform of the social policy in conjunction with the reform of economic organization. It is this idea that has been put forward by James Meade in his book *Agathotopia: The Economics of Partnership* (1989). Agathotopia is "the Good Place", to be compared with Utopia, "the Perfect but Non-existent Place". Meade describes the Agathotopian arrangements as "about as good as one could hope to achieve in this wicked world" (1989: 1).

By "wicked world", Meade refers particularly to the reliance on "self-centred enterprising behaviour in a free competitive economy" (1989: 1) but to this I would add the assumption that there is only a limited degree of altruism in the democratic political process. Once economic and social arrangements have been put in place, there is a distinct unwillingness on the part of the electorate to accept redistributive taxation.

Along with other social scientists, economists have long been interested in the idea of worker cooperatives (see for example Ward, 1958; Vanek, 1970; and Drèze, 1988). The idea of Meade is different in that he envisages labour/capital partnerships in which both capital-owners and workers have shares in the enterprise.

Suppose that in a capitalist enterprise 80 per cent of the value added is paid in wages and 20 per cent is paid in dividends and interest. This could be converted into a labour-capital partnership by issuing capital share certificates *pro rata* to the 20 per cent of capital income and labour share certificates to all employees *pro rata* to the 80 per cent of wage income. Future income would then be allocated according to these shares.[4]

This may not appear to make any significant change. However, for the individual worker there is now security against unemployment. Labour-capital partnerships would mean that a redundant worker retained his or her shares in the enterprise for as long as he or she remained available for work. This availability test might be applied by requiring that a redundant worker could at any time be recalled, on the same terms as previously employed. If the worker is not so available, for example because a job had been accepted in another partnership, then the shares could be cancelled. This security for the worker is obtained by spreading the risk. If there is a business cycle downturn, the reduced revenue to the enterprise leads to a reduced payment to all shareholders – including the holders of labour share certificates. In this way, Meade's proposal is similar to that of Weitzman (1984) for a "share economy".

Concern with unemployment underlies a second feature of Meade's proposals. He envisages that cooperatives would act in a "discriminating" fashion, by which he means that existing share-holders (capital and labour) could offer newly-engaged workers (or newly-invested capital) less attractive terms than those from which they themselves benefit. The terms would have to be sufficient to attract entry but they would not necessarily involve sharing all of the surplus. This feature is designed to overcome the tendency for pure "egalitarian" labour-managed cooperatives to limit the expansion of employment (on the grounds that such expansion would dilute the shares of existing employees). The discriminating form of partnership would not have this obstacle to the expansion of employment.[5] (It would in this respect be similar to profit-sharing.)

3.3 Link between the Partnership Economy and Basic Incomes

There is no reason to expect that a society of such labour-capital partnerships would be egalitarian. Discrimination would lead to identical workers being paid different amounts, in analogous fashion to identical workers being paid different amounts in a segmented economy. Employment may be higher but the distribution of income may shift in favour of capital. For this reason, Meade sees an essential link between such changes in economic organization and the restructuring of income maintenance. Labour-capital partnerships are accompanied in Agathotopia by the introduction of a basic income scheme. In his fictional history of Agathotopia, Meade describes in some detail how the basic income (called "social dividend") came into being. Leaving out the earlier stages,

> the Agathotopians set out gradually to raise rates of taxation until the revenue was sufficient to finance Social Dividends at a level which would be, in general, adequate to maintain citizens who had no other income ... Alas, however, the Agathotopians had to call a halt to this general development long before the Social Dividends had reached an adequate level simply because the marginal rates of tax ... introduced an unacceptably large general disincentive for enterprising work and investment. (Meade, 1989: 36-37)

This is the problem we have already identified – a problem which is particularly likely to arise on account of domestic political pressures or in response to international competition. The solution, however, is novel:

> the Agathotopians found an entirely new and revolutionary source of revenue which much relieved the situation. The source of revenue took the form of the socialization of the beneficial ownership (without incurring any of the management) of some 50 per cent of the national wealth of the community. (Meade, 1989: 386)

The solution lies in endowing the state with a sizeable fraction of the capital stock. As Meade notes, it is a form of topsy-turvy nationalization – ownership rather than control being the primary motive. Simple arithmetic suggests that it can contribute significantly to the problem of financing the basic income. If the share of capital in national income is 30 per cent, with half (or 15% of total income) accruing to the state, then a tax of 40 per cent on the remaining 85 per cent allows a total receipt of 49 per cent. With 20 per cent of the receipt being used to finance other government spending, this would provide a basic income of 29 per cent of the average income – compared to 20 per cent without state ownership of capital. It would be nearly half as high again and this could allow the basic income to provide a realistic safety net for this mixed capital-labour economy.

The implications of this proposal need careful consideration, and it is evident that it raises many of the same analytical issues – in reverse – as does the question of the burden of the national debt. It may be that the citizens would recognize that the state was saving on their behalf and that their own personal saving could be reduced by a corresponding amount. It would be like a funded state pension scheme. On the other hand, there may be a less than off-setting reduction in personal savings, in which case total savings rise and the rate of return may fall. There remains the important question as to how far individual countries can pursue different forms of economic organization in a world of increasing harmonization and where an increasing role is being played by supranational authorities and by multinational enterprises.

The particular set of economic arrangements considered by Meade are not the only ones which may provide an effective intermediate route between market capitalism and centralized socialism. The reason that I have described them here is that he recognizes clearly how the design of economic organization and of social policy are closely interrelated.

4   Concluding Comments

I began by referring to the pure types of centralized socialism and market capitalism, and the associated income maintenance systems. It is tempting to see the changes in Eastern Europe as a transition from one type to the other, and to draw conclusions about the implications for the design of social policy – notably the introduction of social insurance accompanied by a safety net of social assistance. This temptation should be resisted. On the side of Western economies, on which I have concentrated, the reality departs considerably from the pure type. Mass unemployment, and the segmentation of the economy, pose major problems for the system of income support, which has not proved adequate to its task. This has led to radical reconsideration, with ideas for alternative relationships between labour and capital and for basic incomes in place of social security.

The citizens of Eastern Europe may regard experiments with alternative institutional arrangements as a luxury which can only be afforded by rich countries. This is a decision which only they can make, but it should be made on the basis of a clear understanding of the limitations of the Western success and of the close interrelationship between economic and social policy. The choices of economic organization and of social policy are bound closely together. Social policy, such as a safety net, cannot simply be added as an after-thought.

Notes

1   This is a revised version of the paper presented at the "First All-European Dialogue on Social Policies" in Helsinki in March, 1990. I am grateful to the participants, and particularly to Zsuzsa Ferge and Jon-Eivind Kolberg, for their comments.
2   I can recall the horror which greeted the conclusion of Paish (1962) that an increase in the rate of unemployment to around two per cent would be necessary to avoid inflation – yet to propose return to such an unemployment rate today would be regarded as utopian.
3   For a detailed analysis of the cost of a basic income scheme in the United Kingdom, see Atkinson (1989), Chapter 16, and Parker (1989).
4   There would be scope for considerable flexibility in the form of enterprises in that both capital and labour may be employed on fixed payment contracts. Some workers might prefer to remain on a fixed wage or to retain part of their remuneration in that form. Capital could be borrowed at a fixed interest.
5   As it is put by Meade,
"Suppose the inside earnings of [existing workers] is 200 while the outside incomes of many comparable workers in the rest of the economy is only 100. It may well be that an additional worker would add more than 100 but less than 200 – let us say 180 – to the net revenue of the partnership. If the principle of equal pay for equal work were strictly applied in the sense that a newly admitted worker partner must be offered Share Certificates which would earn him or her [200] the admittance of the new worker partner would be to the disadvantage of all existing partners ... On the other hand if the new working partner were offered [150] everyone would gain" (1989: 7-8).

References

Atkinson, A. B. (1989) *Poverty and Social Security.* Hemel Hempstead: Harvester Wheatsheaf.

Atkinson, A. B. (1990) *The Determination of Benefit Scales in Britain: A History of Ambiguity.* Welfare State Programme Discussion Paper 47, LSE.

Atkinson, A. B., Micklewright, J. (1990) 'Unemployment Compensation and Labour Market Transitions: A Critical Review', *Journal of Economic Literature.*

Beveridge, Sir W. (1942) *Social Insurance and Allied Services.* London: HMSO.

Drèze, J. (1989) *Labour Management, Contracts and Capital Markets.* Oxford: Basil Blackwell.

Gordon, D. M. (1988) 'The Un-Natural Rate of Unemployment', *American Economic Review*, Papers and Proceedings 78: 117-123.

Meade, J. E. (1989) *Agathotopia: The Economics of Partnership.* Aberdeen: Aberdeen University Press.

Paish, F. W. (1962) *Studies in an Inflationary Economy.* London: Macmillan.

Parker, H. (1989) *Instead of the Dole.* London: Routledge.

Samuelson, P. A. (1970) *Economics*, 8th edition. New York: McGraw-Hill.

Samuelson, P. A., Nordhaus, W. D. (1985) *Economics*, 12th edition. New York: McGraw-Hill.

Vanek, J. (1970) *The General Theory of Labor-Managed Market Economies.* Ithaca: Cornell University Press.

Veit-Wilson, J. (1989) Memorandum in House of Commons Social Services Select Committee, Minimum Income, *House of Commons Paper 579.* London: HMSO.

Ward, B. (1958) 'The Firm in Illyria: Market Syndicalism', *American Economic Review* 48: 566-589.

Weitzman, M. L. (1984) *The Share Economy.* Cambridge, Mass.: Harvard University Press.

CHAPTER 15

From the Welfare State to a Welfare Society*

Ronald Wiman

1 Legitimacy of Social Welfare Systems

Until the emergence of the welfare state, the interpretation of social problems was based largely on moral and individualistic ways of thinking. The major remedy for social problems was seen in social control and humanitarian work done mainly by voluntary organizations. The individual was considered responsible for the ills of his life but for the sake of social hygiene some help had to be given.

The welfare state saw social problems as deficits in the external resources or conditions of individuals. At the peak of this ideology, at the end of the 1960s and beginning of the 1970s, the theoretical foundations were affiliated to social determinism. Social problems did not, however, become extinct by expanding the economic support for the "not well-to-dos".

A complementary ideology for welfare state social determinism was found in therapeutic approaches. Social problems were viewed through a concept much like the concept of diseases in the health sector. If the individual did not cope with his life, a treatment programme was needed to readapt him to society.

Recently, a compromising model between the individualistic and social-deterministic theory has emerged. It is being realized that the failures of individuals are not only caused by their own actions, nor by external conditions, nor by lack of abilities, but by the interaction of all of these factors.

The actor model of human nature is opening new paths for developing such supporting systems which are based on the understanding of the equal basic human nature of all individuals. This actor model is – in fact – inherent in present Finnish social welfare legislation. Whether the idea has filtered down throughout the system, however, is still doubtful. The individualistic, social-deterministic, and therapeutic approaches coexist with new ways of thinking. This coexistence is not always peaceful. But it is still too peaceful to revolutionize the field.

According to recent research in society at large it is evident that the major value premises of the welfare state (equality; a high level of social welfare; and a strong role for the state) have had and continue to have strong support among the general population.

Until now, the emerging trends towards individualism have not raised any meaningful opposition – possibly due to the fact that there hardly exists any person who would never use social services at all. Social insurance presently covers all population groups, including the self-employed.

One safety measure against social welfare turning into social warfare is the emphasis and obligation of the welfare sector to spread information about its services, to influence public perceptions of the nature of the social service sector, and to influence other societal structures to prevent social problems from arising.

The major danger is still, however, the interest and ideological conflict between the "A" and "B" sections of the population. If, due to financing problems, we turn back to providing support only to some well-defined population groups most in need and leave the majority to rely on private services, a tax revolt is to be expected. Thus, indeed, privatization does not guarantee society against tax revolts. Rather, the opposite may be true.

Such a crisis will be hard to avoid if employment opportunities continue to worsen. Still, today the share of the "inactives" is overshadowed and does not alert the "actives". A small group of "bums" is tolerated; but it is highly doubtful whether, say, unemployment figures reaching one fifth of the population will be understood as external problems of those affected rather than as their own fault.

2   Emerging New Divisions of Political Philosophies

In broad terms, the basic ideological division lines of today are not the same as during the high-growth period of the making of the welfare state. In those days, the major division line was between socialist and bourgeois ideologies. Today, a new dimension is entering the picture. Growth is stagnating and, in the long run, zero economic growth is a possibility. This view of the future is bringing a new dimension into political ideologies. The former issue of a desirable distribution is complemented by the dimension of whether any growth of resources is possible at all. In the following figure, this new segmentation of political ideologies illustrates the new ideological environment where social welfare policies will be formed in the future.

The current policy discussion is focusing mainly on the upper half of the figure:
a) The proponents of the liberalist *laissez-faire* economics are driving at drastic cuts in public social welfare expenditures, firm in their belief that such cuts will lead to a new path of economic growth, and that privatization of services would provide a more effective solution.

Figure 15.1: The New Map of Political Ideologies

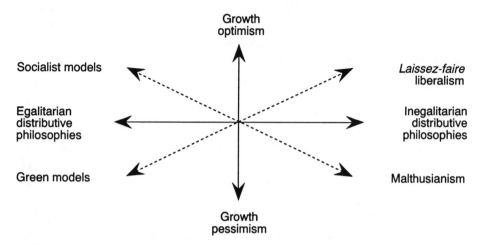

b) The socialist models of egalitarian distributive systems present the other extreme of this dimension; according to this ideology, the performance of the economy and of society as a whole, could be vitalized through the application of more egalitarian structures replacing the need for social welfare systems. This dream has turned into a nightmare.

The ideological area below the horizontal line has long existed within economic philosophies; but it has been forgotten during the high-growth period in Western societies. Both in the case of society as a whole and the social sector in particular, there is a possibility that the future will bring up a new issue: how to distribute *scarce* resources. There are two basic solutions on this side as well:

c) The green model: small is beautiful, decentralized services are provided on a small scale through communities and informal networks.

d) The Malthusian model of natural selection, survival of the fittest: social welfare is cut to the minimum so that the vital segments of society will be able to survive.

Keynesian economics and – consequently – the welfare state ideology, lies in the middle, but still on the growth optimism side. So does the Finnish society and social welfare policy of today on which we will concentrate in the following.

The opinions on the future of the social welfare sector are based on the long tradition of economic and social philosophies. There exist four competing ideologies which set the direction in which we ought to proceed, as well as the direction in which it is possible to proceed within the pressures that the future will bring.

3   Priorities and Possibilities

The current Finnish national planning system of social welfare does not go beyond five years ahead. Since the late 1970s, the Ministry of Social Affairs and Health has made several long-term prognoses which have focused mainly on expenditure and financing issues. The Finnish National Board of Social Welfare has launched a long-term planning process of its own. In this project, qualitative and organizational considerations will be emphasized. In this section, we will first present the established targets up to 1991 and then discuss the long-term priorities.

3.1 The National Five-year Plan for Social Welfare for the Years 1987-91

The general targets of the Plan strive at the following:
a) giving priority to general social services instead of target groups;
b) further diminishing regional differences in the availability of services;
c) making the use of social services easier, more flexible, and laying emphasis on developing services on a district basis; additionally, the access to services will also be improved during weekends and evenings;
d) increasing and supporting the personal initiative of individuals and families;
e) ensuring that the client and his family have a real chance to participate in planning and supportive actions concerning them, and offering a real opportunity for individual choice.

The major quantitative targets are as follows:
a) to increase day care services and subsidies for the home care of children to such an extent that, in 1990, every family has a real chance to choose between either public day care or rearing their children at home, economically supported by an adequate home care subsidy until the child reaches three years of age;
b) to abolish homelessness by the year 1991 and to expand housing subsidies, supported housing, and sheltered housing to meet existing needs;
c) auxiliary services (meals on wheels, transport service, laundry, etc.) will be extended to diminish the need for institutionalization of the elderly and persons with disabilities;
d) for the same purpose, financial subsidy for persons taking care of their elderly or disabled dependents will be further expanded and the adequacy of the subsidy amount guaranteed.

The strategic role of district social welfare offices, as well as the role of academic social workers, will be strengthened to ensure better coordination, integration, and quality of services.

The level of living allowances will be increased and the application and granting procedures made simpler than today.

In institutional care, it is intended to put emphasis on small-scale units and to replace some of these services by out-patient services – by establishing sheltered houses, day centres, and by increasing home help services.

Additionally, the integration of social and health care services will be promoted.

3.2 Long-term Priorities

The orientation expressed in the current five-year plan will be further stressed and strengthened:

a) the gap between day care needs and supply of services will be closed by the year 1995 at the latest;

b) concrete long-term targets include also extending maternity allowances to one year from today's 10 months and finding solutions for shortening the working hours of parents with small children;

c) the quantitative and qualitative needs for housing should be met adequately by the end of the 1990s;

d) needs for institutional care will be partially replaced through expanding non-institutional approaches in the field of services for disabled persons and the elderly: this implies expansion of home-like small units and heavy emphasis on home help services;

e) income security in the form of last-resort living allowance will be improved by increasing the amounts of allowances and by avoiding the means-testing approach;

f) voluntary organizations and client associations will be actively supported to increase the possibilities for popular activity and participation – without, however, cutting the quantity and quality of services.

The strategic all-encompassing tools for action to reach the welfare society model providing *Well-Being for All by the Year 2000,* can be presented as follows:

1) To emphasize structural social welfare policies: influencing all sectors of society, the labour market, economic planning, income policies, city and community planning, etc. in order to work against the threatening possibility of society being split into A and B sections; and to promote real opportunities for popular participation in policy-making and implementation of programmes.

2) The focus of the current five-year planning system will be shifted increasingly towards taking into account – with equal weight – the quality aspects of programmes, instead of staying within the narrow domain of quantitative resource planning.

3) Developing long-term planning processes both within central administration and on the local level.

4) New approaches will be sought throughout the field in accordance with the actor-model philosophy of the new Social Welfare Act of 1984; understanding the potential for an active role inherent in every human being, and supporting the personal identity and undeniable human rights of every individual regardless of his temporary or permanent disabilities.

5) Guiding policies and programmes at all levels and fields from control-oriented and remedial approaches towards active policies striving at an integrated and balanced social development.

There is no doubt that money is needed to reach the targets. But in the efforts to create a new active role for social welfare policies, it is more vital to employ active human resources. The more we are ready to invest into social development today, the cheaper it will be to create well-being for all in the future.

A reorientation of social welfare policies asks for pooling the resources of the innovative capacities of the whole population – especially the clients as well as the administration and the academic field to redefine the role of social welfare policies.

Until recent years, social welfare policies have been subordinated to general economic policies. The social sector has been required to adapt itself to goals and strategies of the national economy.

A new way of thinking of the role of the social sector has arisen first in theoretical discussions at university departments. This has been facilitated by two factors. First, a new cooperation between the administration and Academia was born during the second half of the 1970s, replacing the mutual antagonism of the beginning of the 1970s. Secondly, social welfare is gaining a new status at the universities as an independent subfield of the social sciences, leading to a strengthening interest in, and a rapid theoretical progress of the field. As a result of the interaction of these two developments, the academic discussion has become more practical – and correspondingly, the administrative way of thinking has become more academic. A new common language is in the making.

It is also evident that international cooperation both between countries with similar – and those with different – social problems, policies, and resources, does open new gates for new theoretical and practical developments in the field. Furthermore, through such cooperation, the conception of the role of social welfare policies will be clarified and enriched. And the identity of welfare policy will become stronger.

A new idea fertilized by this increasing cooperation has emerged: social welfare policies should become aggressive tools in overall societal policy-making for creating economic and social processes, which would lead to greater well-being for all – instead of only higher living standards for a majority.

4   Epilogue

On the world scene, the inherited international distribution systems have led to higher living standards for a minority only. Unfortunately, this holds true too often as well within the poorer members of the international community. "Development aid" has not always neutralized this process.

Charity leads to poverty if it destroys local production structures. Humanitarian aid is a necessity but should not be confused with development aid. The most it can do is to maintain the *status quo*: inequality and poverty. Charity is a labile ground for both internal and international solidarity. Wherever possible, aid should be replaced by cooperation in the spirit of equality and joint interest.

The experience of the welfare states has proven that systematic redistribution serves the interests of the rich as well. It has produced higher living standards for the majority. It should be carefully investigated which kinds of redistributive technologies would result in the same outcome on the international level. Redistributing consumption goods is certainly not a sustainable solution.

The physical and social technologies of the rich are often inappropriate for the poor – however rational these technologies may be. The welfare state is a rational redistributive system. It is a European invention which the poor cannot afford. But even the poor can afford a welfare society based on local resources and local human capital.

The technologies for producing societal necessities may differ widely; and they must be tailored to match the local environments, resources, and structures. But as far as the criteria for a good life are concerned, the variation is much smaller. Therefore, it should be possible to produce a limited number of targets and to sketch strategies towards greater well-being for all.

The general target of social welfare systems is to diminish inequality in access to those resources which are needed for a healthy, wealthy, socially sound, and meaningful life. Inadequate health is certainly one of the most basic obstacles for an active life. Consequently, diminishing inequality in health and the length of life is one of the most urgent tasks of our time, both nationally and internationally.

However, lack of or limited access to other necessary resources needed to enable individuals to use their full human potential through purposeful social, economic, and cultural action, should be recognized as an equally burning issue.

The "Health for All"-strategy has been a great example of the productivity of international cooperation. Producing a similar analysis, selecting appropriate indicators, establishing priorities, and designing strategies applicable to social development strategies across the whole spectrum of cultures, is bound to be an even more laborious effort.

To design a strategy to reach *"Well-Being for All"* is a human mission of such an extent, importance, and urgency, that it would deserve as high a priority, as high a political support and publicity, as the health strategy preparation process did. The complexity of social development issues might ask for even more time, skills, money, and devotion. There is doubt that a heavy-enough investment in the social development field may result in unprecedented discoveries of non-depletable, renewable, and even expanding resources: namely, human action itself.

The welfare state does not have mechanisms for utilizing such non-monetary resources. It is a centralized professional system operating from administrative castles and treating clients as passive objects to be provided for from above. The welfare state has certainly been an effective broom for sweeping the leftovers of structural change and economic growth under the carpet. It is a machinery which deals beautifully with averages, average growth, and average people; but it has a tendency to write off the tails of the distributions. For the lower marginal, it has created a highly-professional subsystem employing such strict criteria that one first has to become a professional client to get in. In this sector, one is free not to work but is not free to work. Expanding such a trash bin for the "inactives" makes them even worse off. They will be excluded from society forever. Therefore, such passive solutions should not be accepted as a response to current and future situations when the society is unable to engage the whole population into meaningful activity.

To counteract these trends, the social welfare system must create and adopt a more active theory of itself and of the people. If the world is tough, we must be even tougher to change the world.

We have learnt how to run a welfare state. As the famous jargon goes, "it is not enough to do things right – it is more important to do right things". The right thing to do is to involve the people. That would lead to a sustainable future, a welfare society, a society for all. We are still at square one. But – we are already there.

Note

*   Slightly adapted from Wiman, R. (1987) 'From the Welfare State to a Welfare Society', Helsinki: National Board of Social Welfare, pp. 31-34 and 46-52. Wiman's report was prepared for the Conference of European Ministers Responsible for Social Affairs, Warsaw, Poland, 6-11 April 1987. The theoretical approach has been further developed and adapted to social work practice in Wiman, R. (1990) *Towards an Integrated Theory of Help*. Helsinki: National Board of Social Welfare.

CHAPTER 16

Towards a European Welfare State?
On Integrating Poverty Regimes into the European Community[1]

Stephan Leibfried

Who overcomes
By force, hath overcome but half his foe
(John Milton, Paradise Lost)

1   European Integration and Social Policy: Historical and Analytical Approaches

Europe is more than just a geographical entity. And it is more than a "common market". Europe has a common tradition in war, peace, culture, and, above all, in welfare statism – making it a distinct peninsula on the Asian continent (Schulze, 1990). The legally still-separate Western European nations may be about to merge into a United States of Europe ("USE") – an economical, political as well as cultural entity of its own – analogous to but also quite different from the USA; at least these nations might merge into a steadily increasing "pool" of "shared sovereignties".[2] This process has gained momentum during the past two decades. After several unsuccessful attempts, the Single European Act of 28 February 1986 has moved the European Community (EC) closer to an economic, a political, and to some extent also to a social union.[3] By now, the EC has definitely been developed beyond just a "tariff union" – but where is it moving? Will there be a European welfare state, a "transnational synthesis" (Offe, 1990: 8) of national welfare states, with "European social citizenship" being one backbone of the USE? Or will the welfare state, which is "characteristic only for this part of the world" (van Langendonck, 1991), be irrelevant for "building the new European state"? Will fragmented "social citizenships" remain at the national level, where they might slowly erode?

If European unification were not to be based on "social citizenship", European welfare regimes would remain at the USE's state or "regional" level and stay below the supranational level of visibility. The regimes of poverty policy,[4] the most exposed parts of social citizenship, would then be most likely to slowly and inconspicuously corrode. This may cause phantom pain for social welfare and, in particular, poverty experts. In their respective national contexts they are struggling with the consequences of something that never came to be: a European welfare state built on a European poverty policy.

The options and constraints involved in building a European welfare state are the topic of this essay: I will focus mostly on European poverty regimes and will discuss them historically and typologically.

1.1 From Negative to Positive Integration

If "European social citizenship" or "Social Europe" is to come about, a "positive" mode of integration is required. Such an integration is much more ambitious and complex than a pure and simple "common market" goal. It aims at joined "constructive" action, at a "positive state". However, the evolution of "prefederal" European institutions, of Europe's "incomplete federalism", has been strongly moulded by "negative integration". (A summary of the two modes of integration is given in Figure 16.1.) Negative integration focusses on "deconstruction", on just removing obstacles for a free market, thus being unmindful of inherent social consequences (Kaufmann, 1986: 69).

Figure 16.1: Types of Integration

Modus of Integration	Nature of Tasks	Political System	Examples in Present EC Legislation	Classical and Typical Models
Negative	remove obstacles	weaker; strong reliance on juridical procedures and decisions	free movement of persons, goods, capital, and services ("the four freedoms")	"Tariff Union" ("Zoll-verein") (Germany before 1871 or USA; Italy?)
Positive	create common social space	stronger; reliance on developed executive and parliament	set minimum of essential health and safety requirements	"German *Reich*" (after 1871); Canada[7]

(cf. Dehousse, 1988: 313ff. on the first three columns)

Moving from "freedom" to "social rights" implies a shift in the nature of the political regime in a unifying Europe[5] – a shift from negative to positive integration. The discussion on "Social Europe", on the "social dimension", on the "Social Charter", and on some details of the EC social policy mandate is already testing the limits of the unification regime of the European Community. In this context, the poverty issue is of special relevance, since it is morally clear-cut and marks the "North-South" divide in the Community itself. To address European poverty the EC would have to design programmes which aim at all European citizens. However, the EC mandate is focussed mostly on European employees and their families – and not yet on the European citizen *per se*. Even the EC Social Charter refers mostly to employees,[6] although comparable basic statements of rights at the national level address all citizens.

Interestingly enough, the negative integration modus of the EC was transcended (mostly) in agricultural policy in the Rome Treaty at the very start of European integration (Pinder, 1968: 100f.). In the European Community, as well as in the USA, agriculture was the first "internal"[8] policy domain to be nationalized. This has fundamentally affected the development of a national bureaucracy in the USA[9] (Skowronek, 1982; Dupree, 1957; Rossiter, 1979) and at the EC level, it also incorporated different social policy developments *vis-à-vis* agriculture. More attention could be paid to how universal social welfare components might be systematically intertwined with the agricultural domain at the EC level, and not only to how a "basic income" for certain agricultural producers is or was achieved EC-wide. The US Food Stamps programme might offer a modest example of such a process. Since the EC has been granted legal and administrative competence in this area, it might at first be easier to widen these established policy channels,[10] rather than struggling for a comprehensive EC social policy based on positive integration.

1.2 Historical Models for European Integration in the Social Policy Domain

There are two major examples which highlight the different relevance of "positive integration" or "social unification" for processes of national integration:[11] the German unification of 1871 – and again of 1990 – and the consolidation of the United States of America as a "state" at the turn of the twentieth century.

1.2.1 The German *Reich*[12]

The first German integration of 1871 did not conform to the "normal" (Anglo-Saxon) pattern of evolution of rights, i.e. one expanding from civil to political to social rights (cf. Marshall, 1964). The extension of social citizenship to the working class – not to the poor *per se* – which was the core of Bismarck's social legislation, preceded political citizenship (that is, introduction of universal suffrage after defeat in World War I) by four decades.

Integration of the German *Reich* – as in England – was mainly achieved through social reform. "One nation" grew out of a class-divided "two nations" in a sphere of common social rights. An overdose of social citizenship, mostly granted to men,[13] as well as a homogeneous national bureaucracy,[14] were administered to a nation about to unify – hence identifying the (mostly male) "Second Nation", or the organized working class, with the new, benevolent national state, the "social security state".[15] The new welfare state of the 1880s became the foremost, intermediary (not directly state)[16] bureaucracy, which legitimated an otherwise fragile[17] central government.[18]

Today's German unification repeats, compressed in time, the pattern of 1871: civil and social unification preceded the political union, though – contrary to 1871 – the chances for an improved "integration through social reform" have been mostly bypassed by (West) German politicians.[19]

At first, the German Democratic Republic (GDR) seemed to aim at a synthesis of the "social advantages" of West and East[20] Germany and proposed a "Social Charter"[21]. But in the meantime, the West German social policy model has been simply extended (sometimes in a watered-down version) to the territory of the former GDR, in some cases allowing for transition periods,[22] and now making it "the" German model. There may be some lasting consequences of German social unification in the area of minimum income legislation, since transitory minimum pensions and minimum unemployment benefits have been provided in the Unification Treaty. Many issues which had pointed towards the need for a new era of social reform during the unification period, and which were "displaced" then, resurface now that unification is implemented. West German policy solutions often do not fit reality in the five new states. So, "social cohesion" is an important inner-German issue, which is triggering compensatory action but not comprehensive social reform.

In any case, German unification today will be viewed by others – especially in Europe's southern countries, its Latin rim, and in Ireland – as a leading case for "integration" policy.[23] Perhaps unification can contribute to change Germany's role in the EC in a positive way, too, with Germany now more inclined to promote European social unification instead of blocking it as it did in the past. Other EC countries, especially in the Latin rim, will closely monitor the German "integration experiment"; it may become a "regional observatory" for a possible development of the social dimension of the EC.

1.2.2 USA[24]

In the USA, the historical sequencing of "citizenship" is "normal". This Anglo-Saxon pattern conforms to the one we can also observe in the EC: first come civil, then political, and then social rights. The USA thus offers the best counter-example to the German *Reich* of 1871: it operates with an "underdose" of social rights –

instead political and civil rights are strongly emphasized. *Vis-à-vis* the EC, the USA offers a good comparative case, since it shares central features: both "continents" are unified through federations, and the unification of both is court-led and court-fed,[25] with juridification playing a central role. At the turn of the century, the USA was still just "a state of courts and parties" (Skowronek, 1982) – thus a non-state, at least in the European sense. On the other hand, the EC might be characterized as a "state of the European Court and of Brussels technocrats".

Social policy in the USA was at first only indirectly nationalized. Far before the Great Depression of the 1930s, two classical Departments – War[26] and Agriculture[27] – incorporated social policy functions. Until the Great Depression the national level was otherwise void of social policy competencies, a situation which was first altered by Roosevelt's introduction of social security.[28] The historical legacy of this gaping hole in national social responsibility, is a permanently labile state of nationalization of social policy itself, which today is seen best in "functionally decentralized" poverty policies.[29]

Viewed from the perspective of a USE-to-be, the EC is now confronted by a similar "void". Will the nations of Western Europe be able to cope with this challenge of "social cohesion" faster and more successfully in the twenty-first century than the USA was able to in the twentieth century?

1.2.3 The EC vs. the USA and the German *Reich*

The USA – like the EC, but in contrast to the German *Reich* – has stayed closest to the "tariff union" pattern, the typical model of negative integration. At the same time, the USA has a more highly integrated political structure than the EC might ever achieve. In Figure 16.2, differences in federal development of the USA and the EC are contrasted. For the USE and the USA, there are different fault lines. In the USA the fault line runs between political and social rights, since a "common market" and a political union have developed there in one process. In the sequence of citizenships, social citizenship comes last. The USE, though, has two such fault lines: the same one as in the USA, but also a preceding one that runs between civil and political rights. A European synthesis will thus be especially demanding. The situation of the EC therefore resembles the development in the USA less than it looks like the building of the German *Reich* of 1871 – at that time, Germany also had to deal with two such fault lines at once. But Germany dealt with social citizenship earlier than it did with political citizenship. This reversal of the sequence is also of interest for an analysis of European integration marked by a distinctly lagging "political union".

When we look at the EC compared to the USA or the German *Reich* this question arises: Should and will EC development conform more to the Anglo-Saxon pattern of sequencing citizenship or to the German one? In the former case, European unification will take place without a social foundation but will rest, on the contrary,

**Figure 16.2: Types of Federalism and Lines of Breakage: The USE versus
the USA**

	USE	USA
Type	incomplete federalism	complete federalism
Market ("civil citizenship")	common market	interstate commerce
Parliamentary Governance etc. ("political citizenship")	political union	Congress, Federal Government
Welfare State ("social citizenship")	social union, "Social Europe"	broad federal powers for social regulation
Remarks	Rome Treaty left competency vacuum in social policy and provided for meagre forms of political representation; no EC social citizenship (needle's eye: employment relationship; atrophy of national social citizenship regimes, e.g. welfare, child allowances, youth welfare, housing allowances, etc.).	With the Great Depression, the competency vacuum at the federal level was filled by redefinition of constitutional powers.

on a market-oriented foundation of "possessive individualism". In the latter case, European unification would instead attempt a synthesis of civil, political, and social rights thus confronting both fault lines at once and breaking with the Anglo-Saxon pattern of development. "Social Europe", "social dimensions" of European development, a "Social Charter" (Kommission, 1989; Silvia, 1991; Addison and Siebert, 1991), "Social Fund"[30] – at the moment these are catch phrases in symbolic politics pointing at a social foundation without really building any of the structural prerequisites. Only a confluence of several favourable conditions will contribute to a breakthrough for a truly Social Europe.

2 The Four Social Policy Regimes in the EC

We have seen that positive integration, "social cohesion", is not built into the present structure of the EC: there is no EC welfare state (outside of agriculture). If we look at the different existing welfare systems in Europe may we then realistically expect that a "Social Europe" will come about by an "organic" merging of such systems from the "bottom up"? Positive integration at the EC level would then be a byproduct of ongoing European economic and political integration.

Or are the social and poverty policy regimes of the EC so contradictory that an organic merging from below is not possible and "harmonization" will necessarily have to come "from above", i.e. that it will have to be synthesized and implemented by an authorized EC bureaucracy? Such a European welfare state would, most likely, presuppose a historical North-South compromise within the EC and, surely, a reformulation of the Rome Treaties. Without an EC welfare state, in the long run, regional, national welfare regimes will be in atrophy: their economic and legitimatory bases would slowly erode with the completion and further development of the Common Market – just as they eroded in the USA with the realization of its "common market", interstate commerce.

Whether Social Europe might come about via merging from the "bottom up" can be examined by reviewing typical EC *poverty* regimes. My attention will centre on the interfaces between poverty, social insurance and poverty policy.[31] The different consequences which the introduction of a *basic income* scheme under each regime might have, will be outlined.[32] This is one way to illustrate the practical importance of the differences between these regimes.

Though the discussion of welfare state regimes usually focusses on those policy areas which quantitatively dominate the welfare state – i.e. the social insurance systems (cf. Schmidt, 1988) – I concentrate on the margins of the welfare state: it is here that the limits – and thus the contents – of social citizenship are tested; and it is here that any differences in European social policy will be most obstructive.

In the following, I will distinguish four different social policy regimes – four "worlds of welfare capitalism":[33] the Scandinavian welfare states, the "Bismarck" countries, the Anglo-Saxon countries, and the "Latin Rim" countries.

2.1 The Scandinavian Welfare States

Since World War II, the welfare states of Scandinavia[34] have stressed the right to work for everyone and have centred their welfare state policy on this issue and not on compensatory income transfer strategies. Scandinavia fits the type "modern welfare state".[35] Universalism reigns, though not primarily through income redistribution outside the sphere of work. Here, the welfare state is employer of first resort (mainly for women). Subsidizing "entry" into – or non-exit from – the labour market is the welfare state strategy[36] which conveys the institutionalized notion of social citizenship.

In Scandinavian countries, the basic income debate is likely to be used only as an additional argument for the support of a universalist "work-centred society". The debate might be of some use for improving "income packaging" in the Scandinavian welfare state (cf. Rainwater et al., 1986): Broad-scale issue-specific redistribution, like child allowances, might be improved. Or the rather residual, truly marginal[37] welfare systems there might be improved, in such a way that they match the standards of "Bismarck" countries. But basic income is unlikely to develop into a strong option: to opt out of "work society" as a general strategy will not be condoned.

2.2   The "Bismarck" Countries[38]

For a century, Germany and Austria have relied on a strategy of "paying off" social problems, of subsidizing "exit" from the labour market or even "non-entry" while pursuing a strong policy of economic development only.[39] These countries might be characterized as "institutional welfare states".[40] Here, "compensatory strategies" are prominent which substitute a right to social security for a right to work, and a basic income debate would be most likely to radicalize the present focus on compensation and exit (or non-entry). The welfare state is not the employer but the compensator of first resort, and the institutionalized notion of social citizenship is biased accordingly. Though there is no explicit tradition of universalism in these countries, the "institutionalized full employment promises" and private labour market "practices" (of the 1950s to the early 1970s) have created a fragile tradition of virtual universalism.

The basic income debate here amplifies the pre-existing focus on non-entry or easing-exit from the labour market. Perhaps in the Bismarck countries this debate could lead to something like a universalized non-residual needs approach which might become less and less restrictive in terms of means-testing and might also develop towards an individual instead of a household orientation.[41]

2.3   The Anglo-Saxon Countries[42]

The English-speaking countries have always emphasized the "residual welfare model" (cf. Titmuss, 1987: 262), especially in income transfers.[43] They did not accent, as the Scandinavian countries did, the welfare state as the major employer in a "work society"; rather, they conceived of the welfare state as a work-enforcing coercive mechanism (cf. Lødemel, 1989). The USA, Australia, New Zealand, and also England best exemplify the type of "residual welfare state" (Titmuss, 1987: 267). "Entry" into the labour market was facilitated more by pure force than by subsidization or by training and qualification policy. Here, selectivism reigns as the principal approach of social policy, making the welfare state rather a compensator of last resort. The distance of the Anglo-Saxon model from a "compensatory regime" or a Scandinavian "work society regime" is equally great. Thus, "social citizenship" has remained more of an academic issue in these countries.[44]

The basic income debate in the Anglo-Saxon countries is rather far away from institutionalizing an "option out of work society"; it may support the development of a "normal welfare system" in the Northern European sense. However, the development is not likely to go any further than this. A normal welfare system in the Anglo-Saxon context would mean introducing a universal instead of a categorical welfare system[45] combining such a welfare system with a more prominent role for a public jobs programme that aims at integration into the primary labour market (somewhere between the German and the Scandinavian model), and having adequate ("fair share") and nationally-standardized "welfare" rates.[46]

2.4 The "Latin Rim" Countries[47]

The southern countries of Western Europe, some of them integrated into the EC only in the 1980s, seem to constitute a welfare state regime of their own. This league comprises Spain, Portugal, Greece, to some extent Italy[48] and, least of all, France.[49] This type could be characterized as "rudimentary welfare state".[50] In Portugal, Spain, Italy, and Greece, not even a right to welfare is a given. In some respect, these states are similar to the Anglo-Saxon countries, *de facto* stressing residualism and forced "entry" into the labour market.[51] But in these countries, older traditions of welfare (connected to the Catholic Church) seem to exist on which the Anglo-Saxon and most Northern countries cannot build. Moreover, in these countries certain social security programmes serve as basic income measures – although they were not designed as such (the disability pensions in southern Italy seem to have worked out this way; cf. Ascoli, 1986: 113f., 122). In addition, labour market structures are radically different and often reveal a strong agricultural bias, combined with a "subsistence" economy which provides a different – non-Northern European – "welfare" state background. Finally, these countries do not have a full employment tradition – in particular, one that also fully applies to women – as do some of the Scandinavian countries. But many of these countries have made strong promises pointing towards a "modern welfare state" in their constitutions; it is the legal, institutional, and social implementation which seems to be lacking in the "Latin rim".

It is hard to gauge the effect of a basic income debate in these countries. The development of "normal welfare systems" seems most likely – normal in the sense of the Northern European or German welfare model.

These four types of welfare states are summarized in Figure 16.3. Modern, institutional, residual and rudimentary welfare states start from rather different, in some cases contradictory, goals and are built on quite disparate intervention structures; and they do not share a common policy – and politics – tradition that could serve as a centripetal force. In any case, this divergence of regimes does not lend

Figure 16.3: Types of European Welfare States

	Scandinavian	Bismarck	Anglo-Saxon	Latin Rim
Type of Welfare Regime	modern	institutional	residual	rudimentary
Characteristics	full employment; welfare state as employer of first resort and compensator of last resort	full growth; welfare state as compensator of first resort and employer of last resort	full growth; welfare state as compensator of last resort and tight enforcer of work in the market place	catching up; welfare state as a semi-institutionalized promise
Right to	work	social security	income transfers	work and welfare proclaimed
	backed up by an institutionalized concept of social citizenship		no such backup	only implemented partially
Basic Income Debate	marginal, but may improve income packaging	may somewhat radicalize decoupling of work and income	may support development of "normal" welfare system	may support development of "normal" welfare system

support to the notion that a European welfare state might grow via automatic harmonization, building from the national towards the EC level. A "bottom-up" strategy for EC "social integration" policy, seems stillborn.[52]

3 Whither European Welfare Policy: "Europeanization" from the "Top Down" or "Americanization" from the "Bottom Up"?

What may be the influence of a continuous Europeanization of economic and representational policy on social, especially on poverty policy?[53] Since automatic harmonization of European social policy, building from the national towards the EC level, is not likely, two alternatives remain:
- Policy disharmony in welfare policy may either prevail as a permanent underside of European integration or, worse, be transformed into a process of automatic

disharmonization at the bottom. National policies may be "Balkanized" as the European Common Market solidifies. This process resembles what happened to American poverty policy as the New American national state was built, starting at the turn of the twentieth century.

- Policy disharmony may also provoke – in particular when confronted with more potent pressures for European "social cohesion" – a Caesarian reaction of European institutions. This might prompt a comprehensive European policy frame for poverty policy – or for all social benefits primarily tied to social citizenship.

3.1 Towards "Americanization" of "European" Poverty Policies?

In this part, I will concentrate on "Americanization" as one alternative. Since this path is closest to the given EC situation, I will show how it corresponds with present EC welfare legislation, which is mainly procedural and not substantive (cf. Figure 16.4). The development of EC legislation again fits with the historial model of evolution of poverty policy in European nation-states (cf. Figure 16.5).

In my view, European development will most likely leave all poverty and welfare policy at the local or state – that is, at a sub-European – level. It is impossible to start from a common European denominator. The common ground is missing on which a European welfare regime could be built.

In contrast to poverty policy, some work-centred social policies – "health" and "work safety" issues – would be much easier to "Europeanize", or to "harmonize", since these policies are structured in a rather compatible way to begin with[54] and since the European institutions have a mandate there. Needs-centred social policies are rather difficult to standardize and will have no strong thematic lobby in the European context – unless some poor "Latin rim" states make it a "state issue"[55] – and such policies will also have a hard time finding a mandate. Thus, the most likely outcome is that needs-centred social policies are least likely to be protected by European development.

One might therefore predict that the "Europe to be", in terms of social policy and especially in terms of poverty policy, will look much more like the USA did before the 1930s, or like it does today,[56] than it will look like any of the Northern European welfare regimes. Europe after 1992, as far as poverty policy is concerned, might lead to a shift towards the Anglo-Saxon welfare model; at least, it is likely to lead to a welfare state "Balkanization" quite similar to the USA. If "integration" in poverty policy comes about within these limits it will be of a negative sort, allowing each Member State to have its own regime and creating only procedural rules, perhaps also about how to proceed with "foreign" recipients and with the re-exportation of their burden to their "home" countries.[57]

What is the current situation of EC welfare policy? The few EC rules on welfare which do exist, are only meaningful in "national welfare contexts", where they are

Figure 16.4: Status, EC Residence Permit and Poverty Support in Germany

Status	Residence Permit	Right to Welfare
Self-Employed	for economic activity within EEC Treaty framework (freedom of services and of capital movement; otherwise, see "Others")	yes; only take-up of welfare parallel to economic activity is legitimate; otherwise, take-up results in loss of right to residence and in possible deportation
Employed: Pre-employed	for job search in due time (according to EC law, 3 months)	yes; beyond "due time", take-up of welfare results in loss of right to residence and possibly in deportation[1]
Employed	even in case of sub-poverty-level remuneration	yes; parallel take-up of welfare is legitimate
Unemployed	cf. pre-employed; for the involuntarily unemployed, permit expires as "availability for work" is denied[2]	yes; when permit expires, take-up of welfare results in loss of right to residence and possibly in deportation
Not Employed:[3] Students	if registered for study and insured in case of sickness	only temporarily; costs may be recovered from "home state" of recipient[4]
Pensioners	if insured in case of sickness and in receipt of sufficient (old age, accident, disability) pension to avoid take-up of welfare	yes; but take-up of welfare results in loss of right to residence and possibly in deportation
Others	if insured in case of sickness and in receipt of sufficient resources to avoid take-up of welfare	yes; but take-up of welfare results in loss of right to residence and possibly in deportation

1) Section 10, par. 1, no. 10, *Ausländergesetz* (Alien Bill) stipulates that foreigners may be deported if they cannot support themselves without the take-up of welfare.
2) Section 103 AFG (Employment Bill).
3) In the following, I refer to legislation proposed by the Commission (cf. *Amtsblatt der Europäischen Gemeinschaften*, July 28, 1989, Nr. C 191/2-6; KOM(89) 275 endg.-SYN 199, 200; 89/C 191/02-04). The Council of Ministers agreed to these somewhat modified proposals on December 22, 1989 (cf. *FAZ* Dec. 23, 1989). As yet, the "Not Employed" have no mobility rights which are Community-protected.
4) Such recovery, though, would contradict section 4 of the European Convention on Social and Medical Assistance, ratified by all 12 EC member countries.

meant to become operational. Therefore, I will discuss them in a national – in this case, the "welfare-generous" German – setting.

At present the situation, as it is captured in Figure 16.4, is still at a level where receiving welfare leads to the classic "poor law" remedial procedures: ship the poor back to their place of origin (in the EC). The EC, therefore, compared with the evolution of poverty policy in European nation-states, is still bound to the first of four historical and logical levels of integration of poverty policy, as shown in Figure 16.5.

A second, more refined, stage of social policy development, is realized when a person is permitted to stay in the country granting him or her welfare but the costs of support are charged back to his or her place of origin (Figure 16.5). To channel transfers from many national sources through one national agency is a regular feature of social security networks established in bilateral agreements: for example, when pensions are payed out to an aged migrant worker. Community Law allows for this possibility in welfare policy exclusively for "students",[58] a most temporary status (see Figure 16.4, *"Not Employed"*, "Students"). An internal administrative shifting of costs is still a rare case between national poverty bureaucracies. At the moment, such a solution seems not to be envisioned for the aged (see Figure 16.4, *"Not Employed"*, "Pensioners") – though they are closest to pensioners, where this solution already exists. An aged person moving from Germany to Spain, therefore, has to prove to Spanish authorities that he/she has sufficient resources not to be in need of welfare. Nevertheless, a solution similar to "students" may have to come about for pensioners who did move to another EC country, stayed there for a long time – and then need long-term care arrangements which they cannot afford without welfare co-payments.[59, 60] Rather than destroy the new and last social roots at the place of retirement by insisting that these pensioners return to their country of origin in the EC, it would seem most desirable to recover outlays from that country.

A third step up the evolutionary ladder (see Figure 16.5) is taken when take-up of welfare in Germany – or for that matter in any other EC country which grants a right to welfare – becomes as legitimate for EC citizens as it is for German citizens – or for the citizens of any respective EC country. This is the case only in the immediate vicinity of employment (cf. Zuleeg, 1987): most extremely in case of low-wage employment[61] (see Figure 16.4, *"Employed"*, "Employed"), less in case of joblessness (ibid., "Unemployed") and least in case of non-employment (job search; ibid., "Pre-employed").

The European Court decided in the prejudicial cases of Levin and Kempf[62] that it is only relevant under European law that a person be gainfully "employed" (*Arbeitnehmer*) and "active in wage or salaried employment" (*eine Tätigkeit im Lohn- und Gehaltsverhältnis ausübt*), independent of whether he/she is earning less than the state-defined subsistence minimum (Zuleeg, 1987: 344f.). For the residence permit of an EC citizen "(it) is irrelevant whether such income ... is increased

Figure 16.5: Steps in Integration of Poverty Policy

Step	Characteristic	
1	"Shipping the poor back home"	
2	Shifting only the costs of poor support to the locality of origin	
3	Treatment of EC citizens as national (or local) citizens in each country (or community)	
4	Creation of European substantive and procedural welfare standards	

by other income up to this minimum or whether the person is satisfied with his [or her] below-poverty income, as long as he [or she] is truly active in wage or salaried employment"[63]. This interpretation does not hinge on what the country concerned defines as "employment": it thus holds universally in the EC.

Thus German social security law – Section 8 of the fourth book of the SGB, the Welfare Law Code – levies no pension contributions on "insignificant employment" (*geringfügige Beschäftigung*), defined as being lower than 15 hours per week or earnings less than 470 DM (parameters as of 1 January1990).[64] Looking at the hours only, Kempf – the plaintiff in the European Court case – would not have been considered "employed" according to German law. But according to superior EC law he is "employed" in Germany, and thus has a right of residence and access to all social benefits in Germany, which includes a right to welfare.

Independent of what a national "standard employment relationship" is, the EC and its court set their own Europe-wide principles. A broad interpretation of "employment" through the Court has been one of the avenues of moving towards "social citizenship" under the constraints of an employment-oriented concept of freedom and European integration (cf. most extensively, Steinmeyer, 1990).[65] The same solution obtains in case of self-employment, which does not provide sufficient resources for self-support (see Figure 16.4, "*Self-Employed*"). Again, welfare may be legitimately used as a supplementary benefit for EC citizens. In this case, however, there is no "pre"-[66] and "post"-protective status as it relates to the employment situation (job search, unemployment). Self-employment is thus less shielded in an EC social policy context against the risk of poverty. But there is also less of a necessity to shield it: empirically, these cases are not very significant; and legally, a *Gestaltswitch* of "self-employment" can always be relatively easily converted by the person concerned to a status of "employed, searching for work".

The four steps in integration of European poverty policy have been summarized in Figure 16.5. Presently, Step 1 is still the norm, and Step 2 and Step 3 are the exception. Step 4, which aims more at a European poverty regime, is entirely out of reach.

3.2 *"Europeanization" of Poverty Policy*

European institutions could also define European standards of poverty policy, "social rights" for the European citizens "from the top down" – in a Bismarckian, Napoleonic fashion. These standards could be designed to bring the top – the more generous welfare systems – down or to bring the bottom – the more miserly welfare systems – up. These standards could rely on a uniform European formula (for example, 40 per cent of the average national wage income is to be used as the basic welfare rate of each nation) which could still allow for variance between the different nations.[67] I do not see how the political and juridical base for a beneficial European standardization might be forthcoming. If the EC may not set standards which inform a European right to welfare, it might still subsidize national poverty policy systematically: for example, in underdeveloped or peripheral regions (cf. on the different strategies, Hauser, 1983, 1987).

With social security "harmonized" – or not (cf. Schmähl, 1989: 47)[68] – at the national level and not institutionalized at the European level, it would be a rather peculiar situation to have poverty policy partly centralized supranationally at the EC level. The "showcase" effect *vis-à-vis* the poor produced at the Community level, might even surpass the national "parading of the poor" so well-known from the USA social policy scenery in AFDC (Aid for Families with Dependent Children).

The Europeanization of poverty policy might also take quite a different angle: it may be that certain risks (the "deserving poor") will be Europeanized: as for example, the "poverty of the aged"[69] and, much less likely, of the unemployed.[70] Here, there might be an agreement among all nations for a rather positive means-tested solution. Thus, the "deserving" categories of the poor (*gehobene Fürsorge*) which are already "privileged" in many of the EC member countries (cf. Schulte, 1991) could be Europeanized. All the other poor might be left to be dealt with at the state or local level according to diverging national traditions. This filtering of the poor might permit a cultural construction of an "underclass"[71] at the national level, a *stratum* against which prejudice may then be better directed.

If such a development were to come about, it would lead to another Anglo-Saxonization (in the sense of the USA model) of the European welfare context: the "categorical approach to welfare" (to treat each category differently) will be imported and the universal approaches which are dominant in Northern European states will be slowly subverted. The USA, with its fixation on single mothers' welfare (AFDC), is the most prominent example of the categorical approach – which Germany already discarded in the 1920s. Also, if the EC decides to partly subsidize minimum income developments, then control devices of special revenue sharing, as they have evolved in the USA residual welfare policy regime (especially in AFDC), are likely candidates for Europeanization. Once the benefits of means-tested income transfers cannot be targeted at nationals only,[72] such transfers may either slowly whither away or might have to be delivered directly at the European level or nationally in a strongly harmonized way.

Since European Community law makes national solutions of the categorical sort difficult unless these nations allow "transfer exports" to other European countries – the economic benefits of such transfers may not be sheltered nationally (Zuleeg, 1989)[73] – there is a political and economic incentive for a straightforward European categorical solution.[74]

That a more radicalized version of a basic income might become the European Community approach[75] seems, at this time, rather unlikely – though the discussion of these issues in a European context may be beneficial for a push towards more generous traditional "welfare" solutions at the European level.

4   Conclusion

A unified European poverty regime is no "all-purpose weapon". Surely, Europe should develop its own perspectives on a "War on Poverty" and its standards for a fair distribution of income. Poverty, though, is not limited to the income dimension alone but concerns all sorts of resources – be it education, qualification, or other means of social integration (cf. Friederich et al., 1979: 11-47). To first focus on absent income may be the easiest way to make deprivation and marginalization visible ("social reporting"; cf. Leibfried/Voges, 1990) at the European level and to politicize them, using it as an eye-opener for wider poverty issues.

The road from a common market to a Social Europe, a European welfare state, is barely accessed. It will be a long road. Germany's first unification at the end of the last century led to the creation of the national welfare state. This state was built on a then-timely concept of social citizenship – for workers.

The founding of a United Europe depends mainly, if not totally, on the "four freedoms": the free movement of persons, goods, capital, and services. Thus, "economic citizenship", which does contain some civil aspects of "social citizenship",[76] is at the fore. Political as well as social citizenship are presently relatively marginal in the process of European unification. For this reason, European unification reminds one more of the unification of the USA – a process where political citizenship was pertinent from the beginning and has been complemented by social citizenship only since the 1930s, if at all.

The citizenship on which a unifying Europe must come to rest, seems primarily an economic or civil notion, secondarily a political one, and only lastly a social one.[77] This pattern repeats English and US-American precedents and is not anchored well either in German or in Scandinavian history. Unity in such a restrictive frame, would turn into a unity of "possessive individualism", a unity of markets only. It will not be the unity of an enlightened "Social Europe" synthesizing its traditions of democracy and solidarity, of civil and social rights, and building on its traditions of merging the citizen and the worker.

The coming of such an enlightened "Social Europe" also depends on the challenges provided and the escapes offered by its "environment". Japan and the USA do not offer the EC a better model for social integration. "Social Europe" may lose much of its impetus if Eastern Europe – at least being perceived as "social" pressure in the days of "systems competition"[78] – were to turn into "less Central Europe than *Zwischeneuropa* ... a dependent intermediate zone of weak states, national prejudice, inequality, poverty, and *Schlamassel*." (Ash, 1990: 22).

Notes

1 I am grateful to Lutz Leisering, Chiara Saraceno, Bernd Schulte, Peter Townsend, and to several participants of the 1990 annual conference of the Social Policy Association in Bath for comments and critical remarks. Hannah Brückner, Marlene Ellerkamp, Peter Klein, Jutta Mester and Gitta Stender were helpful in completing this paper.
This paper was first presented at an EC seminar in Florence, in September 1989 and was then redrafted for the First All-European Dialogue on Social Policies in Helsinki, March 15-19, 1990. It was developed further for the EC-Seminar on "Poverty, Marginalization and Social Exclusion in the Europe of the 90s", Alghero, April 23-25, 1990.

2 For general analyses of European unification cf. Hoffmann, 1966; Kaelble, 1987; Keohane and Hoffmann, 1991; Pomian, 1989; Schulze, 1990.

3 The "social" component was an issue between France and Germany already at the time of the Rome Treaty, though not as a "Social Union". Then, the issue was: should social policy expenditures be counted as labour costs in establishing "free markets"? Decades later, in the 1960s, the "Social Union" reemerged in attempts by the Commission to move towards harmonization in social policy, which failed. Finally, in the early 1970s another attempt was made for a "European Social Union", supported by the German government headed by Willy Brandt. Herbert Wehner, head of the parliamentary SPD, envisioned "the United States of Europe constituted as a democratic welfare state" (*Vereinigte Staaten von Europa in der Form eines demokratischen und sozialen Rechtsstaates*). Cf. Henningsen, 1989: 66, for further references.

4 On a definition of poverty policy (vs. "labourist policy"), cf. Leibfried and Tennstedt, 1985, 66ff.

5 The two regime types are not exclusive. The shift from negative to positive integration implies a synthesis: positive integration includes *and* transforms negative integration by relating the latter to concepts of "justice" and "welfare". Positive integration confronts the "social infrastructure" necessary to achieve "negative integration", thus not simply displacing the costs of integration downwards.

6 "Social" policy at the EEC level is structurally narrow (Henningsen, 1989: 56, 70f.) – it is usually understood as "employment" policy only, i.e. programmes for those employed or employable. When Jacques Delors speaks about a "social floor" ("sozialer Sockel") for Europe he does not mean a floor for all citizens but one for the employed only. The "labourer" and the "citizen" (in the nineteenth century: the "poor"; cf. Leibfried and Tennstedt, 1985) are treated as distinct social categories.
In EEC discourse, the meaning of "the social" has always been reduced to employable and divorced from citizenship. If this is not overcome at the EEC level, EEC "social citizenship" will always be tainted by a basic contradiction between these two terms.

7 Maybe Canada – with its entirely different legal regimes in neighbouring Quebec and Ontario, stressing the autonomy of these provinces, but having a strong political and a social union all the same – would also be an interesting example of positive integration. This is especially so when Canada is contrasted with the US on the issue of "social citizenship".

8 The other domain nationalized in the USA was war and foreign policy. This domain is relevant only in the USA, but not yet in the EEC.

9 German unification post-1871 never had such a strong agricultural bias. This area was tugged away in a large Department of the Interior and had, in contrast to the US, no pioneering role in the process of "nationalization".

10 A not too successful version of this was tested in the extremely cold winter of 1987 when the European ministers for agriculture decided to have agricultural surplus products distributed to the needy at no cost. This programme has been continued since then (cf. Henningsen, 1989: 74) and costs more per year than the entire ("other") four-year poverty programme of the EEC. Compared to US Food Stamps this open "in-kind" approach regresses to the tradition of charity. It does not speak too well for a European welfare state based on "social citizenship". At best, this programme offers a "window of opportunity" for a more enlightened way of using the positive integration capabilities of the EEC in agriculture for broad social policy purposes, thus actually implementing a poverty programme more systematically across Europe with an entitlement and a strongly diluted "in-kind" approach.

11 At the time these developments took place they looked much more like "supranational" integration. Only retrospectively and after their success do they look like processes of "national" integration only.

12 For a general overview cf. Tennstedt, 1983.

13 On the gender bias of social policy in Germany, cf. Leibfried and Ostner, 1990.

14 German unification after 1871 was, compared to the US, not particularly influenced by agricultural interests. "Poverty" and "Agriculture" were issues within one Interior Department. After World War I, the *Reich*'s Labour Ministry (*Reichsarbeitsministerium*) evolved as "the" social policy unit out of the Department of the Interior. Agricultural policy in Germany, in contrast to the US, had no pioneering role in the nationalization of social policy competences.

15 In Germany, the political pressures of the working class were not only channelled via social citizenship, as Rimlinger (1971) and Alber (1987) show. Social Reform was also about creating a common, meta-class and meta-regional, state culture, a space for national identity in a unifying Germany. By focussing on the class nature of social policy only, it is often ignored how central social policy was in this respect.

16 The social security bureaucracies are not direct parts of the national German government or of the state governments. They are independent national or state agencies, usually of a corporatist nature, with their governing boards staffed by representatives of labour, employers and of the different levels of the government.

17 Until World War I, the new German national government remained relatively marginal, be it in terms of fiscal power or personnel. In most respects, it was "dependent" on states and local governments ("*Kostgänger*"). Already in the 1880s, the *Reich*'s social security reform broke with this pattern (this is shown in contrast to England by Hennock, 1987).

18 For a comprehensive analysis of these processes in Germany, cf. Huber, 1969: Chapters XVI/ XVIII.

19 If (West) Germany had accepted the challenge, a synthesis might have looked quite interesting. The German Democratic Republic's (GDR) road to a welfare state differed substantially from the West German one: It guaranteed a right to work (and thus did not institutionalize unemployment insurance), with the labour force participation rate of women being far higher than in the FRG. Redistributive policies focussed less on the aged – as they do in West Germany – than on the young. Social policy operated mainly through the provision of public goods ("*Sozial-güterstrategie*"), e.g. through general subsidies for food stuffs and housing (cf. Tennstedt, 1976). With respect to monetary transfers uniform minimum approaches dominated, for example with pensions, leaving less room for inequality among pensioners. Thus the GDR moved from the Bismarck model which it had inherited towards the Beveridge model.

20 On GDR social policy cf. Bonz, 1990; Gehrmann et al., 1990; Winkler, 1988; Winkler and Manz, 1987.
21 Cf. *Sozialcharta*, 1990a; the Social Charter itself is documented in *Sozialcharta*, 1990b.
22 The simple extension of the West German social policy model to East Germany is much easier for pensions or monetary transfers. In unemployment, health and social services, extension is a more difficult strategy. Unification also extends the West German gender policy imbalance to East Germany, driving labour force participation of East German women down – and more towards part-time employment – by withdrawing much of the social infrastructure which allowed more gender balance in East Germany in the first place. A possible drop in labour force participation of women from 90 per cent (GDR) to about 60 per cent (FRG) highlights the scope of social change neccessary.
   Overviews on the development of social unification appear regularly and are rapidly obsolete, cf. Bäcker and Steffen, 1990; Winkler, 1990; Schmähl, 1990b.
23 In Germany, two countries were unified which were much further apart than the extremes within the EEC. The differences between the FRG and the GDR in poverty, for example, are rather similar to the North-South incline obtaining in the EEC (Schmähl [1990a] argues this point differently), but in addition the whole economic system was at variance which is not the case in the North-South incline of the EEC. This EEC-internal tension is amplified when the Latin rim countries are asked to finance German unification via the EEC with their tax monies (cf. Hans im Glück, 1990).
24 On comparisons of the EEC with the US cf. Cappeletti et al., 1986 ff., especially Elazar and Greilsammer, 1986; Garth, 1986; Heller and Pelkmans, 1986; Kommers, 1986; Kommers and Waelbroeck, 1986. On US poverty policy cf. for an overview: Cottingham and Ellwood, 1989 and Palmer et al., 1988.
25 The Supreme Court in the US and the European Court of Justice in Strassbourg are the cores of these integration processes.
26 In the Department of War, a strongly expanding pension system was built up after the Civil War. This system partly stepped in for a then not existing federal welfare state (Skocpol and Ikenberry, 1983).
27 At first, this was just social policy for the farm workers, but with Food Stamps in the second half of the twentieth century the scope of social policy has been extended to the urban population. Food Stamps is still the only programme available to any poor person in the US and it is nationally uniform. For a right to Food Stamps – in contrast to other welfare programmes – it does not matter whether one is working or not, is old or young, has children or not – all that matters is insufficient income. The programme is administered by the Department of Agriculture, even though it is "money" (coupons) and not food which is distributed today (cf. Leibfried, 1989). On the general agricultural policy background of this development cf. Dupree, 1957; Rossiter, 1979.
28 In the US, social citizenship never fully developed. This was recently demonstrated in the abortive debate about "new property" (Charles Reich).
29 An overview is given in Katz, 1989.
30 Cf. Laffan, 1983. Compared to the Social Charter, however, the Social Funds is a real institution, though its scope is modest: The Social Fund of the EC is just as large as Child Allowances in former West Germany alone.
31 Cf. on poverty in Europe: Room et al., 1990; Walker et al., 1984; George and Lawson, 1980; Henningsen and Room, 1990. The most recent empirical discussions of poverty in Europe are increasingly based on the Luxemburg Income Study (LIS), cf. Smeeding et al., 1990.
32 On the structure of "Basic Income Security" in former West Germany cf. Leibfried, 1990.
33 I add another category ("Latin Rim" countries) to Esping-Andersen's (1990) three worlds of welfare capitalism.
34 In fact, the Scandinavian model is essentially a Swedish model, which holds for Norway, Denmark and Finland only with important modifications. At the moment, only Denmark is a member of the EEC. On Sweden as the leading case for international comparisons cf. Baldwin, 1990.
35 Titmuss (1987) would have used the term "institutional-redistributive welfare state". I am substituting the word "modern" to indicate that in these countries "individualization" has no

structural gender barriers: 80 per cent of men and women are integrated into the labour market. When Titmuss coined the term "institutional welfare state" he characterized mostly constellations in which men were individualized but women were not. Titmuss' construction of "institutional-redistributive" is very much influenced by the model of the English National Health System (NHS) which included women *independent* of their work status.

Since this English situation resembles closely to the circumstances obtaining in today's "Bismarck countries" I would use his characterization "institutional" for them only.

36 One is hard put to find a significant "convergence of rhetoric on the goal of integrating all 'working age' citizens into the productive structures of society that cuts across ideology and national boundaries" (Lawson, McFate and Wilson, 1989: 21) in Europe. Only in "modern welfare states" do we find a rhetoric which fits to the reality in the sphere of work. In the "Bismarck" countries ("institutional welfare states") this relationship is already strongly destabilized by compensatory strategies. In Anglo-Saxon countries ("residual welfare states") the rhetoric verges on ideology, while in "Latin Rim" countries ("rudimentary welfare states") the (far-off) promises of development at least resound in such a rhetoric.

37 The "whithering away" of welfare programmes has been an institutionalized hope in many a western welfare state, for example in Germany's major 1961 welfare reform act (BSHG). But only in countries which follow a full employment strategy and have a broad sector of universal transfers is there some real basis for such hope. And, historically speaking, only such countries have a valid excuse for marginalizing welfare programmes in welfare state building.

38 I use a historical typology, which leads back to Germany and Austria as "Bismarckian" social policy countries. One could also start out building a typology from dominant techniques of social policy implementation. It could distinguish a group of "social insurance states" and would also include Belgium, France, Switzerland and the Netherlands in that category.

39 This institutional design differs from aspects of the Italian case. Ascoli (1986: 114) writes about pension policy, which is also the prominent feature of German welfare statism: "(P)ensions have, in the Italian case, many different functions, besides the social security function: (1) they *replace* a policy of economic development devoted to modifying economic imbalances in backward regions, (2) an active manpower policy that deals with unemployment and early retirements, and, finally, (3) specific sectoral policies that cope with agriculture, trade and artisan sector problems." (emphasis and numbering mine) It is in respect to functions 1 and 3 that the German situation differs most.

40 Titmuss would have subsumed these countries under the "industrial, achievement-performance model" (1987: 262) or the "handmaiden model" (1974: 31) rather than under the "institutional-redistributive model of social welfare" (1987: 263). I abandoned this terminology because: (1) in the 1960s and early 1970s the Bismarck countries have "universalized" their "performance model" to a "male citizenship model", which was (2) backed up by a (male) full employment promise. While the independent subsidy of exit or non-entry stresses the strength of social policy institutions, the whole welfare state set-up is not strongly redistributive.

On the first contrast between institutional and residual, cf. Wilensky and Lebeaux, 1958: 138f. Cf. now Leisering, 1989: chapters 2.3, 2.4.

41 In the context of a national institutional welfare state (only) there is the danger that a basic income strategy would support an "opting out of politics". Here the coupling of an income transfer with an employment strategy and possibly a revaluation of work strategy (cf. Mückenberger, Offe and Ostner, 1989) makes most sense, such as to assure the centrality of socio-ethical issues in the political process afterwards.

42 Putting the US and the UK into one league, treating them in effect as if they were "one country", makes more sense today as the effects of Thatcherism on the welfare state become visible. As long as "freedom from want" and Beveridge-style social reform was prominent in England, the divergence from the US was rather pronounced.

43 If one took in-kind transfers into account, the prominent English example of the NHS would highlight the taxonomy in a different way.

44 This is, historically speaking, more so in the US than in England, though England has moved visibly towards the US in the last decade.

45 This need to move away from categorical welfare applies especially to US welfare policy.

46 Again, the need for national standardization applies more to US welfare policy than to England (cf. Petersen and Rom, 1990).

47 Though not a southern country, Ireland also fits with the "rudimentary welfare state" type. Perhaps its peripheral location, its bent towards agriculture, and its latinity in terms of religion are responsible for this similarity.

48 In Italy an integrated look at income transfers *and services* will lead to a different picture than does a concentration just on income transfers, as in this essay. The Italian national health system ("servicio socio-sanitario nazionale") represents a rather singular case of recent "in-kind universalism" – and is, interestingly enough, combined with one of the strongest cases of "income transfer particularism" (or neglect) in European poverty policy. (In England, the inclusion of the NHS would also throw a somewhat different light on residualism as a general welfare state feature.) On an overview about the Italian development and its complications cf. Ascoli, 1986 (on poverty: 126f.). Italy may also be distinctive in the "Latin rim" due to the concentration of poverty in one region only (southern Italy and the islands), whereas in other Latin rim countries (or for that matter in Ireland) poverty is much more an endemic national problem.

49 In France (cf. Haupt, 1989: 271ff.) the heavy family focus of all social policy (and concomitantly of wage policy) probably leads to a special sort of welfare state regime (cf. Schultheis, 1988: 381ff.) which carries some weight even though the structure of *poverty* policy is otherwise very similar (no national but only an optional local general assistance structure, though France, in contrast to Italy, is characterized by a right to those welfare provisions which do exist). On recent national welfare improvements cf. Milano, 1989.

50 This term results from discussions with Bernd Schulte.

51 Though one would have to say that while England is moving downwards, towards a "rudimentary welfare state", the "Latin rim" countries are moving upwards, towards one of the other welfare state types.

52 Even Hauser's (1987: 31ff.) most likely option, which is the low-key harmonization of national law, seems to me an optimistic scenario; cf. also Schulte, l990a; b.

53 On the role of poverty policy at the EC level cf. Hauser, 1980, 1983, 1987; Schulte, 1986; 1989 a-c; 1990 a, b; cf. in general also Schmähl, 1990a-d; Hartmann, 1989.

54 If England's and Germany's pension system are compared one wonders whether harmonization would actually be that simple. However, there may be less need to "europeanize" or harmonize policies here because many of these policies are directly "piggiebacked" to labour market developments. Thus, it would suffice to simply emphasize the integrated development of the European labour market. Schmähl (1990: 47ff.) reflects this disposition and downplays the need for a harmonization of European social security systems.

55 "The economically weaker Member States have stressed repeatedly that the 'cohesion' of the Community ought to be preserved" (Pelkmans, 1988: 376). "At some point, however, a major challenge will have to be faced, for the objective of market integration itself remains unacceptable, politically speaking, for some Member States if it is not accompanied by a specific effort to improve social and economic cohesion within the community" (Dehousse, 1988: 335). Since the economically weaker states will be exposed to problems of "social integration" not so much "in" labour markets and "in" labour-related social security but at the margins of labour markets or within traditional sectors not yet organized in labour markets, poverty policy or the linkages of poverty policy and traditional social security policy are likely to be the focus of their "cohesive" interests in the EEC.

56 Some legal authors, though mostly looking at social security, do not see in this likely European development much of a problem and refer to the US pattern as the leading example, cf. Steinmeyer, 1989: 219; 1982: 101ff.; Zweigert, 1963: 404.
In Zweigert's view, classical motives for legal unification were: the calculability of private and public exchange, the reduction of problems in legal implementation, and the "serious legal philosophy of the radiating effects supranational legal unity would have on a just social order" (404). Zweigert argues that the classical motives for legal unification (*"Rechtsvereinheitlichung"*; *"loi uniforme"*) do not hold for the EEC, since the Community rests on pragmatic, economic

considerations of free competitive markets only – as it appears to him also in the US. Since the political and social union have been added to the EEC ticket in the 1970s and especially the 1980s, his argument would seem to be undercut by EEC development itself. Also, particularly a "social union" should be a centrepiece for a philosophy "of the radiating effects supranational legal unity would have on a just social order".

57 Outside of building social insurance institutions against poverty in old age or of invalids and the sick this was the traditional pattern of poverty policy integration in the building of the German *Reich* from 1871 to World War I. The *"Unterstützungswohnsitzgesetz"* basically left all substantive poverty law to the states or local governments and was only concerned with issues of "free mobility". It dealt with questions like: After how many months is a locality responsible for the welfare of a person? When may the person be shipped back to his community of origin? If not, how may the welfare costs for a recipient, who does not fall into this realm of responsibility, be charged back to the community of origin? Cf. Sachße and Tennstedt, 1980: 195ff.

58 This only holds when national law grants students a right to welfare.

59 This presupposes that the welfare scheme in that nation provides such payments, as it does in Germany.

60 When social assistance is needed to cover the additional costs of institutionalized care, then, as Zuleeg (1987: 343) rightly points out, residence permit and deportation again become an issue.

61 Here the right to welfare is permanent. Naturally it presupposes a universal welfare system like the German one, which also supplements wages. In the American model, where the working poor have no right to welfare (except, mainly, Food Stamps), there would be no such overlap. In the United Kingdom the "family credit" scheme does grant income support to the working poor (when working more than 24 hours per week; otherwise the normal income support scheme applies).

62 The European court has decided in the "Kempf" (EuGHE = E.C.J. 1986, 1741ff.) and "Levin" (EuGHE 1982, 1035ff.) cases that a person has a right to reside in a Community country even though he/she could support him/herself only insufficiently.

In the Kempf case the person was employed as a music teacher for 12 hours a week in the Netherlands. This salary was below the subsistence minimum defined by Dutch welfare law. Among other benefits, Kempf also received welfare payments and, also on these grounds, faced a refusal of his residence permit.

63 EuGHE 1986, 1749ff.

64 The same limit holds true for health insurance. Blue-collar workers working less than 10 hours a week have no right to continued wage payments in case of sickness.

Unemployment insurance does not reach out to certain "part-time employed", e.g. it covers only people working 18 hours and more per week. In this case there is no minimum threshhold in earnings.

65 Steinmeyer (1990: 8, 13) outlines some of the unorthodox ways through which the court has moved towards social citizenship under these conditions. One wonders, why two of the most original decisions in this context come out of France (and arise in connection with tourism). On an overview cf. Zuleeg, 1991.

66 Here three months are seen as a definite upper limit according to EC law (Zuleeg, 1987: 345). There seem to be no clear guidelines which allow for repeated spells of job search and also no clear rules on their duration.

67 Peter Townsend in 1981 has developed such a differentiated concept in more detail, though in view of the Third World. Also he developed a more relative standard just for England in 1979.

68 According to Schmähl (1990) there is no need to harmonize social security by force of (EC) law. A necessity to harmonize social policy may only be argued if one of the following arguments can be made: a) it would implement the four EEC-freedoms; b) it would do away with "unfair" competitive advantages in the market; c) it is a necessary political means to achieve integration ("cohesion"); d) it is a sensible social policy requirement. The political strength of the argument decreases from a) to d). Beyond "harmonization" the option is to leave a plurality of European systems, defining only some minimum standards, be they procedural or substantial. Cf. also Schmähl, 1990b.

69 Cf. sections 24 and 25 ("The Elderly") of the Community Charter for Fundamental Rights, 1990: 56. The original position on "minimum income" taken in the Preliminary Draft of a Community Charter for Fundamental Rights, Brussels, May 1989, was watered down by the conference of the European heads of state in Strassbourg on December 18, 1989, with England being the major opponent.
Cf. on a comparison of the efficiency of European social policy regimes in eradicating poverty in old age: Kohl, 1987, 1988, 1990.

70 Cf. section 10 ("Right to Social Protection") of the Community Charter for Fundamental Rights, 1990: 54, which reads as follows: "In accordance with the situation in the respective country
• each employee within the EC has a right to adequate social protection and must receive, independent of her or his position in and the size of the company, in which she or he works, sufficient social security benefits;
• all those, who have been excluded from the labour market, since entry was barred to them or since they were unable to regain entry, and who do not have sufficient means, must receive such means, as benefits which are suitable to their individual conditions" (translation is the author's).
In the draft this section still aimed at a "minimum income": "Workers who are excluded from the labour market without being able to continue claiming unemployment benefit or who do not have adequate means of subsistence, shall be able to receive a minimum income and appropriate social assistance." (Preliminary Draft of a Community Charter for Fundamental Rights, Brussels, May 1989; translation the author's). This position on "minimum income" has been most radically watered down by the conference of European heads of state in Strassbourg on December 18, 1989, again with England being the major opponent.

71 Cf. on the US Wilson, 1987. The construction of an "underclass" in most *continental* European countries (exceptions might be France and Italy), though, should be rather different from the US, since a strong "'racialization' of the poverty problem" (Lawson, McFate and Wilson, 1989: 7) is not very prominent. In the very *long* run this might become a general continental perspective, depending on the development of real mobility within the European community and on immigration pressures from the African and Arab rim countries *vis-à-vis* the Latin Rim countries within the EEC.
Another angle of *Europeanization* concerns one group of the *undeserving poor*: Immigrants from Eastern Europe and from the African as well as Arab Mediterranean rim – "economic migrants". The EC is presently discussing a uniform immigration policy: One of the issues under consideration is a standardized welfare regime for these groups only.

72 Cf. Hauser's (1987: 23f.) extended discussion of the dangers of national "free rider" strategies, should the EEC opt for financing a minimum income as a subsidiary income of last resort.

73 European law prohibits tying social security entitlements in the wide sense ("social policy advantages"; "*soziale Vergünstigungen*") to residence clauses, thus protecting unfettered personal mobility in the Community. The question is, whether categorical special benefits are closer to "welfare", which may operate with residence clauses nationally, or to "social security", which may not. Zuleeg (1989) presents a series of arguments which make the latter most likely. S. Zuleeg (1987) analyses this legal problem in the context of the then West German welfare system. Cf. also Zuleeg, 1991.

74 Cf. "Bonn wehrt sich gegen Sozialexport. Kritik an der Brüsseler Kommission. 'Untragbare Belastungen'" (= Bonn Struggles against Welfare Exports. Critique of the Brussels Commission. Unbearable Costs), in: *Frankfurter Allgemeine Zeitung*, October 7, 1989: 12; BMA-BMF Position, 1990 and Bundesregierung, 1989.

75 At the European level, basic income is unlikely to become a means to opt out of politics and socio-political issues, since, e.g., there is no European consensus whatever on an institutional welfare state at this level, which would legitimate simply "paying off" social problems. Consensus building at the European level will afford so much in mobilization and political ressources that "opting in" and full focus on socio-ethical issues is necessary to achieve any results at this level.

76 Only those aspects of Marshall's civil citizenship are captured which pass the needle's eye of "free mobility". Freedom of speech, thought and faith, e.g., would play a minor role, the right to own property and to conclude valid contracts, and the pertinent right to justice, would play a major role.

77 On the different levels of citizenship cf. Marshall, 1964: 78ff. He defines: "The civil component is composed of the rights necessary for individual freedom – liberty of the person, freedom of speech, thought and faith, the right to own property and to conclude valid contracts, and the right to justice." (78) "By the political element I mean the right to participate in the exercise of political power, as a member of a body invested with political authority or as an elector of the members of such a body." (78) "By the social element I mean the whole range from the right to a modicum of economic welfare and security to the right to share to the full in the social heritage and to live the life of a civilized being according to the standards prevailing in the society." (78)

78 The necessity to "outcompete" East Germany in social policy was behind much of West German social reform in the mid-1950s. On this "struggle of principles" cf. Hockerts, 1980. This necessity has now withered away. Instead "functional equivalents", internal mechanisms, will have to be developed which serve as forcing mechanisms for social innovation in the future.

References

Addison, J. T., Siebert, W. S. (1991)'The Social Charter of the European Community: Evolution and Controversies', in *Industrial and Labor Relations Review* 44 (4): 597-625.

Alber, J. (1987) *Vom Armenhaus zum Wohlfahrtsstaat. Analysen zur Entwicklung der Sozialversicherung in Westeuropa* (From Poorhouse to Welfare State. Analyses of Social Security Development in Western Europe). Frankfurt a.M.: Campus.

Albrecht, W. R. (1989) 'Europäische Sozialpolitik. Annäherung an ein aktuelles Thema' (European Social Policy. Approaches to a Timely Topic), *Soziale Sicherheit* 7: 198-209.

Anderson, J. J. (1991) 'Sceptical Reflections on a Europe of Regions: Britain, Germany and the ERDF' *Journal of Public Policy* 10 (4): 417-447.

Alston, Ph. (1990) 'U.S. Ratification of the Covenant on Economic, Social and Cultural Rights: The Need for an Entirely New Strategy', *American Journal of International Law* 84 (2): 365-393.

Amenta, E., Skocpol, Th. (1989) 'Taking Exception. Explaining the Distinctiveness of American Public Policies in the Last Century', pp. 292-333 in Castles, F. G. (ed.) *The Comparative History of Public Policy*. Cambridge: Polity Press.

Ascoli, U. (1986) 'The Italian Welfare State Between Incrementalism and Rationalization', pp. 107-141 in Balbo, L., Nowotny, H. (eds.) *Time to Care in Tomorrow's Welfare Systems: The Nordic Experience and the Italian Case*, Vienna: European Centre for Social Welfare Policy and Research.

Ash, T. G. (1990) 'Eastern Europe: The Year of Truth', *New York Review of Books* 37 (2): 17-22.

Bäcker, G. (1991a) 'Sozialpolitik im Vereinigten Deutschland. Probleme und Herausforderungen' (Social Policy in Unified Germany. Problems and Challenges), *Aus Politik und Zeitgeschichte, Beilage zur Wochenzeitung Das Parlament* 3-4 (11): 3-15.

Bäcker, G. (1991b) 'Abbruch statt Aufbruch? Soziale Probleme und sozialpolitische Herausforderungen in den neuen Bundesländern – das Jahr 1990 und ein Ausblick auf 1991' (Destruction or Renewal? Social Problems and Challenges for Social Policy in the New Territories – 1990 and 1991), in Kittner, M. (ed.) *Gewerkschaftsjahrbuch*. Unpublished Manuscript. Köln: Bund Verlag.

Bäcker, G., Steffen, J. (1990) 'Sozialunion: Was soll wie vereinigt werden? Sozialpolitische Probleme des ökonomischen und politischen Umbruchs in der DDR und Anforderungen des Einigungsprozesses' (Social Unification: What is to be Unified?), *WSI-Mitteilungen* 43 (5) (special issue on "Unification"): 265-281.

Baldwin, P. (1990) *The Social Politics of Social Solidarity and the Class Bases of the European Welfare State, 1875-1975*. Cambridge etc.: Cambridge University Press.

Bank, H.-P., Kreikebohm, R. (1991) 'Einige Anmerkungen zu sozialpolitischen Trends im vereinten Deutschland' (Some Remarks on Trends in Social Policy in Unified Germany), *Zeitschrift für Sozialreform* 37 (1): 1-15.

Bank, H.-P., Kreikebohm, R. (1990) '"Deutschland einig Vaterland"? (Sozial-) Politische Betrachtungen zu dem aktuellen Thema' ("Germany's United Fatherland"? (Social) Policy Perspectives on an Current Topic), *Zeitschrift für Sozialreform* 36 (1): 1-10.

Banting, K. G. (1990a) 'Social Policy in an Open Economy. Neo-conservatism and the Canadian State'. Unpublished Manuscript. Kingston, ONT: Queen's University. (paper presented to the Annual Meeting of the American Political Science Association, San Francisco, August 30-September 2.)

Banting, K. G. (1990b) *Canada and the United States in a Changing Environment. Institutional and Policy Response. A Framework*. Unpublished Manuscript, First Draft. Kingston, ONT: Queen's University.

Banting, K. G. (1987) *The Welfare State and Canadian Federalism*. Montreal: McGill-Queens University Press, 2nd ed.

Berenstein, A. (1981) 'Economic and Social Rights: Their Inclusion in the European Convention on Human Rights. Problems of Formulation and Interpretation', *Human Rights Law Journal* 2 (3/4): 257-280.

Berié, H. (1990) 'Sozialcharta. Startschuß für den europäischen Sozialraum oder Beerdigung dritter Klasse?' (Social Charter: Start into a European Social Space or Burial Third Class), *Kompaß* 3: 109-119.

Bercusson, B. (1989) *Fundamental Social and Economic Rights in the European Community*. Florence: EUI, appendix.

Berghman, J. (1990) 'European Integration and Social Security', pp. 1-10 in *EISS (European Institute for Social Security) Yearbook*. Leuven: Acco.

Blackwell, J. (1990) *Some Labour Market Impacts of Social Conventions with Implications for the EC Social Charter*. Unpublished Manuscript, Paris: OECD.

BMA-BMF Position (1990) 'BMA/BMF-Papier zur Europäischen Sozialpolitik mit Blick auf ihre politischen und finanziellen Konsequenzen für die Bundesrepublik Deutschland' (Position of the Department of Labour and of Finance vis-à-vis European Social Policy in View of their Political and Financial Consequences for the Federal Republic of Germany), *Zeitschrift für Sozialreform* 36 (6): 383-394.

Bonz, H.-J. (1990) 'Die Deutsche Demokratische Republik im Aufbruch – Die Sozialversicherung in der DDR und die "Politik der Wende"'(The Transformation of the GDR – Social Insurance and the "Policy of Change"), *Zeitschrift für Sozialreform* 36 (1): 11-35.

O'Brien, M., Hantrais, L., Mangen, St. (1990 ff.) *Cross-National Research Papers*. New Series: The Implications of 1992 for Social Policy. London/Birmingham: Cross-National Research Group, 3 vols. (vol. 1: The Implications of 1992 for Social Insurance; vol. 2: Caring and the Welfare State in the 1990s; vol. 3: Women, Equal Opportunities and Welfare).

Bundesregierung (1989) Antwort der Bundesregierung auf die große Anfrage der Abg. Hellwig u.a. und der Fraktion der FDP "Sozialraum Europäische Gemeinschaft" (Reply of the Federal Government to an Inquiry by a Member of Parliament from the FDP on "Social Europe"), BT Drs. 11/4700 of June 6, 1989.

Cappeletti, M., Secombe, M., Weiler, J. H. H. (eds.) (1986ff.) *Europe and the American Federal Experience*, vol. 1: Methods, Tools and Institutions, Book 1 (1986): A Political, Legal, and Economic Overview; Book 3 (1986): Forces and Potentials for a European Identity; vol. 3 (1987): Consumer Law, Common Markets and Federalism in Europe and the United States; vol. 4 (1988): Legal Harmonization and the Business Enterprise. Corporate and Capital Market Law Harmonization Policy in Europe and the USA. Berlin etc.: de Gruyter.

Castles, F. G., Mitchell, D. (1990) 'Three Worlds of Welfare Capitalism or Four?', *Graduate Programme in Public Policy*. Canberra: Australian National University.

Clever, P. (1990) 'Sozialleistungen im EG-Binnenmarkt außerhalb der Sozialversicherung' (Social Transfers in the Single Market Beyond of Social Security), pp. 191-205 in Schmähl, W. (ed.) *Soziale Sicherung im EG-Binnenmarkt. Aufgaben und Probleme aus deutscher Sicht*. Baden-Baden: Nomos.

Clever, P. (1989) 'Binnenmarkt '92. Die "soziale Dimension"' (The "Social Dimension"), *Zeitschrift für Sozialhilfe und Sozialgesetzbuch* 28 (5): 225-236.

Community Charter (1990) 'Gemeinschaftscharta der sozialen Grundrechte der Arbeitnehmer' (Social Charter of Community Rights of the Employed), *Soziales Europa 1990* 1: 51-56. Brüssel/Luxemburg, December 5/6, 1989.

Cottingham, Ph. H., Ellwood, D. T. (eds.) (1989) *Welfare Policy for the 1990s*. Cambridge and London: Harvard University Press.

Crijns, L. H. J., Tracy, M. B., Uhel, J. Y. (1990) *Social Security in The United States and Canada. Lessons to be Drawn in the Context of European Integration*. Maastricht: European Institute of Public Administration.

Däubler, W. (ed.) (1989) *Sozialstaat EG? Die andere Dimension des Binnenmarktes* (Welfare State EC? The Other Dimension of the Single Market). Gütersloh: Verlag Bertelsmann Stiftung.

Dehousse, R. (1988) 'Completing the Internal Market: Institutional Constraints and Challenges', pp. 311-336 in Bieber, R., Dehousse, R., Pinder, J., Weiler, J. H. H. (eds.) *1992 One European Market? A Critical Analysis of the Commission's Internal Market Strategy*. Baden-Baden: Nomos.

Deubner, Ch. (ed.) (1990) *Europäische Einigung und soziale Frage. Möglichkeiten europäischer Sozialpolitik* (European Unification and the Social Question. Possibilities for European Social Policy). Frankfurt a.M.: Campus.

Deubner, Ch. (1980) 'The Southern Enlargement of the European Community: Opportunities and Dilemmas from a West German Point of View', *Journal of Common Market Studies* 18 (3).

Döring, D., Hauser, R. (eds.) (1989) *Politische Kultur und Sozialpolitik. Ein Vergleich der Vereinigten Staaten und der Bundesrepublik Deutschland unter besonderer Berücksichtigung des Armutsproblems* (Political Culture and Social Policy. A Comparison of the USA and West Germany with Special Regard to Poverty). Frankfurt a.M.: Campus.

Dupree, A. H. (1957) *Science in the Federal Government. A History of Policies and Activities to 1940*. Cambridge, MA: The Belknap Press of Harvard University Press (reprinted 1986).

Elazar, D. J., Greilsammer, I. (1986) 'Federal Democracy: The U.S.A and Europe Compared – A Political Science Perspective', pp. 71-168 in Cappelletti, M., Secombe, M., Weiler, J. (eds.) *Europe and the American Federal Experience*, vol. 1: Methods, Tools and Institutions, Book 1: A Political, Legal, and Economic Overview. Berlin etc.: de Gruyter.

Entzinger, H., Carter, J. P. (eds.) (1990) *Immigration in Western Democracies: The U.S. and Western Europe*. Greenwich, CT: JAI Press. (*International Review of Comparative Public Policy, vol. 1*).

Esping-Andersen, G. (1990) *The Three Worlds of Welfare Capitalism*. Oxford etc.: Polity Press.

Eurostat (1990) *Poverty in Figures. Europe in the Early 1980s*. Study Carried out for Eurostat by the Institute of Social Studies Advisory Service (Issas). Luxemburg: Office for Official Publications of the European Communities.

Flora, P. (1986) 'Introduction' in Flora, P. (ed.) *Growth to Limits. The Western European Welfare States Since World War II, Vol. 1: Sweden, Norway, Finland, Denmark*. Berlin etc.: Walter de Gruyter. (European University Institute, Series C).

Franzmeyer, F., Seydel, B. (1976) *Überstaatlicher Finanzausgleich und Europäische Integration* (Supranational Fiscal Federalism and European Integration). Bonn: Europa Union Verlag.

Friedrich, H. et al. (1979) *Soziale Deprivation und Familiendynamik* (Social Deprivation and Family Dynamics). Göttingen: Vandenhoeck & Ruprecht.

Garth, B. G. (1986) 'Migrant Workers and Rights of Mobility in the European Community and the United States: A Study of Law, Community and Citizenship in the Welfare State', pp. 85-163 in Cappelletti, M., Secombe, M., Weiler, J. (eds.) *Europe and the American Federal Experience, vol. 1: Methods, Tools and Institutions, Book 3: Forces and Potentials for a European Idendity*. Berlin etc.: de Gruyter.

Gehrmann, W., Kleine-Brockhoff, Th., Wernicke, Ch. (1990) 'Deutschland geizig Vaterland' (Germany, Miser's Motherland), *Die Zeit* 9, February 23.

George, V., Lawson, R. (eds.) (1980) *Poverty and Inequality in Common Market Countries*. London: Routledge & Kegan Paul.

Goodin, R. E. (1988) *Reasons for Welfare. The Political Theory of the Welfare State*. Princeton: Princeton University Press.

Hans im Glück (1990) 'Für 'Hans im Glück' zahlen? Die rasche Eingliederung der DDR in die EG gefällt dem Kanzler nicht' (Paying for "Hans im Glück"? The Fast Integration of the GDR into the EC Doesn't Please the Chancellor), *Frankfurter Allgemeine Zeitung*, July 30, 1990: 10.

Hansen, G. (1991) *Die exekutierte Einheit. Vom Deutschen Reich zur Nation Europa* (On Executed Unity. From the German *Reich* to Nation Europe). Frankfurt a.M.: Campus.

Hartmann, H. (1989) Europäische Sozialpolitik und EG-Binnenmarkt als Herausforderung für Wohlfahrtsverbände' (European Social Policy and the Single Market – Challenges for Welfare Associations), *Theorie und Praxis der sozialen Arbeit* 40 (11): 415-422.

Haupt, H.-G. (1989) *Sozialgeschichte Frankreichs seit 1789* (Social History of France since 1789). Frankfurt a.M.: Suhrkamp.

Hauser, R. (1987) *Möglichkeiten und Probleme der Sicherung eines Mindesteinkommens in den Mitgliedsländern der Europäischen Gemeinschaft* (Possibilities and Problems of Assuring Minimum Income in EC Member Countries). Frankfurt a.M. (sfb 3, Working Paper no. 246).

Hauser, R. (1983) *Problems of Harmonization of Minimum Income Regulations Among EC Member Countries*, Frankfurt a.M. (sfb 3, Working Paper no. 118).

Hauser, R. (1980) 'Probleme und Ansatzpunkte einer gemeinsamen Politik zur Bekämpfung der Armut in der Europäischen Gemeinschaft' (Problems of and Strategies for a Common Policy in the Struggle against Poverty in the European Community), pp. 229-251 in Borchardt, K., Holzheu, F. (eds.) *Theorie und Politik der internationalen Wirtschaftsbeziehungen. Hans Möller zum 65. Geburtstag*. Stuttgart etc.: Fischer.

Heclo, H. (1991) *The Search for Social Citizenship*. Unpublished Manuscript. Paris, Maison Suger, January 16-18. (Paper given at the conference on Poverty and Social Marginality).

Heller, Th., Pelkmans, J. (1986) 'The Federal Economy: Law and Integration and the Positive State – The USA and Europe Compared in an Economic Perspective', pp. 245-412 in Cappelletti, M., Secombe, M., Weiler, J. (eds.) *Europe and the American Federal Experience, vol. 1: Methods, Tools and Institutions, Book 1: A Political, Legal, and Economic Overview*. Berlin etc.: de Gruyter.

Henkin, L. (1981) 'Economic-Social Rights as "Rights": A United States Perspective', *Human Rights Law Journal* 2 (3/4).

Henningsen, B. (1990a) 'Politische Rahmenbedingungen einer Europäischen Sozialpolitik' (Political Contexts for European Social Policy), pp.167-187 in Braun, H., Niehaus, M. (eds.) *Sozialstaat Bundesrepublik. Deutschland auf dem Weg nach Europa*. Frankfurt a.M.: Campus.

Henningsen, B. (1990b) 'Social Security and Health', pp. 181-189 in Schweitzer, C.-Ch., Karsten, D. (eds.) *Federal Republic of Germany and EC Membership Evaluated*. London: Pinter.

Henningsen, B. (1989) 'Europäisierung Europas durch eine europäische Sozialpolitik?' (Europeanization of Europe through European Social Policy?), pp. 55-80 in Haungs, P. (ed.) *Europäisierung Europas*. Baden-Baden: Nomos.

Henningsen, B., Krämer, S., Weber, Ch. (1990) *Auswahlbibliographie zur Sozialpolitik in der Europäischen Gemeinschaft* (Bibliography of Publications on European Social Policy). Unpublished Manuscript. Trier, Department of Political Science, University of Trier .

Henningsen, B., Room, G. (eds.) (1990) *Neue Armut in der Europäischen Gemeinschaft* (New Poverty in the European Community). Frankfurt a.M.: Campus.

Hennock, E. P. (1987) *British Social Reform and German Precedents. The Case of Social Insurance 1880-1914*. Oxford: Oxford University Press (Clarendon Press).

Hockerts, H. G. (1980) *Sozialpolitische Entscheidungen im Nachkriegsdeutschland. Alliierte und deutsche Sozialversicherungspolitik 1945 bis 1959* (Social Policy Watersheds in Post-War Germany. Allied and German Social Security Policy from 1945 to 1959). Stuttgart: Klett-Cotta.

272   *Towards a European Welfare State?*

Hoffmann, St. (1990a) 'A Plan for the New Europe', *New York Review of Books* 18: 18-21.

Hoffmann, St. (1990b) *Away from the Past: European Politics and Security 1990*. Unpublished Manuscript. (paper presented to the Aspen Strategy Group directed by Joseph Nye Jr.). Cambridge, MA, CES, Harvard University.

Hoffmann, St. (1966) 'Obstinate or Obsolete? The Fate of the Nation-State and the Case of Western Europe', *Daedalus* 95: 862-915.

Hondrich, K. O. (1990) 'Der deutsche Weg. Von der Heilssuche zum nationalen Interessen-ausgleich' (The German Pathway. From Seeking the Millenium to a National Balancing of Interests), *Frankfurter Allgemeine Zeitung*, June 23, no. 143: 2 (Bilder und Zeiten).

Huber, E.-R. (1969) *Deutsche Verfassungsgeschichte seit 1789* (German Constitutional History since 1789). Stuttgart etc.: Kohlhammer Verlag, 2nd edition.

Jacobs, F.G. (1978) 'The Extension of the European Convention on Human Rights to Include Economic, Social and Cultural Rights', *Human Rights Review* 3: 166-178.

Jencks, C., Peterson, P. E. (1991) *The Urban Underclass*. Washington, D.C.: Brookings.

Jenson, J. (1990) 'Representations in Crisis: The Roots of Canada's Permeable Fordism', *Canadian Journal of Political Science* 23 (4): 653-683.

Joerges, Ch. (1991) *Markt ohne Staat? Die Wirtschaftsverfassung der Gemeinschaft und die Renaissance der regulativen Politik* (Market without State? The Economic Constitution of the Community and the Renaissance of Regulative Politics). Florence: European University Institute. (EUI Wirking Paper LAW no. 91/15).

Kaelble, H. (1987) *Auf dem Weg zu einer europäischen Gesellschaft. Eine Sozialgeschichte Westeuropas 1880-1980* (On the Road to a European Society. A Social History of Western Europe 1880-1980). München: C.H. Beck.

Katz, M. B. (1989) *The Undeserving Poor. From the War on Poverty to the War on Welfare*. New York: Pantheon.

Kaufmann, F.-X. (1986) 'Nationale Traditionen der Sozialpolitik und europäische Integration' (National Traditions of Social Policy and European Integration), pp. 69-82 in Albertin, L. (ed.) *Probleme und Perspektiven europäischer Einigung*. Köln: Verlag Wissenschaft und Politik.

Keohane, R., Hoffmann, St. (1991) 'Institutional Change in Europe in the 1980s', pp. 1-39 in Keohane, R. O., Hoffmann, St. (eds.) *The New European Community. Decisionmaking and Institutional Change*. Boulder etc.: Westview Press.

Ketelsen, J. V. (1990) 'Die soziale Dimension des Binnenmarktes – Gemeinschaftscharta der sozialen Grundrechte der Arbeitnehmer und Aktionsprogrammen der EG-Kommission' (The Social Dimension of the Single Market – The Community Charter of Social Rights for Employees and the Work Agenda of the Commission), *Die Angestelltenversicherung* 37: 139-144.

Kohl, J. (1990) *Minimum Standards in Old Age Security and the Problem of Poverty in Old Age*. Unpublished Manuscript. Florenz, EHI.

Kohl, J. (1988) 'Alterssicherung in Westeuropa: Strukturen und Wirkungen' (Social Security in Old Age – Structures and Effects), pp. 221-250 in Schmidt, M. G. (ed.) *Staatstätigkeit. International und historisch vergleichende Analysen*. Opladen: Westdeutscher Verlag (PVS special issue no. 19).

Kohl, J. (1987) 'Alterssicherung im internationalen Vergleich. Zur Einkommensstruktur und Versorgungssituation älterer Haushalte' (Old Age Social Security Internationally Compared. Income Structures and Supply Situations of Households of the Aged), *Zeitschrift für Sozialreform* 33 (11/12).

Kommers, D. P. (1986) 'Federalism and European Integration: A Commentary', pp. 603-616 in Cappelletti, M., Secombe, M., Weiler, J. (eds.) *Europe and the American Federal Experience, vol. 1: Methods, Tools and Institutions, Book 1: A Political, Legal, and Economic Overview*. Berlin etc.: de Gruyter.

Kommers, D. P., Waelbroeck, M. (1986) 'Legal Integration and the Free Movement of Goods: The American and European Experience', in Cappelletti, M., Secombe, M., Weiler, J. (eds.) *Europe and the American Federal Experience, vol. 1: Methods, Tools and Institutions, Book 3: Forces and Potentials for a European Idendity*. Berlin etc.: de Gruyter.

Kommission 1989: *Kommission der Europäischen Gemeinschaften. Generaldirektion Beschäftigung, soziale Angelegenheiten und Bildung, 1989: Soziales Europa. Der Kampf gegen die Armut* (Social Europe. The War against Poverty). Brussels, Luxemburg: Publications Division of the EEC (CE-NC-89-002-DE-C).

Laffan, B. (1983) 'Policy Implementation in the European Community: the European Social Funds as a Case Study', *Journal of Common Market Studies* 21: 389-408.

van Langendonck, J. (1991) 'The Role of the Social-Security Systems in the Completion of the European Market', *Acta Hospitalia 1991* 1 (in print).

Lawson, R., McFate, K., Wilson, W. J. (1989) *Poverty and Public Policy: American and European Experiences Compared*. Washington, D.C. (discussion paper).

Leibfried, St. (1991a) 'Welfare State Europe?' (paper given at the Second International Symposion of the Sonderforschungsbereich (sfb) 186 Bremen on "Status Passages and their Institutional Regulation", February 20-22, 1991; to be published in Heinz, W. (ed.) *Status Passages and their Institutional Regulation* with UTB. Bremen: ZeS and sfb 186, March.

Leibfried, St. (1991b) *Social Policy and German Unification. The Social Union*. Unpublished Manuscript. New York. (Beitrag zur Konferenz "Consequences of German Unification: Social Policies, Economics, and Education", NYU, 18.-19.8.1990).

Leibfried, St. (1990a) 'Soziale Grundsicherung – Das Bedarfsprinzip in der Sozial- und Gesellschaftspolitik der Bundesrepublik' (Basic Delivery Standards – The Needs Principle in Societal and Social Policy of the FRG), pp. 182-225 in Vobruba, G. (ed.) *Strukturwandel der Sozialpolitik. Lohnarbeitszentrierte Sozialpolitik und soziale Grundsicherung*. Frankfurt: Suhrkamp.

Leibfried, St. (1990b) 'Sozialstaat Europa? Integrationsperspektiven europäischer Armutsregimes' (Welfare State Europe? On Integrating European Poverty Regimes), *Nachrichtendienst des Deutschen Vereins für öffentliche und private Fürsorge* 70 (9): 296-395.

Leibfried, St. (1989) *Nutritional Minima and the State – The Institutionalization of Professional Knowledge in National Social Policy in the U.S. and Germany*. Unpublished Manuscript. Bremen: University.

Leibfried, St. et al. (1985) *Armutspolitik und die Entstehung des Sozialstaats. Entwicklungslinien sozialpolitischer Existenzsicherung im historischen und internationalen Vergleich* (Regulating the Poor and the Genesis of the Welfare State. Lineages of Subsistence Policy in Historical and Comparative Perspective). Bremen: Universität 1985. (Grundrisse sozialpolitischer Forschung, no. 3).

Leibfried, St., Ostner, I. (1991) 'The Particularism of West German Welfare Capitalism: The Case of Women's Social Security', in Adler, M. et al. (eds.) *The Sociology of Social Security*. Edinburgh: Edinburgh University Press (in press).

Leibfried, St., Tennstedt, F. (1985) 'Armenpolitik und Arbeiterpolitik. Zur Entwicklung und Krise der traditionellen Politik der Verteilungsformen' (Poverty Policies or "Labourist" Policies. On the Development and Crisis of Traditional Forms of Redistributional Politics), pp. 64-93 in Leibfried, St., Tennstedt, F. (eds.) *Politik der Armut und die Spaltung des Sozialstaats*. Frankfurt a.M.: Suhrkamp.

Leibfried, St., Voges, W. (1990) 'Keine Sonne für die Armut. Vom Sozialhilfebezug als Verlauf ("Karriere") – Ohne umfassende Information keine wirksame Armutsbekämpfung' (There ain't no Sunshine for Poverty. On Welfare Receipt as a Career), *Nachrichtendienst des Deutschen Vereins für öffentliche und private Fürsorge* 70 (5).

Leisering, L. (1989) *Origins of the Dynamics of the Welfare State. Societal Differentiation and the Formation of Statutory Welfare in England 1795-1847. A Sociological Study*. Ph.D. Thesis, London: LSE, Department of Social Science and Administration.

Lepsius, M. R. (1990) *Die Europäische Gemeinschaft: Rationalitätskriterien und Regimebildung* (The EC: Criteria of Rationality and Regime Building). Unpublished Manuscript. (Paper given at the 25th German Sociological Convention on "Die Modernisierung moderner Gesellschaften" in Frankfurt a.M.).

Lepsius, M. R. (1986) '"Ethnos" und "Demos". Zur Anwendung zweier Kategorien von Emmerich Francis auf das nationale Selbstverständnis der Bundesrepublik und auf die Europäische Einigung' (Ethnos and Demos. On Applying Two Categories of Emmerich Francis to Germany's National Self-Awareness and to European Unification), *Kölner Zeitschrift für Soziologie und Sozialpsychologie* 38: 724-750.

Lødemel, I. (1989) *The Quest for Institutional Welfare and the Problem of the Residuum. The Case of Income Maintenance and Personal Social Care Policies in Norway and Britain 1946 to 1966.* Ph.D. Thesis, London: LSE, Department of Social Science and Administration, June.

Lompe, K. (1990) 'Sozialstaatsgebot und Sozialstaatlichkeit – Vergessene Größen im Einigungsprozeß?' (The "Social State" Principle and the Welfare State – Lost Causes in Unification?), *Gewerkschaftliche Monatshefte* 41 (5/6): 321-332.

Lowe, Ph. (1988) 'The Reform of the Community's Structural Funds', *Common Market Law Review* 25: 503-521.

Majone, G. (1989) 'Regulating Europe: Problems and Prospects', *Jahrbuch zur Staats- und Verwaltungswissenschaft* 3: 159-178.

Majone, G. (ed.) (1990) *Deregulation or Re-Regulation? Regulatory Reform in Europe and the United States.* London.

Mann, M. (1988) 'Ruling Class Strategies and Citizenship', pp. 188-210 in Mann, M. *States, War and Capitalism. Studies in Political Sociology.* Oxford: Basil Blackwell.

Marshall, T. H. (1964) 'Citizenship and Social Class', pp. 71-134 in Marshall, T. H. *Class, Citizenship, and Social Development,* Essays by T. H. Marshall, with an introduction by Seymour Martin Lipset. Chicago: The University of Chicago Press.

Masberg, D., Pintz, P. (1982) 'Die Sozialpolitik der Europäischen Gemeinschaft' (Social Policy of the EC), pp. 51-74 in Hauff, M. von, Pfister-Gaspary, B. (eds.) *Internationale Sozialpolitik.* Stuttgart: Gustav Fischer.

Maydell, B. von (1989) 'Das Recht der Europäischen Gemeinschaften und die Sozialversicherung – Supranationales Sozialversicherungsrecht und Auswirkungen des EG-Rechts auf die nationale Sozialversicherung' (EC Law and Social Insurance – Supranational Welfare Law and the Effects of EC Law on National Welfare Law), *Zeitschrift für die gesamte Staatswissenschaft* 1/2: 1-28.

Milano, S. (1989) *Le Revenu Minimum Garanti dans Les Pays Membres de la C.E.E.* (Guaranteed Minimum Income in EC Member Countries). Paris: Presses Universitaires de France.

Mosley, H. G. (1990a) 'The Social Dimension of European Integration', *International Labour Review* 129 (2): 147-164.

Mosley, H. G. (1990b) *The Welfare State and European Unity.* Unpublished Manuscript. Berlin: Science Centre.

Mückenberger, U., Offe, C., Ostner, I. (1989) 'Das staatlich garantierte Grundeinkommen – Ein sozialpolitisches Gebot der Stunde' (The Guaranteed Basic Income – A Timely Demand), pp. 247-278 in Krämer, H. L., Leggewie, C. (eds.) *Wege ins Reich der Freiheit. André Gorz zum 65. Geburtstag.* Berlin: Rotbuch Verlag.

Offe, C. (1990) *Europäische Dimensionen der Sozialpolitik* (European Dimensions of Social Policy). Unpublished Manuscript. Bremen, Centre for Social Policy Research, July.

Ostner, I., Langan, M. (1991) 'Gender and Welfare. Towards a Comparative Framework', pp. 127-150 in Room, G. (ed.) *Towards a European Welfare State?* Bristol: SAUS.

Palmer, J. L., Smeeding, T., Torrey, B. B. (eds.) (1988) *The Vulnerable.* Washington, D.C.: The Urban Institute Press.

Pieters, D. (1989) 'Naar een eenmaking van de sociale zekerheid in 1992?', *Instituut voor Sociale Zekerheid, de actuele uitdagingen voor de sociale zekerheid,* Seminar at Corsendonk, 31.3.-1.4. 1989 (to be published with Die Keure, Brugge).

Pelkmans, J. (1988) 'A Grand Design by the Piece? An Appraisal of the Internal Market Strategy', pp. 359-382 in Bieber, R., Dehousse, R., Pinder, J., Weiler, J. H. H. (eds.) *1992 One European Market? A Critical Analysis of the Commission's Internal Market Strategy.* Baden-Baden: Nomos.

Peterson, P. E., Rom, M. C. (1990) *Welfare Magnets.* Washington, DC: Brookings.

Pinder, J. (1968) 'Positive Integration and Negative Integration – Some Problems of Economic Union in the EC', *World Today* 24: 88-110.

Pomian, K. (1989) *Europa und seine Nationen* (Europe and its Nations). Berlin: Wagenbach.

Rainwater, L., Rein, M., Schwartz, J. (1986) *Income Packaging in the Welfare State. A Comparative Study of Family Income*. Oxford: Clarendon Press.

Reich, N. (1988) *Schutzpolitik in der Europäischen Gemeinschaft im Spannungsfeld von Rechtsschutznormen und institutioneller Integration* (Protective Policy of the EC: Between Protective Legislation and Institutional Integration). Hannover: Hennis & Zinkeisen.

Reich, N., Ahrazoglou, C. (eds.) (1990) *Deutsche Einigung und EG-Integration* (German Unification and EC Integration). Beiträge und Berichte zur Arbeitstagung deutsch-deutscher Juristen vom 6. & 7. Juni 1990 am Zentrum für Europäische Rechtspolitik (ZERP). Bremen: University, ZERP, (ZERP-DP 6/90).

Reis, C., Wienand, M. (eds.) (1990) *Zur sozialen Dimension des EG-Binnenmarktes* (On the Social Dimension of the Single Market). Frankfurt a.M.: Deutscher Verein für öffentliche und private Fürsorge. (Texte und Materialien 2).

Rimlinger, G. V. (1971) *Welfare Policy and Industrialization in Europe, America and Russia*. New York: Wiley.

Room, G., Lawson, R., Laczko, F. (eds.) (1990) *"New Poverty" in the European Community*. London: Macmillan.

Rossiter, M. W. (1979) 'The Organization of the Agricultural Sciences', pp. 211-248 in Oleson, A., Von, J. (eds.) *The Organization of Knowledge in Modern America 1860-1920*. Baltimore, MD: The Johns Hopkins University Press.

Sachße, Ch., Tennstedt, F. (1980) *Geschichte der Armenfürsorge in Deutschland. Vom Spätmittelalter bis zum Ersten Weltkrieg* (History of Poverty Policy in Germany. From the Late Middle Ages until World War I), vol. 1. Stuttgart: Kohlhammer.

Scharpf, F. W. (1990a) *Kann es in Europa eine stabile föderale Balance geben?* (Thesen) (May Europe Achieve a Stable Federalist Balance? Some Theses). Unpublished Manuscript. Cologne: Max-Planck-Institute for Social Research.

Scharpf, F. W. (1990b) 'Entwicklungslinien des bundesdeutschen Föderalismus' (Lineages of German Federalism). Unpublished Manuscript. Cologne: Max-Planck Institute for Social Research, October, (to be published in the 1991 special issue of *"Leviathan"* commemorating the Fourtieth Anniversary of the Federal Republic of Germany).

Scharpf, F. W. (1989a) 'Regionalisierung des europäischen Raums – Die Zukunft der Bundesländer im Spannungsfeld zwischen EG, Bund und Kommunen' (Regionalization in European Space – On the Future of the (German) Federal States inbetween Supranational, National and Local Government) in Referate Cappenberger Gespräche veranstaltet am 27.9.1988 in Ettlingen, von Lothar Späth und Fritz W. Scharpf, Cappenberger Gespräche der Freiherr-vom-Stein-Gesellschaft, Bd. 23, Köln: Kohlhammer/Grote: 7-33 (abridged version published 1990 in Alemann, U. von, Heinze, R.-G., Hombach, B. (eds.) *Die Kraft der Region: Nordrhein-Westfalen in Europa*. Bonn: Dietz: 32-46).

Scharpf, F. J. (1989b) 'Der Bundesrat und die Kooperation auf der "dritten Ebene"' (The Federal Chamber and Cooperation at the "Third Level"), pp. 121-166 in Bundesrat (ed.) *Vierzig Jahre Bundesrat. Tagungsband zum wissenschaftlichen Symposion in der Evangelischen Akademie Tutzung vom 11. bis 14. April 1989*. Baden-Baden: Nomos.

Scharpf, F. J. (1988) 'The Joint-Decision Trap: Lessons from German Federalism and European Integration', *Public Administration* 66 (3): 239-278.

Scharpf, F. J. (1985) 'Die Politikverflechtungs-Falle: Europäische Integration und deutscher Föderalismus im Vergleich' (The Joint-Decision Trap: German Federalism and European Integration Compared), *Politische Vierteljahresschrift* 26 (4): 323-356.

Schmähl, W. (1990a) 'Harmonization of Pension Schemes in Europe? – A Controversial Issue in the Light of Economics', in Atkinson, A. B., Rein, M. (eds.) *Age, Work and Social Security*. London: Macmillan (in print).

Schmähl, W. (1990b) 'Soziale Sicherung in Deutschland und der EG-Binnenmarkt. Anmerkungen aus ökonomischer Sicht' (Social Security in Germany and the EC Common Market. An Economist's Perspective), pp. 11-38 in Schmähl, W. (ed.) *Soziale Sicherung im EG-Binnenmarkt*. Baden-Baden: Nomos.

Schmähl, W. (1990c) *Zur künftigen Entwicklung der ergänzenden Alterssicherungssysteme in Europa – Ein einführender Problemüberblick* (The Future of Supplementary Old Age Insurance in Europe –An Overview). Bremen: Centre for Social Policy Research, January 1990. (Introductory Statement to the International Colloquium on "Die Zukunft der Alterssicherung in der Europäischen Gemeinschaft – Regel und Ergänzungssysteme nach 1992, Bremen: ZeS, 29./30.1. 1990).

Schmähl, W. (1990d) 'Zur künftigen Entwicklung der ergänzenden Alterssicherungssysteme in Europa' (On Future Developments of Supplementary Old Age Insurance in Europe), *Staatswissenschaften und Staatspraxis* 1 (3): 388-428 (abridged version of 1990c).

Schmähl, W. (1990e) *Alterssicherung in der DDR und ihre Umgestaltung im Zuge des deutschen Einigungsprozesses – Einige verteilungspolitische Aspekte* (Pension Legislation in the GDR and its Transformation in the Process of Unification – Some Distributional Aspects). Bremen: University, CeS, 50 pp. (Arbeitspapier no. 10/90).

Schmähl, W. (1989) 'Europäischer Binnenmarkt und soziale Sicherung – einige Aufgaben und Fragen aus ökonomischer Sicht' (The European Market and Social Security – Some Demands and Questions in Economic Perspective), *Zeitschrift für die gesamte Versicherungswirtschaft*: 29-50.

Schmidt, M. G. (1988) *Sozialpolitik. Historische Entwicklung und internationaler Vergleich* (Social Policy. Historical Developments and International Comparisons). Opladen: Leske & Budrich.

Schmitter, Ph. C., Streeck, W. (1990) *Organized Interests and the Europe of 1992*. Unpublished Manuscript. Stanford University/University of Wisconsin-Madison. (Paper prepared for a conference on "The United States and Europe in the 1990s: Trade, Finance, Defense, Politics, Demographics and Social Policy", American Enterprise Institute, Washington, D.C., March 6-8).

Schulte, B. (1991) 'Das Recht auf Mindesteinkommen in der Europäischen Gemeinschaft, Nationaler Status quo und supranationale Initiativen' (The Right to a Basic Income in the EC. The National Status Quo and Supranational Initiatives), *Sozialer Fortschritt*: 7-23.

Schulte, B. (1990a) '"Konvergenz" statt "Harmonisierung" – Perspektiven europäischer Sozialpolitik' (Convergence instead of Harmonization – Perspectives of European Social Policy), *Zeitschrift für Sozialreform* 36 (5): 273-298.

Schulte, B. (1990b) '"... und für den Arbeitnehmer wenig oder nichts"? Sozialpolitik und Sozialrecht in den Europäischen Gemeinschaften' (" ... and for employees next to nothing"? Social Policy and Welfare Law of the European Community), *Kritische Justiz* 23 (1): 79-97.

Schulte, B. (1990c) 'Europäisches und nationales Sozialrecht' (European and National Welfare Law), *Europarecht*, Special Issue 4 (in print).

Schulte, B. (1989a) 'Soziale Grundsicherung – Ausländische Regelungsmuster und Lösungsansätze' (Basic Income – Foreign Patterns of Regulation and Solutions), in Vobruba, G. (ed.) *Strukturwandel der Sozialpolitik*. Frankfurt a.M.: Suhrkamp (in print).

Schulte, B. (1989b) *Minimum Income Strategies, European Conference on Basic Incomes*. Unpublished Manuscript. London, November 15-17.

Schulte, B. (1989c) 'Sozialhilfe in Europa' (Welfare Systems in Europe), pp. 55-76 in Kitterer, W. (ed.) *Sozialhilfe und Finanzausgleich*. Heidelberg: R. v. Decker's Verlag, G. Schenck.

Schulte, B. (1986) 'Mindestesteinkommensregelungen im internationalen Vergleich: Ansatzpunkte in den Ländern der Europäischen Gemeinschaft und auf Gemeinschaftsebene' (Regulation of Minimum Income Internationally Compared: Potentials for Development at the National and at the EC Level), pp. 118-131 in Opielka, M., Vobruba, G. (eds.) *Das garantierte Grundeinkommen. Entwicklung und Perspektiven einer Forderung*. Frankfurt a.M.: Fischer.

Schultheis, F. (1988) *Sozialgeschichte der französischen Familienpolitik* (Social History of French Family Policies). Frankfurt a.M., New York: Campus.

Schulze, H. (1990) *Die Wiederkehr Europas* (The Return of Europe). Berlin: Siedler.

Schunter-Kleemann, S. (ed.) (1990) *EG-Binnenmarkt – Euro-Patriarchat oder Aufbruch der Frauen* (The EC's Single Market – EuroPatriarchy or Women's Movement). Bremen: Hochschule Bremen, Wissenschaftliche Einheit Frauenstudien und Frauenforschung.

Siebert, H. (1989a) 'Perspektiven zur Vollendung des europäischen Binnenmarktes' (Perspectives on the Completion of the Single Market), *Kyklos* 42: 181-201.

Siebert, H. (1989b) 'The Harmonization Issue in Europe: Prior Agreement or a Competitive Process', pp. 53-75 in Siebert, H. (ed.) *The Completion of the Internal Market*. Tübingen: J.C.B. Mohr.

Sieveking, K. (1990) 'Bildung im Europäischen Gemeinschaftsrecht' (Education in EC Law), *Kritische Vierteljahresschrift für Gesetzgebung und Rechtswissenschaft* 73 (3/4): 344-373.

Silvia, S. J. (1991) 'The Social Charter of the European Community. A Defeat for European Labor', *Industrial and Labor Relations Review* 44 (4): 626-643.

Simonian, H. (1981) 'France, Germany, and Europe', *Journal of Common Market Studies* 19: 203-219.

Skocpol, Th., Ikenberry, J. (1983) 'The Political Information of the American Welfare State in Historical and Comparative Perspective', pp. 87-148 in Thomasson, R. F. (ed.) *The Welfare State 1883-1983*. Greenwich, CN/London etc.: JAI Press. (Comparative Social Research, vol. 6).

Skowronek, St. (1982) *Building a New American State. The Expansion of National Administrative Capacities, 1977-1920*. Cambridge etc.: Cambridge University Press.

Smeeding, T. M., Boyle, B., Rein, M. (1988) 'Patterns of Income and Poverty: The Economic Status of Children and the Elderly in Eight Countries', pp. 89-119 in Palmer, J. L., Smeeding, T., Boyle Torrey, B. (eds.) *The Vulnerable*. Washington, D.C.: The Urban Institute Press.

Smeeding, T. M., O'Higgins, M., Rainwater, L, (eds.) (1990) *Poverty, Inequality and Income Distribution in Comparative Perspective*. The Luxemburg Income Study, New York etc.: Havester/Wheatsheaf.

Sozialcharta (1990a) 'Sozialcharta soll nicht nur das Recht auf Arbeit sichern. Runder Tisch bringt die Vorlage in die Volkskammer ein/Ergänzung zur Wirtschaftsunion' (Social Charter should not just Secure the Right to Work. Round Table Proposes Legislation to Volkskammer to Complement Economic Union), *Frankfurter Allgemeine Zeitung*, March 6, 1990, no. 55: 17.

Sozialcharta (1990b) (Documentation of the original text), *Zeitschrift für Sozialreform* 36 (3/4): 256-266.

Soysal, Y. N. (1991) *Limits of Citizenship: Guestworkers in the Contemporary Nation-State System*. Ph.D. Thesis, Stanford University.

Steinmeyer, H.-D. (1990) 'Freizügigkeit und soziale Rechte in einem Europa der Bürger' (Free Movement and Social Rights in a Europe of Citizens), pp. 63-80 in Magiera, S. (ed.) *Das Europa der Bürger in einer Gemeinschaft ohne Binnengrenzen*. Baden-Baden: Nomos.

Steinmeyer, H.-D. (1989) 'Harmonisierung des Arbeits- und Sozialrechts in der Europäischen Gemeinschaft – Eine Konsequenz aus der Schaffung eines einheitlichen Binnenmarkts?' (Harmonization of Labour and Social Security Law in the EC – A Consequence of Economic Integration), *Zeitschrift für ausländisches und internationales Arbeits- und Sozialrecht* 3 (3), July-September: 208-228.

Steinmeyer, H.-D. (1982) 'Öffentliche und private Sicherungsformen im System der Alterssicherung der Vereinigten Staaten von Amerika' (Public and Private Social Security in US Old Age Security), *VSSR* 10: 101-166.

Streeck, W. (1990a) *More Uncertainties: West German Unions Facing 1992*. Madison, WI: University of Wisconsin, July.

Streeck, W. (1990b) *From National Corporatism to Transnational Pluralism. European Interest Politics and the Single Market*. Madison, WI: University of Wisconsin, July.

Streeck, W. (1989) *The Social Dimension of the European Economy*. Unpublished Manuscript. (A Paper prepared for the 1989 Meeting of the Andrew Shonfield Association, Florence, September 14-15).

de Swaan, A. (1990) *Perspectives for Transnational Social Policy. Preliminary Notes*. Amsterdam/Leiden: PdIS.

Teague, P. (1990) 'European Community Labour Market Harmonisation', *Journal of Public Policy* 9: 1-33.

Teague, P. (1989a) *The European Community: The Social Dimension. Labour Market Policies for 1992*. London: Kagan Page in association with the Cranfield School of Management.

Teague, P. (1989b) 'Constitution or Regime? The Social Dimension to the 1992 Project', *British Journal of Industrial Relations* 27 (3), November: 310-329.

Tennstedt, F. (1983) *Vom Proleten zum Industriearbeiter. Arbeiterbewegung und Sozialpolitik in Deutschland 1800-1914* (From the Proletarian to the Industrial Worker. Social Movements in the Working Class and Social Policy in Germany 1800-1914). Köln: Bund Verlag.

Tennstedt, F. (1976) 'Ökonomisierung und Verrechtlichung der Sozialpolitik' (Rationalization and Juridication of Social Policy), pp. 139-165 in Murswieck, A. M. (ed.) *Staatliche Politik im Sozialsektor*. München: Pieper.

Titmuss, R. M. (1987) 'Developing Social Policy in Conditions of Rapid Change: the Role of Social Welfare', pp. 254-268 in Abel-Smith, B., Titmuss, K. (eds.) *The Philosophy of Welfare. Selected Writings of Richard M. Titmuss*. London: Allen & Unwin. (first published 1972).

Titmuss, R. M. (1974) *Social Policy. An Introduction*. London: Allen & Unwin.

Titmuss, R. M. (1963) 'The Social Division of Welfare: Some Reflections on the Search for Equity', pp. 34-55 in *ibid.*, Essays on 'The Welfare State'. With a New Chapter on the Irresponsible Society. London: Unwin University Books, 2nd edition.

Townsend, P. (1981) *An Alternative Concept of Poverty – How it Might be Applied in National Case Studies in Developing Countries with Special Reference to Social, Educational, and Cultural Forms of Deprivation*. Paris: Division for the Study of Development, UNESCO.

Townsend, P. (1979) *Poverty in the United Kingdom. A Survey of Household Resources and Standards of Living*. Penguin, Harmondsworth.

Turner, B. S. (1990) 'Outline of a Theory of Citizenship', *Sociology* 24 (2), May: 189-217.

Turner, B. S. (1986) *Citizenship and Capitalism. The Debate over Reformism*. London etc.: Allen & Unwin.

Walker, R., Lawson, R., Townsend, P. (eds.) (1984) *Responses to Poverty: Lessons from Europe*. London: Heineman.

Weaver, K. (1990) *The State and the Welfare State in the United States and Canada*. Unpublished Manuscript. Washington, D.C.: The Brookings Institution, January.

Weiler, J. H. H. (1987) *The European Community in Change: Exit, Voice, and Loyalty*. Saarbrücken: University (Vorträge, Reden, und Berichte aus dem Europa Institut no. 109).

Weiler, J. H. H. (1982a) *Supranational Law and Supranational System: Legal Structure and Political Process in the European Community*. Ph.D. Thesis, Florence: EUI.

Weiler, J. H. H. (1982b) 'Community Member States and European Integration. Is the Law Relevant?', *Journal of Common Market Studies* 21: 39-56.

Weir, M., Orloff, A. S., Skocpol, T. (eds.) (1988) *The Politics of Social Policy in the United States*. Princeton: Princeton University Press.

Wilensky, H. L., Lebeaux, Ch. N. (1965) *Industrial Society and Social Welfare: The Impact of Industrialization on the Supply and Organization of Social Welfare Services in the United States*. New York, 2nd edition. (1st edition, 1958): Free Press, LI.

Wilson, W. J. (1987) *The Truly Disadvantaged: The Inner City, the Underclass, and Public Policy*. Chicago, IL: University of Chicago Press.

Winkler, G. (ed.) (1989) *Geschichte der Sozialpolitik in der DDR 1945-1985* (History of Social Policy in the GDR 1945-1985). Berlin (GDR): Akademie Verlag.

Winkler, G. (1988) 'Sozialpolitik in der DDR' (Social Policy in The GDR), *Aus Politik und Zeitgeschichte* 32: 21-28.

Winkler, G., Manz, G. (eds.) (1987) (Lexikon der) Sozialpolitik (Encyclopedia of Social Policy). Berlin (GDR): Die Wirtschaft, XVI: 328, 2nd ed.

De Witte, B. (ed.) (1989) *European Community Law of Education*. Nomos: Baden-Baden.

Zuleeg, M. (1991) 'Die Europäische Gemeinschaft auf dem Weg zur Sozialgemeinschaft' (The European Community en Route to a Social Community), *Nachrichtendienst des Deutschen Vereins für öffentliche und private Fürsorge* 71 (1): 20-29.

Zuleeg, M. (1989) 'Die Zahlung von Ausgleichszulagen über die Binnengrenzen der Europäischen Gemeinschaft' (The Payment of Compensation Transfers across National Borders within the European Community), *Deutsche Rentenversicherung* 10: 621-629.

Zuleeg, S. (1987) 'Zur Einwirkung des Europäischen Gemeinschaftsrechts auf die Sozialhilfe nach dem Bundessozialhilfegesetz' (On the Impact of European Community Law on Welfare Provision According to the Federal Assistance Act), *Nachrichtendienst des Deutschen Vereins für öffentliche und private Fürsorge* 67 (10): 342-347.

Zweigert, K. (1963) 'Grundsatzfragen der europäischen Rechtsangleichung, ihrer Schöpfung und Sicherung' (Basic Questions on the Legal Integration of Europe, its Creation and its Continuity), pp. 401-418 in Caemmerer, E. von, Nikisch, A., Zweigert, K. (eds.) *Vom Deutschen zum Europäischen Recht*. Festschrift für Hans Dölle. Tübingen: JCB Mohr.

CHAPTER 17

The Social Dimension:
A Quest for a European Welfare State[*]

Kåre Hagen

1 Introduction

The new dynamics of integration between the member states of the European Community (EC) must be understood as a reaction to the inability of the Western European nation-states to respond successfully to the new economic environment of the early 1970s. With the benefit of hindsight, we may conclude that neither the economic protectionism which was pursued as a response to the crumbling of the old international trade regime in the 1970s (Bhagwati, 1989; Krauss, 1978), nor subsequent neo-liberal deregulation policies, proved to be successful national solutions to the crisis. Stagflation, chronic unemployment, and "casino capitalism" (Strange, 1987) became tangible symptoms of a common experience in all mixed-economy, liberal states: The legal, economic and social policy measures available to the nation-state, were unable to handle problems of an increasingly, and intrinsically, transnational nature.

The turning of the tide, from crisis and "eurosclerosis" to fervent "euro-optimism", is embodied in the Single European Act adopted by the 12 member countries in February, 1985. The Treaty of Rome (from 1957) was amended and extended, and its goal of a common market was restated by providing a legal base for the Commission to take initiatives and supervise the implementation of a common market from January, 1993. The introduction of majority decisions in the European Council regarding all measures to ensure the free movement of goods, capital, labour, and services across borders, was a significant institutional change. Yet, in all cases of "vital national importance" for any member, unanimity is still required. This implies a built-in institutional bias in favour of a more effective supranational economic deregulation – whereas the ambitions of deepening the community by political and social integration is still at the level of declarations of intent with, at present, little legal basis.

Nevertheless, this chapter argues that the "1992 venture" is an ambitious attempt, at the European level, to create a market responsive to political regulation and to shape a stable supranational institutional framework for private business as well as for social goals beyond the reach of the single nation-state. This implies that, at present, a multitude of motives converge in favour of European integration. Still, conflicts exist both on the issue of ultimate goals, and on the (closely-related) question of how a liberalization of the economy should be accompanied by "a social dimension". How are economic efficiency goals to be combined with welfare ambitions that require political intervention in the play of market forces? And how are common welfare objectives to be decided and incorporated in the single-market regime?

Historically, these questions are basically identical to those problems facing social-democratic movements in search of a political-economical regime to provide "a middle way" between Leninist *coup d'état* socialism and untrammelled capitalism. By subjecting economic forces to democratic political control, welfare capitalism within the boundaries of the nation-state (Myrdal, 1960; Rokkan, 1987) has been an effective regime for transforming the Western part of Europe from economic depression and war to modern welfare societies. However, the economic base of the nation-state has become increasingly dependent on transnational business cycles, and commitments implied by membership in the European Community restrict national sovereignty in economic policies. Therefore, in order to impose common social standards on the internal market, the need arises for a corresponding extension of political powers to supranational bodies. If this process fails, the nation-state could risk being deprived of the means required to implement welfare policies – whereas new and equivalent institutions are not developed at the supranational level.

2   The Present Agenda: Options and Approaches

The question of whether the implementation of a common market should be accompanied by a comprehensive supranational regulation of the same market, or remain "a right-wing ideological totem around which capitalism in Europe, as well as governments, are supposed to dance" (Martin, 1988) is at the very heart of the present debate within the Community (as well as in potential member countries such as Norway and Sweden). Coupled with the omnipresent question of sovereignty and autonomy of national institutions within the supranational polity, the present debate and cleavages within the Community can be condensed to four key questions:

First, should the implementation of the common market proceed towards an economic (and, ultimately a political) union within which the nation-state transfers its control over monetary, and eventually also fiscal policies, to supranational bodies? Or should economic integration aim solely at the completion of the common market?

Second, should economic integration proceed together with the development of a common welfare and suprastate interventionist policy, or should social policy remain the domain of the single member state?

Third, if a supranational welfare policy is to be elaborated, should it be confined to the regulation of paid work only (a "workers' Europe"), or be more ambitious and move towards a "European social citizenship" model by also including redistribution of income and welfare between citizens and regions?

And *fourth*, what institutional design and decision-making processes should move highly divergent national welfare states onto a course towards convergence: a euro-corporatist model in which agreements are made between capital and labour at the level of the European Community, or – by a more democratic procedure – emanating from the European parliament?

These questions can be reduced to four coherent normative views of how social policy should relate to "pure economic" integration.

The most extreme position is to reject any extension of cooperation beyond the implementation of the common market. This strategy can be defended by neo-liberalist economic arguments, but it is also the solution which most vigorously protects national sovereignty in the areas of monetary, fiscal, social, and labour market policies. The advocacy of a free market, combined with a concern for national autonomy, has most forcefully been upheld by the British government – although Britain's entry into the European Exchange Rate Mechanism in October, 1990, and the downfall of Ms Thatcher, may herald a more positive attitude towards a common monetary policy.

The second position is to argue in favour of an inner market which is subject to a common set of social standards and labour market regulations, but without any further political integration. The social standards are regarded as necessary to ensure that extended competition in the market does not encourage a flow of capital (and jobs) to member states with inexpensive and flexible manpower, which could create a downward pressure on the existing social standards in the most developed countries ("social dumping"). A monetary or political union, however, is not regarded as necessary in order to reap the benefits of a common market, as long as common social standards prevent dumping. This position has been championed by Denmark, which wants to combine the maintenance of its advanced welfare state with a high degree of national sovereignty. At present, this model also seems to be the basic idea pursued in the negotiations between the European Community and the member countries of the European Free Trade Association over the "European Economic Space".

The third approach wants to extend the process of economic integration to a monetary union, but without common supranational social policy objectives. The core of this argument is that, in order to function properly, the market needs specific conditions, i.e. a common monetary regime and provisions in the field of competition, which can be provided only by political action. National control over social policy, however, does not impede the possibilities of rational economic action; and thus, a supranational or coordinated social policy is not needed. Not surprisingly, this strategy is advocated by business interests and their representatives in the European Federation of Industries (UNICE).

The fourth, and explicitly federalist position is that of combining a common social policy with economic union – and ultimately, extending the powers of the EC institutions into all policy areas of the member states. At present, the federalist strategy is both the most ambitious vision of the future European Community and the one pursued by the original six member countries – and by the chairman of the Commission since 1984, Jacques Delors. One should, however, note that the federalist strategy is open-ended. There is no clear or well-defined ultimate goal in terms of economic and social policy content, but simply a notion of "the United States of Europe".

The question of what kind of political-economic regime is to replace the cooperation between nation-states, is not likely to be settled in the near future. This question raises both the issue of national sovereignty, and of how (if at all) social objectives should be built into the integrative process. In addition, the pressing issue of legitimacy and democratic accountability of the supranational decisions, has to be solved. At present, the federalist position is the dominant one; it is pursued by major states like France, Germany, and Italy with the support of the new members Spain, Portugal, and Greece. Great Britain has become the sole defender of the European Community, understood as cooperation between independent nation-states. The least articulated view so far is the second approach: namely, to combine a supranationally imposed set of workers' rights and labour market regulations with the common market, with no further political integration. On the other hand, the entry into the Community of firm nation-states such as the EFTA countries, and potentially also by the reborn Central and Eastern European nation-states, may threaten the federalist dominance. These countries might be attracted by the economic gains of participating in the common market, but they still prefer to retain a high degree of national sovereignty in other policy areas.

3   Motives for Integration

In general, and realistically, one might assume that when an impasse in interstate cooperation is suddenly broken, a concurrence of different motives, rather than a genuine consensus of goals, is the major explanatory factor. This applies clearly to the European Community in the mid-1980s, and the following paragraph is a brief outline of the four major motives for economic integration. The first sees integration as a strategy for economic efficiency, the second as a formula for lasting peace. The third regards integration as an approach to boost the global role of European business, and the fourth envisages closer integration as a necessary condition for pursuing traditional social-democratic welfare goals.

The arguments both for a free trade area and a common market, are rooted in Adam Smith's classical postulate of the positive relationship between economic efficiency and the size of the market. By combining the axiom of the division of labour as the core mechanism of productivity with the fact that different states (regions) varied in their natural endowments ("absolute advantages"), he inferred that the abolition of politically-created restraints on economic activity would increase the opulence of any society. In this theory, he had a powerful tool to undermine the mercantilist edifice of trade privileges and protective custom barriers. Later, Smith's theory was elaborated by Ricardo's replacement of absolute with comparative advantages; but the core remains intact in contemporary mainstream economics: abolition of state intervention in the free flow of market transactions ("deregulation") will trigger increased competition and induce more specialization, factor mobility, and other benefits from comparative advantages. The spirit of Smith and Ricardo, coupled with Tayloristic and Fordistic approaches, is clearly surfacing both in the arguments for removing the protectionist measures implemented by most nation-states in the 1970s, and in the econometric forecasts which predict positive impacts of the internal market on economic efficiency (Cecchini, 1988; Baldwin, 1989). However, more critical voices (Pedersen, 1989; Holland, 1988) claim that the postulated economic gains of the European common market are exaggerated – because, they argue, unused comparative advantages do not exist to the extent assumed in the calculations, and because the Fordist conceptions of economies of scale are increasingly outdated in the most advanced segments of the economy.

The creation of a functional economic guarantee for a lasting peace is the second major motive for closer economic integration. The key concept linking peace and free trade, is interdependence. Economic self-sufficiency is a vital precondition for warfare capacity – whereas free trade will, following the market expansion argument above, render the domestic economy dependent on others. The establishment of a supranational regime to remove the option of protectionism from the policy repertoire of the nation-state, is therefore conducive to peace. The very core of the predecessor of the Treaty of Rome, the Coal and Steel Union, was to remove from the hands of the single state (i.e. France and Germany) control over the most strategic commodities needed to wage war. The quest for a peaceful Europe was beyond doubt a fundamental motive in the process culminating in the Treaty of Rome (Swann, 1988). For the last couple of decades, the peace motive has been largely replaced by economic efficiency arguments; but still, if one were to single out a dominant "official" ideology of European integration, it would be that of free markets as a guarantee both for peace and efficiency.

However, a third motive is surfacing when the relationship between the European Community and non-members enters the agenda. Organized interests with considerable leverage in the Commission, envisage a "Fortress Europe" to provide European firms with a large domestic market from which outsiders are excluded – if they are to match the economic clout of Japanese and American firms in global competition. For the past 20 years, the economic performance of the Western European countries has lagged considerably behind that of Japan and the United States, and both hope and fear exists that the common market is part of a strategy to enhance the economic power of Europe at the expense of others (Dahrendorf, 1989; Calingaert, 1988).

The last and most recent argument, is that closer economic integration is the stepping-stone towards a European (social-democratic) super-state. The successful solution to pressing social problems (like unemployment) and new ecological challenges, are beyond the reach of national policy. The creation of a common market with subsequent economic growth, has no justification unless the benefits and costs are distributed fairly: that is, unless it is accompanied by supranational institutions for implementing social ends. Integration is not primarily seen as a process yielding windfall benefits in terms of growth, peace, or globally competitive European firms, but rather as a genuine political process of building new institutions needed to pave the way for a more successful attainment of traditional national welfare state objectives – such as full employment, fair distribution, social security, consumer protection, and sustainable growth. Hence, the legitimacy of economic integration rests on the ability of the new institutions to recreate the interventionist welfare state model at the supranational level. This new motive for integration is largely to be explained as a reaction to the inability of social-democratic governments to develop convincing national strategies out of the economic troubles. What proved wrong in national counter-cyclical policies, was not – according to this perspective – the ability of politics to successfully regulate markets, as neo-liberalists claim, but the impossibility of doing this through the nation-state. European integration has therefore become the social-democratic response to the "new right" policies of deregulation and national welfare state regression. This is clearly illustrated by the "turning European" trend in the social-democratic movements that previously have been less convinced by the benefits of integration, most notably in Britain and in the Nordic countries.

Irrespective of ideological allegiance – whether the internal market is envisaged as an ultimate neo-liberal goal, as a condition for Europe to rise as a world power in its own right, or to serve as an efficient economic base for welfare capitalism – proponents of all strategies agree on the desirability of a rapid implementation of the internal market. However, as we saw in the preceding paragraph, opinions differ on the ultimate goal of integration; and the "social dimension" has already risen a significant, if not the most, critical issue in the integrative process. An influential alliance between the European Federation of Trade Unions and democratic-socialist Euro-MPs, has made its endorsement of the economic integration contingent upon guarantees for a social policy at the Community level (ETUC, 1988). On the other side, the employers' organization (UNICE) has refused to participate in a "social dialogue" if this is to produce concrete proposals (as the Commission wants) for a supranational structure of industrial relations and workers' rights. And on the more extreme right, the "Brugge group" is organized to oppose what they regard as bureaucratic socialism from Brussels (*EF-avisen*, 6/89).

Irrespective of normative positions, the internal market is bound to have social ramifications. A supranational social policy would, as a point of departure, have to cushion undesired social consequences of the implementation of the common market from 1993. Secondly, a more active and deliberate common social policy requires procedures to define the needs, to set the goals, to implement measures, and to have institutions to provide democratic legitimacy to supranational intervention into what has been the domain of the nation-state since welfare policies were invented more than a century ago. These are the questions to which we now turn.

4   Consequences of the Four Freedoms

The "four freedoms" is a bogus label. One could argue that, from the vantage point of the nation-state, a more accurate tag would be the "four restrictions". The pillars of the common market, and what the member states have accepted, is the obligation not to restrict legally, or otherwise impede, the economically-motivated movement of labour, capital, services, and goods across national borders. Consequently, all national welfare measures that – deliberately or indirectly – hamper the free movement of production inputs or final products, have to be abolished. In addition, nation-states are prevented from favouring national producers by subsidies or legal protection, i.e. measures which play an important role in employment policies in many countries. This implies that the social consequences of the inner market are bound to vary between countries. A reasonable assumption is, however, that the more the nation-state and its institutions are interwoven in the present social policy and labour market regimes (as opposed to models that are based on corporate and private agreements between organized interests), the greater the social policy impacts are likely to be – simply because the four freedoms are restrictions on states, and not on private action. Therefore, the assessment of the social impacts on single states, requires a thorough analysis of the means employed in national welfare policies. On the other hand, some consequences involving all member states may be identified: first of all, the impacts of the free movement of workers and capital.

The object of circumscribing the ability of the nation-state to restrict economically-motivated migration, is to reap the benefits of a high mobility of labour.

Measures to promote mobility have therefore been given high priority by the Commission (Social Europe, 1989). These have, however, mainly been attempts to coordinate issues outside the ambit of what is generally considered as social policy – such as common systems of occupational certification. A more significant question is the potential loss of social security and health insurance rights in cases of job mobility across borders for breadwinners and their family members. Both the departure from one's home country and the entry into another state are likely to have an impact on legal rights to benefits. Citizens of welfare states granting entitlement on the basis of residence will, as a general rule, lose rights if they are mobile: whereas these universalist welfare states would be generous to new entrants by automatically including them (as residents) in the systems of health and social insurance. Welfare states based on occupational and contributory schemes, may accommodate the economically active – while leaving family members, students, and unemployed seeking work abroad with less rights. Closely related to these issues is the possible problem of strategic adaptations ("welfare tourism"), be it Danish unemployed boosting the purchasing power of their cash benefits on the sandy beaches of Portugal, or generous national social assistance schemes acting as magnets to residents of less liberal states.

Irrespective of the desirability of eliminating possible hindrances on mobility, of checking welfare tourism, or preventing a drain on generous national schemes from new residents, a demand is likely to arise for a system of social insurance in which rights are more closely tied to the individual – and less to legal citizenship, specific employers, family status, or country of residence. One way to create such individual and perfectly portable rights is, of course, (for the nation-states or the EC) to encourage private social insurance in the market. A second option is a comprehensive and administratively costly system of mutual recognition of rights between the single nation-states. This strategy was pursued by the Commission in the early 1970s (Com. 1408/71). A third alternative is to create schemes deliberately designed, at the supranational level, to accommodate the interests of mobile workers ("a thirteenth state", as advocated by Langendonck, 1989) and eventually, to make it an option also for national employers to insure all their employees in such European arrangements.

Solutions to the interests of mobile workers will probably be more easily found in decentralized, labour-market-based schemes that specify individual and portable rights, than in a policy of harmonizing existing public programmes. Organized labour might press for this option since it is compatible with, and will reinforce, initiatives from the European Trade Union Congress (ETUC) and the Commission to establish a common structure of industrial relations. On the supply side, insurance companies are poised for the common market and will recognize the demand from, and provide solutions for, the most wealthy segments of the labour force. A looming problem, therefore, concerns the rights of the un- and non-employed if a system of contributory, occupational rights is promoted as the social insurance strategy for the Community. One possible scenario is that the interests of the already-employed achieve preponderance ("a workers' Europe"), and that a process of increased social dualism might emerge or be reinforced.

The freedom of capital to seek unhampered the highest profits, is likely to induce two processes with direct social ramifications. The first is related to the problem of social dumping; the second, to the ability of a nation-state to protect their welfare sector from commercialization. Beyond doubt, the fear within the Northern European left that new investments and jobs will be systematically located to regions with less-developed welfare rights for employees, has been a major motive behind the demands for a social policy at the European level. This concern is exacerbated by the possibility that the domestic labour market will be penetrated by immigrant workers paid and insured according to the (lower) standards in their homelands. Although the European Court of Justice has laid down the principle of non-discrimination, a grey area exists in industries which tend to be mobile by nature; for example, haulage and construction. The worry is that the free flow of capital and services generates a pressure for lower wages and social standards, and therefore imposes a trade-off between jobs and social rights for the working class. Moreover, if this sort of pressure varies between different segments in the labour market, it poses a serious threat to the possibilities of implementing a successful solidaristic wage policy within the frame of the nation-state.

The other issue is most relevant to welfare states that, for distributional reasons, have imposed comprehensive legal restrictions on the supply of for-profit welfare goods and services – although it is a common feature of all Western welfare states that market-based social and health insurance is embedded in extensive national legislation. In this case, the Nordic countries are, with their marginalized commercial welfare sector, probably at the extreme end. Political ambitions of providing high- and equal-quality health care to all segments of the population, have required the extensive use of public monopolies that may militate against enterprise freedoms guaranteed by Community legislation. The same applies to state restrictions on private pension insurance and on how their funds are to be managed. In general, any kind of state welfare policy which is deliberately designed to prevent private purchasing power from being reproduced in the consumption of welfare goods supplied by the market, will run counter to the freedoms of the common market.

The problems sketched above highlight two main issues. The first problem, which is most clearly seen in the arguments about social dumping, is that high levels of economic efficiency and profits are often obtainable under socially intolerable conditions. This leads to the question of to what extent interventionist policies should be used in order to accomplish an acceptable balance between efficiency and social goals. The second question is what kind of decision-making processes at the supranational level can possibly replace the role of the democratic institutions of the nation-state in assessing what is an "acceptable" balance: that is, to define the objects of a common social policy. In short, how is the balance between economic efficiency, social equity, and democratic values to be embedded in supranational institutions and decision-making?

5   The Need for Institutional Regulation

Contrary to the pure economic efficiency gains of the integrated market that can be corroborated by scientific methods (Cecchini, 1988), the answers to the above questions are bound to involve conflicting and ideologically-charged views. This chapter surveys five different models found in the current debate on how the relationships between market, nation-state, and superstate – and between individuals, organized interests, and democracy – should be (or not be) institutionalized within the framework of the European Community. The concept of a "social dimension" is used in this broad sense, and the five approaches could be regarded as different outlines of possible supranational welfare-capitalist models, ranging from *laissez-faire* to a European-scale version of the comprehensive citizenship model of the Nordic type.

From the standpoint of economic liberalism, a social dimension is undesirable. State intervention in the economy, like labour market regulations and regional and social policy, is regarded as a rigidity imposed on the free play of market forces. Such interventions will hamper efficiency by diverting the attention of business and labour away from economic and towards institutional parameters in their decisions. When the major motive for the common market is to increase economic efficiency, it is inconsistent to add, at the same time, a social dimension that deliberately reintroduces what is seen as the sources of inefficiency within the European economies (Roberts, 1989). This argument carries a certain self-evident weight. If Portuguese construction workers brought to Denmark are to have the same wages and working conditions as Danish workers (as the Danish Trade Union Congress demands, DLO, 1989), the incentive to employ foreign workers evaporates. A supranational harmonization of working conditions and other social production costs, would therefore neutralize the comparative advantages of some regions (nation-states); and the classical argument for why market integration increases productivity, is ignored.

These arguments against a social dimension are largely a reiteration of the familiar liberalist criticism of political intervention in the play of market forces. But the significance of these arguments in the present European debate is that they justify a high degree of national sovereignty within the European Community. The institutions of the nation-state – i.e. its social legislation, tax system, and industrial relations – are conceived of as mechanisms that generate the sort of differentials in production costs that the market needs to produce higher efficiency and new jobs. A supranational harmonization of the political and social conditions for economic activity, would therefore severely limit the possibility of single nation-states to attract investments by maintaining (or even creating) social conditions that produce comparative advantages in the common market. Consequently, the only supranational institutions needed, are those that enable competition in the common market – whereas all other matters of social and political nature should be left to the nation-state.

The second approach is less concerned with national sovereignity and rejects a social dimension by arguing that there is no need for it. In the same way as wages and social conditions for the workforce differ between single firms and industries within states due to productivity differentials, disparities in welfare efforts between states will also mirror dissimilarities in productivity. Some nation-states can afford generous welfare arrangements and comprehensive state intervention in the labour market because their productivity is high. If a country has a shorter working week than others, this is assessed by the market as a restriction on the supply of labour – to which it adapts with increased productivity or unemployment. If productivity rises, the country can sustain short working weeks and if not, wages will have to be lowered in order to avoid unemployment. Social standards are seen as rewards for productivity, rather than as rigidities imposed on the market. This logic can be extended to any kind of politically-created condition for economic activity, and in no case is there any need for supranational coordination or harmonization of the institutional parameters to which the market has already adapted. A lack of social harmonization and cohesion within the Community might be a political problem (for the federalists), but there are no economic efficiency arguments for a common welfare policy. National regulation is an inherent part of the economy, and supranational intervention would therefore imply unduly interference in the structures of costs and incentives that have been, and are easily, incorporated in the decisions of the economic actors.

Thus, there is no reason for the European Community to regard differences in social standards between single member states as more problematic than those prevailing within states – be it between firms, industries, or federal states (as in the US). Not surprisingly, the above argument was the view of the Federal Republic of Germany when the European Community was founded. Despite French attempts, the Treaty of Rome did not give any significant legal powers to supranational bodies in the field of social and labour market policy. This was left to the single member state, and the economic growth in the following period proved that the lack of a supranational social policy did not hinder a rapid increase in prosperity (Wallace and Hodges, 1981).

The third position is to argue that, even if social harmonization is desirable, a supranational social policy is superfluous – because political-economic forces within the market will, by themselves, initiate a gradual process towards convergence. When the single market is opened, increased competition is assumed to put a downward pressure on prices. Efficient producers will gain market shares, irrespective of whether technological superiority or cheap labour explain their competitiveness. The common market may therefore bring into play two different processes. The first of these is a pressure for productivity increases in the rich and developed welfare states; and the second, that investments and new jobs will be located in states with less costly and more flexible manpower. If rising productivity in the rich countries can compensate the fall in prices, we may envisage a divided Europe with permanent social and economic divisions between North and South. However, with the reasonable assumption that capital and technology are more mobile than labour, and that increases in productivity in the rich countries will not fully compensate for falling prices (for example, because high social standards frustrate it), employment will fall in the richer regions and increase in the poor, i.e. social dumping will take place. However, the prospects of job losses may force the workers in the richer countries to accept lower wages and social standards – whereas the new investments in the South will boost employment and consequently improve the bargaining position of organized labour. By this process, the high social standards in the richer countries are modified, whereas they are improved in the poorer countries. A gradual convergence of social standards within the Community will consequently emerge, with decentralized bargaining between labour and capital (within the single states) as the driving force. The bargaining position of both unions and capital is determined by the local demand for labour and a trade-off between employment and labour costs. Thus, there is no need for the single nation-state or for a supranational body to intervene in this process. The competition in the single market automatically affects the power structure in the national systems of industrial relations in a way conducive to a dynamic process towards harmonization. As a minimalist approach to a more active policy, this view could be extended by arguing that supranational legislation could be used to strengthen the bargaining position of labour – or more correctly, to actively guarantee the rights of workers to organize, to take industrial action, and to be represented in enterprise boards, irrespective of national legislation.

These three arguments against the need for a social dimension all confine the role of supranational bodies to that of creating and enforcing conditions for optimal economic efficiency. The two remaining views do not accept leaving social issues to the nation-state or to the market forces. In this respect, they are the only strategies deliberately responding to the restrictions put on the nation-states by demanding new institutions at the supranational level. The first strategy is to establish a "European social market economy", and the second is to create a "European welfare superstate". Both views depart from the notion that the single integrated market is a stepping-stone to a more effective realization of social goals than is possible by the institutions of the nation-state. Economic efficiency is no goal in its own right but must be balanced by welfare and distributive objectives.

Both views call for supranational institutions to carry out this judgement, but they differ as to whether corporatist cooperation or democratic decision-making processes should produce these institutions.

Whereas neo-liberalists accept social dumping as a natural and desirable process of factor mobility, the intention of the social market economy is to restrict competition that, untrammelled, would press wages down and flexibility up by treating labour as any other commodity. Intensified competition is accepted as a measure to ensure efficient usage and allocation of resources, but it must be based on a set of institutional restrictions which guarantee a socially satisfactory use of labour. Consequently, no company and no single nation-state should have the option to gain economic advantages by maintaining low social standards for its workforce. It is therefore necessary that the implementation of the single market is accompanied by a comprehensive set of workers' rights to ensure that competition takes place within a common institutional framework that guarantees socially-acceptable working conditions and industrial relations throughout the whole market.

This political intervention may be composed of several types of deliberately imposed "rigidities" on the labour market and the work contract: first, as a supranationally guaranteed set of workers' rights, for example, to paid vacations, to unionize, to minimum wages, to maternity leave, to certain rights in case of dismissals, etc.; second, as common legislation that enables workers to take legal action against single firms or nation-states that violate supranationally-agreed principles of equal pay, equal opportunity, physical work, and environmental conditions; and third, as mergers and acquisitions add to the transnational nature of modern companies – and are assumed to increasingly do so in the single market –, a need arises for common legislation that enables collective bargaining, industrial action, and worker participation within transnational enterprises and across nation-state borders and legal restrictions.

This model of a common labour market regime is supposed to serve a dual purpose: to protect and ameliorate the conditions for workers in the less-developed countries and, simultaneously, raise the cost of labour in these countries in order to erode the profitability of capital mobility from rich to poorer regions of the market. Companies with insufficient productivity to adapt to the standards, and thus unable to pay a relatively high cost of labour, should not be allowed to survive in the market. This, of course, may easily constitute a conflict of interest between workers in the North and in the South. A labour market regime that increases the cost of labour in the regions where it is less expensive, implies to them a loss of a comparative advantage and rising unemployment. The incentive for capital to direct investment to the South will be eroded by a social policy that equalizes production costs at a high level. The better a common regime protects the interests of the workers in the most advanced states by imposing high and restrictive common standards for the inner market, the more difficult will it be for the South to attract new investments and jobs. Portuguese and Greek unions may share the view of German and Danish workers who demand common standards at the highest level as an ultimate goal, but they probably hesitate to endorse an immediate effectuation.

An additional problem of giving the single market a social dimension solely by labour market regulations, is that the benefits and social protection offered by this approach exclude non-participants in the labour market. The social-market model may lay the foundation for a "workers' Europe" and cover roughly one third of the EC population (126 out of 320 million) with supranationally-agreed welfare guarantees. The needs of those permanently or temporarily outside the labour market, are not taken into account. This model of a "workers' Europe" could therefore contribute to the social divisions between the economically active and non-active.

As an alternative welfare strategy, one could envisage a "citizens' Europe" approach in which the object of supranational social legislation is not the worker, but the citizen. The economic benefits of the single market should, according to this view, not be shared exclusively between labour and capital, but by all, independent of position in the formal economy. The breaking-up of traditional family patterns and old, non-institutionalized forms of social care and responsibilities, the ageing of the population, and the growing numbers of students, are all factors that add to the inadequacy of a social policy exclusively tailored to the needs of the worker. The idea of satisfying social needs of women, children, people with disabilities and other economically non-actives by covering the breadwinner (and assuming a fixed traditional sex division of unpaid work) is outdated; and in this perspective, the social market economy strategy is unmistakably the expression of the social interests of male employees as long as labour force participation patterns differ across sex. A regulation only of the conditions under which labour is traded, is therefore insufficient. To distribute the benefits of the single market to all, would require a set of universal social rights; such as a guaranteed minimum income, pension rights, health insurance, education, and training – in short, a development of supranational distributive measures for the reallocation of resources between individuals and regions. A social dimension to the inner market is, according to this approach, inadequate as long at it only guarantees that production takes place in a socially acceptable way – and as long as the distribution of income is not accompanied by common social goals. This leads to the questions of how a welfare policy for a "citizens' Europe" should be institutionalized: for example, the relationship between present national systems of social protection and new supranational bodies; the financing of EC expenditures to distributive programmes; and what kind of decision-making process should precede and determine the content of "European social citizenship".

In contrast to the social market strategy, the social citizenship approach is significantly less elaborated. At present, it is more a vision than a concrete policy proposal. The social interests of the economically non-actives are less, if at all, organized at the European level; and they require democratic and representative institutions to a larger extent than do the interests of organized labour in order to gain influence: for the latter, corporatist systems of bargaining, a social dialogue is always an alternative arena to pursue social objectives. Secondly, the "social citizenship" approach to welfare never replaced the "industrial achievement" model in the continental European member states, as it did to a large extent in Great Britain and in the Nordic countries. This historical legacy implies that the politically most influential segments of the working class in the continental countries, already have their need for social insurance taken care of in the occupational schemes to which they belong. They are consequently more concerned with the fear that their welfare is undermined by the economic aspects of European integration rather than through a confined role for the nation-state. Conversely, unions in the Nordic countries are more concerned with the future ability of the nation-state to provide and finance its welfare commitments in the integrated market. Denmark illustrates the case, where the EC proposals for harmonization of indirect taxes will have immediate impacts on its welfare state – because it is financed by taxation, and not by contributions from the insured.

The question of whether the social dimension to the common market should take the form of a social market economy, or be developed as a set of citizen rights, is – of course – a normative issue. On the other hand, the future development of the legal constitution of the Community may significantly influence the prospects of success for the two respective approaches. The choice of a bureaucratic, a corporatist, or a democratic decision-making process, is of vital importance for whose social interests will be taken into account in supranational legislation. If the initiatives are still to rest in the Commission (and the lobby surrounding it), or even if the social dialogue is revitalized, the needs of the non-employed and less-organized interests are likely to be subdued. Inferring from the historical development of national welfare states, we could assume that, without a considerable increase in the legal powers of the European Parliament, a social policy based on social citizenship and universal benefits has meagre prospects.

6   The Development of a Common Social Policy

The need for a common social policy was first raised in the wake of the Coal and Steel Union in the early 1950s and in the process preceding the Treaty of Rome. The issue was whether national differences in social legislation could impede the process of economic integration. The problem was left to experts, who concluded (ILO, 1956) that market forces would be able to adapt to interstate variations in social legislation without negative effects for the integrative process. On the other hand, the French feared that their, at that time, more protective system of workers' rights would prove a competitive disadvantage *vis-à-vis* German companies. They therefore demanded that social guarantees should be included in the Treaty of Rome. As a compromise, the clauses in Articles 119 and 120 are expressions of this disagreement. In short, in the first 15 years of the Community no significant attempts to coordinate or generate a common policy took place. Langendonck (1989) summarizes the period by stating that "Social security had become for the European Commission an area of study and exchange of ideas, instead of an area of European policy" – a conclusion that seems to be shared by Collins (1975), Taylor (1983) and Brewster and Teage (1989).

A significant shift in attitudes appeared in the beginning of the 1970s, when social goals were – for the first time – officially given the same status as economic objectives. At their meeting in Paris in 1972, the member states jointly declared that they "attached as much importance to vigorous action in the social field as to the achievement of economic union"; and the year after, a Social Action Programme was adopted. The initiatives can be grouped into four policy areas: equal treatment of men and women in the labour market, harmonization of labour law including working time legislation, common standards for physical working conditions, and a supranational employment and regional policy.

Opinions differ as to why these efforts to broaden the scope of integration occurred in the early 1970s. Lodge (1978) explains it as an increased interest among national economic and political élites for integration as an answer to the emerging international economic problems, whereas Nielsen (1989) sees the efforts as attempts on the part of the Community to coordinate the active process of social and labour legislation within the nation-states. On the other side, Shanks (1977), Brewster and Teage (1989), and Langendonck (1989) emphasize changes at the ideological level. The "growth-at-any-price" ideology was increasingly challenged by new social movements in this period, and the EC had to provide an answer to this criticism.

The answer came as attempts from the Commission to harmonize national legislation by imposing directives. This strategy proved most successful in the field of equal treatment of men and women, and several member countries amended their national legislation in order to comply with supranational standards (Landau, 1985; Hoskyns, 1986). In the field of labour market regulation, some progress was made regarding common standards for physical working conditions. However, in all areas where the directives affected the power relations between workers and management as well as the competence of national legislation in this field, the attempts to impose common rules (and workers' rights) produced more conflict and resistance than harmonization. The initiatives finally ended in a stalemate at the beginning of the 1980s (Hepple, 1987). Here, one should also keep in mind the declining interest in economic integration during the 1970s in the member states – a period in which economic protectionism rather than cooperation was the response to the economic slump.

The adoptions of The Single Act and a time schedule for the internal market, the entry of three new member states, and – not least – the election of the French socialist Jacques Delors as Chairman of the Commission in 1984, broke the impasse. However, the problems facing the Commission was complex: on the one side, the implementation of the four freedoms was bound to have social impacts, which, if not accompanied by concrete proposals for common social policy measures, would imply a concession to the liberalist vision of a deregulated Europe. Consequently, the support from the European trade union movement for the common market, would be put at risk. On the other side, past experience had shown that the Commission's strategy of imposing directives on member states and organized interests, met with considerable resistance. The Commission's response to this predicament was Delors' concept of a "European Social Area". Rather than proposing concrete objectives for a supranational social policy, Delors drew attention to how it should be developed: namely, through a "social dialogue" between labour and capital at the European level. The initiative was handed over to the "social partners", with the hope that they would agree on concrete proposals for a common social policy. However, this deliberate shift from a bureaucratic to a corporatist process of supranational decision-making, has so far been stranded by reluctance on the part of the employers to participate in a process (the Val Duchesse talks) intended to prepare the ground for EC legislation. As Brewster and Teage (1989) conclude, "the idea of a social dialogue between management and labour being the cornerstone of the 'l'espace social' appears to be in ruins", and this deadlock has returned the initiative to the Commission. The Commission's proposal for a "Social Charter" in September, 1989, should be judged against this background.

7   The Social Charter

The conflicts over what, if any, kind of supranational welfare regime is to accompany the common market, are most clearly seen in the disputes over the Social Charter. These are most properly understood as surfacing signs of conflicting ideological undercurrents. On the other hand, top-level decisions in the European Community are outcomes of a mixture of bargaining, lobbying, tactical compromises, and manœuvres – which to the general public is a largely hidden process of decision-making. In order to distinguish the various motives involved in the debate over the social dimension, it could be useful to present four different assumptions on what underlies the debate over the Charter. The first is that the disputes about the Social Charter are not actually over social policy at all but rather reflect the basic debate over national sovereignty within the Community. Social policy has become the battleground because those who envisage the internal market as a grand-scale neo-liberal deregulation, do not, understandably, link national sovereignty to the competence of the nation-state to implement *"dirigiste"* policies. This hypothesis could be corroborated by the fact that the actual content of the present proposal for a Social Charter should be palatable even to zealous free-marketers. The British government rejects the Charter – not primarily because it objects to its content, but due to its opposition to establishing what could easily be turned into the legal foundation of a supranational welfare policy. During autumn 1989, the Commission watered down the original draft and clearly conceded to the British position by proposing "subsidiarity" as the guiding principle of future EC social policy. This federalist concession to national autonomy did not, however, produce unanimity – and at present, the Charter is nothing but a declaration by 11 of the 12 member states.

The second assumption is to regard the Social Charter as a tactical manœuvre from eurocratic forces in order to placate those who fear that the integrated market is a process of pure economic deregulation. One might ask why a Social Charter is proposed at all, when it is blocked by predictable British resistance and – even if endorsed – still would have no legally-binding force. The content of the Charter is largely a reiteration of principles to which all member countries have already committed themselves, by accepting the Social Charter of the Council of Europe (from 1965 and explicitly mentioned in the preamble of the Single Act) and the European Convention of Human Rights, in addition to a large number of ILO conventions from 1930 and onwards. To adopt another solemn declaration of social rights and welfare principles, should thus be unnecessary. The core of this argument is, however, that the prestige attributed to the Charter by the Commission and its Chairman Delors, is intended to assuage the concerns both of a suspicious European trade union movement and of electoral minorities within the member states who are sceptical to the neo-liberal elements of the common market. At the same time, the lack of concrete policy proposals in the Charter is both deliberate and intended to defuse resistance from the business community. "Like this, the Commission hopes to leave itself more time and space for manœuvre over the next two or three years", according to EIRR (1990). In short, the Social Charter is a lure deployed to buy time for the implementation of the integrated market, and not primarily an initiative to prepare the ground for a comprehensive welfare policy from Brussels.

The third angle from which the Social Charter can be assessed, is to focus on conflicting economic interests between workers and regions likely to be accentuated by the internal market and the prospects of social dumping. The demand for a supranational welfare regime within which the interests of workers are guaranteed by high common standards, could be explained as an expression of the self-interest of the most privileged groups in the Northern regions of the market. Supranationally-imposed high social standards would tend to lessen the incentives to locate new investments in less-developed areas. Consequently, the importance of other factors – such as labour productivity, physical infrastructure and proximity to the most prosperous consumers – become relatively more important for enterprises, and the threat of job losses for workers is avoided. In a "logic of capital"-type of argument, Amoroso (1989: 62) claims that "the content given to social dumping reflects the view of the richest European countries on what development is all about. That Greece might use its comparative advantages (more labour and less capital) to produce cheaper goods, is considered dumping (social dumping). But the mass production of cheaper goods in other European countries (e.g. West Germany) by high technology is not considered dumping in the Greek market". The former British Prime Minister, Ms Thatcher, advocating the case of Britain as a low-wages, flexible labour market "dumping ground", used in essence a similar argument when she explained her opposition to the Charter by saying that "it will stunt the creation of wealth. It will in fact put extra burdens on business. It would suit some people in the Community well to hoist their high costs on to everyone else, then you get no competition within the Community" (*Times*, 24.11.89). And she continues, "The mystery to me is why Portugal and other countries are agreeing with it (the Charter) because when I speak to them they say it is absurd".

This remark is an apt point of departure for the fourth hypothesis: namely, that the Social Charter is, in fact, a first and cautious, but still sincere, attempt to combine a mainly neo-liberalist strategy of economic integration with welfare ambitions attainable only through institutionally-imposed restrictions on the functioning of the internal market. A new (second) Social Action Programme has been proposed (Com, 89/568), and the structural funds (though still small compared to agricultural subsidies) are supposed to double their expenditures in the period from 1987 to 1992. Problems of poverty and youth unemployment have enjoyed increased attention and measures are being discussed and prepared (Social Europe 2/89). Common social standards – even if they are moderate compared to those prevailing in the most advanced countries – combined with more or less extensive income transfers to economically weak regions, could represent initial moves towards an active welfare policy. Judged against this background, the Social Charter is nothing but a beginning of a deepening of the integrative process, with all the hopes and fears that this may nurture. All four hypotheses of just what underlies the debate on the Social Charter, can be reasonably substantiated. None can easily be rejected on empirical grounds. They represent different motives pursued by different actors whose self-interest is related to different aspects of the internal market. The social dimension as a legitimation of the internal market, combined with deregulatory measures to boost labour market mobility, is in line with traditional economic interests of private business. The ambition of widening the concept of social policy and using it as justification for political intervention in the marketplace, is familiar social-democratic ideology. At present, this "right-left" dimension largely parallels the pattern of opinions on national autonomy within the Community. The most zealous proponents of the Social Charter are found among the federalists, whereas the defenders of national sovereignty reject the implicit (and moral) granting of powers to the Commission that a unanimously-endorsed charter inevitably would imply. This has put a small country like Denmark in a difficult position. It wants to retain a high level of sovereignty (which in the EC results in an uneasy alliance with British conservatives); but at the same time, its allies in pursuing welfare ambitions are the most eager federalists (Germany and the Be-Ne-Lux countries). This predicament is, however, most likely to be shared by the other Scandinavian countries if they were to enter the Community. They need guarantees for a high degree of sovereignty in order to retain command over policy measures essential to maintain their comprehensive welfare states – whereas as export-dependent economies, they fear exclusion from the common market. In addition, a third dimension can be traced: namely, a potential conflict of interest between the prosperous North and the less-developed South. This conflict does not express itself directly in the question of whether the present version of the Social Charter should be adopted, but is bound to be accentuated when questions come to the level of standards. High standards may rob the Southern countries of their major comparative advantage, while at the same time protecting the interests of the workers in the North.

8   A "Guesstimate" for the Near Future

Many controversial issues must be settled before a full-fledged social dimension is embedded in the internal market. But if the European Community is to become something more than economic cooperation between nation-states, the members will have to agree on an institutional edifice which combines to an acceptable degree core values of social welfare, democratic decision-making procedures, and po- litically-disciplined welfare capitalism. A European Community without these three traits is, of course, conceivable (in principle) but highly implausible. Is it possible to be more precise in assessing the future?

What is the best guess we can make for the development of the coming decade or so, assuming that the present dynamic is not choked by fundamental conflicts over national sovereignty (as it was in the 1960s); that economic integration does not run out of steam (as in the 1970s); and that the macro-political situation in the whole of Europe does not shift dramatically (as it did in the 1980s)?

My guess is this: the social dimension will in the coming years emerge as a framework for a euro-corporatist variant of the social market economy with moderate ambitions. This conclusion is not reached by an analysis of the power resources of specific parties or alliances but rather is corroborated by what seems to be the least common denominator. The European Community is, despite the federalist ambitions of the forces that have succeeded in establishing themselves as transnational actors at the European level, still a family of single nation-states. My conclusion is that the regulation of the market will emanate from the formal (and informal) corporatist structures emerging in Brussels. The principle of a social dialogue is already established in the Single Act and operating in the Social Fund and Economic and Social Committee. The Val Duchesse talks between employers (UNICE) and the trade union (ETUC) still exist, and the present stalemate may be broken as the Commission's proposals for a Social Action Programme are likely to demand a more active attitude from organized interests. A vitalization of the social dialogue could provide legitimacy for the process of economic integration, Delors' *"espace sociale"* can be concretized, and British interests are represented by the Trade Union Congress and the employers' organization, parties that are more in favour of European integration than is their government.

The guiding principle for supranational market intervention is most likely to be the social market economy. The emphasis will be on the regulation of working and production conditions rather than on common (European) citizens' social rights. The first is more in line with the national tradition of the major continental members; whereas, and more importantly, citizens' rights implies redistribution of income and therefore a reopening of an old dispute: namely, the need to devise a formula for allocating expenditures among the member states. To the extent that individual rights will be granted, it will probably take place as a continuation of the present silent acceptance of rulings from the European Court of Justice. By passing sentences based on the general intentions of EC declarations, its rulings are predictably pro-integration; and by declaring the direct applicability of EC laws within the member states, national legislation has to be amended without any discussions in the national parliament or disruptive vetoing in the European Council.

The supranational regulation of the market will, in general, take the form of moderate ("minimum") social standards, though above the lowest existing in the less-developed countries. This is a compromise between North and South. In the Southern (and also most recent) member countries, EC membership has to prove tangible social pay-offs, whereas the common standards are too high to induce a halt in investment and job creation in the more prosperous countries. These countries will – by and large – probably be able, through productivity increases, to maintain present standards. Taken together, the social policy likely to emanate from a supranational level for the next decade or so, still leaves substantial room for national priorities. The nation-state will, for a considerable time to come, remain the primary setting for political choice on "the big trade-off" between welfare and efficiency.

Note

* I am indebted to professor Jon Eivind Kolberg for useful comments and criticism on an earlier version of this chapter.

References

Amoroso, B. (1989) 'How Will the Labour Market and the Social and Educational Institutions be Affected by the EEC and the Internal Market', in Pedersen, J. S., Greve, B. (eds.) *The Internal Market in EEC: A Debate on Eurotrends*. Roskilde: Forlaget Samfundsøkonomi og Planlægning.

Baldwin, R. (1989) 'The Growth Effects of 1992', *Economic Policy* 9.

Bhagwati, J. (1989) *Protektionismen*. Stockholm: SNS Forlag.

Brewster, C., Teage, P. (1989) *European Community Social Policy*. London: Institute of Personnel Management.

Cecchini, P. et al. (1988, 1992) *The Benefits of a Single Market*. London: Wilwood House.

Calingaert, M. (1988) *The 1992 Challenge From Europe*. Washington, DC: National Planning Association.

Commission (1971) 'On the Application of Social Security Schemes to Employed Persons, to Self-employed Persons and to their Families Moving within the Community'. Brussels: Directive No. 1408/71.

Collins, D. (1975) *The European Communities. The Social Policy of the First Phase*. London: Martin Robertson.

Dahrendorf, R. (1989) 'The Future of Europe', in Dahrendorf, R. (ed.) *Competing Visions for 1992*. London: Institute of Economic Affairs.

DLO (1989) *EF, det indre marked og den sociale dimensjon – Dansk fagbevægelses position, målsætning og strategi*. Copenhagen: Landsorganisasjonen i Danmark.

EF-Avisen (1989) 'Det indre marked mellom Skylla og Scarybdis', No. 6, June. Copenhagen: EF-Kommisjonen.

European Industrial Relations Review (EIRR) (1990) No. 192, January. London.

European Trade Union Congress (ETUC) (1988) *The Social Dimension and the Internal Market*. Info, Nos. 25 and 26. Brussels: ETUC.

Hepple, B. (1987) 'The Crisis in EEC Labour Law', *Industrial Labour Law*.

Holland, S. (1989) 'Competition, Cooperation and the Social Dimension: Reviewing the 1992 Proposals', in Pedersen, J. S., Greve, B. (eds.) *The Internal Market in EEC: A Debate on Eurotrends*. Roskilde: Forlaget Samfundsøkonomi og Planlægning.

Hoskyns, C. (1986) 'Women, European Law and Transnational Politics', *International Journal of the Sociology of Law* 14.

International Labour Organization (ILO) (1956) *Social Aspects of Economic Cooperation, Studies and Reports*. New Series No. 46. Geneva: ILO.

Krauss, M. B. (1978) *The New Protectionism: The Welfare State and International Trade*. New York: New York University Press.

Landau, E. (1985) *The Rights of Working Women in the European Communities*. Brussels: European Perspectives.

Langendonck, J. (1989) *The Role of the Social Security Systems in the Completion of the European Internal Market*. Paper. Leuven: European Institute of Social Security.

Lodge, J. (ed.) (1978) *The European Community and the Challenge of the Future*. London: Pinter Publishers.

Martin, D. (1988) *Bringing Common Sense to the Common Market: A Left Agenda for Europe*. London: Fabian Society.

Myrdal, G. (1960) *Beyond the Welfare State*. London: MacMillan.

Nielsen, R. (1989) *EF-Arbejdsret*. Copenhagen: Jurist- og Økonomforbundets Forlag.

Pederson, J. S. (1989) 'The Internal Market and European Political and Economic Integration', in Pedersen, J. S., Greve, B. (eds.) *The Internal Market in EEC: A Debate on Eurotrends*. Roskilde: Forlaget Samfundsøkonomi og Planlægning.

Roberts, B. (1989) 'The Social Dimension of European Labour Markets', in Dahrendorf, R. (ed). *Competing Visions for 1992*. London: Institute of Economic Affairs.

Rokkan, S. (1987) *Stat, Nasjon, Klasse*. Oslo: Universitetsforlaget.

Shanks, M. (1977) *European Social Policy Today and Tomorrow.* Oxford: Pergamon Press.

Social Europe (1989) *The Fight against Poverty,* Supplement No. 2. Brussels: The Commission.

Strange, S. (1987) *Casino Capitalism.* Oxford: Blackwell.

Swann, D. (1988) *The Economics of the Common Market.* London: Penguin.

Taylor, P. (1983) *The Limits of European Integration.* Beckenham: Croom Helm.

Wallace, W., Hodges, R. (1981) *Economic Divergence in the European Community.* London: Macmillan.

CHAPTER 18

The Strategy of Social Citizenship

Laura Balbo

Introduction

The purpose of this chapter is twofold: to describe the sequence of political decisions and social changes that we call the "welfare state", which has made social citizenship a basic component element and a key reference in Western European societies in the postwar period; and to raise questions as to future developments. In short, the chapter focuses on strategies concerning social citizenship in our future all-European system.

Starting from the strong commitment to, and measures taken towards, the implementation of the welfare state in some countries after World War II, and growing with conditions of economic growth in subsequent years, basic citizenship rights became established; and a "needs-oriented culture" came into being. By this, I mean a widely-shared experience of entitlements, daily practices, and expectations (including social security for life).

I shall dwell upon this concept, a needs-oriented culture, because it is crucial in several respects. Firstly, it links the welfare state and social citizenship as traits of the political system to people throughout their daily life and needs; secondly, it forces us to view the years and decades following World War II, the decades of the welfare state as a process during which both the political scenario and the organization of everyday life in Western Europe underwent deep changes; thirdly, such a perspective brings women into the picture. Women, in fact, have been assigned a key position and have played an active role in the process of the welfare state. All along, they have been in charge of the organization of daily life while entering the human service professions in large numbers. It is important to keep these features in mind in order to analyse the development of a needs-oriented culture and its implications (Balbo, 1987).

We are now, at the beginning of the 1990s, at a turning point. Throughout the 1980s, highly diversified paths have been followed by governments in the Western world with regard to social policies. Some went as far as dismantling and de-legitimizing what had been a collective hope and, in part, a promising reality. Presently, in face of a common European future, there seem to be no shared strategies as to social citizenship rights and no common model of social organization. It seems to me extremely threatening that little or no room is created for these issues on the political agenda.

But because of these diversified responses and choices (ranging from Thatcher's Britain to the Nordic countries), and because of ongoing developments in the East, we need to address issues of social citizenship within the all-European scenario with a full understanding of discontinuities between earlier stages, the present, and future scenarios. Models of linear development are of no use (such as we used to rely upon, i.e. early, limited rights would develop into stronger and more widely recognized rights for all; social citizenship, or the needs-oriented culture, would result in a widespread, homogeneous, shared heritage of values and daily patterns). This has not been the case so far, nor is it likely to be in the future.

The second part of the chapter suggests alternative scenarios for the years ahead. These reflect previous processes, but also take into account projections and trends not only in the European region but internationally, placing Europe in the context of rapidly-changing and predictable worldwide/planetwide processes.

Which scenario is the most likely for the region of Europe in the coming years? There is no answer to such a question. Actually, even to ask it is "unscientific". But I am convinced that trying to look ahead is essential; and in that sense, my focus is political. I attempt to anticipate alternative outcomes and – if at all possible – to contribute to a better understanding of the present and perhaps the future as well.

1   The Coming of a "Needs-Oriented Culture"

Throughout the early part of the postwar period, all over the Western world the welfare state/social citizenship model of access to, and organization of, social resources was a shared perspective and a crucial concern to all main institutional actors (such as left-wing parties, unions, associations, intellectuals) – as well as to collective movements, social research and debate. Criticism and efforts at reanalysis and redefinition, strong though they were and coming from many perspectives (from the left, in the "fiscal crisis" debate; and from the women's movement, as expressed in the analysis of the state as a system of "patriarchy"), shared a common assumption: that largely unaccomplished and distorted though it was, it would be possible and, indeed, highly desirable, to bring this process to a conclusion. I believe that this attitude was of the greatest importance in characterizing the first part of the story. It is also important to remember that these were years of unprecedented economic expansion. Patterns of consumption improved and general conditions became better for great numbers of people throughout

Western Europe. Furthermore, up to the oil crisis of 1973, this trend was taken as irreversible, the promise of unending progress in economic and social conditions being the cornerstone of the Western model.

Within this relatively short time-span, unprecedented social changes took place and were implemented on a mass basis. I shall briefly dwell upon these newly-emerging circumstances of social citizenship – or as I prefer to say, upon the coming of a needs-oriented culture, i.e. upon social citizenship as it actually took shape in everyday life.

All those in the younger generations went to school and stayed in school for an increasing number of years; there actually was full employment; a (relatively generalized) safety net system of social policies was put into place; and an expanding network of public social services, as well as a universalist health system, were developed in several countries.

I do not mean to say that the goals of the original ideal of citizenship were fully implemented. Of course they were not. In the daily experience of those who lived their adult lives after the war and reconstruction, however, many were in a position to compare present conditions to what pre-war/pre-welfare Europe had been. More people had a higher level of education than ever before; access to information became widespread; more people were in good health and had access to conditions of physical and mental well-being; levels of consumption and well-being that the previous generation could not even have imagined, came to be taken for granted. All this was true for a large majority. Furthermore, conditions were expected to improve. Most importantly, people became increasingly aware of and concerned with *personal needs* not in terms of the abstract definition, important as it had been, of rights as to employment, housing, education, but their specific, diversified needs, as they were experienced in daily life. In Britain, to give a particularly telling example, families who had twins received special home help.

The point I want to make is that expectations and actual ways of living changed for the better. Most importantly, the process through which this change was brought about, was pervasive, giving legitimacy and recognition, and perceived as part of common experience. Also in those years, issues of daily life and reproduction acquired the status of rights: new family laws came into being, a less punitive approach to abortion resulted in new "reproductive rights", and sex education and greater freedom as for sexual choices were accepted.

Increasing numbers of service workers and professionals – as well as public administrators, intellectuals, and volunteers – were involved; and they have developed know-how, professional expertise, and social values. Clients and consumers were part of this emerging structure and culture: as opposed to the image of the client as a passive recipient of social services, the end-point of a bureaucratic chain, professionals' movements and organizations in the social services took an active part in developing awareness of personal needs and rights.

1.1   Actors and Strategies for Social Citizenship

Client movements and consumer movements in the personal social services; self-help and lay care groups in health; environmental groups; and those involved in adult education programmes in a great variety of fields: these have become active in many countries as part of a transformed pattern of personal living and societal organization. Such groups and associations dealt with a variety of personal, daily needs, but most of them also developed a critical approach to professionalization and bureaucratization within the dominant agencies and professions.

What I wish to stress is that ways of meeting needs developed not only out of professional expertise and specialized knowledge but often actually against, or parallel to, them on the basis of daily grass roots: to parallel, complementary, and counter-cultures (in health and mental health in particular).

Let me now come to one further element that I consider to be crucial to these processes. In doing research on adult women in the context of European welfare states, I have come to describe them as knowledgeable as to needs (their own and their family's) and resourceful as to the organization of daily life. In modern society, adult women are "skilled actors", a term I borrow from Anthony Giddens to stress how they have come to master the complexities of our social system. They experience "full immersion" in the multiple and often contradictory life circumstances and institutions they are part of: family and jobs, emotions and rationality, the logic of love and the logic of money, public and private, the time of daily routine and the time of anticipating and planning ahead (Balbo, 1986 and 1987).

Their daily tasks require that they develop organizational and professional know-how as to personal needs and service work. They relate to a variety of service agencies, to the heterogeneous institutions of our mixed service economy, to rules and bureaucracies of both the market and the public sphere.

We also know that women constitute the great majority of workers in service jobs, as well as of clients and consumers. They do the caring work in families and households, and they make up a large share of those involved in neighbourhood networks and in volunteering/third-sector agencies.

I am not suggesting that women are biologically, or psychologically, more apt to do the caring work of society (and that they should hence continue doing their wonderful job). What I am arguing is that, in our contemporary societies, the circumstances of their caring work place them strategically in relation to a needs-oriented culture and to needs-oriented institutions – and that because of that (among other things), women no longer are peripheral, invisible, voiceless, or powerless in the social and political arena. Actually, they have become strategic actors.

1.2 Politics and Policies as to Social Citizenship: Three Western European Models

In spite of common processes and experiences in previous years, deeply different outcomes have resulted in the European scene of the 1980s. Margaret Thatcher became Prime Minister in 1979 and Thatcherism, "a project to reverse the whole postwar drift of (British) society ..." (Hall and Jacques, 1987), has since become the symbol of an unfriendly, actually hostile, state. It soon became painfully clear that in the very country that had first committed itself to the goals and practices of the welfare state and of citizenship rights, a full reversal was actually taking place. Both in her political principles and in dismantling through subsequent steps the British welfare state, Margaret Thatcher lanced a strong ideological attack against its landmarks (full employment, equality of opportunity, and welfare support), emphasizing free market values – the market as the measure of everything – and "Victorian" social values (family and patriarchism, imperialist nostalgia, and a shift towards a "law and order" model of political and social organization).

In the long run, only the Nordic social-democratic governments continued to consider the original welfare state project as expressing fundamental values and as being the best way to achieve them: though adjustments were considered necessary, the direction and basic goals remained the same. In some instances (the Finnish "welfare society" model being such an example), a new vision emerged, contributing to the international debate and quest for solutions. Most European countries, though neo-conservatism was now a highly visible and increasingly legitimized option, did not openly reverse their previous commitment to social citizenship. What have been labelled as "mixed" approaches to socio-economic policies, progressively became the dominant model. There is a high degree of inconsistency among different sets of goals and different aspects, but little seems to be planned. The private sector has been given increasing recognition and support, but commitment to the public sector is still a main element of the "package". Social policies have become means-tested, without actually redefining goals and tools. Budgetary cuts or, at any rate, the slowing down of investments into the welfare budget have meant that conditions of access and use of the social sector are radically different from what they were a decade before. Market values and market mechanisms are given full legitimation. Behind "mixed" approaches and in spite of governments' commitment to social justice and basic citizenship rights, creeping strategies of privatization came into being – shifting the balance from state to market, from universalism to selectivity, from expectations of citizenship rights to the problems of everyday life in a deeply unequal, dual system (*Eurosocial*, 1987).

2   The Future of Social Citizenship: Alternative Scenarios

"In times of controversy ... we would do better to compare various possible futures than to concentrate on one basic forecast ... this method enables us to consider possible alternative futures before choices are made or plans elaborated" (Commission of the European Communities, 1987).

I would also argue that when attempting to deal with future processes, it helps to organize our thinking around simplified, synthetic, provocative statements. For this reason – though I am well aware of the difficulties and shortcomings of scenario writing, particularly in a very simplistic way – strategies for social citizenship in the future will be ranged around three "scenarios": a "user-friendly Europe", a "land of privilege", and the "Blade Runner" model. Trying to look forward is something we badly need to do.

The British "case", where the attack against the social citizenship model appears to have been fully successful, suggests that the outstanding achievement of Thatcherism has been to disorganize the opposition and to undermine "traditional" citizenship consensus. The waste of potentialities and actual resources, the disarray, the human costs have become increasingly visible.

At the other extreme, criticisms and increasing political difficulties notwithstanding, the Nordic countries still embody welfare state – or better yet, *welfare society* – goals, as key components of a cultural and political model to be preserved and strengthened. In comparative terms at least, one cannot but be struck by the continuity and accumulation in policies and strategies as opposed to the successful attack by Thatcherism and the weak, inconsistent policies regarding social citizenship in all other European countries.

Against this background, a number of crucial questions remain unanswered – such as, has the social citizenship/needs-oriented culture made any difference as to these different outcomes? Has it been a platform for political organization and resistance? What actors (institutional actors such as the welfare state, political parties, and unions or other organizations/collective movements) have been relevant as to the policy decisions? What about alliances, such as between clients and service workers, political parties and organizations committed to social citizenship values, and intellectuals and research?

And finally, now facing a common European future, is there any shared vision of society or long-term project for social change in which social citizenship and needs-orientation can be taken as crucial values and as a valued past experience? The answer being "no", how can we contribute to bringing these issues onto the European agenda?

2.1 A User-Friendly Society

A caring society, a "welfare society", a "user-friendly society", are all terms which have been in use for some time now in the political and cultural world of the Nordic countries (and more recently, in Italy). They come from, or in any case draw upon, feminist thinking on issues of social organization, relationships between citizens and the state, and future models of daily living. Adding one more – indeed, very appealing – definition, Helga Maria Hernes has made this statement:

> I wish to make the claim here that Nordic democracies embody a state form that makes it possible to transform them into woman-friendly societies ... non-repressive and non-violent, and thus friendly to women (or children and men, for that matter). It would be ... a state where injustice on the basis of gender would be largely eliminated without an increase in other forms of inequality ... (Hernes, 1987).

I see the Nordic debate, and actual policies being attempted in those countries, as hopeful examples of what we all badly need: vision, a pragmatic approach to possible solutions, a new public agenda (which includes issues such as caring work as well as how to meet growing needs and guarantee basic entitlements in a "society with care"). In this perspective, alternative resources (noticeably time), and, hence, flexibility and decentralization in the delivery of services (Swedish Secretariat for Future Studies, 1984); flexibility in working time and life scheduling (Best, 1980); giving support and recognition to individual actors; personal coping strategies (National Board of Social Welfare, 1989), receive crucial attention. One can point here to a positive relationship between the social citizenship/needs-oriented heritage which has been discussed above and policy decisions as to our European future. Furthermore, what women – both women's collective movements and women in their individual, daily-life experiences – have contributed to public discourse and the political agenda in welfare and post-welfare systems, comes into the picture.

Using "invisible" resources is a key strategy in this scenario. Caring work, third-sector (voluntary and self-help) agencies, individual life strategies, reorganizing time – all become assets for the individual, local, national well-being.

The philosophy in this model, however, has nothing to share with the pervasive economic reductionism in social thinking. The aim is to satisfy basic human needs, taking into account, on the one side, their variety and complexity in contemporary – and future – societies, and, on the other, a creative use of social innovation, organizational flexibility, and new technologies. Some examples are as follows: solving health and welfare problems closer to the source as against the trend towards growing professionalization and bureaucratization; increasing the number of available options (as in the Finnish "welfare society" model – a particularly remarkable effort towards this aim – which allows parents the choice of either sending their babies to nursery school or staying at home to care for them until they are three); promoting all forms of self- and mutual aid; and stressing personal responsibility and lay know-how and expertise (Hatch and Kickbusch, 1983).

Thirdly, the issue of redistributing rights and obligations in caring work, which have always been asymmetrically distributed between men and women, younger and older people, and different subgroups in the population, is of crucial relevance.

Nobody should be exempted from the obligations of a "caring society". This policy would result in an unprecedented step towards democratization of everyday life. I do want to stress that reducing traditional constraints upon women's use of time (daily time, across their lives) would result in an enormous amount of freedom, but also in bringing new "intelligent" resources into the system that may well contribute to further radical change and innovation in social processes.

There are several reasons for taking this model – which corresponds to the structure and culture of a limited and privileged part of Europe – as a possible, indeed highly desirable, scenario. In face of diminishing resources and increasing constraints, the answer is not to renounce the goals of the overall system as well as of individual rights. As Crozier (1987) has suggested, this latter model is a *punitive* response to social and economic change. Actually, most of the Western world has accepted it as the only possible response to the "welfare state crisis" and to social change. As opposed to this punitive attitude, I wish to stress the user-friendly character of an approach whose basic challenge is finding ways to increase available resources. It is a radical shift from widespread unconcern with people's expectations and entitlements: it actually puts people – citizens, men, and women in their daily life circumstances – with their needs and their resources at the centre, as skilled, intelligent social actors.

My question then is, under what conditions could we share this perspective in building an all-European project, or scenario, for the coming years?

2.2   Europe, a Land of Privilege, a Fortress

Profiting from the internal market of 1992, and from the integration of some Eastern European countries into its economic mechanisms, and because of privileged relationships with the rest of the Western world (including Japan), Europe will improve its economic position and become highly competitive internationally. According to a projection of an EEC economic research group early in 1989, the rise in total income, following the internal market recognition, was expected to be in the range of 2.6-6.5 per cent over a time span of five to seven years. A "Marshall plan" for Eastern Europe, public and private investments, the advantages of a skilled labour force that may in part at least take the place because of Third World migration, and a widely enlarged market for consumption goods and services, are all likely to contribute to even greater economic growth. Under such circumstances, Europe's (both Western and Eastern) long-standing commitment to social citizenship rights may well be reinforced. Whether, however, a universalist "citizenship rights", or a "US-like" model will prevail, remains to be seen (Agnelli Foundation, 1990). Yet another possibility is the "Latin-Americanization" of Eastern Europe. Within a common system of rules and market exchanges, the unified Germany – or some of the most powerful Western countries – may take the role the US has traditionally played within the American continent: a hegemonic role, establishing privileged relations with some, playing the interests of one against the other, keeping control over all economic and political decisions.

I wish to turn now to yet another aspect that I consider to be extremely relevant. In Europe, a wealthy region of the world with strong democratic traditions and a culture of social citizenship, there is a growing fear of threatening worldwide processes. Because it is a land of such extreme privilege – both economic and social – Europe feels under siege. Here are some possible implications of this fortress scenario:

1) The borders of Europe are closed to new immigrants, under strict police and military control. Border police and the army, as well as other officials and employees at all levels of the public administration, are involved in keeping out "aliens". Computerized screening devices and data banks are developed at the European level.

2) Only selected categories are allowed into the region: for example, those from other European or Western countries, or those – no matter where they come from – who can invest or in other words buy their right to entry, or perhaps top-ranking students and professional people. Refugee status is severely restricted. All this takes place in a situation of increasing, dramatic pressure for millions to move out of their countries of origin, either for economic or political reasons, or simply because the right to mobility has come to be considered as a basic right in contemporary societies.

3) Citizenship is granted according to similar criteria, a strict hierarchy of desirability. Already both in Europe and in the US, "... a dual membership structure has emerged ..." (Brubaker, 1989) where increasing numbers of residents live as second-class political and social actors. It is obvious that illegal immigration will continue, leaving those in this category deprived of all rights and protection, tolerated at best, exploited and threatened, depending upon the circumstances.

What is at issue is the following question: how could the legitimate expectations and strategies aimed at well-being and social citizenship of European people, be fulfilled without Europe becoming a white-centred (and Christian-centred), monocultural fortress, defensive of Western values and the Western model, with its democratic tradition being very much at risk?

2.3 The Blade Runner Model

If current trends continue, we may witness an increasingly dual system worldwide. Though Europe is a relatively sheltered region of the world, the majority of its population would not escape conditions and problems common to the underprivileged all over the world. Inequalities (between rich and poor, those living in ecologically "clean" areas and those living in areas of pollution and high-risk exposure, whites and non-whites, young and old, men and women, those in secure/satisfactory jobs and careers and those in occasional/marginal employment, lifestyles of the worldwide élites and living conditions of the majority) will grow worse. Patterns of worldwide social control are created, and international agencies cooperate in narco-wars, in anti-AIDS politics, in policing borders of rich countries and exclusive neighbourhoods. Increasingly intolerant and repressive social norms control youth lifestyles, women's choices, and sexual behaviour. The death penalty is widely accepted. No civil and legal rights are guaranteed. There is no right to privacy or to any decent standard of care.

The scenario reminds us of a movie, *Blade Runner,* a Bronx-like technological, police-run urban society, in which a small minority tries to keep control and all others – masses of men and women of different races and backgrounds and having different roles and social functions – are destitute, alienated, and powerless.

The United Nations Report of May 1990 (1991) indicates that in the near future, the world population will concentrate in huge urban cities (25 cities will grow to 7-24 million; only one, Paris, will be in Europe). At present already, 40 per cent of the urban population in Third World cities have no water provision; 1,175 million have no health care whatsoever, 926.6 million persons – one quarter of the adult world population – are illiterate, and one billion live in extreme poverty. One commentator reminds us that "Europeans – though their numbers have increased four times in the last two centuries – constitute a tiny island in the ocean of the world population, that has doubled since 1950 and is going to double again before 2050" (Julien, 1990).

One should also consider trends as to violence, disease, environmental catastrophes, racism, and wars.

"Each day in New York city five persons are murdered, nine are sexually assaulted, 256 robbed, 367 cars disappear (...). Though nationwide statistics are not available yet, many [US] cities are showing sharp increases in killings for the first months of 1990 compared to a year ago (...). If the trend continues, U.S. homicides in 1990 could reach the record 23,040 killings in 1980. That would be 9.2 murders per 100,000, more than seven times the rate in England or Japan" (*Newsweek*, 16 July 1990).

How far are we from the Blade Runner model?

Concluding Remarks

Both because of the methodology I have chosen and because of substantive reasons, there are no conclusions to be drawn.

It can be easily seen that I like the user-friendly Europe best – a quite unlikely scenario, however, as I see things at the time of this writing, during the Summer of 1990. At the other extreme, Blade Runner – or some milder form along those lines – is not a totally implausible perspective. The fact that nobody ever mentions this scenario makes one guess: is our land of privilege – and, perhaps, even of social citizenship rights – becoming, eventually, an armed fortress? Aren't we, the Europeans, lucky?

References

Agnelli Foundation (1990) *Globalization and Welfare Systems*. Turin.

Balbo, L. (1986) 'The Culture of Caring and the New Daily Rights', in Balbo, L., Nowotny, H. (eds.) *Time to Care in Tomorrow's Welfare Systems: the Nordic Experience and the Italian Case*. Vienna: European Centre for Social Welfare Policy and Research.

Balbo, L. (1987) 'Crazy Quilts: Rethinking the Welfare State Debate from a Woman's Point of View', in Showstack Sasson, A. (ed.) *Women and the State. The Shifting Boundaries of Public and Private*. London: Hutchinson.

Best, F. (1980) *Flexible Life Scheduling*. New York: Praeger.

Brubaker, W. R. (1989) *Immigration and the Politics of Citizenship in Europe and North America*. New York.

Commission of the European Communities (1987) FAST (Forecasting and Assessment in Science and Technology). Brussels, Occasional Paper No. 137, April.

Crozier, M. (1987) *État modeste, État moderne, Strategies pour un autre changement*. Paris: Fayard.

Ehrlich, P. R., Ehrlich, A. H. (1990) *The Population Explosion*. New York: Simon and Schuster.

Eurosocial (1987) *Social Policies Beyond the 1980s in the European Region*. Vienna: European Centre for Social Welfare Policy and Research.

Eurostat (1988) *Demographic and Labour Force Analyses*. Luxembourg.

Giddens, A. (1987) *Social Theory and Modern Sociology*. Stanford: Stanford University Press.

Hall, S., Jacques, M. (1987) *Our Common Future. Report of the World Commission on Environment and Development*. Oxford: Oxford University Press.

Hatch and Kickbusch, L. (eds.) (1983) *Self-help and Health in Europe. New Approaches to Health Care*. Copenhagen: WHO Regional Office for Europe.

Hernes, H. (1987) *Welfare State and Women Power*. Oxford: Oxford University Press.

Julien, C (1990) *Le monde diplomatique no. 434*, May 1990.

National Board of Social Welfare in Finland (1990) *Clients or Coproducers? The Changing Role of Citizens in Social Services*. Helsinki.

Swedish Secretariat for Future Studies (1984) *Time to Care*. Oxford: Pergamon Press.

United Nations Dept. of Economic and Social Affairs (1991) *World Urbanization Prospects 1990*. New York: United Nations.

List of Contributors

Anthony B. Atkinson is Tooke Professor of Economic Science and Statistics at the London School of Economics, England

Laura Balbo is Member of Parliament and Professor of Sociology at the University of Ferrara, Italy

Robert J. Brym is Professor at the Department of Sociology and the Centre for Russian and East European Studies of the University of Toronto, Canada

Richard A. Cloward is Professor at the Columbia University School of Social Work, New York, USA

Zsuzsa Ferge is Professor of Sociology and Head of the Department for Social Policy at the Eötvös Loránd University, Budapest, Hungary

Frances Fox Piven is Professor at the Graduate School and University Center of the City University of New York, USA

Ana M. Guillén is a postgraduate student at the Centro de Ciencias Sociales of the Juan March Foundation in Madrid, Spain

Kåre Hagen is Research Fellow at the Department of Political Science of the University of Oslo, Norway

Jan Hartl is researcher at the Institute of Philosophy and Sociology of the Czechoslovak Academy of Sciences, Prague, Czechoslovakia

Jean-Pierre Jallade, Economist, is Director of the European Institute of Education and Social Policy, Paris, France

Lena Kolarska-Bobinska is researcher at the Institute of Philosophy and Sociology of the Polish Academy of Sciences, Warsaw, Poland

Jon Eivind Kolberg is Professor of Sociology at the University of Bergen, Norway

Stephan Leibfried is Professor at the Centre for Social Policy Research of the University of Bremen, Germany

John Myles is Professor at the Department of Sociology and Anthropology of the Carleton University, Ottawa, Canada

Veljko Rus is Senior Research Fellow at the Institute for Social Research of the University of Ljubljana, Slovenia

Vladimir Shubkin is Professor and Head of Department at the Institute of the International Labour Movement of the Academy of Sciences, Moscow, Russian Federation

Adrian Sinfield is Professor at the University of Edinburgh, Scotland

Hannu Uusitalo is Professor and Deputy Director General of the National Agency for Welfare and Health, Helsinki, Finland

Jiri Vecerník is researcher at the Institute of Philosophy and Sociology of the Czechoslovak Academy of Sciences, Prague, Czechoslovakia

Ronald Wiman is Social Affairs Officer, seconded by the Government of Finland, at the Centre for Social Development and Humanitarian Affairs of the United Nations Office at Vienna, Austria

Tatiana Zaslavskaya is Professor and Director of the Center for Public Opinion Studies, Moscow, Russian Federation